Language, Culture, and Society

An Introduction to Linguistic Anthropology

Second Edition

Zdenek Salzmann

Westview Press
A Member of the Perseus Books Group

Copyright © 1998 by Westview Press, A Member of the Perseus Books Group

Published in 1998 in the United States of America by Westview Press, 5500 Central Avenue, Boulder, Colorado 80301-2877, and in the United Kingdom by Westview Press, 12 Hid's Copse Road, Cumnor Hill, Oxford OX2 9JJ

Library of Congress Cataloging-in-Publication Data
Salzmann, Zdenek.
    Language, culture, & society : an introduction to linguistic
anthropology / Zdenek Salzmann.—2nd ed.
        p.   cm.
    Includes bibliographical references and index.
    ISBN 0-8133-3404-7 (pb)
    1. Anthropological linguistics.   I. Title.   II. Title: Language,
culture, and society
P35.S18   1998
306.44'089—dc21   97-53076
                                                                                      CIP

The paper used in this publication meets the requirements of the American National Standard for Permanence of Paper for Printed Library Materials Z39.48-1984.

10   9   8

Contents

Illustrations

Boxes

Trees

Map

Preface to the Second Edition

To write a preface to the second edition of a textbook is a gratifying experience for an author. It means that a book has been successful enough to merit what revisions and additions may be needed and that to have written it in the first place was a worthwhile undertaking.

In preparing this second edition, I benefited from several reviews of the original work—reviews both published in professional journals and requested for my benefit by the publisher. The reviewers did not always agree as to what should or should not be covered in an introductory textbook of linguistic anthropology, but their views were taken into consideration and a number of their suggestions accepted.

Besides reorganizing several chapters and changing the placement of others to make the sequence of topics easier to follow, I have provided many additional examples and increased the number of languages referred to or cited from 126 to 140. Among the topics introduced in this edition are linguistic typology, taboo words, means of expressing politeness and deference, evolution of basic color terms, and the Ebonics controversy.

One reviewer must be singled out by name—Harriet Ottenheimer of Kansas State University. She provided a most helpful ten-page commentary on what should be retained, changed, deleted, or added, based on her experience in using the book. Not all of her suggestions could be adopted, but many were, and she deserves special thanks for being constructive, explicit, and detailed in her comments.

I must also express my appreciation to members of the staff of Westview Press, who have been very helpful in bringing this new edition into being, and to my wife, Joy Salzmann, who as always has been of great help.

Zdenek Salzmann

Preface and Acknowledgments to the First Edition

For more than twenty years I taught an introductory course in linguistic anthropology. During those years I made use of various textbooks, supplementing them with selected readings and always wishing for a comprehensive text that would introduce students to linguistic anthropology in its full scope and with due credit given to those who paved the way. Several years ago I decided the time had come to write such a text, and this book is the result.

In preparing the text, I had several objectives in mind. I wanted the book to be a broad survey of linguistic anthropology including, for example, a discussion of such topics as writing systems, oral folklore, communication among nonhuman primates, proxemics, and several others not always covered in a standard course. Another of my objectives was to acquaint readers with some of the classical writings of anthropologists who were also linguists before linguistic anthropology became established as a field in its own right. So many good recent or contemporary writings are discussed in class that the work of scholars from the early part of the century is frequently neglected. Third, because the contributions to linguistic anthropology have come from physical anthropologists, cultural anthropologists, biologists, sociologists, linguists, and scholars from still other fields, I have felt that the book should not be written from any particular theoretical point of view but should reflect instead the healthy eclecticism that has always characterized the field.

A few additional remarks are called for. Even though well over 100 languages or dialects are referred to in the text, examples have been drawn primarily from English. It would have been easy to exemplify the various concepts discussed by using the many languages of the world, but I am convinced that most students who are being introduced to linguistic anthropology will gain the clearest understanding if examples are taken from a language they know well. (The map on pp. 322 and 323 illustrates where the languages and dialects mentioned in the text are spoken.) Some users of the book may consider the treatment of certain topics to be too concise. My own feeling is that a textbook for use in an introductory course should be supplemented by original readings assigned either to all members of a class or to students according to their individual interests. The boxes with extended quotations from original sources are designed to stimulate such interest. The notes and suggestions for further reading that follow each chapter should aid instructors in selecting supplementary original materials. The several linguistic problems appended to Chapters 3 and 4 will give students an opportunity to try their hand at simple linguistic analysis.

There are many people to whom I am indebted for useful suggestions or simply for asking good questions. They include some of my former students at the University of Massachusetts at Amherst and more recently at Northern Arizona University in Flagstaff. They also include Charles F. Hockett of Cornell University, some of my former colleagues whom I asked for opinions on specific topics—George Armelagos, a physical anthropologist, in particular—and the two reviewers (anonymous to me) engaged by the publisher. Furthermore, I am greatly indebted to members of the editorial staff at Westview Press who gave me advice at various stages of the project and who expertly saw the book through the process of editing and printing—Dean Birkenkamp, Diana Luykx, Shena Redmond, and Alice Colwell.

My greatest indebtedness, however, is to my wife, Joy Salzmann, who through the years has always been my first editor. Because she is not a trained anthropologist or linguist, she has been able to read the several drafts of each chapter from a student's point of view; what was not clear to her was likely to be puzzling to even the best of students. And because she is a native speaker of English (which I am not) who is concerned that ideas be expressed clearly and well, her suggestions have found their way onto every page. I owe her a large debt of gratitude.

I hope that the book will prove to be of value to students and instructors alike as well as to other readers who are interested in gaining some understanding of communicative behavior in general, the use of speech in different societies, and the relationship between language, culture, and society.

Z. S.

1

Introducing Linguistic Anthropology

A very simple definition of **anthropology** might read as follows: Anthropology is the study of humankind. Many other fields of study, of course, are also concerned with aspects of the human condition. Among these fields are anatomy, physiology, history, political science, economics, art history, linguistics, literature, and sociology. With all these specialized areas focusing on the human experience, why would there be a need for such a broad discipline as anthropology? What do anthropologists do that is different? A few brief comments concerning the history of modern anthropology will help to answer these questions.

In the United States modern anthropology began during the nineteenth century mainly as a study of subjects that were not already claimed by scholars in other fields. Early anthropologists focused especially on the nonliterate tribal peoples others considered "primitive" or "savage" and therefore of little interest or importance. These humble beginnings are reflected to the present day in the popular conception of anthropologists as people who supply museums with exotic specimens from societies in remote parts of the world or who dig up the remains of past human life and cultures.

Because the early anthropologists were interested in peoples other specialists neglected, they concerned themselves with all aspects of a society. German-born Franz Boas (1858–1942)—a dominant figure in modern anthropology and holder of the first academic position in anthropology in the United States (at Clark University in Worcester, Massachusetts, 1888–1892)—authored, coauthored, or edited more than 700 publications ranging from articles on Native American music, art, folklore, and languages to studies in culture theory, human biology, and archaeology. Boas's direct influence was felt until his death at the age of eighty-four, and the course of American anthropology after him was shaped to a great extent by scholars who had served their apprenticeships under Boas at Columbia University—among them Alfred L. Kroeber (1876–1960), Edward Sapir (1884–1939), Ruth Benedict (1887–1948), and Margaret Mead (1901–1978). Kroeber was another of the rare anthropologists whose interests and contributions to the field were encyclopedic.

By World War II, anthropology was well established as an academic field and taught at major U.S. universities. The four main subfields then recognized were physical (or biological) anthropology, cultural anthropology, linguistic anthropology, and archaeology. More specialized areas of concern and research have developed within the subfields—among them political, economic, urban, feminist, medical, nutritional, visual, and psychological anthropology, and the anthropology of Latin America, of Europe, and of law, to mention a few.

The one commitment that anthropologists profess regardless of their specialization is the holistic approach. The term **holistic** refers to concern with a system as a whole rather than with only some of its parts. Because studying a whole culture in full detail could easily become a lifetime project, anthropologists focusing on only certain of its aspects invariably study and discuss them in full cultural context. In the study of humanity, applying the holistic approach means emphasizing the connections among the many different facets of the human condition so that humankind can be understood in its full complexity—cultural, social, and biological.

One characteristic that sets apart anthropology from the other social sciences is a strong fieldwork component, which in archaeology and physical anthropology is supplemented by work in the laboratory. Archaeologists survey land for sites, excavate remains of past cultures, and then analyze some of their findings in the laboratory. There they date excavated material remains by radioactive decay methods (for example, carbon 14 or potassium-argon dating) or by comparing growth rings in trees and aged wood; reconstruct features of past environments by identifying fossil pollen or spores; and analyze pottery for hardness, firing methods, porosity, and other qualities. Physical anthropologists study not only the behavior of nonhuman primates (chimpanzees, gorillas, and others) in their natural habitats or search in particular locations of the world for skeletal remains relating to human evolution, but they also conduct research in the laboratory—examining fossil remains for ancient diseases, calculating through the examination of blood samples gene frequencies in a gene pool, analyzing the fossil dentitions of early humans in order to be able to draw inferences concerning their dietary habits, and so on.

For some time now, anthropologists have not been limiting themselves to the study of tribal societies, peasant villages, or bands of hunter-gatherers in remote parts of the world but are also exploring modern societies. This is certainly as it should be: If anthropology is truly the study of humankind, then it must concern itself with all of humankind.

Anthropology, Linguistics, and Linguistic Anthropology

By drawing on what one of my colleagues and I have said elsewhere (Pi-Sunyer and Salzmann 1978:3), I might summarize the overall scope of anthropology by the following propositions:

1. Because members of the *Homo sapiens* species are biological organisms, the study of human beings must try to understand their origin and nature in the appropriate context.
2. As humans strove to adapt to a great variety of natural and self-made conditions, they engaged in a long series of innovations referred to by the term *culture.*
3. In the course of their cultural evolution during the past million years, humans were immeasurably aided by their developing of an effective means of communication, the most remarkable and crucial component of which is human language.

Linguistic anthropology is concerned with the consequences of the process referred to in the third proposition.

A terminological note is appropriate here. Although *anthropological linguistics* has frequently been employed to refer to the subfield of anthropology otherwise known as linguistic anthropology, and a respected journal exists under that name (*Anthropological Linguistics*), the term **linguistic anthropology** is to be preferred, as Karl V. Teeter argued some years ago (1964). Briefly, if anthropology is the study of humanity, and language is one of the most characteristic features of humankind, then the study of language is an obvious and necessary aspect of anthropology as a whole. To modify the noun *linguistics* by the adjective *anthropological* is clearly redundant because even though members of all animal species communicate, so far as is known no other species uses anything comparable to human language. Only if, say, members of the cat family (Felidae) or of the class of birds (Aves) had something like human speech (not just some system of communication, no matter how intricate) would it make sense to speak of anthropological linguistics to distinguish it from some such field of study as felid or avian linguistics (that is, the study of the language of cats or birds). As we have already seen, there are several subfields of anthropology; just as the subfield concerned with culture is referred to as *cultural anthropology,* the one concerned with language is aptly referred to as *linguistic anthropology.* This is the term used throughout this book: It states exactly what the subfield is about—the study of language (or speech) within the framework of anthropology.

Another discipline that also focuses on the uniquely human attribute of language is **linguistics,** the scientific study of language. *Linguistics* does not refer to the study of a particular language for the purpose of learning to speak it; rather, it refers to the analytical study of language, any language, to reveal its structure—the different kinds of language units (its sounds, smallest meaningful parts of words, and so on)—and the rules according to which these units are put together to produce stretches of speech. There is a division of labor, then, between linguists and linguistic anthropologists: The interest of the linguist is in language structure; the interest of the linguistic anthropologist is in speech use and the relations that exist between language on the one hand and society and culture on the other (see Box 1.1). As for the prerequisite training, the linguist does not need to study anthropology in order to become fully proficient in linguistics; a linguistic anthropologist, in contrast, must have some linguistic sophistication and acquire the basic skills of linguistic analysis to be able to do significant research in linguistic anthropology.

The Fieldwork Component

Research concerning the cultures and languages of contemporary societies is for the most part conducted in the field. Exposure of anthropologists to the societies or communities they wish to study is usually not only prolonged (lasting at least several months and frequently a full year) but repeated (once accepted by a group, anthropologists tend to return for follow-up research). The immersion of anthropological field-workers for an extended period of time in the day-to-day activities of the people whom they study is referred to as **participant observation.** To be able to communicate in their own language with the people under study is very helpful to the anthropologist. Lacking such skills, the anthropologist must rely on interpreters who, no matter how eager they are to help, may unwittingly simplify or distort what is being said by those who supply cultural or linguistic data. Because members of a society who are fluent in two languages are sometimes culturally marginal people, they should be selected with care: Individuals who have adapted to or borrowed many traits from another culture could have lost a substantial number of traits from their own. To be sure, studies of how and to what extent individuals or whole groups may have modified their culture by prolonged or vigorous contact with another society are of great importance and interest, but these studies cannot be carried out satisfactorily unless the traditional base of the culture undergoing change is well understood.

The availability of someone who can communicate with the anthropologist does not excuse the researcher from needing to become acquainted with the language of the group. The knowledge of a language serves the

---

BOX 1.1   Linguistics Contrasted with Linguistic Anthropology

Unlike linguists, [linguistic] anthropologists have never considered language in isolation from social life but have insisted on its interdependence with cultural and social structures. In this sense, their technical linguistic analyses are means to an end, data from which it is possible to make inferences about larger anthropological issues. Hence, under the ... label "language and culture," anthropologists study topics such as the relations between world views, grammatical categories and semantic fields, the influence of speech on socialization and personal relationships, and the interaction of linguistic and social communities. ... As Hymes has aptly remarked, "language is not everywhere equivalent in communicative role and social value ... [and] no normal person, and no normal community is limited in repertoire to a single variety of [style], to an unchanging monotony which would preclude the possibility of indicating respect, insolence, mock-seriousness, humor, role-distance, etc. by switching from one code variety to another." Consequently, the relation between languages and social groups cannot be taken for granted, but is a problem which must be ethnographically investigated.

from Pier Paolo Giglioli, ed., *Language and Social Context*
(1972), 9–10

---

anthropologist as an invaluable tool for gaining an informed understanding of the many aspects of a culture—for example, enabling the researcher to judge the relative standing of members of a community on the basis of how they address one another. As early as 1911 Boas emphasized this point in his introduction to the first volume of the *Handbook of American Indian Languages* when he insisted that "a command of the language is an indispensable means of obtaining accurate and thorough knowledge [of the culture that is being studied], because much information can be gained by listening to conversations of the natives and by taking part in their daily life, which, to the observer who has no command of the language, will remain entirely inaccessible" (Boas 1911:60).

What Boas insisted on was underscored by Bronislaw Malinowski (1884–1942), the Polish-born anthropologist who pioneered participant observation during his fieldwork in Melanesia and New Guinea between 1914 and 1920. In discussing the advantage of being able to speak one of the local languages, he wrote: "Over and over again, I was led on to the track of some extremely important item in native sociology or folklore by listening to the conversation of ... Igua [his young helper] with his ... friends, who used to come from the village to see him" (Malinowski 1915:501). And seven years later, in his introduction to *Argonauts of the*

Western Pacific, Malinowski offered additional reasons why the command of the native language is useful: "In working in the Kiriwinian language [spoken on the island of Kiriwina in the Trobriand Islands], I found still some difficulty in writing down . . . [a] statement directly in translation . . . [which] often robbed the text of all its significant characteristics— rubbed off all its points—so that gradually I was led to note down certain important phrases just as they were spoken, in the native tongue" (Malinowski 1922:23).

For linguistic anthropologists, reasonably good speaking knowledge of the language of the society being studied is indeed indispensable. ("Reasonably good" speakers are those who can express themselves comfortably on nontechnical subjects; fluency, if it refers to nativelike command of a language, is very difficult to attain even after an extended period of fieldwork.) It is also necessary for linguistic anthropologists to learn a great deal about the culture of a foreign society, for much of what they study concerns the sociocultural functions of linguistic behavior. In short, both a knowledge of the language and a fair acquaintance with the culture are called for if inquiries made in the field are to be relevant and statements about the relationship between language and culture or society accurate and valid.

The native speaker from whom the researcher collects linguistic (or cultural) information is referred to as an **informant.** In recent years the term *consultant* has been used with increasing frequency, in part because some members of the public confuse *informant* with the uncomplimentary term *informer.* More importantly, though, the term *consultant* gives recognition to the intellectual contribution made to linguistic and anthropological studies by those native speakers who work with anthropologists or linguists. The collaboration between members of a society and outsiders who study various aspects of that society is reflected in the growing number of coauthored articles. Another way of using to advantage the native speakers' insights into their own language is to enable interested individuals to receive training in linguistics and anthropology and then encourage them to use the acquired skills and knowledge not only for the benefit of linguistic anthropology in general but for the benefit of their own societies. Perhaps the most prominent among those who have urged that language informants be brought fully into collaboration is Kenneth Hale of the Massachusetts Institute of Technology. He has pioneered this approach for over a quarter of a century. As early as 1969 Hale made the points that "for some linguistic problems [it is doubtful] whether the traditional arrangement, in which the linguistic problem is formulated in one mind and the crucial linguistic intuitions reside in another, can work at all—or, where it appears to work, whether it can be said that the native speaker is not, in fact, functioning as a linguist," and, a little further, that the distribution of linguistic talent and interest which is to be found [for example] in an American Indian community does not necessarily correspond in any way to the distribution of formal education in the Western sense. If this talent is to flourish and be brought to bear in helping determine the particular relevance of the study of language to the communities in which it is located, then ways must be found to enable individuals who fit such descriptions . . . to receive training and accreditation which will enable them to devote their energies to the study of their own languages. (Hale 1974:387, 393)

Data for the analysis of a language or of language use can of course be collected away from the area where the language is spoken if an informant lives within reach of the linguistic anthropologist. Linguistic data obtained in such a manner can be quite useful if the informant's native language skills have remained good and the goal of the research is to make a preliminary analysis of the language. Determining how a language functions in a society, though, cannot be accomplished with the help of only one native speaker removed from those with whom he or she would normally communicate. (Special circumstances may merit exceptions. The description of the grammar of Tunica, a Native American language formerly spoken in northern Louisiana, was based on the speech of the only individual who could still speak the language "with any degree of fluency." The author of the grammar, Mary R. Haas [1910–1996], who did most of her fieldwork in 1933, noted that her informant "has had no occasion to converse in Tunica since the death of his mother in 1915" [Haas 1941:9]. In this case, the only available informant was clearly preferable to none at all.)

In the 1990s there are likely to remain only a few languages in the world about which nothing is known. However, there are still hundreds of languages about which linguists and anthropologists know relatively little. For the most part these languages are in Irian Jaya (West Irian) and Papua New Guinea (the western, Indonesian, and eastern, independent, halves of New Guinea, respectively) and the basin of the Amazon. According to recent estimates, some 850 languages are reported for Papua New Guinea, some 670 for Indonesia, and about 210 for Brazil—a total of nearly three-tenths of the world's languages (Krauss 1992:6). As a result of the great amount of fieldwork done the world over following World War II, it is now increasingly common for anthropologists to study communities or societies whose languages have already been described at least to some extent (and for which a system of writing may even have been devised, although speakers of such languages may have little if any need for writing). Such scholars are fortunate to be able to prepare in advance for their fieldwork by reading the relevant publications or unpublished manuscripts, listening to tape recordings made in the field by others, or even studying the language from native speakers if they are readily available. But occasions still arise in which the linguistic anthropologist must or does start from scratch.

The following description, then, has two functions: first, to indicate very briefly how potential field-workers who lack any knowledge of the field language should proceed and, second, to indicate how linguists and anthropologists have coped with unknown languages in the past.

Besides being fluent in their native language, informants should be active participants in their culture. In most instances ideal informants are older men and women not significantly affected by other languages and outside cultural influences. Such people almost always know their language better than the younger members of the society, who are likely also to use the language of whatever dominant culture may surround them. The situation of course varies from one part of the world to another. In many Native American societies in the United States, for example, young parents are no longer able to speak to their children in the language that was native to their own parents or grandparents. Not only do older members of a society tend to remember traditional narratives, which invariably preserve grammatical forms, words, and phrases that do not occur in everyday conversation, but they also are knowledgeable about the traditional aspects of their culture—ceremonies, rules of kinship, artifacts, foods, and the like—and therefore have a good command of the corresponding vocabulary.

Informants should be able to enunciate clearly. The speech of men and women missing most or all of their front teeth may be distorted to the point that a description of the sounds of their speech would not be representative of the typical pronunciation of the society's members. Most commonly, male anthropologists use male informants in the initial stages of their fieldwork and female anthropologists use women simply because individuals of the same gender usually work more comfortably with each other, especially in traditional societies. At some point during the field research, however, it is essential to obtain data from informants of the opposite gender as well, because in some societies the language of women has certain sounds or words that differ from those heard in men's speech. All such differences should be accounted for and described. It is also important to include younger members of a society among the informants in order to find out whether and how linguistic variation is related to the age of speakers and to what extent their speech may be influenced by other languages or dialects used in the area or by the official language of the country in which the group is located. For example, even though typical American teenagers and their grandparents speak the same language, their dialects differ somewhat, especially as far as vocabulary is concerned; older speakers are not likely to be acquainted with teenage slang and, even if they are, may not want to use it. Speakers of Badaga (a Dravidian language of southern India) who learned to speak the language prior to the 1930s make use of twenty distinctive vowel sounds, whereas the younger Badaga use only thirteen (Samarin 1967:61). The result of this simplification of the Badaga vowel system is an increased number of homonyms, words pronounced alike but different in meaning (like the English words spelled *meet* and *meat, rode* and *rowed,* and *soul* and *sole*). In general, variations in speech may be due to differences in age, gender, socioeconomic class, caste, religion, and various other factors.

In eliciting data—that is, in obtaining from informants words, utterances, texts, and judgments concerning their language—the field-worker should strive to collect material that is dialectally uniform and spoken in a natural tone of voice and at a normal rate of speed. Unnaturally slow speech used by an informant to enable the linguist to transcribe utterances more easily tends to distort sounds, stress, and the length of vowels; when sentences are spoken too rapidly, there is a tendency to leave out sounds or even to change them (consider the English *Gotcha!* 'I got you!' and *Betcha!* 'I bet you!'). Because dialects of a language may have somewhat different repertories of sounds and words, using informants who speak different dialects could prove confusing for the field-worker in the initial stages of research. Eventually, of course, dialectal variation is worth noting, as are also the sound modifications that words undergo when they are pronounced rapidly.

During the initial stages of fieldwork, eliciting is accomplished by asking the informant relatively simple questions such as "How do you say 'I am hungry' in your language?" "What does - - - - mean in your language?" "Am I repeating correctly the word you have just said?" and the like. Once the linguistic anthropologist has become accustomed to hearing the language and working with it, more spontaneous and richer data can be obtained. Informants are then asked to talk without prompting on topics of personal interest to them—for example, "Please tell me how your father taught you to hunt when you were young" or "When you were a child, what was your favorite way of helping your mother?"—or to give an eyewitness account of some memorable experience, narrate a traditional tale, or engage in a conversation with another native speaker. Utterances longer than just a few sentences are best recorded on tape. The recordings can later be replayed as many times as needed to ensure accurate transcription. When first used, the tape recorder may inhibit informants somewhat, but if it is used often enough, informants become accustomed to it and their speech should not be appreciably affected.

If field-workers wish to include in their studies so-called body language (eye movements, gestures, or shrugs), which may be a very important component of communicative behavior, video cassette recorders are useful. They not only record the sounds of speech and the body motions of the individuals speaking but also the reactions of the audience and the overall setting, making it possible for the linguistic anthropologist to arrive at an accurate and comprehensive description of the communicative behavior characteristic of ceremonies, conversations, and encounters of other kinds.

What should be the size of a corpus, the collection of language data available to the linguist? A corpus is adequate for the study of the sounds and grammar of a language once several days of recording and analysis have passed with no new sounds or grammatical forms noted. As for vocabulary, it would be impractical or impossible to collect every word that members of a society know or use. Quite commonly, words heard in everyday conversation among the members of a group do not include words heard in such traditional contexts as the telling of myths, praying, conducting ceremonies, and the like. A comprehensive description of a language (its sound system, grammar, and sentence formation) should therefore be based on data drawn from both casual and noncasual speech, that is, speech of different styles—everyday conversations, speech of both young and old and women and men, speech of traditional storytelling, language used in formal affairs, and so on.

Linguistic anthropologists are of course interested in much more than just the sounds, grammar, and vocabulary of a language, as the following chapters of this book show. However, both practical speaking skills and knowledge of the structure of a language are prerequisite for the full understanding of the relations between a language on the one hand and the society and its culture on the other.

From what has just been said, it would appear that doing anthropological fieldwork is a challenging but interesting undertaking: The anthropologist makes many friends in an environment that is usually—at least in the initial stages—exciting and even mysterious and becomes caught up in a discovery procedure that builds from the first day until the project is completed. The overwhelming majority of anthropologists engage in fieldwork repeatedly because they enjoy being away from the paperwork and routine of teaching and being among those whom they are eager to learn about.

Many demands, however, are placed upon field-workers that require adjusting to. The common response to exposure to unfamiliar cultural surroundings and people who speak a different language is culture shock. It manifests itself at least initially in disorientation and some degree of anxiety on the part of the field-worker, particularly if he or she is the only outsider in an otherwise close-knit community and a conspicuous outsider at that. There are many things to adjust or conform to: different foods, almost invariably the absence of personal privacy, poor hygiene, and the lack of physical comfort. There can also be a variety of threats to a field-worker's well-being: excessive heat, humidity, or cold; ever-present insects (some alarming in size or number); larger animals to beware of (snakes, for example); and bacteria and viruses to which the visitor is not immune, with no physician to consult if the need arises. Then, too, it can be frustrating to have no one with whom to discuss the puzzling issues that frequently develop in the course of research. But even if the picture is somewhat mixed, all the anthropologists I have known—students and colleagues alike—consider their times in the field to be among the most memorable experiences of their lives.

The Beginnings of Modern Linguistic Anthropology

When Herodotus, a Greek historian of the fifth century B.C., wrote briefly about the ethnic origin of the Carians and Caunians of southwestern Asia Minor and took into consideration the dialects they spoke, he engaged in (stretching the point a bit) what could be called linguistic anthropology. During the Age of Discovery, European scholars became intrigued by the many different peoples of the American continents and the languages they spoke. Nevertheless, linguistic anthropology in the modern sense is a relatively recent field of study that developed in the United States and has been practiced predominantly by North American academics.

The stimulation for the earliest phases of what was to become linguistic anthropology came from the exposure of European immigrants to Native Americans. The cultures and languages of these peoples were studied by educated Americans of varying professions—physicians, naturalists, lawyers, clerics, and political leaders. Among these amateur linguists, for example, was Thomas Jefferson, who collected vocabularies of Native American languages. In his *Notes on the State of Virginia* (1787), Jefferson wrote, "Great question has arisen from whence came those aboriginals of America" and then offered the following suggestion: "Were vocabularies formed of all the languages spoken in North and South America . . . and deposited in all the public libraries, it would furnish opportunities to those skilled in the languages of the old world to compare them with these, now, or at any future time, and hence to construct the best evidence of the derivation of this part of the human race" (Jefferson 1944:225–226). In this passage Jefferson referred to more than just the comparative study of languages; he must have had in mind using linguistic evidence to address questions concerning the cultural prehistory of humankind.

During the nineteenth century, the study of Native Americans and their languages once again occupied both distinguished Americans and a number of European explorers who traveled in the western part of the United States. Some of them collected and published valuable data on Native Americans and their languages that would otherwise have been lost. Serious and purposeful study of Native American languages and cultures, however, did not begin until after the establishment of the Bureau of (American) Ethnology of the Smithsonian Institution in 1879. John

Wesley Powell (1834–1902), perhaps better known as the first person to run the Colorado River throughout the entire length of the Grand Canyon, became its first director. It was Powell who in 1891 published a still-respected classification of American Indian languages north of Mexico. Twenty years later, Boas edited the first volume of the *Handbook of American Indian Languages* (1911), followed by two other volumes (1922 and 1933–1938) and part of a fourth (1941). Even though Boas emphasized the writing of grammars, the compiling of dictionaries, and the collecting of texts, research concerning both the place of languages in Native American societies and the relation of languages to cultures began to be undertaken with increasing frequency. After World War II the study of the relationship between language and culture (or society) was fully recognized as important enough to be considered one of the four subfields of anthropology.

Modern Myths Concerning Languages

This may be as good a place as any in this text to provide information about languages in general in order to set some basic matters straight. Every human being speaks a language, and some speak fluently two, three, or even more. What people think about languages—particularly those about which they know little or nothing—is quite another matter. Let us briefly consider a few of the misconceptions concerning languages that appear to be widespread, even among those who are otherwise well educated and knowledgeable. These misconceptions we can refer to as **myths,** in the sense of being unfounded, fictitious, and false beliefs or ideas.

The most common misconception is the belief that unwritten languages are "primitive," whatever that may mean. Those who think that "primitive" languages still exist invariably associate them with societies laypeople refer to as "primitive"—especially the very few remaining bands of hunter-gatherers. Now there are of course differences in cultural complexity between hunting-and-collecting bands and small tribal societies on the one hand and modern industrial societies on the other, but no human beings today are "primitive" in the sense of being less biologically evolved than others. One would be justified in talking about a primitive language only if referring to the language of, for example, the extinct forerunner of *Homo sapiens* of half a million years ago. Even though we do not know on direct evidence the nature of the system of oral communication of *Homo erectus*, it is safe to assume that it must have been much simpler than languages of the past several thousand years and therefore primitive in that it was rudimentary, or representing an earlier stage of development.

Why are certain languages mistakenly thought to be primitive? There are several reasons. Some people consider other languages ugly or "primitive sounding" if the languages make use of sounds or sound combinations they find indistinct or "inarticulate" because the sounds are greatly different from those of the languages they themselves speak. Such a view is based on the ethnocentric attitude that the characteristics of one's own language are obviously superior. But words that seem unpronounceable to speakers of one language—and are therefore considered obscure, indistinct, or even grotesque—are easily acquired by even the youngest native speakers of the language in which they occur. To a native speaker of English the Czech word *scvrnkls* 'you flicked off (something) with your finger' looks quite strange, and its pronunciation may sound odd and even impossible because there is no vowel among the eight consonants; for native speakers of Czech, of course, *scvrnkls* is just another word. Which speech sounds are used and how they are combined to form words and utterances vary from one language to the next, and speakers of no language can claim that their language has done the selecting and combining better than another.

Another myth has to do with grammar. Some think that languages of peoples whose societies are not urbanized and industrialized have "little grammar," meaning that such languages have few if any of the sort of grammar rules students learn in school. According to this misconception, members of simple societies use language in rather random fashion, without definite pattern. To put it differently, grammar in the sense of rules governing the proper use of cases, tenses, moods, aspects, and other grammatical categories is erroneously thought to be characteristic of "civilized" languages only. Once again, nothing could be further from the truth. Some languages have less "grammar" than others, but the degree of grammatical complexity is not a measure of how effective a particular language is.

What sorts of grammars, then, characterize languages spoken by members of tribal societies? Some of these languages have a fairly large and complicated grammatical apparatus, whereas others are less grammatically complex—a diversity similar to that found in Indo-European languages. Sapir's description of the morphology of Takelma, based on material collected in 1906, takes up 238 pages (Sapir 1922). In Takelma, the now extinct language spoken at one time in southwestern Oregon, verbs were particularly highly inflected, making use of prefixes, suffixes, infixes, vowel changes, consonant changes, and reduplication (functional repetition of a part of a word). Every verb had forms for six tense-modes, including potential ('I can'. . . or 'I could . . .'), inferential ('it seems that'. . . or 'I presume that . . .'), and present and future imperatives (the future imperative expressing a command to be carried out at some stated or implied time in the future). Among the other grammatical categories and forms marked in verbs were person, number, voice (active or passive), conditional, locative, instrumental, aspect (denoting repeated, con-

---

BOX 1.2   Sapir on Linguistic and Cultural Complexity

All attempts to connect particular types of linguistic morphology with certain correlated stages of cultural development are vain. Rightly understood, such correlations are rubbish. ... Both simple and complex types of language of an indefinite number of varieties may be found spoken at any desired level of cultural advance. When it comes to linguistic form, Plato walks with the Macedonian swineherd, Confucius with the head-hunting savage of Assam.

It goes without saying that the mere content of language is intimately related to culture. A society that has no knowledge of theosophy need have no name for it; aborigines that had never seen or heard of a horse were compelled to invent or borrow a word for the animal when they made his acquaintance. In the sense that the vocabulary of a language more or less faithfully reflects the culture whose purposes it serves it is perfectly true that the history of language and the history of culture move along parallel lines. But this superficial ... kind of parallelism is of no real interest to the linguist except in so far as the growth or borrowing of new words incidentally throws light on the formal trends of the language. The linguistic student should never make the mistake of identifying a language with its dictionary.

from Edward Sapir, *Language* (1921), 234

---

tinuing, and other types of temporal activity), and active and passive participles. Sapir's description of verb morphology fills more than 147 pages—yet is not to be taken as exhaustive. Although the brief characterization here is far from representative of Takelma verb morphology, it clearly indicates that Takelma grammar was anything but simple. A similar and more detailed demonstration of morphological complexity could easily be provided for hundreds of other so-called primitive languages.

When it comes to the vocabulary of languages, is it true, as some suppose, that the vocabularies of so-called primitive languages are too small and inadequate to account for the nuances of the physical and social universes of their speakers? Here the answer is somewhat more complicated. Because the vocabulary of a language serves only the members of the society who speak it, the question to be asked should be, Is a particular vocabulary sufficient to serve the sociocultural needs of those who use the language? When put like this, it follows that the language associated with a relatively simple culture would have a smaller vocabulary than the language of a complex society (see Box 1.2). Why, for example, should the Eskimo have words for *chlorofluoromethane, dune buggy, lambda particle,* or *tae kwon do* when these substances, objects, concepts, and activities have no part in their culture? By the same token, however, the language of a tribal society would have elaborate lexical domains for prominent aspects of the culture even though these do not exist in complex societies. The Agta of the Philippines, for example, are reported to have no less than thirty-one different verbs referring to types of fishing (Harris 1989:72).

For Aguaruna, the language serving a manioc-cultivating people of northwestern Peru, Brent Berlin (1976) isolates some 566 names referring to the genera of plants in the tropical rain forest area in which they live. Many of these genera are further subdivided to distinguish among species and varieties—for example, the generic term *ipák* 'achiote or annatto tree (*Bixa orellana*)' encompasses *baéŋ ipák, čamíŋ ipák, hémpe ipák,* and *šíŋ ipák,* referring respectively to 'kidney-achiote,' 'yellow achiote,' 'hummingbird achiote,' and 'genuine achiote.' Very few Americans, unless they are botanists, farmers, or nature lovers, know the names of more than about forty plants.

Lexical specialization in nonscientific domains is of course to be found in complex societies as well. The Germans who live in Munich are known to enjoy their beer and, accordingly, the terminology for the local varieties of beer is quite extensive. Per Hage (1972) defines ten different "core" terms for Munich beers according to strength, color, fizziness, and aging. But when local connoisseurs also wish to account for the degree of clarity (clear as against cloudy) and the Munich brewery that produced a particular beer, the full list exceeds seventy terms. Such a discriminating classification of local beers is likely to impress even the most experienced and enthusiastic American beer drinker.

Even though no languages spoken today may be said to be primitive, there are linguistic anthropologists who believe that not all languages can be considered equal. In the view of Dell Hymes (1961), languages are not functionally equivalent because the role of speech varies from one society to the next. One example he gives is the language of the Mezquital Otomi, who live in poverty in one of the arid areas of Mexico. At the time of Hymes's writing most of these people were monolingual, speaking only Otomi, their native language. Even though they accepted the outside judgment of their language as inferior to Spanish, they maintained Otomi and consequently were able to preserve their culture, but at a price. Lack of proficiency in Spanish, or knowledge of Otomi only, isolated the people from the national society and kept them from improving their lot. According to Hymes, no known languages are primitive, and all "have achieved the middle status [of full languages but not] the advanced status [of] world languages and some others. . . . [But though] all languages are potentially equal . . . and hence capable of adaptation to the needs of a complex industrial civilization," only certain languages have actually done so (Hymes 1961:77). These languages are more successful than others not because they are structurally more advanced but because they happen to be associated with societies in which language is the basis of literature, education, science, and commerce.

Summary and Conclusions

In its modern form, linguistic anthropology was the last subfield of anthropology to be developed and recognized and was practiced primarily by North American anthropologists. Its beginnings go back to the interest of nineteenth-century scholars in the great variety of Native American societies and the languages they spoke. Linguistic anthropologists view language in its cultural framework and are concerned with the rules for its social use; the analysis of its structure is therefore only a means to an end. By contrast, linguists in their study of languages emphasize linguistic structure and the historical development of languages.

Just as in the rest of anthropology, the data for linguistic anthropology are for the most part obtained in the field. Over the decades field-workers have developed techniques and methods to the point that anthropology departments with a sizable program in linguistic anthropology now offer courses in linguistic field methods.

Suggestions for Further Reading

For a book-sized guide to linguistic fieldwork, see Samarin 1967. Quite possibly the earliest article discussing the training of linguistic anthropologists is Voegelin and Harris 1952. Useful although somewhat dated comments on obtaining a linguistic sample and a guide for transcribing unwritten languages may be found in Voegelin and Voegelin 1954 and 1959. Eliciting and recording techniques are discussed in Hayes 1954 and Yegerlehner 1955.

For contributions to the history of linguistic anthropology, see Hymes 1963, somewhat revised in Hymes 1983; Hallowell 1960; and Darnell 1992. Readers on language in culture and society and on language in the social context are Hymes 1964 and Giglioli 1972.

2

Communication and Speech

It is now generally accepted that communication among members of animal species is widespread and that most vertebrates transmit information by acoustic signals. The variety and ingenuity of these communicative systems have stimulated a great deal of research in animal communication and its comparison with human speech. If we accept the single modern human species (*Homo sapiens*) as one of the very recent results of the evolution of living organisms over more than a billion years, then we may also be likely to assume that human speech is the end result of a long, cumulative evolutionary process that shaped communicative behavior throughout the animal kingdom.

In his book dealing with the biological foundations of language (1967), Eric H. Lenneberg (1921–1975) includes an extended discussion of language in the light of evolution and genetics. Language development, he points out, may be viewed from two sharply differing positions. One, which Lenneberg calls the continuity theory, holds that speech must have ultimately developed from primitive forms of communication used by lower animals and that its study is likely to reveal that language evolved in a straight line over time. According to this view, human language differs from animal "languages" only quantitatively, that is, by virtue of its much greater complexity. Although the proponents of a variant version of this theory argue that differences between human and animal communication are qualitative rather than merely quantitative, they also believe that all communicative behavior in the animal kingdom has come about without interruption, with simpler forms from the past contributing to the development of later, more complex ones.

The second theory, referred to as the discontinuity theory of language evolution and favored by Lenneberg, holds that human language must be recognized as unique, without evolutionary antecedents. Its development cannot be illuminated by studying various communicative systems of animal species at random and then comparing them with human language.

One statement concerning the antiquity of language, however, can be made with some assurance: Because all humans possess the same biological potential for the acquisition of any language, the capacity for speech must have characterized the common ancestors of all humans before populations adapted to different environments and diversified physically (racially).

Lenneberg rejects the continuity theory of language development for several reasons. Even though the great apes are the animals most closely related to humans, they appear to have very few if any of the skills or biological prerequisites for speech. Frequently cited examples of animal communication have been drawn from insects, birds, and aquatic mammals, but the evolutionary relationships of these animals to humans vary greatly. That only a few species within large genera or families possess particular innate communicative traits indicates that such species-specific behavioral traits have not become generalized and therefore are likely to be of relatively recent date. In the following discussion, human speech and the several representative communicative systems of other animals should therefore be viewed as having no evolutionary continuity. There is, in short, no evidence to suggest that human speech is an accumulation of separate skills throughout the long course of evolution. If it were so, gibbons, chimpanzees, orangutans, and gorillas would not be as speechless as they are.

Communication and Its Channels

Communication among members of animal species is universal because it is important to their survival; it takes place whenever one organism receives a signal that has originated with another. An early (from the 1940s) but serviceable model of communication makes use of five components: the sender (or source), the message, the channel, the receiver (or destination), and the effect. These components take into account the entire process of transmitting information, namely, who is transmitting what by what means to whom and with what effect. The model appears to be rather simple and straightforward, but because communication is by no means uniform, some discussion is in order.

Although communication among members of any particular species is to be expected, interspecific communication—that is, transmission of signals between members of different species—is far from rare. An experienced horseback rider transmits commands to a horse and expects them to be received and followed. A dog whining outside its owner's door conveys its wish to be let in. Communication between people on the one hand and their pets or work and farm animals on the other is in fact very common and not limited to sounds. Touching (stroking, patting, holding, and grooming) animals is frequently more effective than talking to them, and the dog who wags its tail and vigorously rubs its muzzle against a human knee leaves no doubt as to its feelings of satisfaction and pleasure. The means of sending messages clearly vary and are not limited to sounds (as in speech) or visible signs (as in books or by hand gestures), although these two channels, or media selected for communication, are the means humans most frequently employ.

The most common and effective channel of human communication is the *acoustic channel,* used whenever people speak to each other as well as in so-called drum language or whistle speech (discussed in Chapter 11). Writings, gestures, and pictorial signs make use of the optical channel, relating to vision. Braille, a writing system for the blind that uses characters consisting of raised dots, is received by the sense of touch, the tactile channel. The olfactory channel is chosen whenever one wishes to communicate by the sense of smell: People sometimes use room deodorizers before receiving guests and put perfume or deodorant on themselves when they expect to spend time with other individuals at an intimate distance. By the same token, most Americans consider garlicky or oniony breath to be a signal that reflects unfavorably on its senders.

The olfactory channel is especially important among social insects, who do much of their communicating by means of odors in the species-specific substances known as pheromones they secrete. Regardless of the channel used, animals send out messages for a variety of reasons, such as to guide individual organisms of the same species to one another or to help synchronize the behaviors of those who are to breed. In other words, communication enables organisms to maintain certain relationships that are of advantage to them individually as well as to their species as a whole.

Members of any animal species may use several kinds of signaling behavior. The signals familiar to humans are patterns of behavior known as displays. They may take the form of birdsongs, croaking (among frogs), chirping (among crickets), spreading fins or changing color (among certain fish), chest beating (among gorillas), and so on. Some signal units are cooperative, involving at least two individuals; others are rather formalized. A male hawfinch touches bills with a female, and during courtship the male bowerbird builds a chamber or passage decorated with colorful objects to attract a mate. Some animals (for example, dogs and wolves) use urine marking as a chemical signal delimiting territory, whereas others (skunks and bombardier beetles, to mention just two) use chemical signals for defense. Some of the findings in the field of animal communication have been quite unexpected, stimulating continued research.

Communication Among Social Insects

Social insects include certain species of bees and wasps and all ants and termites. Among the many species of social insects, the temperate-zone honeybee (*Apis mellifera*) is genetically endowed with fairly elaborate communicative behavior. For our understanding of the so-called bee dance language, we are especially indebted to the Austrian zoologist Karl von Frisch (1886–1982), who spent many years doing painstaking research on the subject and shared with two other scholars the 1973 Nobel prize for physiology or medicine.

One of several pheromones the queen of a honeybee colony secretes is ingested by bees that constantly attend and groom her. These bees subsequently spread the pheromone throughout the beehive to suppress the ovarian development of the worker bees and thus prevent the rearing of new queens. As the distribution of this pheromone begins to lag as a result of the queen's death or the colony's excessive size, new queens are reared and preparations made for swarming. When the developing potential queens communicate from their cells their readiness to assume their duties, their vibrations are received by detectors located in the hollow legs of the beehive population (bees feel rather than hear the vibrations because they have no ears). Swarming itself is triggered by an acoustic signal sent out by a worker bee. As soon as the first new adult queen hatches, she locates the cells containing her potential royal rivals and destroys them. Then she leaves the hive to mate with drones, attracting them by secreting another pheromone.

The most interesting aspect of the communicative behavior of honeybees has to do with foraging for food (see Figure 2.1). A scout bee can communicate the location of an especially abundant source of food by means of a dance inside the hive. The distance of the nectar source from the hive is indicated by the form of the dance the scout bee performs on the vertical surface of the honeycomb. If the source is quite close to the hive, the bee performs a round dance. If the source is farther away, about 100 yards or so, the scout bee dances in the shape of a figure eight. In this performance, the bee elaborates on its roughly circular dance by adding a tail-wagging walk across the circle, moving its abdomen from side to side. The length of time given the tail-wagging portion communicates the distance of the food source from the hive: the greater the distance, the longer the duration. The angle between the direction of the tail-wagging run and an imaginary line directed to the center of earth's gravity corresponds to the angle between the sun and the nectar source, with the hive used as a point of reference. If the sun happens to be above the food source and in direct line with it, the tail-wagging portion of the dance is vertical and the bee dances upward; if the sun is in line with the food source but on the opposite side of the hive, the crucial portion of the dance is again vertical but is danced downward. On partly cloudy days the scout bees are able to infer the position of the sun from the polarization of skylight. In addition to distance and direction from the hive, the richness of the food source is indicated by the amount of liveliness that

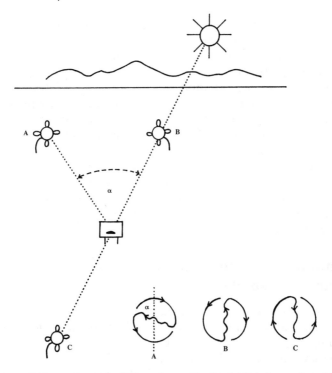

FIGURE 2.1 Communication of Honeybees. The beehive is located at the center, with three sources of nectar (A, B, and C) appearing in various directions from the hive. The three tail-wagging dance diagrams at bottom right show how the direction of the food source from the hive is communicated, using the sun as a point of reference.

characterizes the dance. It further appears that the length of the special buzzing sound a bee makes during the tail-wagging portion of the dance contributes to the information concerning distance. Experiments have established that the location of a food source as distant as 7 miles from the hive can be accurately communicated through the bee dance.

The honeybee's communication system is innate, that is, young bees do not have to learn how to use it. However, the more experienced the bee, the more precise is its reporting. Then, too, the dance language of the honeybees varies somewhat from one variety to another. For example, black Austrian honeybees perform a somewhat different dance from the honeybees of Italy. These differences are similar to the dialectal variation in human languages, but with one important difference: Dialects of human languages are aspects of a behavior that is learned whereas the variations in the communicative behavior of honeybees are inherited.

The communicative behavior of ant species may not be as intricate as that of honeybees, but it includes a wide variety of signals. Secreting pheromones from different glands to lay down scent trails to lead other ants to food or to trigger alarm-defense behavior is common to several species. More specifically, a pheromone secreted from the mandibular glands of male carpenter ants synchronizes the nuptial flights of males and females; a female pharaoh ant sexually stimulates a male by a pheromone and by touching him with her antennae or by presenting the enlarged part of her abdomen to him; certain species of ants who conduct slave raids on other ants discharge pheromones for various purposes, among them to disorient the ants under attack; and workers of several species make tactile signals with the antennae and forelegs to stimulate workers returning to the nest to regurgitate food to share.

Insects are commonly considered to be among the lower organisms of the animal kingdom, but their communicative behavior—especially that of the social insects—is highly specialized and efficient.

Communication Among Nonhuman Primates and Other Vertebrates

The amount of research concerning communicative behavior of vertebrates other than humans has been considerable; only a few representative examples can be given here, in brief and very general terms.

Of the several channels by means of which birds communicate, the vocal channel is best known to humans. Bird vocalizations are of two major classes: songs and calls. Consisting of several subparts, birdsongs are typically sung only by males and are longer and more complex than calls. Their two main functions are to establish and hold territory by repelling other males and to attract females during the breeding season. Depending on the species, birdsongs are either innate, learned, or in part innate and in part learned. The learning ability of many species of birds is at its maximum during the individual's first few months of life, but birds learn only the song characteristic of their own species. Birdcalls, in contrast, are short (single notes or short sequences of notes) and are used to signal alarm, feeding, distress, imminent takeoff or landing, and the like. For the most part, birdcalls are innate, but in some species a degree of learning is involved. Dialectal differences exist, especially in birdsongs.

For some time much scholarly and popular attention has been focused on the communication of cetaceans, an order of aquatic mammals that includes dolphins and whales. Despite the number of studies concerning bottle-nosed dolphins, our understanding of their acoustic communicative behavior is still insufficient. Members of this species of dolphins produce clicks, barks, yelps, and moans as well as whistles and squeals. The function of these different vocalizations is not fully understood: Some appear to express emotional states, others may be used for echolocation and navigation, and still others may identify individual dolphins. As yet, however, no evidence suggests that dolphins communicate with each other to a greater extent than do birds, for example.

In addition to various other sounds, humpback whales produce "songs" consisting of several ordered subparts and lasting as long as half an hour. All whales of a particular area sing the same song, although in the course of time these songs may be somewhat modified. Song sessions of whale groups are known to have lasted several hours. Our understanding of whale communication, too, is still far from adequate.

The greatest amount of research on animal communication since World War II has been devoted to nonhuman primates, especially the chimpanzees. In the wild, besides visual and other signals, apes use a variety of vocal sounds, including grunts, pants, barks, whimpers, screams, squeaks, and hoots. Each vocalization is associated with one or several circumstances. The physical similarity between the great apes and humans has long intrigued observers, suggestions that apes could be taught to speak having been made several centuries ago. Of the various experiments to teach chimpanzees to talk, the best documented was the one begun by Keith J. Hayes and Catherine Hayes in the late 1940s. They adopted a newborn female chimpanzee, Viki, and brought her up in their home as if she were a human child. Despite all the Hayeses' efforts to teach Viki to speak, after six years Viki had learned to approximate only four words (*mama, papa, cup,* and *up*), and poorly at that. It appears from the disappointing results of this and similar experiments in home-raising chimpanzees that the ability to speak is unique to humans and that the principal channel of communication for apes is the optical one—postures, facial expressions, and gestures.

In a more recent experiment, Washoe, an infant female chimpanzee, was taught the form of gestural language used by the American deaf. Toward the end of the second year of the project, Washoe was reportedly able to use over thirty signs spontaneously. After five years of training, she was said to be actively proficient in about 150 hand signs, was able to understand more than twice that many, and could use combinations of several signs. At about the same time, another chimpanzee, Sarah, was taught to write and read by means of plastic tokens of various shapes, sizes, and colors, each token representing a word. According to a report published in 1972, Sarah acquired a vocabulary of about 130 terms that she used with a reliability of between 75 and 80 percent. Her performance included the use of a plastic symbol that stood for the conditional relation *if-then*, as in "If Sarah takes a banana, then Mary won't give chocolate to Sarah" (Premack and Premack 1972).

Studies of communicative behavior among the great apes are continuing, and important new findings have been reported. Some of these studies concern the pygmy chimpanzees (*Pan paniscus*), whose habitat is the dense equatorial forest south of the Congo (Zaire) River in Zaire. Because their population is relatively small, the species may be considered endangered. The behavior of the pygmy chimpanzee is noticeably different from that of the common chimpanzee (*Pan troglodytes*). Pygmy chimpanzees appear to be more intelligent and more sociable and are faster learners; there is also evidence that they are more bipedal, less aggressive, and more willing to share food. Adult males and females associate more closely, and those in captivity seem to enjoy contact with humans. Of interest is a recent study by E. S. Savage-Rumbaugh (1984) based on two pygmy chimpanzees observed at the Language Research Center of the Yerkes Regional Primate Research Center in Atlanta, Georgia. At the time the study was made, the center had two pygmy chimpanzees, a twelve-year-old female born in the wild and her "adopted" son, Kanzi, then one and a half years old. When Kanzi wanted something, he intentionally used a combination of gestures and vocal sounds to draw the attention of a member of the center's staff. His wishes included being taken from one area to another, being helped with a task he could not perform alone (for example, opening a bottle), and the like. He would point to strange objects with an extended index finger, sometimes accompanying such pointings with vocal signals and visual checking, and would lead his teachers by the hand to where he wanted them to go, pulling on their hands if he wanted them to sit down. On occasion Kanzi expressed frustration by fussing and whining. If we judge from the behavior of the small sample of pygmy chimpanzees at the center and elsewhere, they appear to be better able to comprehend social situations than are common chimpanzees, and communicate correspondingly. In other words, their behavior is more reminiscent of human behavior than is the behavior of other species of apes.

In another project research assistants were requested to teach signs for objects to the young chimpanzee Nim, rewarding him for correct responses but not treating him like a human child. In contrast to a human child, Nim preferred to act upon his social environment physically rather than communicatively and was little interested in making signs simply for the sake of contact. Several years later an experiment was performed to test the hypothesis that social context can influence the communicative performance of a sign-using chimpanzee. The results of the experiment established that Nim adjusted his conversational style according to whether the interaction with humans was social or instructional (as in drill sessions). For example, in a social context, Nim made more than four times as many spontaneous contributions in sign language as he did when he was being trained. Apparently chimpanzees, just like children, tend to interact spontaneously when the situation is relaxed; in testing situations they are repetitive, imitative, and do not elaborate their contributions. If the communicative behavior of chimpanzees does indeed vary according to context, earlier reports on the cognitive capacities of chimpanzees may not tell the whole story.

Another noteworthy finding, made at the Institute for Primate Studies at the University of Oklahoma, involved Loulis, the young male Washoe adopted when he was ten months old. Although staff members were requested to refrain from signing to Loulis, or even to other chimpanzees when Loulis was present, Washoe and several chimpanzees in contact with Loulis freely used signs they had learned earlier from their human teachers. Five years and three months later, when Loulis's "vocabulary" consisted of fifty-one signs, the restriction on human signing was lifted. During the subsequent two years Loulis learned to use an additional nineteen signs. Independent observers acquainted with American Sign Language (ASL) were able to recognize the signs Loulis had learned from the other chimpanzees and could identify over 90 percent of them (Fouts, Fouts, and Van Cantford 1989; Fouts and Fouts 1989).

Some of the great apes also have been observed to indulge in generalization, that is, they made a response to a stimulus similar but not the same as a reference stimulus. To give a few examples: Washoe extended the sign for "dirty" from feces and dirt to a monkey who threatened her and also to Roger Fouts, who had raised her, when he refused to accede to a request. The female gorilla named Koko generalized "straw" from drinking straws to hoses, plastic tubing, cigarettes, and other objects of similar shape. And Lucy, a chimpanzee, signed "cry hurt food" to mean radishes (Hill 1978).

These and other experimental results are naturally of considerable interest, but one must keep in mind that the chimpanzees were learning to communicate in an artificial setting and for the most part were carefully directed by humans. It would have been of greater significance if some of the human-trained chimpanzees had subsequently been able, on their own, to add new signs to their "vocabulary" and to understand conversational turn-taking. Scholars have argued that at least some of the reported animal responses may have been due to unconscious nonverbal cueing by those who studied them. Although this may be true, there is little doubt that apes can learn the communicative behavior a number of researchers have described. But even at that, the nearly sexually mature chimpanzee is quite limited in what it can sign compared to a human child of six, who is capable of communicating verbally about a large variety of subjects. In short, the proficient use of the repertory of gestural signs of which chimpanzees are highly capable is a far cry from the conscious linguistic processing common to all humans from childhood on.

Design Features of Language

If human language is unique among the many known systems of communication that exist in the animal kingdom, then it must possess some features of design not to be found elsewhere. For the first modern attempt to develop a list of design features that characterize speech, we are indebted to Charles F. Hockett (1958). The discussion that follows is based on an expanded version, in which Hockett raises the number of design features from the original seven to sixteen (Hockett 1977).

1. *Vocal-auditory channel.* Some sounds produced by animals are not vocal (for example, the chirping of crickets) or are not received auditorily (as mentioned, bees have no ears). Writing, of course, is excluded by definition: The channel used for written messages is optical rather than vocal-auditory. Among mammals, the use of the vocal-auditory channel for communication is extremely common. One important advantage of using the vocal apparatus to communicate is that the rest of the body is left free to carry on simultaneously various other activities.

2. *Broadcast transmission and directional reception.* Speech sounds move out from the source of their origin in all directions, and the sender and the receiver need not see each other to communicate. Binaural reception (involving both ears) makes it possible to determine the location of the source of sounds.

3. *Rapid fading.* Speech sounds are heard within a very limited range and only at the time they are being produced. After that they are irretrievably lost. (By contrast, writing is relatively permanent, some written records having been preserved for several thousand years.) There is both a disadvantage and an advantage to this feature: Wise words have merely a fleeting existence when spoken but, fortunately, so do foolish ones.

4. *Interchangeability.* In theory, at least, human beings are capable of uttering what others say (if, of course, the language used is familiar). This is not true of many animal species where the nature of messages varies between males and females or according to other natural divisions. For example, in some species of crickets only the males chirp by rubbing together parts of their forewings, and the dance language of worker honeybees is not understood nor can it be performed by a queen or the drones of the same colony.

5. *Complete feedback.* Speakers of any language hear what they themselves are saying and are therefore capable of monitoring their messages and promptly making any corrections they consider necessary or appropriate. By contrast, a male stickleback cannot monitor the changing of the color of his eyes and belly that serves to stimulate the female fish of the species.

6. *Specialization.* Human speech serves no other function than to communicate. By contrast, the primary purpose of, say, the panting of a dog is to effect body cooling through evaporation, even though panting produces sounds that carry information (for example, the location of the dog or the degree of its discomfort).

7. *Semanticity.* Many communicative systems in the animal kingdom have semantic components. For example, some features of honeybee dance language denote the distance of a food source from the beehive and others give the direction in which the food is to be found. However, in no system other than human language is there such an elaborate correlation between the vast number of words and possible sentences and the widely different topics humans talk about.

8. *Arbitrariness.* There is no intrinsic relationship between the form of a meaningful unit of a language (for example, a word) and the concept for which the unit stands. The common domestic animal that barks—*Canis familiaris* by its scientific Latin name—is referred to as *dog* in English, *Hund* in German, *chien* in French, *perro* in Spanish, *pes* in Czech, *cîine* in Romanian, *sobaka* in Russian, *köpek* in Turkish, *kutya* in Magyar, *łééchąąʔí* in Navajo, *pohko* in Hopi, *heθ* in Arapaho, and *inu* in Japanese, even though one and the same animal species (in all its varieties, to be sure) is involved. Even the sounds of a dog's barking (*bowwow*) are heard differently by different peoples: *wanwan* by the Japanese, *haf haf* by the Czechs, *wauwau* by the Germans, and so on.

9. *Discreteness.* Messages in human languages do not consist of sounds that are continuous (like a siren, for example) but are made up of discrete—that is, individually distinct—segments. The difference between the English questions "Would you care for a piece of toast?" and "Would you care for a piece of roast?" is solely due to two discrete sounds at the same place in each sentence, one written and pronounced as *t* and the other as *r*. By contrast, bee dance language is continuous; it does not make use of discrete elements.

10. *Displacement.* Humans can talk about (or write about, for that matter) something that is far removed in time or space from the setting in which the communication occurs. One may, for instance, describe quite vividly and in some detail the military campaign of the Carthaginian general Hannibal against ancient Rome, even though the Second Punic War took place more than 2,000 years ago on another continent. Or people may talk about where they plan to live after retirement some twenty or thirty years in the future. Displacement of this kind exists nowhere else in the animal kingdom.

11. *Openness* (or *productivity*). Humans are capable of making completely unprecedented statements and having them understood by the listener. To be sure, this does not happen frequently in everyday life, but thinking up a novel sentence is not difficult (as, for example, "Our two cats argue about approaches to linguistic anthropology whenever they are left at home alone"). Good poets quite regularly use language in innovative ways.

12. *Duality (of patterning).* The smallest meaningful parts of a language, such as the eight units of the English phrase *the ir-repar-able type-writ-er-s* (here given in conventional spelling), are made up of sounds characteristic of the language. The number of different contrastive sounds in English is relatively small—between three and four dozen, depending on the dialect and analysis—but the total number of the smallest meaningful units these sounds make up runs into many tens of thousands, including all those words that cannot be further subdivided (for example, *cat, soup, hammer, elephant*). A limited number of linguistic units of one kind make up a vast number of units on another level, much as the atoms of only about ninety naturally occurring elements make up the molecules of millions of different compounds.

13. *Cultural* (or *traditional*) *transmission.* One does not inherit a particular language genetically; children learn language from parents or others who speak to and with them. Speaking a particular language is therefore a part of one's overall cultural behavior, that is, behavior acquired through learning.

14. *Prevarication.* What a person may say can be completely false (as if someone asserts that the moon is made of green cheese or that Washington is an hour's leisurely walk from Leningrad). Among animals, the opossum may feign death (play possum) if surprised on the ground, or a bird may pretend to have a broken wing to lead predators away from her nest. On the whole, however, attempts at simulation are not common among animals.

15. *Reflexiveness.* Humans can and do use language to discuss language or communication in general, as one may do in a class or over coffee. Nonhuman animals do not appear to be capable of transmitting information about their own or other systems of communication.

16. *Learnability.* Speakers of any language can learn a second language or even several languages in addition to their mother tongue. Some communicative behavior among nonhuman animals is also the result of learning, either by experience or from humans. No other animals, however, possess the ability to learn one or several systems of communication as complex as language.

Human languages possess all these design features, whereas the communicative systems of other animals possess only some. For example, according to Hockett (1960), calls produced by gibbons are characterized by the presence of design features 1 through 9 but lack displacement, productivity, and duality of patterning (Hockett is unsure about traditional transmission). One shortcoming of the original list of design features when applied to communicative systems of nonhuman animals is that it calls for yes-or-no, or present-or-absent, answers rather than for the degree to which a particular feature might be present. A revision of the design-feature approach (Hockett and Altmann 1968) allows for indicating the degree to which any one of the design features is employed and in addition calls for the use of five frameworks having to do with features of the social setting, the behavioral antecedents and consequences of communicative acts, the channel or channels employed, continuity and change in communication systems, and the structure of messages and their repertories in specific systems. Accordingly, if one is to study a particular communicative system or transaction, one should include inquiries concerning who the participants are and where and under what circumstances they communicate, what channel or channels they use, what the structure of their messages and of the code as a whole is, and so on.

These and related concerns not only are necessary for a fuller understanding of subhuman communication but are equally important for the study and appreciation of human language in the context of society and culture.

Language Acquisition

As most students know only too well, learning to speak a foreign language is a demanding undertaking that means coping with unfamiliar sounds and sound combinations, mastering grammatical rules different from those of one's native language, and learning a new vocabulary with thousands of words. But if for most adults learning a foreign language is a major task and only relatively few attain actual fluency in a second language, how is it that small children learn a language, or even two or more, as effortlessly as they do?

In order to be able to reproduce the speech sounds of any particular language when they begin to speak, infants must learn to discriminate among sounds that may be quite similar. Among the sounds in English considered to be alike or to closely resemble each other are the initial consonants of such pairs of words as *bill* and *pill* or *thin* and *sin,* the final consonants of *sin* and *sing* or *dose* and *doze,* and the vowels of *pet* and *pat, pen* and *pin,* or *mill* and *meal.* The ability to discriminate among sounds that have the same magnitude of acoustic difference when they are contrastive (but perceiving them to be the same when they are not contrastive) is referred to as categorical perception.

How soon and how well do infants discriminate among speech sounds and can they perceive speech categorically? One of the techniques to test infants' acuity of sound perception is high amplitude sucking. A pacifier connected to a system that generates sounds when a child sucks records the rate of sucking. When infants begin to hear sounds, they suck energetically, but they gradually lose interest if the sound continues to be the same. When the sound changes, however, vigorous sucking is resumed.

Infants only one month old appear to be able to distinguish two synthetic consonant-vowel syllables different only in the initial consonants *p* and *b*. Other tests have established that infants are born with the ability to differentiate between even closely similar sounds, but that this ability diminishes or is lost by the age of about one year in favor of perceiving only the differences crucial to the native language. The acuity of voice perception in newborn babies has also been attested. It has been established that three-day-old infants are able to distinguish their mothers' voices from among other female voices. And it has also been shown that newborn infants prefer to listen to their mother tongue rather than another language.

Although the rate of speech development in normal children varies somewhat, it is possible to generalize about the stages that characterize language acquisition. Only reflexive (basic biological) noises such as burping, crying, and coughing are produced during the first eight or ten weeks; these are supplemented by cooing and laughing during the next dozen or so weeks. Vocal play, consisting of the production of a fairly wide range of sounds resembling consonants and vowels, becomes noticeable by about the age of six months. The second half of an infant's first year is characterized by babbling. According to some observers, sounds made during this stage are less varied and tend to approximate those of the language to be acquired. Babbling appears to be largely instinctive because even children who do not hear go through the babbling stage. In general, even before the onset of babbling, infants show eagerness to communicate and begin to process the information they are receiving through various channels. It also appears that regardless of the language they are acquiring, children learn to use the maximally distinct vowel sounds of their language (usually *a, i,* and *u*) before other vowels, and the consonants articulated with the help of the lips and teeth (commonly *p, b, m, t,* and *d*) before those produced farther back in the mouth (Jakobson 1968). Although subsequent research has indicated that the order in which the sounds of languages are acquired is not universal, Roman Jakobson (1896–1982) must be credited as having discovered significant statistical tendencies.

Intonational contours (such as those characteristic of questions) begin to appear around the end of the first year, at about the same time as the one-word stage (for example, *mama, cup,* and *doggie*). This stage is succeeded around the age of two by the multiword stage. At first the child combines two words (for example, *see doggie, baby book, nice kitty,* and *daddy gone*) but soon expands such phrases to short sentences. On the average, the spoken vocabulary of two-year-olds amounts to 200 words or more, although they understand several times that many. Initial consonants of words tend to be pronounced more distinctly by this age group than the consonants toward word ends. By the age of five or so, all normal children the world over are able to ask questions, make negative statements, produce complex sentences (consisting of main and subordinate clauses), talk about things removed in time and space, and in general carry on an intelligent conversation on topics they are able to comprehend (but they have yet to learn to tie their shoes). Even though much of the speech to which children are exposed is quite variable and casual, they gain command of the many sounds, forms, and rules so well that they are able to say, and do say, things they have never before heard said—and all of this without the benefit of any formal teaching.

There are several theories of language acquisition. One of them, the behaviorist psychology theory based on the stimulus-response-reward formula, is not unlike the popular view of language acquisition. According to this theory, the human environment (parents, older peers, and others) provides language stimuli to which the child responds, largely by repetition of what he or she is hearing. If the response is acceptable or commendable, the learner is rewarded (by praise or some other way). Children do imitate, of course, but not as consistently as is generally thought; otherwise they would not produce such analogical but ungrammatical forms as *sheeps, gooses,* and *taked* instead of *sheep, geese,* and *took.* Such forms as *sheeps, gooses,* and *taked* in fact show that rather than imitating others, children derive these forms on the assumption of grammatical regularity—by extending the "regular" plural and past-tense markers to words to which they do not apply.

Another theory, referred to as cognitivist, links language acquisition with a child's intellectual, or cognitive, development. Introduced in the early writings of Jean Piaget (1896–1980), a Swiss psychologist, this theory holds that not until a child develops general (nonlinguistic) knowledge of the environment does it apply this knowledge to speech behavior, and that knowledge of word meanings is prerequisite to achieving mastery of the grammatical structure of language. What is difficult to demonstrate precisely in an infant or small child, though, is the relationship between cognitive development and speech behavior.

Among the latest theories of language development is the innatist theory stimulated since the late 1950s by the writings of Noam Chomsky. Chomsky believes children are born with a capacity for language development (see Box 2.1). However, the nature of the language acquisition device, with which all infants are equipped, cannot at present be specified. According to some, it consists only of general procedures helping the child to discover how to learn any natural language; according to others, this device provides children with a knowledge of those features that are common to all languages. Chomsky (1986), for example, speaks of a genetically built-in "core grammar" that besides a number of fixed rules also contains various optional rules; it is up to the child to discover which of these options apply to a particular language. This would help to explain how children manage

BOX 2.1 Chomsky on Language Acquisition

We can think of every normal human's internalized grammar as, in effect, a theory of his language. This theory provides a sound-meaning correlation for an infinite number of sentences. ...

In formal terms ... we can describe the child's acquisition of language as a kind of theory construction. The child discovers the theory of his language with only small amounts of data from that language. ... Normal speech consists, in large part, of fragments, false starts, blends, and other distortions of the underlying idealized forms. Nevertheless, as is evident from a study of the mature use of language, what the child learns is the underlying ideal theory. This is a remarkable fact. We must also bear in mind that the child constructs this ideal theory without explicit instruction, that he acquires this knowledge at a time when he is not capable of complex intellectual achievements in many other domains, and that this achievement is relatively independent of intelligence or the particular course of experience. These are facts that a theory of learning must face. ...

... It is unimaginable that a highly specific, abstract, and tightly organized language comes by accident into the mind of every four-year-old child.

from Noam Chomsky, "Language and the Mind" (1968), 66

to overcome what is referred to as "poverty of stimulus"—that is, their ability to learn to speak a language effectively in a relatively short time, regardless of how complex it may be grammatically, even if much of what they hear happens to be largely fragmentary or repetitious.

It would probably oversimplify the explanation of how young children are able to acquire so rapidly the knowledge of such a complex symbolic system as language if one were to accept any one of these or other theories to the exclusion of the others. There is little doubt that children do imitate, but certainly not to the extent some claim; and it is also quite likely that the earliest phases of language learning are not completely divorced from the child's mental development. However, many of the aspects of the innatist theory are quite convincing, and the theory has received much acceptance. It is indirectly supported by the somewhat controversial critical-period (or critical-age) hypothesis that language is acquired with remarkable ease during brain maturation, that is, before puberty. By this time the brain has reached its full development, and the various functions it performs have been localized in one side or the other (lateralization). According to recent research, though, lateralization may already be complete by the end of the fifth year, by which age children have acquired the grammatical essentials of their mother tongue.

Until recently, language acquisition was treated as if it were unaffected by sociocultural factors and, correspondingly, the process of children's learning their culture was usually studied without giving attention to the role language plays in the process. Among those linguists and anthropologists who have called for the integration of the two approaches are Elinor Ochs and Bambi B. Schieffelin. In one of their works concerning language acquisition and socialization (1982), their view of the subject is expressed in terms of the following two claims: "The process of acquiring language is deeply affected by the process of becoming a competent member of a society [and] the process of becoming a competent member of society is realized to a large extent through language, through acquiring knowledge of its functions . . . i.e., through exchanges of language in particular social situations" (Ochs and Schieffelin 1982:2–3). In the main body of the article, the authors make use of their fieldwork experiences in Western Samoa and Papua New Guinea (among the Kaluli) and for comparative purposes draw on data pertaining to the communicative development of children of the Anglo-American white middle class. To simplify matters I present only the comparison between the Kaluli and the Anglo-American children.

According to Ochs and Schieffelin's study (which is more than a decade old), Anglo-American white middle-class infants interact mainly with their mothers. This dyadic (two-party) interaction is in part the consequence of the typical family form, postmarital residence, and physical setting characteristic of middle-class apartments or houses—nuclear family, separate home for the young married couple, and a separate bedroom for an infant. Mothers (or caregivers) hold infants face-to-face and treat them as social beings and communicative partners, frequently taking the perspective of the child or displaying interest in what may have been meant by a child's incomplete or unintelligible utterance. To accommodate young children and protect them from injury the environment is adapted to their needs. Consider the availability of baby food, high chairs, and baby walkers as well as books and toys designed for specific ages, and the parental concern shown for the safety of the child by the cushioning of sharp edges, the placing of protective gates at stairs, and the like. The gap between the caregiver's and the child's verbal competence is reduced by a generous interpretation of the child's utterances or is masked by attempts to elicit stories from the child by posing questions it can answer with brief responses. In short, the child is the focus of attention and quite frequently the starting point of social interaction.

Among the Kaluli, a small, nonliterate, egalitarian society, the process of language acquisition and socialization is different. Kaluli babies are considered helpless and unable to comprehend the world around them; their unintelligible utterances tend to be ignored and no attempt is made to interpret them. Infants' needs are of course attended to, and a mother nurses her child even if she is involved in other activities. Nor are infants ever left alone: Mothers carry babies with them in netted bags whenever they happen to be gathering wood, gardening, or simply sitting and talking with others. But despite the physical proximity of a mother and her child, there is little communicative interaction between them. Infants are carried facing others, not their mothers. When infants approaching the age of one year do something they should not, they are reprimanded with such questions as "Who are you?" or "Is it yours?" meaning, respectively, "You are not someone to do that" and "It is not yours." Not until a child begins to use the words *nɔ* 'mother' and *bo* 'breast' is it considered ready to be "shown how to speak." Because adult men and women are involved in extensive networks of obligation and reciprocity as they organize their work and manipulate social relations, the primary goal of socialization at the time when children begin to talk is to teach them how to talk effectively. Among the conventions of adult speech is avoiding gossip and indicating the source of information by noting whether something has been heard or seen and by quoting others directly. Children are expected to follow these conventions. Very little language is directed to Kaluli children before they begin to speak, but the verbal environment in which they grow up is rich, and children acquire verbal skills from listening to others. Although the one large village longhouse, where all villagers once lived together, is no longer in general use, at least two or more extended family groups share living space. The presence of a dozen or more individuals in one semipartitioned dwelling leads to frequent multiparty interaction. To teach the Kaluli language as spoken by adults, mothers constantly correct children for faulty pronunciation, grammar, and use of words so that they bypass the stage of baby talk.

Evaluating the available information as to how children develop their communicative skills for functioning in different societies or subcultures, the authors are led to assume that "infants and caregivers do not interact with one another according to one particular 'biologically designed choreography' . . . [but] there are many choreographies within and across societies . . . that contribute to their design, frequency and significance" (Ochs and Schieffelin 1982:44). This means, for example, that dyadic exchanges are accorded a varying degree of significance in different societies: Among the Kaluli, children are exposed to multiparty interaction much more frequently than to dyadic interaction. The authors further propose that the "simplifying features of caregiver speech that have been described for white middle class speakers are not necessary input for young children to acquire language," and on the basis of these two proposals the authors suggest that "a functional account of the speech of both caregiver and child must incorporate information concerning cultural knowledge and expectations . . . [and] generalizations concerning the relations between behavior and goals of caregivers and young children should not presuppose the presence or equivalent significance of particular goals across social groups" (Ochs and Schieffelin 1982:46, 50).

Without language no child could adequately learn all aspects of the culture and worldview of his or her society. It follows, then, that normal communicative exchanges in which caregivers and small children engage must in some way relate to the behavior patterns expected of adult members of a society. Are situations adapted to the child, or must the child adapt to situations? And if there is a shift from one to the other of these two orientations in any given society, when does it take place?

The authors make it clear that their model does not exclude the role biological predisposition may play at the expense of culture and that they do not view socialization as a process that is inflexible over time or during an individual's lifetime. But they insist that "our understanding of the functional and symbolic interface between language and culture" can only be furthered by studies of "how children are socialized through the use of language as well as how children are socialized to use language" (Schieffelin and Ochs 1986:184).

Language and the Brain

Even though our understanding of how the human brain operates is steadily increasing, our knowledge of its functions is still far from complete. Among the reasons are that the brain is tremendously complex and that experimentation with the brain is still somewhat limited. Some of what is known about its functions has been learned from the location and extent of brain injuries; however, a great deal of information has recently been gained from new experimental techniques (for example, neuro-imaging, the use of tachistoscopes, and the stimulation of the cerebral cortex or nerve centers below it by electric current).

Neurolinguistics—the branch of linguistics concerned with the role the brain plays in language and speech processing—explores questions on which parts of the brain control language and speech, how the brain encodes and decodes speech, and whether the controls of such aspects of language as sounds, grammar, and meaning are neuroanatomically distinct or joint.

In relation to body mass, the human brain is the largest in the animal kingdom. It is also the most complexly organized. The largest part is the cerebrum, situated at the top of the brain and consisting of two lobes—the left and right cerebral hemispheres—and connecting structures. Each of the two hemispheres fills different functions. For example, the left is specialized for associative thought, calculation and analytical processing, the right visual field, temporal relations, and other functions; the right hemisphere for tactile recognition of material qualities, visuospatial skills,

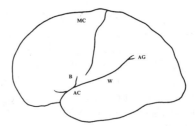

FIGURE 2.2   The Human Brain. Side view of the left hemisphere of the human brain, with its front on the left. The locations of the areas mentioned in the text are indicated as follows: AC = auditory cortex; AG = angular gyrus; B = Broca's area; MC = motor cortex; W = Wernicke's area. The thalamus is not seen from this view.

nonlinguistic auditory stimuli (including music), the left visual field, some use of language in social context, and others. In an overwhelming majority of right-handed individuals, the left hemisphere controls language, speech, writing, and reading. In more than one half of left-handed people, it is also the left hemisphere that either controls language or is significantly involved, but in other left-handers language specialization is located in the right hemisphere. Apart from the cerebral cortex—the surface layer of gray matter of the cerebrum—several other parts of the brain contribute to language processing. One such part is the left thalamus, the largest subdivision of the posterior of the forebrain.

Injuries to specific areas of the language-dominant hemisphere from such causes as gunshot wound, tumor, stroke, or infection result in different aphasias or other impairments of linguistic capabilities. To give a few examples, Broca's aphasia, also referred to as expressive or motor aphasia, is caused by a lesion in what is known as Broca's area (see Figure 2.2) and is characterized by omission of function words (such as articles, prepositions, demonstratives, and conjunctions) and past-tense and plural endings, as well as by faulty word order and distortions of sounds. Wernicke's aphasia (also known as sensory or receptive aphasia) is due to a lesion in Wernicke's area; it is characterized by circumlocutions, impaired ability to understand written and spoken language, and occasional substitutions of inappropriate words, leading in severe cases to nonsensical utterances. Individuals affected by anomic aphasia have difficulty naming objects presented to them. Impairment of this type is associated with lesions in the dominant angular gyrus, one of the characteristic ridges of gray matter at the surfaces of the hemispheres.

Wernicke's area appears to generate the basic structure of sentences, which are then encoded in Broca's area; the articulation of sounds is directed by certain motor areas of the cortex. Comprehension of speech takes place in Wernicke's area after acoustic signals are transferred there from the ear by the auditory cortex. In general, speaking and writing are more likely to be affected by damage to the front part of the brain, listening and reading to damage to the rear part.

From what is now known, lesions in different parts of the language-dominant hemisphere result in different language and speech impairments. But much is yet to be learned about the human brain, both in general and concerning its role in communicative behavior.

Summary and Conclusions

Speech is only one of several means by which humans communicate, but it is the most common and efficient one. Besides the acoustic channel employed in speaking, people make use of other channels, especially the optical one; they do so whenever they make gestures or facial expressions and, of course, when they write.

Communication is common among animals of all species and in some cases is surprisingly elaborate, as when a worker honeybee signals to other bees in what direction and at what distance from the hive an abundant source of nectar is to be found. To a considerable extent, animals are genetically endowed with communicative behavior, that is, they do not have to learn it. Although the capacity for speech is also a part of human genetic makeup, the particular language or languages an individual happens to speak must be learned. Among the design features that distinguish speech from the communicative behavior of other animals, the most striking are productivity, displacement, and reflexiveness.

Learning to speak a foreign language is a formidable task, and most adults fail to achieve fluency even after many years of trying. Children, however, learn their native language with no apparent effort and without instruction before they reach school age. One widely accepted theory concerning language acquisition holds that infants are born with an abstract language model already programmed into their brains. Endowed with such a language acquisition device, they apply it as they learn the particular mother tongue they hear spoken around them. Acquisition of language should not be studied without considering the sociocultural context in which it takes place. Knowing how to use their native language effectively helps individuals cope with their culture, and learning to use it appropriately is an important part of enculturation (the process of learning one's culture).

Among the many activities the human brain controls are speech, writing, and reading. Even though much is still to be learned about the workings of the brain, it has long been known that different parts of the brain contribute to different aspects of language processing. Injuries to these areas result in corresponding language and speech impairments.

Suggestions for Further Reading

Informative sources concerning communication among animals include Sebeok 1977, Bright 1984, and Roitblat and others 1992. The dance language of bees is described in Frisch 1967. For communication of nonhuman primates, see Schrier and Stollnitz 1971, which contains articles by Keith J. Hayes and Catherine H. Nissen, Beatrice T. Gardner and R. Allen Gardner, and David Premack, who trained Viki, Washoe, and Sarah, respectively. For an extensive and richly illustrated recent report on the chimpanzees of Gombe National Park in Tanzania, see Goodall 1986; and for a book-size discussion of Nim, see Terrace 1979. Savage-Rumbaugh 1986 discusses at length the various projects, including her own, to teach chimpanzees to communicate; and Susman 1984 deals with the evolutionary biology and behavior of pygmy chimpanzees. For a survey of works and bibliography concerning apes and language prior to 1978, see Hill 1978.

Useful surveys of child language acquisition and the neurological basis of language can be found in Crystal 1991a. See Chomsky 1959 for an extensive and now classic review and critique of a book concerning verbal behavior by the influential advocate of behaviorist psychology, B. F. Skinner. Jakobson 1968 is an English translation of Jakobson's German original published in Sweden in 1942. For a detailed account of language socialization of Kaluli children, see Schieffelin 1990. More information on language development, language disorders, and language and learning may be found in Menyuk 1988 and Berko Gleason 1989. For a classic (though no longer the latest) account of the biological foundations of language, see Lenneberg 1967.

3
Language and Culture

The nature of the relationship between language and culture was under consideration long before anthropology became recognized as a scholarly field in its own right. Wilhelm von Humboldt (1767–1835), a well-known German diplomat and scholar, was one of those who had very definite thoughts on the subject. He wrote, "The spiritual traits and the structure of the language of a people are so intimately blended that, given either of the two, one should be able to derive the other from it to the fullest extent. . . . Language is the outward manifestation of the spirit of people: their language is their spirit, and their spirit is their language; it is difficult to imagine any two things more identical."

In the past, language, culture, and race were often lumped together as though any one of them automatically implied the other two. Modern anthropologists find Humboldt's statement unacceptable in the form in which it was made. One of the tasks and accomplishments of anthropology has been to demonstrate that culture, race, and language are historically separable. Although it is true that human culture in its great complexity could not have developed and is unthinkable without the aid of language, no correlation has yet been established between cultures of a certain type and a certain type of language. In fact, there were and still are areas in the world where societies share a very similar cultural orientation yet speak languages that are not only mutually unintelligible but completely unrelated and structurally different. Such was the case, for example, of the North American Indians of the Great Plains, who possessed many of the same or very similar cultural characteristics but whose languages belonged to at least six different language families: Algonquian (for example, Arapaho and Cheyenne), Siouan (for example, Crow and Dakota), Uto-Aztecan (for example, Shoshone-Comanche), Athapaskan (Sarcee and Kiowa Apache), Caddoan (Wichita and Pawnee-Arikara), and Kiowa-Tanoan (Kiowa). The opposite may also hold true: Estonians and Lapps speak related languages (both belong to the Finnic branch of the Finno-Ugric subfamily of the Uralic family of languages), but their cultures are quite different. The absence of any intrinsic (inherent) relationship among a people's physical type, culture, and language was repeatedly declared by Boas, particularly in his eighty-page introduction to the first volume of the *Handbook of American Indian Languages* (1911).

The subject of language-culture relationship was also prominent in the work of Edward Sapir. Although Sapir was convinced, just as Boas had been earlier, that "language and culture are not intrinsically associated," he nevertheless believed that "language and our thought-grooves are inextricably interwoven, [and] are, in a sense, one and the same" (Sapir 1921:228, 232). If the distinction between Boas's view and Sapir's contention, as cited, sounds like hairsplitting, let me try to clarify the difference. Both Boas and Sapir had no doubt that the association of a particular culture, physical type (race), and language was not given by nature but was a historical coincidence. If this were not so, how could it happen that peoples of different physical types speak the same language or closely related languages and that peoples of the same or similar physical type speak a variety of different and completely unrelated languages? The same sort of random association holds true for language and culture as well as for language and physical type. However, both Boas and Sapir believed that inasmuch as each particular language serves a particular society and is instrumental in helping the youngest members learn to operate within the society's culture, some relationship between the language and the culture could be expected to develop.

Because Sapir's writings aroused a great deal of interest in the question of how languages influence the culture of their speakers, it is important to take up the recent history of this subject in more detail and also to examine it from the perspective of contemporary anthropology.

The Stimulus of Sapir's Writings

Sapir, who had come to the United States at the age of five, became acquainted with Boas at Columbia University while doing graduate work. Impressed by Boas's breadth of knowledge and field experience, he switched from Germanic studies to anthropology. From that time on, most of his energies were devoted to the study of Native American languages. He published prolifically, his book *Language* (1921) remaining a classic to the present day.

In *Time Perspective in Aboriginal American Culture* (1916), Sapir discusses various methods that can be employed to develop cultural chronologies for aboriginal America whenever native testimonies and historical or archaeological records are either lacking or of little or no help. Sapir observes that compared to changes in culture, linguistic changes come about more slowly and evenly, and that language is far more compact and self-contained than culture taken as a whole and therefore is largely free of conscious rationalization on the part of its speakers. Major revolutions, whether violent or not, usually change profoundly the structure of the societies in which they occur, yet languages remain unchanged except for relatively minor adjustments in vocabulary.

Two examples from the many Sapir gives illustrate his use of language as a key to the cultural past of a society. Mount Shasta in northern California was visible to a number of Native American tribes. Among these, members of the Hupa tribe referred to the mountain by the descriptive term *nin-nis-ʔan ɬak-gai* 'white mountain,' whereas the Yana name for it was *wa'galu·*, a word no longer translatable or analyzable. According to Sapir, the Yana word is therefore undoubtedly much older, and one may assume that the country dominated by Mount Shasta was home to the Yana long before the Hupa came to the region. Turning to the Northwest Coast, Sapir considers the Nootka word *ɬo·kwa·na*, which refers to the wolf ceremonial complex of the tribe. Because Nootka words characteristically consist of one syllable (made up of a consonant-vowel-consonant sequence) rather than three syllables, the form of the term suggests that it, along with the ceremony, may have been borrowed from another tribe. And indeed the neighboring Kwakiutl people have a wolf dance to which they refer by a term that appears to be the source of the Nootka word. Linguistic data in this case indicate not only that at least some aspects of a culture complex may have been borrowed by another tribe but also the likely source of the influence.

What caught the imagination of a great many scholars and inspired active research for several decades, however, was a particular paragraph of a paper Sapir read in 1928 at a scholarly meeting in New York attended by both linguists and anthropologists:

> In a sense, the network of cultural patterns of a civilization is indexed in the language which expresses that civilization. . . . Language is a guide to "social reality." Though language is not ordinarily thought of as of essential interest to the students of social science, it powerfully conditions all our thinking about social problems and processes. Human beings do not live in the objective world alone, nor alone in the world of social activity as ordinarily understood, but are very much at the mercy of the particular language which has become the medium of expression for their society. . . . The fact of the matter is that the "real world" is to a large extent unconsciously built up on the language habits of the group. No two languages are ever sufficiently similar to be considered as representing the same social reality. The worlds in which different societies live are distinct worlds, not merely the same world with different labels attached. (Sapir 1929:209)

The most provocative statement was the assertion that humans are at the mercy of the language they happen to speak.

The Whorf Hypothesis of Linguistic Relativity and Linguistic Determinism

Whereas Boas's and Sapir's ideas concerning the relationship between language and culture primarily influenced only their students and other scholars, the writings of Benjamin Lee Whorf (1897–1941) caught the attention of the educated public. Whorf, a chemical engineer by training, was a fire prevention inspector and later an executive of a New England fire insurance company. Although he continued to work for the company until his untimely death, in 1931 he enrolled in a course at Yale University in order to do graduate study under Sapir, who had just been awarded a professorship at Yale. Among Whorf's numerous subsequent publications, the best known are those in which he expounded on what some have referred to as the Sapir-Whorf hypothesis (see Box 3.1).

Expanding on Sapir's ideas, Whorf wrote that

> the background linguistic system (in other words, the grammar) of each language is not merely a reproducing instrument for voicing ideas but rather is itself the shaper of ideas. . . . We dissect nature along lines laid down by our native languages . . . organize it into concepts, and ascribe significances as we do, largely because we are parties to an agreement to organize it in this way—an agreement that holds throughout our speech community and is codified in the patterns of our language. . . . [Not] all observers are . . . led by the same physical evidence to the same picture of the universe, unless their linguistic backgrounds are similar. (Whorf 1940a:231)

He further asserts that "users of markedly different grammars are pointed by their grammars toward different types of observations . . . and hence are not equivalent as observers but must arrive at somewhat different views of the world" (Whorf 1940b:61). In these passages Whorf sets forth a double principle: the principle of **linguistic determinism,** namely, that the way one thinks is determined by the language one speaks, and the principle of **linguistic relativity,** that differences among languages must therefore be reflected in the differences in the worldviews of their speakers.

Many of the examples Whorf uses to support his contention came from Hopi, a language spoken by Native Americans in the pueblos of northeastern Arizona. Although Whorf briefly visited the Hopi villages in 1938, the data for his grammatical sketch of the language (1946) were obtained from a native speaker of Hopi who lived in New York City. In an article dealing with grammatical aspects of Hopi verbs, Whorf puts forth the claim that the Hopi "have a language better equipped to deal with such vibratile phenomena [that is, phenomena characterized by vibration]

BOX 3.1 How Words Affect Behavior

It was in the course of my professional work for a fire insurance company, in which I undertood the task of analyzing many hundreds of reports of circumstances surrounding the start of fires, and in some cases, of explosions. My analysis was directed toward purely physical conditions, such as defective wiring, presence or lack of air spaces between metal flues and woodwork, etc., and the results were presented in these terms. ... But in due course it became evident that not only a physical situation *qua* physics, but the meaning of that situation to people, was sometimes a factor, through the behavior of the people, in the start of the fire. And this factor of meaning was clearest when it was a LINGUISTIC MEANING, residing in the name or the linguistic description commonly applied to the situation. Thus, around a storage of what are called "gasoline drums," behavior will tend to a certain type, that is, great care will be exercised; while around a storage of what are called "empty gasoline drums," it will tend to be different—careless, with little repression of smoking or of tossing cigarette stubs about. Yet the "empty" drums are perhaps the more dangerous, since they contain explosive vapor. Physically the situation is hazardous, but the linguistic analysis according to regular analogy must employ the word 'empty,' which inevitably suggests lack of hazard.

from Benjamin Lee Whorf, *Language, Thought, and Reality* (1956), 135

---

than is our latest [English] scientific terminology" (1936:131). Among his examples are the verb forms *wa´la* 'it (a liquid) makes a wave, gives a slosh,' *ti´ri* 'he gives a sudden start,' and *ʔi´mï* 'it explodes, goes off like a gun.' These and others can be changed from their punctual aspect (a term used to refer to a verb action concentrated into a very short period of time) to the segmentative aspect by repeating (reduplicating) their last two sounds and adding the ending *-ta* to produce the forms *wala´lata* 'it is tossing in waves,' *tiri´rita* 'he is quivering, trembling,' and *ʔimï´mïta* 'it is thundering.' Whereas in English the difference between something happening once briefly and something occurring repeatedly over time may call for different phrases (for example, "it explodes" as against "it is thundering" or "it makes a wave" as against "it is tossing in waves"), the Hopi express it by the use of a simple grammatical device. In Whorf's words, the example illustrates "how the Hopi language maps out a certain terrain of what might be termed primitive physics ... with very thorough consistency and not a little true scientific precision" and "how language produces an organization of experience" (1936:130–131).

In another article, written in the mid-1930s but not published until nine years after Whorf's death, the author states that "the Hopi language is seen to contain no words, grammatical forms, constructions or expressions that refer directly to what we call TIME, or to past, present, or future . . . or that even refer to space in such a way as to exclude that element of extension or existence that we call TIME" (1950:67). Instead, the grand coordinates of the universe for the Hopi are manifest, objective experience and the unfolding, subjective realm of human existence.

Whorf illustrates his notion of linguistic relativity by using as an example the Apache equivalent of the English utterance "It is a dripping spring" (referring to a source of water): "Apache erects the statement on a verb *ga:* 'be white (including clear, uncolored, and so on).' With a prefix *nō-* the meaning of downward motion enters: 'whiteness moves downward.' Then *tó,* meaning both 'water' and 'spring,' is prefixed. The result corresponds to our 'dripping spring,' but synthetically it is: 'as water, or springs, whiteness moves downward.' How utterly unlike our way of thinking!" (Whorf 1941a:266, 268).

Following up on the hypothesis that a language and the culture it serves mirror each other, Whorf compares the Hopi language with western European languages (labeled SAE for "Standard Average European"). According to him, the differences in linguistic structure between Hopi and SAE are reflected in "habitual thought" and "habitual behavior." For example, "the Hopi microcosm seems to have analyzed reality largely in terms of *events* (or better[,] 'eventing'), referred to in two ways, objective and subjective" (1941b:84); the emphasis is on being in accord, by means of thoughtful participation, with the unfolding forces of nature. Speakers of SAE, in contrast, conceive of the universe largely in terms of things and of time in terms of schedules. SAE languages use tense to mark the time at which an action takes place (as in the past, present, future, or, even more specifically, as in "I had eaten," to express the completion of an action before a specific past time). No wonder, then, that speakers of western European languages tend to be preoccupied with "records, diaries, book-keeping, accounting . . . calendars, chronology . . . annals, histories . . . [and] budgets" (1941b:88).

The implications of Whorf's ideas concerning linguistic relativity and determinism are quite serious. If the worldview and behavior of a people are significantly affected by the structure of the language they speak, and if languages differ in structure, then cross-cultural communication and understanding are likely to be noticeably impaired, if not impossible to achieve. This is why Whorf's ideas received a great deal of attention and stimulated much discussion for a number of years after World War II. From a contemporary standpoint, however, it appears that Whorf overstated his case. Let us next consider how.

Language, Culture, and Worldview:
A Relationship Reconsidered

Critical comments on Whorf's writings were soon to appear. Eric H. Lenneberg pointed out that "a demonstration that certain languages differ from each other suggests but does not prove that the speakers of these languages differ from each other as a group in their psychological potentialities" (1953:463), and on the following page appears his comment on Whorf's well-known example of "empty drums" (see Box 3.1): "Clearly, English is capable of distinguishing between a drum filled with an explosive vapor, one that contains only air, and one which is void of any matter. . . . The person who caused the fire could have replaced the word *empty* by *filled with explosive vapor*."

Others decided to put the principle of relativity to the test, among them Brent Berlin and Paul Kay. According to them, "the prevailing doctrine of American linguists and anthropologists has . . . been that of extreme linguistic relativity," meaning that "each language is semantically arbitrary relative to every other language . . . [and] the search for semantic universals is [therefore] fruitless in principle" (Berlin and Kay 1969:1–2). Their research during the late 1960s, based on the examination of ninety-eight languages from all parts of the world, came up with some unexpected findings.

1. There is a universal inventory of eleven basic color categories from among which the basic color terms in different languages are drawn: These categories are white, black, red, green, yellow, blue, brown, purple, pink, orange, and gray.

2. If a language encodes fewer than the eleven basic color categories, then there is a sequence in which the color terms are encoded: All languages contain terms for white and black; the third term is for red; the fourth term is for either green or yellow; the fifth term is for the other of the previous two; the sixth term is for blue; the seventh is for brown; and the remaining four terms are for the remaining color categories or some combination thereof. (A basic color term consists of one morpheme, is not included in any other color term, and is a general term; accordingly, the English color terms *bluish*, *crimson*, and *blond* would be excluded by definition.)

The second major conclusion of Berlin and Kay is that "there appears to be a fixed sequence of evolutionary stages through which a language must pass as its basic color vocabulary increases" (1969:14). In addition, a positive correlation appears to exist between the complexity of the color vocabulary and cultural complexity.

Berlin and Kay's findings should not be taken as a total refutation of the concept of linguistic relativity but only of its extreme form. What their conclusions point to, though, is that when it comes to the domains of color vocabulary, there does exist a semantic feature that is universal, or at least nearly universal.

For the purposes of further discussion concerning the relationship between language and culture, the two terms must be carefully defined. The term *language,* as we have already seen, refers to the complex of universally human potentialities for vocal communication or, simply, to the gift of speech. By contrast, **a language** refers to any one of the several thousand systems of oral communication used by different human societies. Language is a part of human genetic endowment, whereas *a* (particular) language must be learned during childhood along with the many nonverbal facets of the particular culture. In a sense, then, *a* language is just as culture-bound as are the traditional habits and value orientations characteristic of the society whose members use it. Furthermore, when discussing particular languages in this context, it is convenient to distinguish between at least two aspects of any language—its lexicon (or vocabulary) and its structure (conventionally referred to as grammar).

The term **culture** also is all-inclusive. Taken comprehensively, it is understood to refer to the total pattern of human learned behavior transmitted from generation to generation. When one talks about **a culture,** however, the explicit mention of language is, strictly speaking, redundant because any particular language is a form (even though autonomous) of learned behavior and therefore a part of the culture. A solution to this terminological overlap would be to distinguish between a nonverbal culture and the corresponding language. Nonverbal culture can be further divided into mental culture (for example, worldview or value orientations), behavioral culture (for example, wiping one's feet before entering a house or performing a heart transplant), and—according to some anthropologists—material culture, that is, the material products of behavior (for example, a pull-open beer can or a radio telescope). Items of material culture are usually the result of the application of behavioral (manual skills) and mental culture (knowledge).

If it is true that all languages, regardless of the superficial differences among them, share some universal features—or in other words, if the structure of language is in some way determined by the structure of the human brain—then one could envision the possibility of a common organization of human experience. In such case, on a deep level the question of the relationship between language and culture would cease to exist.

According to a strong version of this proposition, grammatical categories of a language determine how its speakers perceive the world around them. According to a weak version, there is simply some sort of correlation between a language and its speakers' worldview (the philosophical dimension of a society's culture).

There is no question that the lexicon of any language mirrors whatever the nonverbal culture emphasizes; that is, those aspects of culture that are important for the members of a society are correspondingly highlighted in the vocabulary. For example, words conveying the various characteristics of camels (age, breed, gender, function, condition, and so on) are undoubtedly more plentiful in a language spoken by bedouins who depend on camels than they are in English; the vocabulary of American English, for its part, is replete with the names of makes and models of automobiles, with new names of models of the various makes being added every year. In Pintupi, one of the aboriginal languages of Australia, there are at least ten words designating various kinds of holes found in nature or in manufactured objects: *mutara* is a special hole in a spear, *pulpa* is a rabbit burrow, *makarnpa* is a burrow of a monitor lizard, *katarta* is the hole left by a monitor lizard after it has broken the surface after hibernation, and so on. This example also shows that even though a language may not have a one-word equivalent for a word of another language, it is possible to provide an adequate translation by a descriptive phrase (which in the case of *katarta* may take as many as fifteen English words). To avoid wordiness or the use of borrowed words, many languages coin new words. Some years ago an American anthropologist thought a kinship term was needed to include the meanings of both *nephew* and *niece* and coined the word *nibling*, using the word *sibling* (brother or sister) as a model. However, to conclude that the absence of equivalent terms between different vocabularies must always be associated with a different perception of the world would be farfetched.

Whorf's examples from Hopi also call for comment. According to Charles F. Voegelin, Florence M. Voegelin, and LaVerne Masayesva Jeanne (1979), the relationship between the punctual and segmentative aspects is not as straightforward as Whorf describes it: For example, not all nonreduplicated (not doubled) stems without the ending *-ta* can be said to express the punctual aspect. Furthermore, although speakers of Hopi make little of the division between future and nonfuture, they do indicate tense by temporal adverbs, the suffix *-ni* (future), and the gnomic suffix *-ŋʷɨ* (meaning that something is generally true).

Whorf claimed that the Apache way of thinking is "utterly unlike" that of speakers of English because the utterance "It is a dripping spring" translates literally from Apache into English as "As water, or springs, whiteness moves downward." But suppose that speakers of a foreign language were to interpret literally *breakfast* as "breaking the fast (abstinence from food)," *bonfire* as "a fire of bones, bone fire," and *spinster* as "a woman whose occupation is spinning" and as a result saw a profound difference between their own way of thinking and that of English-speaking people.

Certain lexical differences between languages may, though, have as a consequence different categorizations of the corresponding part of the environment. Speakers of English use the personal pronoun *you* whether they are addressing one or several children, adults, old persons, subordinates, or individuals much superior to themselves in rank. Only when addressing God in prayer or in certain very limited contexts—for example, in the language of the Friends (the Quakers) or in poetry—does one use the pronoun *thou* (which is singular only). The typical situation in other languages, including most of those spoken in Europe, is more complex. When addressing someone, speakers of Dutch, French, German, Italian, Russian, Spanish, and other languages must choose between the "familiar" personal pronoun (T form) and the "polite" personal pronoun (V form) and/or the corresponding verb form. (The symbols T and V are derived from the French *tu* and *vous*, the familiar and polite second-person pronouns, respectively.) In Czech, for example, to address an individual who is closely related, someone socially close and of long acquaintance, or a child below the age of puberty, one commonly uses the personal pronoun *ty*. But in addressing a casual acquaintance, a stranger, or a person deserving respect, one uses the pronoun *vy*, which also serves as the plural of *ty*. A speaker may occasionally wonder, for example, which of the two forms to use when addressing an adult whom the speaker knew as a child and referred to repeatedly as *ty*. A translation from Czech into English, or vice versa, that involves these pronouns (and/or the corresponding verb forms) is therefore not equivalent. The Czech phrases "ty a já" and "vy a já" both translate into English as "you and I," even though the first one makes use of the informal, familiar—even intimate—pronoun and would not be used in situations in which the formal, polite pronoun of the second phrase would be appropriate. The English translation, then, can only be approximate, as it cannot fully convey the nature of the relationship between the speaker and the addressee.

Let us consider another example, one with more significant consequences. Among the Arapaho, a Native American tribe of the Great Plains, the term for "my mother" is *néínoo*. This Arapaho term for "my mother" also applies to ego's mother's sister, a person referred to in the American kinship system as "my aunt" (*ego* is the person of reference to whom others are shown to be related). However, the term by which ego calls his mother's brother is *nési*, roughly equivalent to "my uncle." Similarly, the term for "my father," *neisónoo*, also refers to ego's father's brother, whereas father's sister is referred to as *nehéi*, roughly equivalent to "my aunt." Now if ego's father's brother is termed *neisónoo*, as is also ego's father, it follows that father's brother's wife would be referred to by the same term as ego's father's wife, that is, *néínoo*. And by the same token, ego's mother's sister's husband is referred to in Arapaho as *neisónoo* 'my father.' Whereas in the American kinship terminology biological parents are distinguished from uncles and aunts, the Arapaho and many other peoples lump together lineal relatives with some of their collateral relatives—the biological mother, her sister, and father's brother's wife on the one hand, and the biological father, his brother, and mother's sister's husband on the other (see Figure 3.1). It follows, then, that anyone who calls some relatives of the parental generation by terms that apply to the biological mother and father is in turn called by all these relatives by terms that apply to biological sons and daughters.

Is one to conclude from the Arapaho kinship terminology that the Arapaho are unaware of the difference between a biological mother (or father) and her sister (or his brother)? Of course not. What it means is that the extension of the Arapaho kinship terms *neisónoo* and *néínoo* from ego's biological parents to additional relatives is paralleled by an extension of ego's behavior toward his or her biological father and mother to all those relatives who are referred to by the same kinship terms. All Arapaho terminological "fathers" and "mothers" have the same obligations toward their terminological "sons" and "daughters," and vice versa, even though opportunities to fulfill them may sometimes be limited by circumstances. Among those "parents" and "children" whose interaction is limited by distance, the emphasis is on extending the relevant attitudes rather than behavior. It is clear that the kinship terminology by which one classifies relatives also governs the type of behavior patterns and attitudes applied to them.

Do grammatical features have any influence on how speakers of a language perceive and categorize the world around them? In some instances they do, at least to some extent. In others the influence is negligible, if any at all. In English the word *teacher* refers to a person who teaches, whether it is a woman or a man. From a pupil's remark, "Our teacher is too strict," there is no indication of the teacher's gender, though in subsequent conversation gender may be disclosed by the use of the teacher's name or the gender-specific personal pronoun (*she* or *he*). Such ambiguity is not so likely to occur, for example, in German, which distinguishes between the masculine form of *teacher* (*Lehrer*) and the feminine form (*Lehrerin*). Similarly, the suffix -*in* in German changes *Arzt* 'male physician' to *Ärztin* 'female physician' and *Professor* 'male professor' to *Professorin* 'female professor.' English clearly differs from German in that what is optional in the former is obligatory in the latter. But the claim that this and similar distinctions between the two languages have an influence on the outlook of their speakers would be hard to prove; no one would argue, for example, that sexism is more or less common in countries that speak German, in which the marking of gender is more common (but in these and most

50

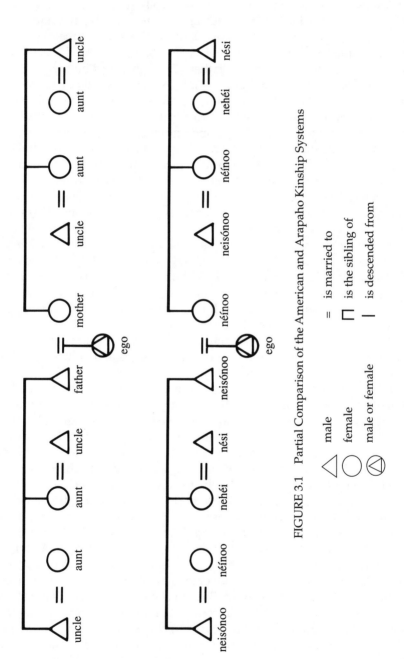

FIGURE 3.1   Partial Comparison of the American and Arapaho Kinship Systems

other languages, the feminine form is derived from the masculine, as in *lioness* from *lion*, and *Löwin* 'lioness' from *Löwe* 'lion' in German).

Like some other Indo-European languages, German has three genders—masculine, feminine, and neuter—that for the most part have nothing to do with maleness, femaleness, or absence of sexual characteristics. In German, for example, window (*das Fenster*) is of neuter gender, as are girl (*das Mädchen*) and woman (*das Weib*); blackboard (*die Tafel*) is feminine, as is crowbar (*die Brechstange*); and bosom (*der Busen*) is masculine, as are the season of spring (*der Frühling*) and skirt (*der Rock*). Do German-speaking people believe that crowbars and blackboards are feminine in the same way as mother (*die Mutter*) or a woman with whom someone is in love (*die Geliebte*) is? I invite the reader to guess.

With only very few exceptions, in English the plural forms of nouns differ from the corresponding singular forms, as in *child* and *children*, *mouse* and *mice*, *horse* and *horses*, *book* and *books*, and *pen* and *pens*. There is no such distinction in many languages and dialects spoken in the People's Republic of China: The same form of a noun stands for both the singular and the plural. Yet the lack of marked grammatical number in nouns and hence no need to differentiate between one or more entities has obviously not prevented the Chinese from making achievements in mathematics and science. In some languages, however, in addition to singular and plural there is also dual, and in a relatively few languages trial and even quadrual, referring respectively to two, three, or four. For the most part, societies whose languages mark these additional distinctions in the grammatical category of number make little use of mathematics.

Still, several studies do indicate that grammatical features may have some influence on nonverbal behavior. Among the best-known studies of this type is the report on an experiment administered to Navajo and white American children by John B. Carroll and Joseph B. Casagrande (1915–1982). A speaker of Navajo must choose from among several forms of Navajo verbs of handling according to the shape or some other characteristic of the object being handled—for example, solid roundish (rock), slender and flexible (rope), flat and flexible (cloth), slender and stiff (stick), noncompact (wool), and so on. Even though the use of the appropriate forms is obligatory, the selection operates below the level of conscious awareness on the part of the speakers, and even children as young as three or four make no errors. (In a somewhat similar fashion, in English one *shrugs* one's shoulders and *nods* one's head, and no native speaker would ever use one term for the other.) One of the hypotheses of the investigators was that this feature of Navajo affects the perception of objects and consequently the behavior of speakers.

Ten pairs of objects were used, each pair significantly differing in two characteristics. The 135 Navajo children who took part in the experiment included some who spoke only Navajo, some who were more proficient in Navajo than in English, some who were balanced bilinguals, some who spoke predominantly English, and some who spoke only English. Each of these children was presented with one of the pairs of objects, shown a third object similar to each member of the pair in one characteristic only (for example, a pair represented by a yellow stick and a piece of blue rope of comparable length, with a yellow rope as the third object), and then asked to match one of the paired objects with the third. The matching on the part of the Navajo-dominant children was predominantly on the basis of shape rather than color, this tendency increasing with the age of the child. Among the English-dominant Navajo children, color appeared to be more important among the youngest, but by the age of ten the two groups had almost converged, with the selection dominated by shape.

The performance of white children in the Boston area was more similar to that of the Navajo-dominant than the English-dominant Navajo children. According to the two investigators, this result may be due at least in part to the early and continued play of white children with toys of the form-board variety, stressing form and size rather than color. On the basis of the difference between the Navajo-dominant and English-dominant groups of Navajo children, the investigators concluded:

> The tendency of a child to match objects on the basis of form or material rather than size or color increases with age and may be enhanced by . . . learning to speak a language, like Navaho, which because of the central role played by form and material in its grammatical structure, requires the learner to make certain discriminations of form and material in the earlier stages of language learning in order to make himself understood at all. (Carroll and Casagrande 1958:31)

The Navajo are among the most extensively studied Native American peoples, and the depth of our understanding of Navajo culture is due in large measure to those individuals who were exposed to the culture for an extended period of time. One such person is the anthropologist Gary Witherspoon, who made the Navajo country his home for over ten years. Prior to his academic career, he worked for Navajo communities and local boards of education and became an interested and concerned participant in the life of the local communities. He learned the Navajo language by listening to Navajos and talking with them.

In *Language and Art in the Navajo Universe* (1977), Witherspoon shares some of the results of his unique experience with the Navajo language and culture. "In the Navajo view of the world," writes Witherspoon (1977:34), "language is not a mirror of reality; reality is a mirror of language." Ritual language in Navajo culture is powerful, its primary purpose being to maintain or restore *hózhǫ́* (the symbol ['] marks high tone; ǫ is nasalized *o*). Although this word refers to the central theme of Navajo worldview and religious thinking, its use is not restricted to ritual contexts—the word is heard frequently in everyday speech. What is *hózhǫ́*? The stem *-zhǫ́* refers to a state characterized by goodness, peace, order, happiness, blessedness, health, beauty (of the natural surroundings), satisfaction, perfection, well-being, deliberation, care, success, and harmony in one's relations with others (the list is not exhaustive but should serve). The form therefore refers not only to aesthetic but also to moral, emotional, and intellectual qualities, and it is difficult to translate into English by a single word or even a phrase. The verbal prefix *ho-*, which is part of *hózhǫ́*, adds to the meaning of the stem the idea of "total environment"— the whole, the general, the abstract, the indefinite, the infinite. As Witherspoon puts it, "Navajo life and culture are based on a unity of experience, and the goal of Navajo life—the creation, maintenance, and restoration of *hózhǫ́*—expresses that unity of experience" (Witherspoon 1977:154).

For the second illustration I let Witherspoon speak for himself (see Box 3.2).

The next example is from Japanese. According to Agnes M. Niyekawa-Howard (1968), the Japanese passive consists of two different constructions. One of these, the ordinary passive, is neutral in meaning. The other, referred to as adversative passive, implies that the grammatical subject of a sentence has been adversely affected, that is, subjected to something undesirable. When the adversative passive is combined with the causative, the resulting connotation is that the subject of the sentence is not responsible for what happened because he or she was "caused" to take the action expressed by the main verb. This connotation is not one that speakers of Japanese are usually conscious of.

The first part of the study consisted of the examination of all passive constructions in about twenty Japanese short stories translated into English by native speakers of English, and twenty English short stories translated into Japanese by native speakers of Japanese. As hypothesized, the connotation of the adversative passive tended to be lost in the translations into English, but it appeared in the translations into Japanese, the Japanese translators having read it into the English original.

The second part of the study compared the interpretations by Japanese and Americans of cartoons depicting situations of interpersonal conflict. As hypothesized, the Japanese were found to attribute responsibility for the negative outcome of events to others to a greater extent than did Americans. Could such an attitude have derived support from the traditionally authoritarian Japanese culture rather than from the structure of the Japanese language? To answer this question, Niyekawa-Howard

BOX 3.2 Classifying Interaction Through Language

The sentence 'the girl drank the water'

At'ééd	tó	yoodlą́ą́'
(girl)	(water)	(it-it-drank)

is acceptable, but the sentence 'the water was drunk by the girl'

Tó	at'ééd	boodlą́ą́'
(water)	(girl)	(it-it-drank)

is unacceptable and absurd in the Navajo view of the world. ...

It is rather evident ... that we need some nonlinguistic data or information in order to interpret these rather unusual linguistic patterns properly. They are not generated by a set of operations at the deep structural level of Navajo grammar; they are generated by a set of cultural rules which are ultimately derived from more fundamental metaphysical propositions which the Navajo take to be axiomatic.

Taking a cultural approach to the explanation of this pattern in Navajo syntax, some years ago I asked my wife why it was so absurd to say *tó at'ééd boodlą́ą́'* 'the water was drunk by the girl.' She thought long and hard about this matter, unable to see why it was not absurd to me. Finally, she said, "The sentence attributes more intelligence to the water than it does to the girl, and anyone [even you—was the implication] ought to know that human beings are smarter than water." Therein I had a lead to solve this riddle, but I was not sure what to make of it. She went on to say that the water does not think, so how could it have the girl drink it. But, I insisted, the water was not acting or thinking, it just got drunk. She countered by saying that the way I had constructed the sentence made it appear that the water was the cause of the drinking action, not the girl.

From the discussion above I later surmised that maybe the sentence should be translated 'the water caused the girl to drink it.' I tried this translation out on several Navajos who knew English. They said it was much closer to the Navajo meaning of the sentence than 'the water was drunk by the girl' but they were still a little uncomfortable with it. After some further thought and discussion, we came up with the translation 'the water let the girl drink it.' Therein we had captured in English not just the covert meaning of the Navajo sentence but the overt absurdity that the meaning expressed.

from Gary Witherspoon, *Language and Art in the Navajo Universe*
(1977), 65–67

tested a sample of Germans, another group with a tradition of authoritarianism. Their responses differed from those of the Japanese but were very close to those of the Americans. The study indicated, therefore, that a particular grammatical feature can at least significantly contribute to the reinforcement of a perceptual habit or cultural outlook.

In general, those examining the relationship between language and culture in recent years have advocated more experimental vigor. They have argued that research concerning this relationship must be comparative, that is, contrast two or more languages, preferably widely differing; that it must use some "external nonlinguistic reality" (stimulus) as a standard for determining by comparison the content of linguistic and cognitive categories; that it must contrast the languages of the respective speech communities to determine how they differ in understanding a common stimulus; and that it must make plain the implication of differences in language for differences in thought between the members of these speech communities (summarized from Lucy 1992).

John A. Lucy applied these four components that he considered requisite for adequate empirical research to Yucatec (a Mayan language) and American English. The focus of his study has been on the marking of the grammatical category of number (for example, the pluralization of nouns): Is there any correspondence between the grammatical treatment of number and the habitual thought (cognition) of the speakers of Yucatec on the one hand and those of American English on the other?

For example, in English the marking of the plural is obligatory for a very large number of "thing" nouns, or countables, such as *child, horse,* or *chair;* the only exceptions in nontechnical contexts are mass and abstract nouns, or uncountables, such as *sand, water, butter,* and *honesty.* By contrast, speakers of Yucatec mark plural optionally and for a relatively small number of nouns. The two languages also differ fundamentally in the use of numerals. In English, numerals modify a noun, as in *one candle* and *two baskets.* In Yucatec, numerals must be accompanied by a special piece of structure, a classifier, that identifies the counted object as to its material properties, as in *un-tz'íit kib'* 'one long thin wax,' referring to a candle.

In nonverbal experimental tasks, speakers of both English and Yucatec were responsive to the number of objects presented to them according to how the objects were treated grammatically in the respective language. Speakers of English were aware of the number of animate entities and objects but not of the substances represented by mass nouns; speakers of Yucatec were sensitive to number only for animate entities. In classifying three test objects as to which two of the three were more similar (a small cardboard box, a plastic box similar in form, and a piece of cardboard), speakers of English preferred to classify them according to shape (selecting the cardboard box and the plastic box), whereas the speakers of Yucatec preferred to classify them according to material (selecting the cardboard box and the small piece of cardboard). Although Lucy considers his study exploratory in nature, his findings suggest that "language patterns do affect cognitive performance" or, in other words, that "there is good preliminary evidence that diverse language forms bear a relationship to characteristic cognitive responses in speakers" (Lucy 1992:156, 158).

The fairly general agreement at the present time appears to be that differences in thought that are responsive to differences in grammatical structure exist but tend to be superficial. However, the field-worker engaged in ethnography or linguistic anthropology must always remember that "language, culture, and meaning have inextricably contaminated each other" (Hill and Mannheim 1992:382–383). (For yet another comment on linguistic relativity, see Box 3.3.)

Ethnoscience

Whorf's interest in the relationship between language and culture was responsible for the development in the 1950s of several closely related analytical approaches to the study of culture. However, Whorf's main focus seems to have been on grammatical categories, whereas the new approaches have focused on lexical classification of the social and physical environments of speakers of a language by means of its word-stock (lexicon). Discussed here under the widely used term **ethnoscience,** they include cognitive anthropology, componential analysis, ethnosemantics, folk taxonomy, and the so-called new ethnography. Ward H. Goodenough had these approaches in mind when he wrote in 1957, "We learn much of a culture when we learn the system of meanings for which its linguistic forms stand. Much descriptive ethnography is inescapably an exercise in descriptive semantics. . . . Relatively little [systematic] attention is devoted . . . to isolating the concepts or forms in terms of which the members of a society deal with one another and the world around them, and many of which are signified lexically in their language" (Goodenough 1964:39).

The term *ethnoscience* can easily be misinterpreted. It does not imply that alternative approaches to the study of culture are necessarily unscientific, nor does it suggest that folk classifications—that is, classifications by members of a particular culture—are more scientific than those developed by Western science. Rather, the term refers to a method of studying parts (domains) of a culture primarily on the basis of how they are lexically encoded by native speakers. The assumption is that as a rule what is culturally discriminable is also lexically differentiated.

What ethnoscience is about has been neatly illustrated by William C. Sturtevant in one of the earliest surveys of ethnoscientific research, in which he refers to a book published in 1897 by Walter E. Roth, a Victorian

---

BOX 3.3 Carroll on Linguistic Relativity

The speakers of one language ... may tend to ignore differences which are regularly noticed by the speakers of another language. This is not to say that they *always* ignore them, for these differences can indeed be recognized and talked about in any language, but they are differences which are not always salient in their experiences. The effect of any one language category is to lead language users to assume, perhaps mistakenly, that there is uniformity of some sort within the category. ... For example, historians have pointed out that the use of the term "the Middle Ages" may lead to the false impression that the period between the fall of Rome and the Italian Renaissance was in truth a distinct historical period which had uniform characteristics, throughout its length, which set it apart from other periods. ...

Let us now analyze a simple cross-linguistic example. In English, it is possible to report about someone, "He went to town." Nothing is said about his mode of travel: he might have walked, run, rode a horse, driven a car, or taken a bus or even a boat or a helicopter. It is well known that in German one would have to specify at least a minimum of information about the mode of travel. Use of the verb *gehen* (as a cognate of *go,* apparently the most direct translation) would imply walking or some other form of self-propelled movement; use of *fahren* would imply going in a vehicle; of *reiten,* going on horseback; etc. Russian, and, it so happens, Navaho, could use an even longer list of verbs to distinguish modes of transportation. Thus, in English, it is possible to focus attention on the mere fact of someone's having departed in the direction of town, even though the speaker of English can be more specific if he wants to: *walked, ran, drove, rode, flew, bicycled, rowed, helicoptered* could be substituted for *went* in the sentence indicated. ... As compared with German speakers, English speakers are sometimes benefited, sometimes disadvantaged by the possible lack of specificity in the meaning of the English term *go.*

from John B. Carroll, "Linguistic Relativity, Contrastive Linguistics, and Language Learning" (1963), 12–13

---

ethnologist. According to Sturtevant, Roth "titled the last chapter of his monograph on Queensland aboriginal culture 'ethno-pornography,' warned that 'the following chapter is not suitable for perusal by the general reader,' and described under this heading such topics as marriage, pregnancy and childbirth, menstruation, 'foul language,' and especially genital mutilations and their social and ceremonial significance" (Sturtevant 1964:100). The point Sturtevant makes is not so much that what today is considered pornography in the United States and other complex societies has changed drastically from what it was a century ago but that the aboriginal Queenslanders, and for that matter many other societies, may not have a concept corresponding to pornography at all, or if they do, it is likely to be somewhat or even quite different from that of the anthropologist's own culture. Consequently, in the opinion of the proponents of ethnoscience, describing other societies in terms of categories not applicable to them is likely to lead to serious distortions.

A good example of viewing a domain of another culture with the help of native categories is the discussion by Charles O. Frake concerning how disease is diagnosed among the Eastern Subanun, slash-and-burn farmers of western Mindanao in the Philippines (Frake 1961). Sickness is one of the most frequent subjects of conversation among these people, and consequently their language has many terms related to disease. Frake's paper is a partial analysis of 186 disease names, one of the numerically more modest terminological sets in Subanun. (The following English labels briefly explain but do not define Subanun terms.) Among the names of human diseases Frake recorded, some were descriptive phrases such as *meŋebag gatay* 'swollen liver,' but most of the disease names were expressed by a single Subanun word. Let us consider the term *nuka* 'skin disease,' which contrasts with, for example, *samad* 'wound,' and *pasuʔ* 'burn.' There are several varieties of *nuka*: *pugu* 'rash,' *meŋebag* 'inflammation,' *beldut* 'sore,' *buni* 'ringworm,' and others. A *beldut* 'sore' is further classified according to depth (shallow as against deep), distance from the point of origin or attachment (away from, or distal, as against close to, or proximal), severity (severe as against mild), and spread (single as against multiple), with each of the existing varieties referred to by a Subanun term—for example, *telemaw glai* 'shallow distal ulcer (considered severe),' *selimbunut* 'multiple sore,' and the like. The diagnosis of any particular disease may require advice from different people who judge, among other things, whether a particular *bagaʔ* 'proximal ulcer' is shallow (*bagaʔ*) or deep (*begwak*). But proper diagnosis is not an end in itself; it is

> a pivotal cognitive step in the selection of culturally appropriate responses to illness by the Subanun [and] bears directly on the selection of ordinary, botanically-derived, medicinal remedies from 724 recorded alternatives. The results of this selection . . . influence efforts to reach prognostic and etiological decisions [decisions having to do with the causes of a disease and the prospect of recovery], which, in their turn, govern the possible therapeutic need for a variant of one of 61 basic, named types of propitiatory offerings. (Frake 1961:131)

To sum up: To diagnose and classify Subanun diseases from the vantage point of Western medicine may be appropriate for an article to be published in a medical journal. However, for an anthropologist such a description would fail to reveal or at least would obscure the linkages that the Subanun believe to exist between the method of diagnosing diseases and the application of remedies to them. This is so because the final diagnosis and choice of appropriate treatment have important social and economic consequences in Subanun society.

One of the methods of semantic analysis the so-called new ethnographers have used is componential analysis. It is a technique applied to a set of terms (lexical items) that belong to a highly patterned and well-defined cultural domain (color terms, disease names, kin terms, terms for daily meals or for liquids taken in by humans, and the like); the aim is to discover the semantic distinctions that make these terms contrast with one another, and this aim is accomplished by analyzing lexical items into their component parts (a lexical decomposition of sorts). The value of a semantic dimension (range of meaning) may be represented by means of binary contrast—that is, the presence (+) or absence (−) of a feature—or simply by opposite characteristics of a dimension. Accordingly, if gender and relative age were among the semantic dimensions selected to analyze kinship terms, *grandmother* would be female + and old +, whereas *grandson* would be female − and old − (or, alternatively, *grandson* would be male + and young +, whereas *grandmother* would be male − and young −), or the two kin terms would be contrasted simply as female against male and old against young.

Some anthropologists who employ componential analysis seek to discover psychological reality—that is, their descriptions are intended to reflect the folk taxonomies used by the members of the society being studied. Frake took essentially this approach in his account of the diagnosis of disease among the Subanun. Other anthropologists are more concerned with producing the most efficient and elegant formal account possible rather than trying to discover the cognitive world of the people they study. Fred W. Householder, Jr. (1913–1994), referred to a somewhat parallel difference in attitudes toward linguistic analysis as the "God's truth" position and the "hocus-pocus" position, depending on whether the linguist (or, by extension, the anthropologist) believes that the task is to discover the inherent structure in a language or a culture (God's truth position) or that the task is only to impose on the mass of available information some kind of structure that does not conflict with the data at hand (hocus-pocus position; Householder 1952:260).

To discuss the method of componential analysis in detail is beyond the scope of this book, but a few examples are in order. In American kinship terminology, the gender (or sex) of the speaker is never a distinctive variable (component). Whether male or female, the speaker refers to individual kin as *my sister, my brother, my nephew, my niece,* and the like. By contrast, in the kinship terminology of the Arapaho, the gender of the speaker is a distinctive variable in the case of certain kin: The term *neíhʔe* 'my son' is used by a man to refer not only to his own son but also to his brother's son and to certain other kinsmen, but not to his sister's son, who is instead referred to as *néθeʔéθe* 'my nephew.' In contrast, *neíhʔe* 'my son' is used by a woman to refer not only to her own son but also to her sister's son and to certain other kinsmen, but not to her brother's son, who is referred to as *néθeʔéθe* 'my nephew.' Similarly, *neyóo* 'my brother-in-law' is used only by men and *notóʔu* 'my sister-in-law' only by women, and the term *neiθébi*, used by both women and men, is best glossed in English as 'my sibling-in-law of the opposite gender,' that is, as 'my sister-in-law' when used by a man and as 'my brother-in-law' when used by a woman.

Another example: In American kinship terminology, on the one hand, the term *cousin*, whether it refers to the child of one's uncle or aunt or someone descended from a grandparent or more distant relative, is used regardless of whether the individual spoken of is male or female. In other words, gender is not a distinctive component of cousin terminology in English. In Czech kinship terminology, on the other hand, a female cousin is terminologically distinguished from a male cousin, the former being referred to as *sestřenice* and the latter as *bratranec*.

For a final example, let us anticipate the brief discussion of semantics in Chapter 5. The following list of terms applied to domestic animals is not intended to be complete but is large enough to illustrate the method of componential analysis as applied to a domain. The terms and their meanings are characteristic of the speech of the majority of native speakers of English; however, readers who use the terms with somewhat different senses or who wish to enlarge the list are encouraged to make the necessary changes to accommodate their own dialect. These are the terms: bitch, boar, buck, bull, calf, cat, chick, chicken, cock, colt, cow, doe, dog, donkey, drake, duck, duckling, ewe, filly, foal, gander, gelding, goat, goose, gosling, hen, hog, horse, jack, jenny (jennet), kid, kit(ten), lamb, mare, ox, piglet, pup(py), rabbit, ram, rooster, sow, stallion, swine, tom-cat, and turkey. (For the most part the terms have been limited to words consisting of a single morpheme; not included are such constructions or phrases as *she-cat, turkey hen,* and *male dog,* or terms little known or used, such as *wether* 'male sheep or goat castrated when young.')

The major difference among the domestic animals represented by the forty-five terms is that the majority (thirty-three of them) are four-legged (mammals) and the others (twelve of them) are two-legged (birds). In both groups some terms refer specifically to the young of the species (for example, *colt* and *duckling*), other terms only to adult animals (*mare, ram*), and a few are ambiguous (*chicken, rabbit*). Gender is commonly differentiated in the case of adult domestic animals (for example, *stallion* as against *mare* or *jack* as against *jenny*) but much less frequently in the case of the young (*filly* as against *colt*). We have thus far established three binary contrasts: four-legged + (for example, *horse*) as against four-legged – (*hen*), adult + (*gander*) as against adult – (*gosling*), and male + (*rooster*) as against male – (*hen*). The prominent distinguishing features in folk classification between the domesticated goose and duck, both of which belong to the same bird family (Anatidae), are the larger size and longer neck of the goose; we may therefore set up the length of the neck as a contrastive feature. Similarly, the horse and donkey (domestic ass) belong to the same genus (*Equus*), but donkeys are smaller and have longer ears and smaller hoofs than horses. Most of the species of domestic animals and their varieties, however, are distinguished from each other by an aggregate of their physical traits. To avoid Latinate terms such as *bovine* and *equine*, we will use the adjectives *catlike, cattlelike, doglike, fowl-like, goatlike, gooselike, horselike, piglike, rabbitlike, sheeplike,* and *turkeylike.* In Table 3.1 the forty-five terms for domestic animals are componentially defined by means of seventeen semantic distinctions.

All terms in Table 3.1 are uniquely defined except for two, *cock* and *rooster,* which many speakers of English think of as synonymous. Because one of the senses of the former term can be considered vulgar, however, most people prefer to use the word *rooster.* (This pair of words supports the claim that absolute synonyms do not exist or at least are extremely rare.) The use of minuses in all columns is not necessary because, for example, doglike + clearly implies the absence of physical traits characteristic of cats, cattle, fowl, goats, and the other domestic animals.

Applying componential analysis to an English terminological set as we have just done may reveal little if anything that native speakers do not already know, at least implicitly. But to discover the underlying semantic differences among the terms of domains from other cultures helps anthropologists determine what is culturally significant in those societies and how their members structure their experience linguistically.

It would be incorrect to think that ethnoscientists (or New Ethnographers) were the first cultural anthropologists to insist on the importance of discovering how a culture is seen from the perspective of the society's members. Such a view has had a long tradition in American anthropology. Nevertheless, the practitioners of these recent approaches have made some valuable contributions to the study of culture; they have elicited helpful data by making the language of those they study a rich source of information rather than merely the means of communicating. At the same time, however, it must be mentioned that the peak of ethnoscientific research was reached in the 1960s. The main shortcoming of the ethnoscientific method is that its emphasis on understanding culture through language results in the neglect of nonverbal behavior and those aspects of culture that lie outside the domains accessible through terminological sets.

TABLE 3.1 Componential Analysis of English Terms for Domestic Animals

	Four-legged	Adult	Male	Long-necked	Long-eared	Altered	Cat-like	Cattle-like	Dog-like	Fowl-like	Goat-like	Goose-like	Horse-like	Pig-like	Rabbit-like	Sheep-like	Turkey-like
Bitch	+	+	−						+								
Boar	+	+	+											+			
Buck	+	+	+			−									+		
Bull	+	+	+			−		+									
Calf	+	−	±					+									
Cat	+	+	±			±	+										
Chick	−	−	±							+							
Chicken	−	±	±							+							
Cock	−	+	+							+							
Colt	+	−	+		±								+				
Cow	+	+	−					+									
Doe	+	+	−												+		
Dog	+	±	±			±			+								
Donkey	+	±	±		+								+				
Drake	−	+	+	−								+					
Duck	−	+	±	−								+					
Duckling	−	−	±	−								+					
Ewe	+	+	−													+	
Filly	+	−	−										+				
Foal	+	−	±		±								+				
Gander	−	+	+	+								+					
Gelding	+	±	+		±	+							+				
Goat	+	+	±								+						
Goose	−	+	±	+								+					
Gosling	−	−	±	+								+					

	1	2	3
Hen	−	+	−
Hog	+	+	±
Horse	+	±	±
Jack	+	+	+
Jenny (jennet)	+	+	
Kid	+	−	±
Kit(ten)	+	±	±
Lamb	+	−	±
Mare	+	+	−
Ox	+	+	+
Piglet	+	−	±
Pup(py)	+	−	±
Rabbit	+	±	+
Ram	+	+	+
Rooster	−	+	+
Sow	+	+	−
Stallion	+	+	+
Swine	+	±	±
Tomcat	+	+	+
Turkey	−	±	±

Summary and Conclusions

There is no question that languages differ—if only superficially, as contemporary linguists would add. They differ in sounds, structure (grammar), and in the ways their vocabularies classify the conceptual world of
those who speak them. But despite the differences among the lexical systems of different languages, most linguists would agree that any nontechnical utterance can be expressed with reasonable accuracy in any language, although usually not on a word-by-word basis. When it comes to
technical subjects, some languages have highly specialized terminologies
that may be lacking in others—one could hardly expect to give a report
on quantum chromodynamics in, say, Hopi. Yet Hopi has specialized areas in its lexicon that are not matched in English. In general, those aspects
of any culture that are worked out in some detail receive corresponding
attention in the vocabulary of the language in order for the speakers of
the language to be able to discuss them with ease and accuracy.

Whorf concerns himself with the important question of language-
culture dependency in several of his papers, but he overstates his case.
Some of his evidence is anecdotal, that is, short and amusing but not necessarily representative of a specific language taken as a whole. One may
also wonder how reliable for the purposes of Whorf's illustrations was
his Hopi informant, who resided in New York City and must have been
nearly or fully bilingual: If the perception of one's environment is affected
by the particular language one speaks, then fluency in both Hopi and
English might obscure the contrast between the two. According to Whorf,
"the Hopi language contains no reference to TIME, either explicit or im-
plicit" (Whorf 1950:67). Hopi may indeed not have tenses in the same
sense that English has (as in *I go, I went, I will go, I had gone,* and so on), but
speakers of Hopi are able to refer to the time at or during which an action
takes place by using morphemes or words that pertain to such time references as "today, late morning, noon, last night, towards evening, yesterday, tomorrow, day after day, once in a while, from tomorrow on until the
next day" and "next year" (Voegelin and Voegelin 1957:24).

Noting that speakers of a particular language might neglect objects or
events that speakers of another language normally take into account, John
B. Carroll restates the hypothesis of linguistic relativity and determinism in
a more modest but acceptable form: "Insofar as languages differ in the
ways they encode objective experience, language users tend to sort out and
distinguish experiences differently according to the categories provided by
their respective languages. These cognitions will tend to have certain effects on behavior" (Carroll 1963:12; for his examples, see Box 3.3).

The relationship between language and culture has been put to
methodological use by the proponents of cognitive anthropology, who

believe that even minute structural distinctions in a culture are likely to be encoded in the vocabulary of the corresponding language. No one questions the contribution these ethnoscientists have made to a better understanding of the peoples they have studied, but their insightful research has invariably been limited to particular domains of culture.

Notes and Suggestions for Further Reading

The citation from Humboldt, from *Wilhelm von Humboldts Werke* (1907:7:42), is my own translation. The references to the linguistic affiliation of the Native American languages of the Great Plains are according to Voegelin and Voegelin 1966; the hyphenated names of languages identify dialects.

For representative selections from the writings of Sapir and Whorf, see Sapir 1949 and Whorf 1956. The two examples in the text referring to Hupa and Nootka words may be found in Sapir 1949:436–437 and 446–447.

The Pintupi examples are from Crystal 1991a and the Arapaho examples from Salzmann 1983. The acute accent over an Arapaho vowel marks prominent stress and higher pitch; long vowels are written doubly.

For additional discussion of the interrelations of language and other aspects of culture, see Hoijer 1954, Fishman 1960, Gumperz and Levinson 1996, and Lucy 1997. And for a survey of works on language and worldview and the relevant bibliography, see Hill and Mannheim 1992.

Goodenough's comment made in 1957 is quoted here from Hymes's reader (1964). For a book of readings in cognitive anthropology, see Tyler 1969. It supplements two special issues of *American Anthropologist* devoted to cognitive studies and formal semantic analysis; one was edited by Romney and D'Andrade (1964), the other by E. A. Hammel (1965).

4

The Structure of Language: Phonology

The nature of ethnographic fieldwork makes it essential for anthropologists to acquire a working knowledge of the language of those whom they study, to learn something about its structure, and to be able to write it down in order to record words, utterances, or traditional narratives. American anthropologists have long been concerned with language, in large part because of the great number and variety of Native American languages spoken in their own linguistic backyard.

Each language represents a particular variety of the general language code—in other words, no two languages are alike, although some are structurally similar whereas others are quite different. Understanding the workings of a foreign language rather than simply learning to speak it requires some acquaintance with the plan according to which a particular language code is constructed. Such acquaintance cannot be gained by using as a framework the traditional grammar of English or some other language taught in schools. There are several important reasons for a more systematic and specialized approach.

One major reason has to do with converting to written form a language that has previously been only spoken. To accomplish this task, one must learn the principles of phonetic transcription. The use of the conventional spelling system of the anthropologist's own language is invariably out of the question: Not only should one expect the sounds of one language to differ from those of another, but the sounds and the orthographic conventions that represent them in the written language are not likely to correspond to each other on a one-to-one basis. English spelling is notorious for its lack of correlation with spoken English. For example, the sound "sh" of *shy* is written in English in twelve additional ways, as in *chef, conscience, fuchsia, issue, mansion, nauseous, ocean, potion, pshaw, schist, sugar,* and *suspicion*. The two sentences "The sun's rays meet" and "The sons raise meat" sound exactly alike despite their different meanings and orthographic representations, and in "Where do these lead pipes lead?" the two words written as *lead* are pronounced differently depending on their meaning. It should be obvious that the writing systems of languages with a literary tradition, English in particular, are not suitable for careful linguistic work.

The second major reason for a specialized approach has to do with grammatical structure. Each language has a structure of its own that cannot be analyzed or grasped in terms of the investigator's own language. Many languages, for example, do not possess the definite and indefinite articles corresponding to the English *the* and *a(n)*. And English does not distinguish in the first person of the plural between the exclusive and inclusive forms that are common in other languages, for example, the Algonquian languages of Native North Americans. Where in English one would simply say *we, us,* or *our,* speakers of these languages must specify whether both the addressee (hearer) and perhaps others are included (as when a boy talks to his sister about "our mother"), or whether others are included but the addressee (hearer) is excluded (as when a mother talks to a visitor about "our children," referring to those belonging to her and her husband). In sum, each language has its own distinctive structural characteristics, and these are likely to be overlooked if its structure is accounted for through the grammatical categories of the investigator's mother tongue or some other language serving as a model. Many grammars of American Indian languages compiled in earlier centuries by well-meaning missionaries strongly resembled Latin or Greek even though the Native American languages could not have been more different; the descriptions betrayed their authors' thorough grounding in the classical languages and the resulting dependence on their structures.

There are many benefits to understanding the structure of a system, not only with respect to becoming acquainted with a foreign language but in regard to other learning situations as well. One practical benefit is that if we are able to understand how the parts of a system function and what kinds of relationships exist among them, we are then spared having to memorize, or at least pay undue attention to, details that may well be trivial. In order to illustrate this point, let me use a simple example.

Bontok is a language spoken by a people in the mountains of northern Luzon in the Philippines. Among the many words corresponding to English nouns and adjectives are the following four stems: *fikas* 'strong,' *kilad* 'red,' *bato* 'stone,' and *fusul* 'enemy.' To express the idea that someone is becoming what the noun or adjective refers to, the Bontok would use the following words derived from the four stems above: *fumikas* 'he is becoming strong,' *kumilad* 'he is becoming red,' *bumato* 'he is becoming stone' (as in a myth), and *fumusul* 'he is becoming an enemy.' Those not trained in linguistics may find these forms a bit confusing, perhaps expecting, as a result of being native speakers of English, that in each case several words would be needed to indicate that an individual is undergoing some sort of change—becoming strong, red, stone, or an enemy. An examination of the Bontok data reveals a simple rule that accounts for the meaning 'he is becoming – – – –' (in stating the rule I am avoiding terminology that might be unfamiliar to readers): Insert the sounds (written here as *um*) after the initial consonant of the stem. This rule produces *f-um-ikas* from *fikas* and so on. Now that we know this particular piece of Bontok structure, we can guess at the word that would most likely mean 'he is becoming white,' given *pukaw* 'white'—namely *pumukaw*; and, conversely, we can guess what the stem meaning 'dark' would be from the word *ŋumitad* 'he is becoming dark'—namely *ŋitad*.

Focusing on recurring patterns of behavior of members of a society—in other words, trying to discover the structure of a cultural system—helps us to become familiar with how the system operates. This is particularly true of the thousands of communicative systems we call languages.

The Anatomy and Physiology of Speech

The capacity for speaking and speech itself are taken so much for granted that very few individuals ever stop to wonder how sounds are produced and why they vary as much as they do. Although it is true that speakers use their mother tongue automatically, without concentrating, it is equally true that the production of a dozen to a score of speech sounds per second requires extremely well-coordinated and precise movements and positionings of various parts of the speech apparatus located between the diaphragm and the lips (see Figure 4.1).

The extent of these elaborate gymnastics is all the more remarkable when we remind ourselves that the primary functions of the various parts of the speech apparatus are not those associated with the production of sounds. For example, the tongue, rich in tactile sensory nerve endings, is the seat of the sense of taste and helps in swallowing food, and the main purpose of teeth is to bite off food (incisors) and then chew it (molars). In short, speech is a secondary function for what we refer to as the vocal tract, or vocal organs.

The production of speech sounds, which is a complex process involving about 100 muscles as well as other tissues, requires precise coordination. When one speaks, air is taken into the lungs more rapidly than in the normal course of inbreathing and then exhaled in a slow and steady stream. It is forced from the lungs through the trachea (windpipe) and undergoes important modifications in the larynx, located at the upper end of the trachea. The larynx, the position of which is marked externally by the Adam's apple, houses two bands of muscular tissue known as the vocal cords, or vocal folds. The vocal folds stretch from front to back and

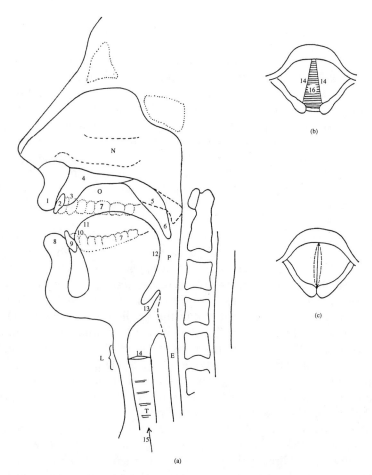

(a)

FIGURE 4.1 The Speech Apparatus. (a) A cross-section of the human head showing the principal parts of the vocal tract. The lungs and the diaphragm below them are not shown.

E	esophagus (gullet)	5	velum (soft palate)
L	larynx (voice box)	6	uvula
N	nasal cavity	7	molars
O	oral cavity	8	lower lip
P	pharynx	9	lower teeth (incisors)
T	trachea	10	tongue tip
1	upper lip	11	tongue blade
2	upper teeth (incisors)	12	tongue root
3	alveolar ridge	13	epiglottis
4	(hard) palate	14	vocal cords
		15	direction of outgoing air

(b) A view of the glottis (16), with a vocal cord on each side, during normal breathing. (c) The same view, but with vocal cords vibrating during speech. Adapted from Bohuslav Hála: Uvedení do fonetiky češtiny, Prague, 1962, p. 63.

regulate the size of the elongated opening between them, the glottis. During swallowing, in addition to being protected by the folded epiglottis from above, the vocal cords are drawn together, with the glottis closed, to prevent liquids or food particles from entering the lungs; for the production of **voiced** sounds, such as those making up the word *buzz*, the cords are drawn together and made to vibrate as the airstream forces its way between them; in whispering, they are brought close together, with the glottis narrowed; for the production of **voiceless** sounds, such as those heard at the beginning and end of the word *ship*, they are spread apart but tensed; and during normal breathing, they are relaxed and spread apart. The tension of the vocal cords determines the frequency of their vibration and therefore the pitch, whereas the force of the outgoing air regulates the loudness of sounds.

Having passed through the larynx, the air proceeds outward through the pharynx toward the oral and nasal cavities. When the soft palate (velum) in the rear upper part of the mouth, just above the uvula, is lowered and the lips are closed, the air is released through the nose, producing nasal sounds, such as the three different ones in the Spanish word *mañana* 'tomorrow' or the final one in the English word *king*. If the soft palate is lowered but the air allowed to escape simultaneously through both the nose and the mouth, nasalized sounds are the result, as in the French *bon* 'good.' The majority of sounds in the languages of the world are oral, with the air escaping only through the mouth because the soft palate is fully raised, making contact with the back wall of the pharynx and shutting off the entrance to the nasal cavity.

As the air passes through the upper part of the speech tract, numerous modifications of the vocal channel, involving such articulators as the soft palate, tongue, and lips, make possible the tremendous variety of sounds heard in the several thousand of the world's languages. These sounds are customarily classified according to the manner and place of articulation and transcribed by means of phonetic symbols, which are enclosed in square brackets [ ].

Articulation of Speech Sounds

The two main classes of speech sounds are **vowels** and **consonants** (see Notes). In the production of vowels, the air that escapes through the mouth (in the case of oral vowels) as well as through the nose (in the case of nasalized vowels) is relatively unimpeded. Vowels are classified according to the part of the tongue that is raised, the configuration of the lips, and the extent to which the tongue approaches the palate above it (see Table 4.1). Another variable is the degree of muscular effort and movement that goes into the production of vowel sounds. If the tension in the

TABLE 4.1 Types of Vowels According to Place and Manner of Articulation

Place and Manner of Articulation	*Vowel Types* — oral, nasal(ized)				
	front		**central**	**back**	
	unrounded (spread)	rounded	unrounded	unrounded	rounded
If the air escapes through the mouth			*oral*		
If the air escapes *also* through the nose			*nasal(ized)*		
high (close)	i *beat*	ü German *kühl* 'cool'	ɨ Russian быть 'to be'	ɯ occurs in Turkish	u *boot*
lower high	ɪ *bit*		ᵻ as in *just* (*you wait*)		ʊ *book*
mid	e *bait*; German *See* 'sea'	ö German *schön* 'lovely'	ə the second vowel of *sofa*		o *boat*; French *beau* 'beautiful'
lower mid	ɛ *bet*	œ French *peur* 'fear'		ʌ *butt*	ɔ *bought*
low (open)	æ *bat*		a *body*		ɒ *pot*; in London English, *not*

It is not easy to illustrate various vowel types by examples from English because of wide dialect variation. For example, people native to eastern New England, the central Atlantic seaboard, and the coastal South pronounce the words *Mary, marry,* and *merry* differently, whereas in the rest of the United States, these three words are usually pronounced alike.

tongue muscles is prominent, vowels are said to be *tense*, as in *beat* or *boot*; if it is lacking or scarcely noticeable, they are said to be *lax*, as in *bit* or *book*.

Even though an utterance may be viewed as a succession of individual sounds, most speakers tend to subdivide utterances naturally into somewhat larger units, syllables. In order to be fully serviceable, the term *syllable* needs to be defined separately for each language, but in general one may say that a syllable consists of a nucleus—usually but not always a vowel (V), with or without a consonant (C) or consonants before or after it. All of the following English words—*a, on, me, pin, spin, drift,* and *strengths*—consist of one syllable and may be represented as V, VC, CV, CVC, CCVC, CCVCC, and CCCVC(C)CC, respectively. In the word *button*, the nucleus of the second syllable is the nasal [n], because the orthographic vowel *o* is not pronounced. A consonant functioning as the center of a syllable is said to be syllabic.

The vowels of American English dialects occur for the most part singly, as in the words *linguistic anthropology* [-ɪ-ɪ-ɪ- æ-ə-ɒ-ə-i]. However, sometimes there is a change in vowel quality within a syllable, as in the words *bite, bout,* and *boy*. What occurs in each of these three words and others like them is a movement from the first, more prominent vocalic part to the second, which is shorter and less distinct. A change in vowel quality within the same syllable is referred to as a diphthong.

In the production of consonants, places of articulation range all the way from the glottis to the lips, the last place in the vocal tract where the outgoing air can be modified (see Table 4.2). The manner of articulation refers to the several kinds of constriction that may be set up at some point along the speech tract by the articulators (see Table 4.3).

The vowel and consonant types surveyed here include only the basic ones. Just as sounds can undergo lengthening or nasalization, they can be modified by secondary articulations. These give rise to labialized, palatalized, velarized, pharyngealized, and otherwise modified sounds. Some consonants may also be followed by aspiration, that is, accompanied by an audible breath. Relatively rare are clicks, sharp suction sounds made by the lips or the tongue, and ingressive sounds, those produced on the inbreath rather than the outbreath. The most common speech sounds and their modifications are represented by the **phonetic** symbols and diacritics of the International Phonetic Alphabet (IPA). Its various symbols and diacritics can be used to represent a great many (but by no means all) sounds occurring in the world's languages. Because the special characters and diacritical marks used by the IPA are not always readily available, for the sake of economy and convenience many U.S. linguists use some symbols that do not correspond to those of the IPA. One should remember, in this connection, that phonetic symbols are arbitrary; therefore, in principle one phonetic alphabet used for transcription is just as acceptable as

TABLE 4.2 Types of Consonants According to Place of Articulation

Place of Articulation	General Description	Consonant Type	Example(s)
Glottis	Vocal folds are positioned so as to cause a closure or friction.	Glottal	glottal stop that in some dialects of English replaces the *t* sound (-*tt*-) in such words as *bottle*
Pharynx	Back wall of the pharynx articulates with the root of the tongue.	Pharyngeal	common in Arabic
Uvula	Back of the tongue articulates with the uvula.	Uvular	the *r* sound frequently heard in German (voiced variety) or French (voiceless)
Velum, or soft palate	Back of the tongue articulates with the soft palate.	Velar	initial sound of *calf*
(Hard) palate	Front of the tongue articulates with the hard palate.	Palatal	the final sound of the German *ich* 'I'
Area where the palate and the alveolar ridge meet	Blade of the tongue (and sometimes the tip) articulates with the palato-alveolar area.	Palato-alveolar	initial sound of *ship*
	Tip of the tongue, curled back, articulates with the palato-alveolar area.	Retroflex	typically, *t* and *d* sounds in English as spoken by East Indians
Alveolar ridge	Front of the tongue articulates with the alveolar ridge.	Alveolar	the initial sound of *sit*
Teeth	Tongue tip articulates with the upper teeth.	Dental	*t* and *d* sounds of Irish English
	Tongue tip is positioned between the upper and lower teeth.	Interdental	the initial sounds of *thin* and *this*
Lower lip and upper teeth	Lower lip articulates with the upper teeth.	Labiodental	the initial sounds of *fan* and *van*
Lips	Both lower and upper lips articulate.	Bilabial	the initial and final sound of *bob*

TABLE 4.3 Types of Consonants According to Manner of Articulation

Type of Constriction	Subtype of Constriction	General Description	Consonant Type	Examples with Description
CLOSURE	Total	complete closure at some point in the vocal tract, with soft palate raised; sudden release of air pressure	Plosive, or stop	the initial sound of *pick*; closure at the lips
	Total	complete closure at some point in the mouth, with soft palate lowered and air escaping through the nose	Nasal	the initial and final sound of *mom*; closure at the lips
	Total	complete closure at some point in the mouth, with soft palate raised; gradual release of air pressure	Affricate	the initial and final sound of *judge*; the tongue blade forms closure with the front of the hard palate
	Intermittent	an articulator flapping loose or one articulator tapping against another	Trill	the *r* sound in Scottish pronunciation or in the Spanish *perro* 'dog'; the tongue vibrates against the alveolar ridge
	Intermittent	a single tap by one articulator against the roof of the mouth	Flap	the *r* sound in British English pronunciation of *very* or in the Spanish *pero* 'but'; the tongue taps the alveolar ridge
	Partial	partial closure in the mouth allowing the air to escape around one or both sides of the closure	Lateral	the initial sound of *law*; the middle part of the tongue touches the top of the mouth
NARROWING		at some point in the vocal tract the opening is narrowed so as to produce audible friction	Fricative	the initial and final sounds of *fuss*; air is forced between the lower lip and upper teeth, and between the front of the tongue and the alveolar ridge, respectively

another so long as each sound is represented by one symbol only and all the symbols are carefully defined.

Articulatory phonetics, the study of the production of speech sounds by the vocal organs, is not the only way to examine the raw material of language. It is also possible to examine speech sounds for their physical properties, that is, from the perspective of acoustic phonetics. This approach requires the use of the sound spectrograph, a device that visually represents acoustic features of speech sounds in the form of spectrograms, or voiceprints. Spectrograms show three dimensions of sounds: Duration (time) is displayed horizontally, frequency vertically, and intensity by the degree of darkness. For example, each vowel is characterized by several resonance bands, referred to as formants, which represent the overtone structure of a vowel produced by the shape of the vocal tract. Because the position of the tongue changes with the production of different vowels, the formants vary correspondingly.

Prosodic Features

Vowels and consonants that combine into words and sentences may be thought of as segments, or segmental units, that is, as discrete units that can be identified in the stream of speech and separated from other such units (as in *part* = *p-a-r-t* and *slept* = *s-l-e-p-t*). But there is more to speech than just ordering these segments according to the rules of a particular language. Additional features are essential for an utterance to sound natural and to be fully meaningful, especially stress and pitch, the two sometimes lumped together under the term *accent*.

Stress refers to the degree of force, or prominence, associated with a syllable. In the word *under*, the prominent stress is on the first syllable, whereas in *below*, it is on the second. In the sentence "Will you permit me to use your permit?" the word *permit* functioning as a verb is stressed differently from *permit* used as a noun. Some linguists claim that to describe English adequately, as many as four degrees of stress are needed, ranging from primary (1) to weak (4), as in *dictionary* (1–4–3–4) and *elevator operator* (1–4–3–4 2–4–3–4). In English the placing of stress is not completely predictable, as it is in Czech, where as a rule the main stress falls on the first syllable, or in Polish, where it falls on the penultimate, or next to the last, syllable.

A distinctive pitch level associated with a syllable is referred to as tone. Among the several dialect groups in China, Mandarin Chinese provides a good example of a tone system. Simpler than the systems of other Chinese tone languages or dialects, it employs four relative pitch contours, or tones, to distinguish among normally stressed syllables that are otherwise identical (see Table 4.4).

By contrast, the use of pitch in English is not associated with individual syllables but with utterances in a variety of intonation patterns. The into-

TABLE 4.4   The Four Distinctive Tones of Mandarin Chinese

Syllable	Tone Number	Description	Tone Letter	Pitch Contour	Pinyin Transcription	Meaning
ma	1	high and level	⌐	5–5	—	mother
ma	2	rising	⟋	3–5	/	hemp
ma	3	falling, then rising	⟍⟋	2–1–4	∨	horse
ma	4	high falling	⟍	5–1	\	to scold

The tone letter provides a simplified time-pitch graph of each syllable under normal stress. The time-pitch graph is drawn from left to right, with the vertical line serving as a reference scale for pitch range. Similarly, the pitch contour represents pitches by numbers from 1 to 5, with 5 being the highest.

nation that accompanies the question "Who ran off, Mother?" addressed to the speaker's mother, may elicit some such answer as "Your sister." With the appropriately different intonation, the question "Who ran off— Mother?" addressed to some other member of the family, may elicit some such answer as "Yes, without even leaving a note."

The physical duration of a sound is referred to as its quantity, or length. In English the difference between the short vowel in *bit* and the longer one in *beat* is not strictly or primarily a difference in length because the two vowels vary in other respects. Yet the consonant written as *-tt-* in *cat-tail* is somewhat longer than that written as *-tt-* in *cattle*. In Czech, though, length is contrastive; such word pairs as *lak* 'varnish' and *lák* 'pickle (brine)' or *dal* 'he gave' and *dál* 'farther' are alike except for the considerable lengthening of the vowel in the second word of each pair (marked in conventional Czech spelling by the diacritic ´ over the vowel).

Some linguists also distinguish phonetic features that mark the joining of one grammatical unit to another—so-called junctures. English examples include the audible difference between the members of such pairs as *nitrate* and *night rate, I scream* and *ice cream,* and *an aim* and *a name.*

From Phones to Phonemes

The smallest perceptible discrete segment of speech is a **phone,** a speech sound considered as a physical event. A succession of phones in a particular language makes up a stretch of speech, or utterance. Each utterance is unique, occurring if not under different circumstances at least at a different point in time. Yet people do not respond to each instance of speech as though it were different from all others. Such utterances as "Where have you been?" or "I have no time just now" are treated as if they were much the same every time they are said regardless of whether the voice belongs to a woman, man, or child, or happens to be clear or hoarse. Because there is so much likeness in what is objectively different it is possible to represent speech sounds, phones, by means of written symbols of a suitable phonetic alphabet. Linguistic anthropologists make phonetic transcriptions of words or utterances whenever they wish to obtain a sample of speech for subsequent analysis.

Let us now consider the English words written as *papaya, pepper, pin, spin, up,* and *upon.* The *p* sound of *pin* is followed by a distinct puff of air, which is completely absent in *spin.* The difference between the two *p* sounds can be easily demonstrated if one holds a sheet of ordinary paper vertically between thumb and finger about 2 inches from one's lips and says the two words. The puff of air, or aspiration, following the *p* sound of *pin* sends a ripple through the sheet, whereas the word *spin* leaves the sheet motionless. We find that the same difference obtains between the *p*'s of *pair, peck, peer,* and *pike* on the one hand and those of *spare, speck, spear,* and *spike* on the other.

In the word *upon,* the *p* sound is about as distinctly aspirated as in *pin.* In *papaya,* however, it is only the second *p* that is strongly aspirated, with the first one aspirated only slightly, if at all; in *pepper,* it is the other way around. In the word *up,* especially if it stands at the end of a sentence, as in "Let's go up!," the *p* sound may remain unreleased, that is, the lips simply stay closed in anticipation of the silence that follows.

To generalize about the occurrence of these phonetically similar segments, we may say that in English there are at least four varieties of the *p* sound: an aspirated [pʰ] before a stressed vowel unless preceded by an *s* (as the second *p* in *papaya,* the first in *pepper,* and in *pin* and *upon*); a very slightly aspirated [p] before a weakly stressed vowel (the first in *papaya,* the second in *pepper*); an unaspirated [P] with a relatively small degree of muscular effort and breath force, after an *s* of the same syllable and before a vowel (*spin*); and an unreleased [p꜒] in the sentence-final position, where [pʰ] or [p] may also occur. (In order to illustrate a principle rather than to account for numerous other details, the description of the varieties of the English *p* sound and their occurrence has been simplified.)

Let us next consider the words *pin, spin,* and *bin,* which we may transcribe phonetically as [pʰɪn], [sPɪn], and [bɪn]. The difference between the *p* of *pin* and *b* of *bin* is clearly of another kind than that between [pʰ] and [p] or [pʰ] and [P]. By choosing either *b* or *p* for the initial sound, the speaker is distinguishing between two meaningful items of the English vocabulary, *bin* and *pin*. Even if one were to interchange the pronunciation of the *p* sounds in *pin* and *spin* and say [Pɪn] and [spʰɪn] instead, one would no doubt be understood, though the listener would probably suspect that either English is not the speaker's native language or the speaker is trying to imitate a foreign accent. As a matter of fact, native speakers of English never have to choose consciously between [P] and [pʰ]. They employ automatically the former before a vowel whenever the sound *s* precedes within the same syllable, and the latter if it occurs before a strongly stressed vowel.

With specific reference to English—because all languages must be examined and analyzed only on their own terms—linguists establish the *b* sound of *bin* and the *p* sound of *pin* as two contrastive sound units, or **phonemes,** and they classify the several varieties of the *p* sound—[pʰ], [P], [p], and [pʼ]—as allophones of the phoneme /p/. (Note the use of slant lines around the symbol to indicate its phonemic status.) To put it differently, when *p* is used to represent the English phoneme /p/, it serves as a cover symbol for a class of phonetically similar sounds that are in complementary distribution or free variation. Phones are in complementary distribution if they never occur in the same phonetic environment—for example, simplified, [P] is found always after *s*, where [pʰ] never occurs. Phones are in free variation if substituting one for another does not cause a change in meaning. But if two phones contrast, as does [b] in *bin* with [pʰ] in *pin*—that is, if substituting one for another causes a change in meaning—they are assignable to two different phonemes (or, phrased differently, they are allophones of two different phonemes).

The simplest way to establish phonemic contrasts in a language is by means of minimal sets, in which each word has a different meaning but varies from the rest in one sound only. From the foursome of words *bit, bet, bat,* and *butt,* we establish phonemic contrast among all four vowels. As for consonants, all the initial sounds (not letters!) of the following set of words contrast with one another and are therefore assignable to different English phonemes: *by, die, fie, guy, high, lie, my, nigh, pie, rye, shy, sigh, thigh, thy, tie, vie,* and *why,* yielding /b, d, f, g, h, l, m, n, p, r, š, s, θ, ð, t, v, w/.

To demonstrate the fundamental principles underlying phonemic analysis, we have, for obvious reasons, used English. But linguistic anthropologists typically face a different situation as they study peoples whose languages have never before been written. A thorough phonemic analysis of a language involves more than just compiling minimal sets; it takes weeks of painstaking listening for contrasting sounds, repeating words and utterances and recording them on tape, and phonetically transcribing a good deal in the initial stages of work. The following need to be established: the distinctive sounds, or phonemes, of a language; the prosodic features that characterize its utterances; the main allophones of each phoneme and the phonetic environment in which they occur; the pattern of phonemes—vowels, consonants, and their subclasses; and the rules for their combinations among each other and in higher-level units. Next, the practical task for the linguistic anthropologist is to devise an appropriate alphabet so that the language can be transcribed phonemically, without the many phonetic details of the initial transcription that have now become easily retrievable: When we write /p/ in English, we know under what circumstances this phoneme is physically realized as one of its four allophones, [pʰ], [p], [P], and [p˺].

It is important to remember that the same phonemes do not necessarily characterize every speaker of English. It is common knowledge that British, Australian, and other forms of English differ from American English, and that each of these exists in several dialectal varieties, particularly as far as vowels are concerned. In general, though, each language has its own particular overall system of distinctive sounds. In Spanish, for example, a certain vowel sound approximates that heard in the English word *beat*, but there is no Spanish parallel to the English vowel of *bit*. This and similar differences are the source of the "natural" mispronunciations of native speakers of Spanish learning English, as when they pronounce the word *mill* as though it were *meal*. Their Spanish speech habits carry over into a language they are learning or are not familiar with.

The study of the phonetics and phonemics of a language and of the sound changes that take place over time in a language or in several related languages is referred to as **phonology.**

Phonemes of English

The dialects of English vary somewhat with respect to vowels even within the United States. The repertory of vowel phonemes in Table 4.5 is representative of a great many speakers of American English, though not all. The list is supplemented by three diphthongs.

The list of consonant phonemes in American English is shown in Table 4.6 (whenever possible, the occurrence of each phoneme is exemplified for the word-initial, word-medial, and word-final positions).

Comparative Phonology

How does the phonemic system of English compare with the systems of other languages? In terms of the number of segments, it belongs in the middle range, along with the large majority of the world's languages. According to a survey based on the phonemic inventories of a sample of 317 languages (Maddieson 1984), some languages have no more than a dozen

TABLE 4.5 Typical Vowel Phonemes in American English

Phonemic Symbol	Example
Single vowels	
/i/	bead
/ɪ/	bid
/e/	bade (rhyming with *made*)
/ɛ/	bed
/æ/	bad
/ʌ/ (unstressed = /ə/)	bud
/a/	body
/u/	boot
/ʊ/	book
/o/	bode
/ɔ/	bought
Diphthongs	
/aɪ/	bite
/aʊ/	bout
/ɔɪ/	boy

TABLE 4.6 Consonant Phonemes in American English

Phonemic Symbol	Examples
/p/	*p*it, su*pp*er, ri*p*
/b/	*b*it, fi*b*er, ri*b*
/t/	*t*ip, mea*t*y, ki*t*
/d/	*d*ip, o*d*or, ki*d*
/k/	*c*ap, lo*ck*er, pi*ck*
/g/	*g*ap, so*gg*y, pi*g*
/č/	*ch*in, it*ch*y, ri*ch*
/ǰ/	*g*in, pu*dg*y, ri*dge*
/f/	*f*at, go*ph*er, belie*f*
/v/	*v*at, i*v*y, belie*v*e
/θ/	*th*in, e*th*er, brea*th*
/ð/	*th*en, ei*th*er, brea*the*
/s/	*s*eal, i*c*y, hi*ss*
/z/	*z*eal, co*z*y, hi*s*
/š/	*sh*ow, po*ti*on, ru*sh*
/ž/	–, lei*s*ure, rou*ge*
/h/	*h*asp, a*h*oy, –
/m/	*m*oon, si*mm*er, loo*m*
/n/	*n*oon, si*nn*er, loo*n*
/ŋ/	–, si*ng*er, ki*ng*
/l/	*l*imb, mi*ll*er, ree*l*
/r/	*r*im, mi*rr*or, rea*r*
/w/	*w*et, lo*w*er, –
/y/	*y*et, la*y*er, –

segmental phonemes (for the most part they are members of the Indo-Pacific and Austronesian language families), while a few languages are reported to have in excess of 100 (members of the Khoisan family in southern Africa). The mean number of consonants per phonemic inventory is in the low twenties (22.8), that of vowels close to nine (8.7). In most languages, the total of consonants is more than twice as large as the number of vowels. The most common consonantal subsystem includes five to eleven plosives (stops), including affricates; one to four fricatives; two to four nasals; and four consonants of other types. The most common vowels are those classified as high front unrounded, high back rounded, mid front unrounded, mid back rounded, and low central unrounded. The inventory of segmental phonemes in English appears to be much like the systems characteristic of the bulk of the world's languages. This is not to say, however, that English is a typical language. Although all natural languages are indeed distinct variations on a common theme—human language—each has its own peculiar features of structure that make it unique.

Etics and Emics

Let us first briefly review the distinction between phonetics and phonemics. A phonetic transcription (or description) of a particular language is an attempt to account for all the audible or perceivable differences among the sounds of that language. For example, the phonetic transcription of English words would register the difference between the *p* sounds of *pike* and *spike* (the first, [pʰ], is aspirated whereas the second, [p], is not) or between the initial consonants of *shoot* and *sheet*, both conventionally written as *sh* (the first, [š°], is pronounced with the lips rounded in anticipation of a rounded vowel; the second, [š], is pronounced with the lips spread in anticipation of an unrounded vowel). By contrast, the phonemic transcription of these four sounds in the two pairs of words would be simply /p/ and /š/ because in English neither the sounds [pʰ] and [p] nor [š°] and [š] distinguish meaning in the manner in which /n/ and /ŋ/ do, for example, in *sin* and *sing*, words given different meaning by virtue of /n/ versus /ŋ/.

The terms *etic* and *emic* (and the corresponding nouns *etics* and *emics*) were derived from phon*etic(s)* and phon*emic(s)* and coined by the linguist Kenneth L. Pike in a work in which he attempted to relate the study of language to a unified theory of the structure of human behavior (1954). According to Pike (1967), there are several important differences between the etic and emic approaches to language and culture. For example, social scientists who study behavior (including language) from outside a particular system are following the etic approach because the units they use are available in advance (as are the numerous phonetic symbols representing the great variety of different sounds occurring in the many languages of the world). By contrast, the emic approach involves a study from within: The emic units must be discovered by subjecting a particular system to analysis (a linguist arrives at the phonemes of a language only as a result of an analysis). Moreover, the etic approach is potentially cross-cultural and comparative in that it may be applied to several languages or cultures at a time; the emic approach is language- or culture-specific because it can be applied to only one at a time. And furthermore, etic criteria are directly measurable and may be considered absolute: For example, both English and Czech include sounds that are phonetically represented as [m], [n], and [ŋ]. Emic criteria, however, are relative to one particular system: In English /m/, /n/, and /ŋ/ are phonemically distinct, as in *sum, sun,* and *sung,* but in Czech only /m/ and /n/ are, because [ŋ] in Czech is an allophone of /n/ (it occurs before velar consonants). Native speakers of a language of course do not know and do not have to know the phonemic system of their mother tongue; they internalize it when they learn their language in early childhood.

Another way to exemplify the difference between etics and emics is to point out that native speakers of English encode their messages etically— although unaware that they aspirate some *p*'s strongly, others weakly, and still others (after an *s* of the same syllable) not at all—but unconsciously decode them emically, paying attention only to distinctive features (such as the voicing that distinguishes /b/ from /p/ in *bunch* and *punch, best* and *pest,* and other such pairs.

Pike's extension of the concepts of etics and emics to the study of culture stimulated other scholars to apply these concepts to the fields of their own specialization. James Deetz, an archaeologist, suggests (1967:83–93) that in archaeology one may wish to distinguish among facts, factemes, and allofacts (and among forms, formemes, and alloforms). To illustrate what Deetz means by these terms, let us use his example concerning arrowheads. Some have straight sides whereas others have notches near the base. Because the notches are used to attach the arrowhead to the shaft, they have a functional significance and may be said to constitute a facteme (by analogy to phoneme). But the notches vary in form: Some are squarish, others triangular, still others rounded, and so on. These variations in notchings constitute allofacts (by analogy to allophones), and any individual notching, regardless of shape, can be termed a fact (by analogy to phone). In this terminology, fact is an etic unit, facteme is an emic unit, and allofact represents a group whose etic members constitute an emic unit.

In similar fashion, the folklorist Alan Dundes coined the terms *motifeme* and *allomotif* to supplement the established term *motif*. For example, folk narratives from all parts of the world contain a motifeme that could be described as "the hero is subjected to a difficult or dangerous test." The test can take a great many forms, each of which would be an allomotif of the motifeme—for example, swallowing red-hot stones, tricking a woman who kills her husbands and lovers by means of her toothed vagina, hatching boiled eggs, carrying water in a sieve, and hundreds of other means of testing the hero. Each actual telling of a hero's test would represent the occurrence of a motif in the narrative (Dundes 1962).

How is the study of nonverbal behavior to be approached—etically, emically, or both—and which of these possible approaches is most appropriate for describing culture? That these and related questions are far from having been settled among anthropologists is evident from a controversy that has persisted for over a quarter of a century. A recent debate on the subject took place during the annual meeting of the American Anthropological Association in 1988, when eight scholars representing several fields contributed to an etics-emics symposium (their papers have since been published; see Headland, Pike, and Harris 1990).

The crux of the controversy has to do with the status of etics. Is etic description no more than a prerequisite for discovering an emic system, or are the etic and emic analyses of equal importance? From the cultural materialist research strategy in anthropology, of which Marvin Harris is the foremost proponent, "etic analysis is . . . a steppingstone . . . [only] to the discovery of etic structures. The intent is neither to convert etics to emics nor emics to etics, but rather to describe both and if possible to explain one in terms of the other" (Harris 1979:36). And further, "*etics* for Pike, even at the phonetic level, is in part the observer's emics incorrectly applied to a foreign system. . . . If Pike had meant by *etics* nothing but the emics of the observer, why did he bother to introduce the term *etics?* Why not simply be content with the opposition: 'emics of the observer' versus 'emics of the native participant'?" (Harris 1990:49). A good anthropological report, according to Harris, should distinguish between, on the one hand, what the observer has seen and heard to the best of his or her objective ability (and which can therefore be independently verified) and, on the other hand, what is in the heads of the native informants when they comment on their own culture. Etic analysis is therefore to be considered an end in itself.

The finer points of the etics-emics debate are quite technical and therefore outside the scope of an introduction to linguistic anthropology. On the whole it seems that the distinction between the etic and emic approaches is more easily applicable to linguistic data than to nonverbal cultural behavior.

Summary and Conclusions

In order for ethnographic research to be conducted as participant obser-vation, anthropologists should have a working knowledge of the lan-guage spoken by the people they study. For a linguistic anthropologist, acquaintance with the methods of linguistic analysis and appreciation of structural differences among languages are essential.

Speech sounds are produced by various modifications of the vocal channel as the outgoing airstream passes between the vocal cords and the lips. The two main classes of speech sounds are vowels and consonants, each consisting of various types according to the place and manner of ar-ticulation. Vowels are usually associated with accent, which may take the form of stress, pitch, or a combination of both. Languages that make use of distinctive pitch levels are referred to as tone languages, some of those spoken in China being the best-known examples.

Analysis of the sounds of a language involves determining which pho-netic differences are contrastive (distinctive, significant), that is, phone-mic (for example, [b] and [pʰ] in English, differentiating between *bull* and *pull*), and which are predictable, or allophonic (for example, [P] and [pʰ] of *span* and *pan*). Each language has a characteristic phonemic system: Sounds that are assignable to two or more distinct phonemes in one lan-guage may be allophones of a single phoneme in another. Although phonemes have been defined traditionally as the minimal units in the sound system of a language, they can be further analyzed into distinctivə features, of which each phoneme is a bundle. The number of segmental phonemes per language varies from a mere dozen to as many as 100 or more, but the inventories of the great majority of languages (70 percent) range between twenty and thirty-seven segments.

The phonetic and phonemic analytical approaches have been extended from the study of language to nonlinguistic aspects of culture under the terms *etic* and *emic*. Although the techniques of both etics and emics have been employed for several decades, not all scholars agree on their status and mutual relationship.

Chapter Appendix:
Distinctive Features and Phonological Rules

Even though the phoneme continues to be defined and used for purposes of tran-scription as the smallest unit of speech—much as the atom refers in nontechnical usage to the smallest particle of matter—the view of the phoneme as a bundle of distinctive features appears to go back to the early 1930s. The concept derives from the recognition that in any language certain phonemes have some phonetic features in common despite being perceived by speakers as discrete units of contrast. In English, for example, both /p/ and /b/ are bilabial (rather than velar), oral (rather than nasal), and plosive (rather than fricative), but /p/ is voiceless whereas /b/ is voiced—hence the contrast between *pin* and *bin*, *pit* and *bit*, and the like. A distinctive feature is usually regarded as a binary attribute, with a plus (+) value indicating the presence of a feature and a minus (–) value its absence. General agreement has not been reached whether to characterize distinctive features primarily in acoustic terms, in reference to articulatory criteria, or as a combination of the two.

Among the consonantal phonemes of English, each of the four plosives, or stops /p, b, t, d/, and the four fricatives /f, v, s, z/ can be uniquely defined in terms of articulatory features as follows:

	/p	b	t	d	f	v	s	z/
voiced	–	+	–	+	–	+	–	+
plosive	+	+	+	+	–	–	–	–
alveolar	–	–	+	+	–	–	+	+

To define the remaining segments would require the introduction of additional features. For example, the inclusion of consonantness would distinguish all eight segments, as well as other consonantal phonemes, from all English vowels, which would be characterized as "– consonantal." The addition of the phoneme /n/ to the eight consonants would require the introduction of the feature of nasality, with "+ nasal" for /n/, "– nasal" for the other eight.

To describe economically the systematic relationships among sounds or classes of sounds, linguists summarize them by means of phonological rules. One such rule, applicable to English, can be expressed in formal notation as follows:

$$/p/ \rightarrow [- \text{aspirated}]/[s]\_\_,$$

where the arrow ($\rightarrow$) is to be read as "become(s)" and the slash (/) as "in the environment of," that is, the phoneme *p* becomes unaspirated if it follows an *s*. Alternatively, one may state the rule as

$$/p/ \rightarrow [+ \text{aspirated}]/\$ \_\_ \acute{V},$$

or

$$/p/ \rightarrow [p^h]/\$ \_\_ \acute{V},$$

where the symbols $ and $\acute{V}$ stand for syllable boundary and any stressed vowel, respectively. According to this rule, the phoneme *p* becomes aspirated if it follows a syllable boundary and precedes a stressed vowel. Because this same rule applies in English also to /t/ and /k/, one may include the two by generalizing the rule as follows:

$$\begin{bmatrix} + \text{plosive} \\ - \text{voiced} \end{bmatrix} \rightarrow [+ \text{aspirated}]/\$ \_\_ V\ [+ \text{stress}].$$

Notes and Suggestions for Further Reading

Textbooks of linguistics are fairly numerous. The two classics are Sapir 1921 and Bloomfield 1933; two excellent postwar but pre-Chomskyan introductions to linguistics are Hockett 1958 and Gleason 1961. From about a score of recent or contemporary texts, a representative selection ranging from a slender introduction to a fairly comprehensive text might include Lehmann 1983; Hudson 1984; Akmajian, Demers, Farmer, and Harnish 1995; and Parker 1986. For general reference, one may wish to consult Crystal 1991b and especially the excellent Crystal 1991a. For more specialized topics, see Ladefoged 1982 on phonetics, Lass 1984 on phonology, and Chomsky and Halle 1968 on the phonology of English. Bright's four-volume encyclopedia of linguistics (1992) is an excellent and reliable source on all aspects of linguistics.

Some linguists distinguish between vocoids and vowels on the one hand and contoids and consonants on the other. When this distinction is made, vocoids and contoids refer to speech sounds defined in phonetic terms and considered as phonetic entities, whereas vowels and consonants refer to segments defined in terms of the sound structure of a particular language, that is, considered as phonological entities.

There is by no means agreement about how best to analyze the system of English vowel phonemes. In one widely accepted analysis, for example, the vowels of *pit* and *peat* are phonemically represented as /i/ and /iy/, respectively; in another, they are interpreted as /ɪ/ and /i/; and in still another as /i/ and a long /i:/. For our purposes, however, it is enough to note that alternative interpretations exist.

Problems

In order to make it possible for the reader to apply the discussion in some of the sections of this chapter to non-English data, five simple problems are included below. Solutions can be found following the bibliography at the end of the book.

Problem 1

Based on Wonderly 1951a and 1951b, this problem is taken from Zoque, a language spoken in southern Mexico that belongs to the Mixe-Zoque group of languages. Among the sounds of Zoque are [c], a voiceless alveolar affricate (similar to the consonants in the word *tsetse* [*fly*]), and [ʒ], a voiced alveolar affricate. From the data below—to be taken as representative of the language—are [c] and [ʒ] allophones of one phoneme (that is, are they in complementary distribution), or are they assignable to two different phonemes (that is, do they contrast)? Support your conclusion.

1. ʔakaʔŋʒʌhk-	'to be round'	7. nʒʌhku	'I did it'
2. ʔaŋʒoŋu	'he answered'	8. nʒima	'my calabash'
3. camʒamnayu	'he chatted'	9. nʒin	'my pine'
4. cap	'sky'	10. pac	'skunk'
5. caʔ	'stone'	11. puci	'trash'
6. cima	'calabash'	12. wanʒʌʔyu'	he quit singing'

Problem 2

Czech is a West Slavic language of the Indo-European language family, spoken in the Czech Republic. In Czech, among the various stops (plosives) are two alveodental stops, [t] and [d], articulated by the tongue tip against the boundary between the upper incisors and the alveolar ridge behind them, and two palatal stops, [tʸ] and [dʸ]. To how many phonemes are these four sounds assignable? Consider the data below and support your conclusion.

1. dej	'give!'		9. tʸelo	'body'
2. dʸedʸit	'to inherit'		10. teta	'aunt'
3. dʸej	'action'		11. tikat	'to be on a first-name basis'
4. dʸelo	'cannon'		12. titul	'title'
5. kotel	'kettle'		13. tʸikat	'to tick (clock)'
6. kotʸe	'kitten'		14. vada	'flaw'
7. tedi	'hence'		15. vana	'bathtub'
8. tele	'calf (animal)'		16. vata	'absorbent cotton'

Problem 3

Based on Echeverría and Contreras 1965, this problem is taken from Araucanian, a language spoken by Native Americans of Argentina and Chile. Is the main stress, marked by ['], distinctive, or is it predictable by rule? Support your conclusion.

1. elúmuyu	'give us!'		4. nawél	'tiger'
2. kimúfaluwulay	'he pretended not		5. putún	'to drink'
	to know'		6. θuŋúlan	'I do not speak'
3. kurám	'egg'		7. wuyá	'yesterday'

Problem 4

Based on Wolff 1952, this problem is from Osage, the Siouan language of a Native American people who originally lived in what is now western Missouri. [ð] is a voiced fricative formed with the tip of the tongue against the teeth or the teethridge; [ĩ], [ã], and [õ] are nasalized vowels; [ʔ] is the glottal stop; and ['] marks stress. From the data below, are [d] and [ð] allophones of one phoneme or are they assignable to two different phonemes? Support your conclusion.

1. ðíe	'you'		8. dálĩ	'good'
2. ðíški	'to wash'		9. nõpá	'two'
3. dakʔé	'to dig'		10. cʔéðe	'he killed it'
4. lóðĩ	'drunk'		11. dacpé	'to eat'
5. ðéze	'tongue'		12. daštú	'to bite'
6. ðužá	'to wash'		13. mãðĩ	'he walked'
7. tapé	'ball'		14. ĩtáci	'father'

Problem 5

Based on Postal 1969, this problem is from Mohawk, the Iroquoian language of a Native American people who live mainly in southern Ontario and extreme north-

ern New York. On the basis of the data below, what is the status of vowel length—
is it predictable or is it distinctive? Length is indicated by doubling a symbol—
that is, *éé* is a long *e*. [ʔ] is the glottal stop; ['] marks stress; [ʌ] is an unrounded
back lower mid vowel, as in the English word *bud*; and [ɔ] is a rounded back
lower mid vowel.

1. ranahéézʌs	'he trusts her'	7. wahrehyáára?ne?	'he remembered'
2. ragéédas	'he scrapes'	8. ɔwaduniza?áshege?	'it will be ripen-
3. rayʌ́thos	'he plants'		ing repeatedly'
4. waháágede?	'he scraped'	9. yékreks	'I push it'
5. wísk	'five'	10. royó?de?	'he works'
6. rehyáára?s	'he remembers'		

5

Structure of Words and Sentences

Because many of the languages they encounter have only been spoken, never written, anthropologists must adequately identify all of the sounds before they can transcribe and later analyze what speakers of these languages have said. Since accurate transcription cannot be made at the speed at which people talk, magnetic tape recorders have been of great help in modern fieldwork. When ethnographic reports are published in which native words or texts are to be cited, a reliable method of writing down the language must be devised. Phonemic transcription is the most economic and at the same time accurate way of recording utterances ranging from short comments to long ceremonial speeches.

A good transcription is essential for an analysis because only with a reliable text in hand can the linguistic anthropologist determine its grammatical structure and exact meaning. Full understanding requires the identification of even the smallest *meaningful* segments (morphemes) that make up the text. Every language has its own stock of morphemes and arranges them into words, phrases, and sentences in a particular way, and every language has its own grammatical categories which vary from one language to the next.

In what units do people communicate? The answer depends on the approach one takes to the study of speech. An important unit of linguistic analysis is the sentence, which is in turn subdividable into smaller constituents—for example, noun phrases and verb phrases or the subject, verb, and object. The principal analytical unit of communicative behavior in linguistic anthropology is **discourse.** The concept of discourse is not easy to define because individual scholars use it differently. Discourse may be as short in duration as a greeting or as long as a protracted argument or the telling of a traditional narrative; it can be oral or written, planned or unplanned, poetic or lacking in poetic qualities; and it can be exemplified by any one of the genres characteristic of the speech behavior of a particular culture. A great deal of any culture is transmitted by means of discourse, and discourse may be said to constitute a significant part of any culture. As Joel Sherzer puts it,

> Discourse is the broadest and most comprehensive level of linguistic form, content, and use . . . [and] the process of discourse structuring is the locus of the language-culture relationship. . . . It is in certain kinds of discourse, in which speech play and verbal art are heightened, as central moments in poetry, magic, politics, religion, respect, insult, and bargaining, that the language-culture-discourse relationship comes into sharpest focus and the organizing role of discourse in this relationship is highlighted. (Sherzer 1987:305–306)

Linguistic theories and methods have undergone great changes in the course of the current century, with the transformational-generative approach of recent decades rapidly gaining followers. And although linguistic anthropologists are more concerned with the relationship between language and culture and society than with linguistic structure in and of itself, they nevertheless follow current linguistic research with interest and when applicable use its results in their own work.

Morphemes and Allomorphs

An overview of phonetics and the fundamental principles of phonemic analysis has been presented in the previous chapter. Let us now shift to the level of analysis conventionally referred to as grammar. Consider the phrase *shockingly disgraceful acts,* which can be subdivided into the following *meaningful* segments (to simplify matters, conventional spelling instead of phonemic transcription is used below):

shock, meaning "to startle, offend, distress,"
-ing, an adjectival segment meaning "causing to . . . ,"
-ly, an adverbial segment meaning "in a . . . manner,"
dis-, meaning "not, opposite of,"
grace, meaning "propriety, decency,"
-ful, meaning "characterized by,"
act, meaning "deed," and
-s, meaning "more than one," that is, marking the plural.

It appears that the three-word phrase consists of eight meaningful segments of English, none of which can be further subdivided without the loss of the original meaning (it cannot be claimed, for example, that the word *grace* is made up of *g-* plus *race*). Linguistic units that have a meaning but contain no smaller meaningful parts are termed **morphemes.** To put it differently, a morpheme is the smallest contrastive unit of grammar.

The search for such units in a particular language is called morphemic analysis. And the study of word structure, including classification of and interrelationships among morphemes, is referred to as **morphology.**

There are many thousands of morphemes in any language. The large majority are commonly free morphemes because they may occur unattached to other morphemes, that is, they can stand alone as independent words—in the example above, *grace, shock,* and *act.* Some morphemes, but usually relatively few, are bound morphemes because they normally do not occur on their own but only in combination with another morpheme—for example, *dis-, -ing, -ly,* and *-s.* A base form of a word that cannot be further analyzed is referred to as a root. Removing *dis-* and *-ful* from *disgraceful* leaves the root, or root morpheme, *grace.*

A concept related to root is stem, which is that part of a word to which inflectional affixes (such as the plural) are attached. A stem may coincide with a root (as in *bird*), but it may also consist of two roots (as in the compound *blackbird*) or a root followed by certain endings (as in *speaker* from *speak* and *-er*). Not all roots are free morphemes: In *cranberry* and *cranapple,* for example, *cran-* is a root that happens to be a bound morpheme but not a prefix.

In English and other languages, bound morphemes occur in limited numbers. There are languages, though, in which most morphemes are bound; Eskimo is usually cited as an example of such a language. In still other languages, those noun stems that stand for objects that are typically possessed do not occur as free morphemes. This is true, for example, of Arapaho nouns referring to body parts, kinship relationships, and a few other referents. (In Arapaho, the acute accent ['] marks stressed vowels with higher pitch; long vowels are written doubly.) Examples of dependent nouns are *bétee* '(someone's) heart,' *wonotóno?* '(someone's) ear,' *notóóne* 'my daughter,' *béiteh?éí* '(someone's) friend,' and *betéí* 'louse, flea,' because there is no such thing as a heart or an ear apart from a human or an animal, a daughter without a mother or father, a friend unattached to another by affection, or a louse or flea who could survive without deriving benefits from a host. The forms *bétee, wonotóno?, notóóne, béiteh?éí,* and *betéí* consist of either the first-person possessive morpheme *n-* in the case of *notóóne* or the indefinite personal possessor morpheme *b-* or *w-* in the case of the other four nouns. None of these four or some 200 other nouns ever occurs as a free (unpossessed) stem.

Some but not all bound morphemes in a language are affixes; attached to other morphemes, they modify meaning in some way and make more complex words. If an affix is attached before a root or stem, it is called a prefix; if it follows a root or stem, it is a suffix; and if it is placed within another morpheme, it is called an infix. In English only the first two types of affixes occur: Examples of prefixes are *be-, de-, in-, pre-, re-,* and *un-* as in *befriend, debug, inlay, prewash, rewrite,* and *undo;* examples of suffixes are *-en, -er, -hood, -ish, -ize,* and *-ward* as in *oxen, smaller, childhood, bookish, equalize,* and *skyward.* An example of an infix may be taken from Chontal, a language spoken by a people in southern Oaxaca, Mexico: *akán'ó?* 'woman,' *kón'í?* 'grandchild,' *sewí?* 'magpie,' and several other stems form the plural by inserting an infix in the form of *-ɬ-* (a voiceless lateral continuant) before the second consonant, yielding *akáɬn'ó?* 'women,' *kóɬn'í?* 'grandchildren,' and *seɬwí?* 'magpies.' Infixation is fairly common in Native American, Southeast Asian, and African languages.

What about such "irregular" plurals in English as *feet, geese, men,* and *mice?* Rather than by adding a suffix to the stems *foot, goose, man,* and *mouse,* the plural is formed by changing the stem vowel, for example, in the case of *foot* → *feet* and *goose* → *geese* by fronting and unrounding it. Pluralization in these cases is effected by what is sometimes referred to as a process morpheme and is quite different from the addition of a suffix after the stem (as in *cat* plus *-s*).

A particular morpheme does not have to have the same shape every time it occurs. The plural of English nouns offers an excellent example of the considerable variation in the phonemic shape of a morpheme. Noun stems ending in a so-called sibilant (an *s*-like or *sh*-like fricative) form their plural by adding a vowel plus a *z* sound, very commonly [əz], as in *box-es, pass-es, buzz-es, bush-es, garage-s, patch-es,* and *judge-s.* The great majority of noun stems ending in voiced nonsibilant sounds add a voiced [z], whereas those ending in voiceless nonsibilant sounds add a voiceless [s], as in *bear-s, can-s, comma-s, lathe-s, pad-s, pill-s, rib-s, rig-s,* and *song-s* on the one hand, and *cat-s, laugh-s, lip-s,* and *tick-s* on the other. But there are a number of noun stems that form their plural differently—among them *alumna, alumnus, child, crisis, criterion, datum, kibbutz,* and *ox;* their plurals are, respectively, *alumnae, alumni, children, crises, criteria, data, kibbutzim,* and *oxen.* And then there are a relatively few noun stems the plurals of which are not overtly marked, for example, *sheep* and *swine.* These and other such nouns are said to have their plurals marked by a *zero* (written as Ø), that is, by the absence of an overt linguistic feature. The variant forms of a particular morpheme are referred to as its allomorphs (just as the varieties of a phoneme are called allophones), or morpheme alternants. Allomorphs of a given morpheme, then, are different forms of the morpheme, depending on the context in which they occur.

In summary, then, one may say that the plural morpheme in English has a number of allomorphs, ranging from the most common ones of /-z/, /-s/, and /-əz/, through several others associated especially with loanwords, to zero. And in the case of pluralizing the noun *man* to *men,* one would represent the plural allomorph as /æ/→/ɛ/. The plural morpheme in English is by no means an exception in that it has morpheme alternants. For example, the stem *child* has a different phonemic shape in its plural form (*children*) from when it occurs by itself or when it is suffixed by *-hood*, *-ish*, and *-like* (in *childhood, childish,* and *childlike*).

Morphemes also vary considerably in length. Some consist of a single phoneme: For example, the three English morphemes marking the plural, the possessive, and the third-person singular (as in *apes, ape's,* and [*he*] *apes* [*someone*]) have /s/ as one of their several allomorphs. Others, like *caterpillar* or *hippopotamus,* consist of several syllables. Words, too, in English vary in length: *a* is the shortest, but it is impossible to list the longest. Suppose you would wish to refer to a lineal paternal male relative from the sixteenth century: He would be your *great-great-* . . . . *great-grandfather.*

Morphological Processes

Just as languages differ in their phonemic systems, they differ in their morphologies. Some morphological processes, however, are quite common throughout the world even though they may be applied differently in specific languages. One such process is derivation, by means of which new words are formed from existing ones, frequently by changing them from one word class to another. In English this process of word formation is frequently accomplished by the use of derivational affixes. For example, affixes change the adjective *modern* to the verb *modernize,* the noun *friend* to the adjective *friendly,* the verb *speak* to the noun *speaker,* and the adjective *abrupt* to the adverb *abruptly.* They also produce such words as *kingdom, outbid,* and *despite.*

The other common morphological process is inflection, the use of affixes to indicate grammatical relationships (number, case, person, tense, and others). In English all inflectional affixes are suffixes and are limited to the plural and possessive markers in nouns (as in *mother*s and *mother*'s), comparative and superlative markers in adjectives (as in *tall*er and *tall*est), and the third-person singular present-tense marker and the past-tense, progressive, and past-participle markers in verbs (as in *wait*s, *wait*ed, [*is*] *sing*ing, and *beat*en).

Derivational and inflectional morphemes may have the same phonemic shape: One *-ing* in English serves as the derivational suffix changing a verb into a noun as in "Excessive eating is harmful," whereas another *-ing* is an inflectional suffix marking the progressive verb form as in "They were eating voraciously." In English inflectional suffixes always follow derivational suffixes, as in *reader's, organizers,* and *friendliest* (*read-er's, organ-iz(e)-er-s,* and *friend-li-est*).

As languages go, English has very few inflectional affixes compared with, for example, Latin. As against the handful of different forms of an English verb (*speak, speaks, speaking, spoke,* and *spoken*), a Latin verb has scores. As regards number, English distinguishes formally only between the singular and the plural, whereas some languages have special forms also for the *dual* to refer to two of a kind, and even forms to refer to three and four of a kind. Old English marked the dual number in its personal pronouns: Besides *ic* 'I' and *wē* 'we,' there was *wit* 'we two'; besides *mē* '(to) me' and *ūs* '(to) us,' there was *unc* '(to) the two of us'; and so on. These dual forms gradually disappeared during the second part of the thirteenth century, halfway through the Middle English period. However, derivational suffixes in English are plentiful: *-able* (as in *reasonable*), *-ade* (*blockade*), *-age* (*breakage*), *-al* (*coastal*), *-ance* (*assistance*), *-ant* (*servant*), *-ar* (*linear*), *-ard* (*drunkard*), *-ary* (*budgetary*), *-ate* (*activate*), *-atic* (*problematic*), and scores of others.

Some languages distinguish nouns according to several genders, each of which may require corresponding forms in pronouns, adjectives, and even verbs. Frequently there is no correlation between grammatical and natural gender. In English all inanimate objects are referred to by the pronoun *it;* in German, however, *der Löffel* 'spoon' is masculine, *die Gabel* 'fork' is feminine, and *das Messer* 'knife' is neuter, as are also *das Weib* 'woman' and *das Mädchen* 'girl.' In Old English, *stān* 'stone' and *wīfman* 'woman' were masculine, *duru* 'door' and *sunne* 'sun' feminine, and *word* 'word' and *wīf* 'woman, wife' neuter. The substitution of natural for grammatical gender also took place during the Middle English period.

Although Old English had three different case forms for, say, *stān* 'stone' in the singular (nominative and accusative *stān*, genitive *stānes*, and dative *stāne*) and three in the plural (*stānas, stāna,* and *stānum,* respectively), Modern English manages quite well with only two forms—*stone* and *stones.* Latin has six cases in both the singular and the plural, Czech seven, and Finnish more than a dozen. It is not surprising, therefore, that so many people around the world learn English and manage to speak it remarkably well.

Another morphological process is reduplication, the doubling or repetition of a phoneme or phonemes. In Isthmus Nahuat, a dialect of Nahuatl spoken by Native Americans in eastern Mexico, verb stems are derived from roots by reduplication to mark different kinds of repetitive action: *-kakalaki-* 'enter a house many times' from *-kalaki-* 'enter,' *-pahpano-* 'pass by many times' from *-pano-* 'pass by,' *-poposteki* 'break many times' or 'break in many pieces' from *-posteki* 'break,' *-papaka* 'wash many times' and *-pahpaka* 'wash many things' from *-paka-* 'wash,' and the like. The compounds *goody-goody, helter-skelter, teeny-weeny,* and *wishy-washy* are reduplications of sorts, but the process in English is quite limited.

One could go on illustrating various other grammatical categories found in the thousands of the world's languages (aspect, mood, tense, voice, and so on) and the processes by which they are marked, but the examples already given should suffice. However, one important point must be made. Whether or not a language formally marks a particular grammatical category does not make it superior (or inferior) to others. If it were so, Old English would have to be rated as much superior to Modern English—something no one can seriously maintain. All languages are fully adequate because they enable native speakers to express all that they wish to say about the society and culture in which they live.

Morphophonemics

Sound alternations like the one between /f/ and /v/ in *knife* and *knives*, *life* and *lives*, *loaf* and *loaves*, and *wife* and *wives* are common in English and other languages. Alternations of this kind are changes in the phonemic shape of the allomorphs of a morpheme, and as such they represent important processes in the structure of language. The study of the relations between morphology and phonology or, to put it in other words, the study of the phonemic differences among allomorphs of the same morpheme, is referred to as **morphophonemics** or morpho(pho)nology, and the generalizations concerning the occurrence of the various shapes of morphemes are called morphophonemic rules. To formulate such a rule one usually selects a particular allomorph as the base form and then describes the conditions under which other allomorphs of the same morpheme occur. To refer to an example used earlier in this chapter, nouns in English (except for those specifically exempt) form the plural by adding /z/ to their stem (as in *leg, legs*) but insert /ə/before the plural suffix if the stem ends in a sibilant (/s/, /z/, /š/, /ž/, /č/, or /ǰ/) (as in *kiss, kisses*) or change the voiced /z/ to voiceless /s/ if the stem terminates in a voiceless nonsibilant (as in *neck, necks*).

Morphophonemic rules in any language are statable even if they are fairly complex. For example, in Arapaho, an Algonquian language spoken by Native Americans in Wyoming and Oklahoma, the word *néíʔibéheʔ* 'my grandmother' is regularly changed to *hiníʔiiwóhoʔ* to mean 'his/her grandmother.' (The explanation of why this change takes place is fairly complex, but to satisfy the curious, here it is: In addition to the two common word-initial prefixes marking possession ['my' and 'his/her'], the differences between the two forms are also regular. The final *-oʔ* in *hiníʔiiwóhoʔ* is the obviative suffix [a morpheme that marks the so-called fourth person when two third persons are referred to, in this case a grandmother and the person who claims her as grandmother]. The vowel of the obviative, *o*, influences the selection of a like vowel in the diminutive suffix before it, and *b* regularly changes into *w* before a back vowel [in this case *o*]. The word apparently means 'his/her little one [mother]'—a rather gentle way of referring to one's grandmother.)

Another example of a morphophonemic rule is found in Turkish, one of the languages with vowel harmony, the requirement that vowels within a word have a certain similarity. With relatively few exceptions, Turkish suffixes containing high vowels have

$\left.\begin{array}{l} /\text{i}/ \\ /\ddot{\text{u}}/ \\ /\text{i}/ \\ /\text{u}/ \end{array}\right\}$ if the preceding syllable has $\left\{\begin{array}{l} /\text{i}/ \text{ or } /\text{e}/ \text{ (front unrounded vowels)} \\ /\ddot{\text{u}}/ \text{ or } /\ddot{\text{o}}/ \text{ (front rounded)} \\ /\text{i} \text{ or } /\text{a}/ \text{ (back unrounded)} \\ /\text{u}/ \text{ or } /\text{o}/ \text{ (back rounded)} \end{array}\right.$

whereas suffixes containing low vowels have

$\left.\begin{array}{l} /\text{e}/ \\ /\text{a}/ \end{array}\right\}$ if the preceding syllable has $\left\{\begin{array}{l} /\text{i}/, /\text{e}/, /\ddot{\text{u}}/ \text{ or } /\ddot{\text{o}}/ \text{ (front vowels)} \\ /\text{i}/, /\text{a}/, /\text{u}/, \text{ or } /\text{o}/ \text{ (back vowels).} \end{array}\right.$

However, on occasion morphophonemic changes are irregular in the sense that they are limited to one morpheme and are not repeated elsewhere in the language. Examples are the forms *am, are, is* from (*to*) *be*, the past tense form *went* from (*to*) *go*, and the comparative form *better* or superlative *best* from *good*. The occurrence of phonemically unrelated allomorphs of a morpheme is referred to as suppletion and the specific instances of it suppletive forms. Suppletion seems to occur in all natural (as opposed to artificial) languages; however, it is never extensive because any irregularity on a large scale would tend to hinder communication.

Syntax: The Sentence Patterns

Just as speech sounds normally do not occur in isolation, neither do words. As a rule, human utterances are made up of larger units—phrases and sentences. It is not easy to define these two terms rigorously; for our purposes let us say that a sentence is the largest structural unit of the grammar of a language and that a phrase—for example, *tomorrow evening, in the sky, the wicked witch*—is a structural unit larger than a single word but smaller than a clause.

The number of different sentences that can be produced in any language is infinite. For example, it is most unlikely that the sentence "Whenever the moon is full, bats gather to discuss the state of the local economy" has ever been said before. One could easily generate novel sentences by the thousands. How is it possible that speakers of a language can and do produce and understand sentences conforming to the rules of grammar even though they have never been said or heard before? The answer is quite simple: Native speakers know the **syntax** of their language—the internal structure of sentences and the interrelationships between the various sentence elements.

All speakers have a largely unconscious knowledge of the system of grammatical rules that characterizes their native language or a language in which they are truly fluent. This knowledge is referred to as competence. What language users actually do with this knowledge in speaking or comprehending speech, however, is somewhat different and is referred to as performance. Although an individual's competence may be expected to remain fairly stable for a long period of time, performance tends to suffer when a speaker is sleepy, tired, ill, preoccupied, or under the influence of alcohol. Sentences that conform to the syntactic rules of a language are grammatical sentences; those that do not are ungrammatical (as when a speaker's performance has noticeably suffered). Grammatical sentences may be meaningless, as in "Jabberwocky," the poem Alice was able to read by using the mirror in *Through the Looking-Glass:*

> *'Twas brillig, and the slithy toves*
> *Did gyre and gimble in the wabe.*

Yet some ungrammatical sentences may be meaningful, as when a foreigner says, *"I not speak English good" (an asterisk is placed before a sentence to show that it is ungrammatical or unacceptable). Then there are sentences that are grammatical but structurally ambiguous, that is, having more than one meaning—for example, "Visiting in-laws can be very trying": Is it very trying to visit in-laws, or are in-laws who visit very trying?

To gain some understanding of English sentence structure we might look at the sentence "The stream carries the boat." This sentence (S) has two major constituents: The first, corresponding to the traditional subject of the sentence, is the noun phrase (NP) "the stream"; the second, corresponding to the traditional predicate, is the verb phrase (VP) "carries the boat." These constituents consist ultimately of lexical categories: an article (Art), a noun (N), and a verb (V). The tree diagram of the sentence (see Tree 5.1) gives three kinds of information: the linear order of words that make up the sentence, the lexical category of each word, and the grouping of the words into structural constituents.

The longer sentence "The boats in the stream will enter the ocean from the bay" may be diagramed as shown in Tree 5.2. In Tree 5.2, *Aux* refers to the auxiliary verb, *PP* to a prepositional phrase, and *Prep* to a preposition.

The two sentences diagramed in Trees 5.1 and 5.2 may also be represented in general by the following phrase-structure rules (elements enclosed in parentheses are optional):

$$S \rightarrow NP \ (Aux) \ VP$$
$$NP \rightarrow Art \ N \ (PP)$$
$$PP \rightarrow Prep \ NP$$
$$VP \rightarrow V \ NP \ (PP)$$

These rules are, of course, only a few of those governing English syntax. Others would include VP → V (NP) as in "[The child] eats (a meal)," NP → (Art) N as in "Mother . . . [has come]," but not NP → N Art because in English an article does not follow its noun (as it may in other languages).

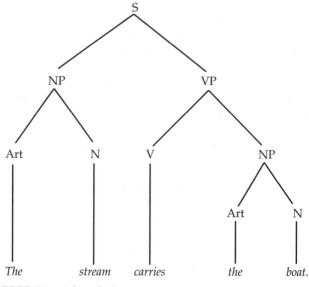

TREE 5.1   A Simple Sentence

The sentence "The ship will be sinking" has the structure

$$S \rightarrow NP \ Aux \ VP$$

typical of simple English declarative sentences. But what of the corresponding interrogative sentence, "Will the ship be sinking?" The rule that changes the declarative sentence to the corresponding interrogative sentence requires moving *will* to the front of the sentence. An operation that adds, deletes, or changes elements in one structure to produce another is referred to as transformation and the general statement describing such an operation as a transformational rule. An English declarative sentence is transformed into an interrogative sentence by placing the first auxiliary verb that follows the subject of the sentence immediately to the left of the subject: NP Aux VP → Aux NP VP. This rule, which applies to sentences with auxiliary verbs (forms of the verbs *be, have, do,* and such other verb forms as *can, could, will, would, may,* and *must*), does not apply to other types of sentences. In some sentences an appropriate form of the verb *do* is placed at the beginning of the sentence and appropriate changes are made in the main verb, as in "Mother knows best" → "Does Mother know best?"

This is only a very brief illustration of how one approaches the study of sentence structure. A complete description of the great variety of sentence types in English and the processes of their derivation would easily fill a sizable book. Such a description would include transformations having to

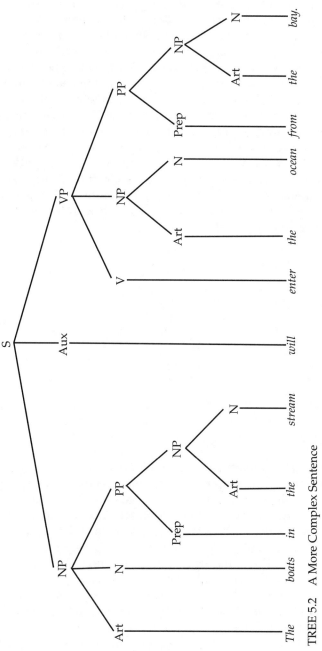

TREE 5.2 A More Complex Sentence

do with commands, exclamations, complex sentences (consisting of a main clause and at least one subordinate clause), embedding (as in "The man who suddenly appeared in the door was my first cousin," in which "The man suddenly appeared in the door" is embedded in the matrix sentence "The man was my first cousin"), and many other constructions.

As shown in Trees 5.1 and 5.2, analysis is motivated by empirical evidence, that is, it can be verified or rejected on the basis of observation or inquiry. Not only do linguists reject utterances (sentences) native speakers consider ungrammatical, but they may occasionally ask if two closely similar utterances have the same meaning (for example, "Don't you want some soup?" and "Don't you want any soup?"—many speakers would consider them to be slightly different) or account for structural ambiguities (for example, the phrase "French history professor" may mean "a history professor who is French" or "a professor who teaches French history," and accordingly it would be represented as

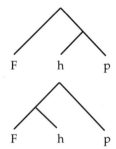

or

depending on what the speaker had in mind).

Semantics

We have so far given attention to the formal aspects of language structure—phonemes (and allophones); morphemes (and allomorphs); and the ways the meaningful units (morphemes) combine to produce words and, in turn, the ways words combine to form sentences (syntax). A second important aspect of the study of language has to do with the point of view of its users. This particular focus is referred to as pragmatics. Linguistic anthropologists deal with the topics related to pragmatics in the ethnography of communication (see Chapter 10). A third aspect of language study is concerned with meaning—the meaning of words (for example, *daisy*), compound words (*daisy wheel*), and phrases (*he is pushing up daisies*). The study of meanings is referred to as semantics.

When children acquire language, they not only learn the phonemic shapes of morphemes and the manner of putting morphemes together to form words and sentences, they also learn what these morphemes, words, and sentences mean. For many people, learning new words and their meanings is a lifelong process. The speaker of any language shares the large majority of meanings with those who speak the same language; not to do so would cause frequent misunderstandings and greatly impeded communication. The total stock of morphemes and the words they make up—the lexicon of a language—is invariably so large that no one speaker has full command of it. Therefore users of written languages occasionally have to look up a word in a dictionary if they are not sure of its meaning.

Each word commonly has some semantic properties on which speakers of a language are in agreement. For example, among the semantic properties of the word *widow* are the attributes of being human, female, and adult. Technically, elements of a word's meaning have been referred to as semantic features. Most words in any language belong to one of a large number of semantic fields—for example, color terms, kinship terms, bird names, names of foods (dishes) and drinks, and the like. For example, most speakers of English would analyze the words *horse, stallion, gelding, mare, colt,* and *filly*—all of which belong to the same semantic field, or area of meaning—as follows:

	horse	*stallion*	*gelding*	*mare*	*colt*	*filly*
adult	±	+	+	+	−	−
male	±	+	+	−	+	−
castrated	±	−	+	−	−	−

where + refers to the presence of a feature listed on the left, − to its absence, and ± to presence or absence. One should note that each of the examples except the first one (*horse*) is uniquely defined, that is, each excludes any of the other four. If one were to contrast these six words with additional ones, say, *bull, cow, calf, ram, ewe,* and *lamb,* it would be necessary to introduce additional semantic features, for example, "equine," and then to distinguish *cow* from *ewe* by such a feature as "bovine" (*cow* is −equine but +bovine while *ewe* is −equine and −bovine).

Semantic relations between words are of many different kinds, and analyzing them can be complicated. Their study, however, can be helpful to ethnographers, who strive to understand what members of the societies they study consider culturally important and how different aspects of culture appear to relate to one another. Among the semantic relations that may prove revealing are such relationships as part of *X*, related to *X*, used for *X*, different from *X*, same as *X*, and consequence of *X*. That a semantic feature may be predicted on the basis of another feature can be formalized as a redundancy rule. For example, the redundancy rule [+ female] → [+ animate] states that any word containing the feature [+ female] automatically contains the feature [+ animate]. A word may include information in addition to its basic meaning: If someone or something flies, it is taken for granted that the action occurs in the air. To formalize this meaning postulate one may write it as the rule

(x) flies → (x) in the air.

Homonyms—separate words pronounced or spelled alike despite their different meanings and listed in dictionaries as distinct entries—may create ambiguity if the hearer or reader is not sure from the context which of two or more meanings is intended. For example, does *bank* by itself refer to a financial institution or the rising ground bordering a body of water, and does the sentence "My mother can no longer bear children" mean that she is too old to give birth *or* that she can no longer put up with children? Interestingly enough, some homonyms have originated from the same source: Both *sole*, the underside of a foot or shoe, and *sole*, any flatfish of the family Soleidae, derive ultimately from the Latin *solea*, 'sandal.' Homonymy, the condition of being homonymous, must be distinguished from polysemy, the condition of having multiple meanings. Polysemy is a property of a single item in the vocabulary of a language. Many English words are polysemous (having several different senses), as is the word *seat*, which may refer to a chair or bench, the buttocks, a center of authority or capital, a place of residence, or the manner in which a rider sits a horse.

Synonyms are words in a language that have the same or nearly the same meaning. Absolute synonyms are rare: Not only must all their meanings (senses) be identical, but they must also be synonymous in all contexts and equivalent in all dimensions of meaning (and I will not attempt to list one because there are usually regional, stylistic, and other differences to consider). Near synonyms are more or less similar, for example, *mist* and *fog* or *stream* and *brook*. Partial synonyms may be exemplified by the words *big* and *large*. In the sentence "They put up a large/big tent," the meaning of *large* and *big* is the same. In the sentences "I will tell my big brother" and "I will tell my large brother," however, the meanings of the two words differ: *big* would most likely be understood as 'older,' *large* as 'stout, bigger than average in size,' presumably because the speaker's other brother (or brothers) is of normal size. Antonyms, in contrast, are words that are opposite in meaning: *good* and *bad*, *dead* and *alive*, and *buy* and *sell*.

A good example of the use of nonliteral meaning is the metaphor, which suggests a likeness or analogy between two objects or ideas. Metaphors are not only common in poetry but also in everyday speech, as when someone says, "The car I had before this one was a lemon" or "She is drowning in money." An expression whose meaning is not determined by the meaning of its constituents and their syntactic relations is an idiom. The sentence "My uncle kicked the bucket last week" contains an idiom if what is meant is that he died; the alternative interpretation, that he struck a cylindrical vessel forcefully with his foot, would be literal.

Even though much important work in semantics has already been done, linguistic meaning is the least understood aspect of grammar. The reason for the lag in our understanding of the semantic component is the complex nature of meaning and the difficulties in analyzing it. This should not come as a surprise: There are many words in English (as well as in other languages) that have multiple senses, each of which may refer to a different system of linguistic relationships. For example, in *Webster's Third New International Unabridged Dictionary* (1961), the verb *go* has twenty-one senses given and defined in its intransitive form, nine in its transitive form, and over thirty additional run-on entries such as *go about, go for broke,* and *go to pieces.* Moreover, most of the senses and run-on entries have several subsenses.

When at the beginning of this chapter I referred to the shifting from one level of analysis to another, I did not mean to imply that the levels are detached from each other and structurally unrelated; they do interweave. For example, in the simple but acceptable definition of a word—a word is an arbitrary association of sound and meaning—we emphasize the connection between the phonological and semantic levels. And when we list allomorphs of a morpheme to show how the concrete occurrences of a morpheme may vary in different sound environments (consider, for example, the morpheme written as *child* in *childlike* and *children*), we refer to phonological factors that affect morphology. In languages that have a fixed stress—that is, those in which stress always falls on a particular vowel in a word and is therefore completely predictable—we can use this prosodic feature to determine word boundaries (in Swahili, for example, in which stress regularly falls on the next-to-last vowel of a word, the utterance *kibándakínamilángomiwíli* 'the hut has two doors' can be segmented into the following words (not morphemes): *kibánda kína milángo miwíli*). However, because the so-called levels are major dimensions of the structural organization of languages, for the sake of convenience their analysis usually proceeds more or less independently. The linguist focuses on and analyzes units on one level, making references to other levels as necessary.

Transformational-generative Grammar

The study of languages and linguistics has been documented for ancient Greece as early as two and a half millennia ago. At about that time, the earliest preserved scientific grammar was compiled in India. The work is Pāṇini's grammar of Sanskrit, written around the fifth century B.C. or even earlier and described by a distinguished American linguist as "one of the greatest monuments of human intelligence" (Bloomfield 1933:11). Not a great deal is known about the development of linguistics during the Middle Ages, but both pedagogical and philosophical studies of languages continued. In Europe attention was given almost exclusively to classical Latin rather than to the living languages spoken by the different peoples. By contrast, Arab grammarians furnished a number of excellent descriptions of their own language.

Although the roots of modern linguistics go back to the end of the eighteenth century, most of the revolutionary developments did not come about until the beginning of the twentieth. To simplify matters considerably one may say that the first half of the 1900s was characterized primarily by structural and descriptive approaches in the study of language. Structural because language—any language—was considered to be a complex system of elements that were interrelated and could be studied and analyzed only as such; descriptive because the aim was to describe actual usage rather than what, according to a traditionalist view, usage ought to be. During the second half of the 1900s, linguistics departed radically from these earlier approaches as a result of the contribution of the American linguist Chomsky, whose theoretical perspective and methodology are referred to as **generative** or **transformational** (or transformational-generative) **grammar.**

Using the descriptivist approach, linguistic analysts would begin by writing down words and phrases of a language phonetically, and when sufficient phonetic data had been collected, proceed to determine the phonemes of the language. Once they had completed phonemic analysis and devised transcription, the analysts would phonemically transcribe words, phrases, sentences, and whole utterances in order to understand the morphology of the language as well as the meanings of its different morphemes. Sentence structure would usually receive only secondary attention.

By contrast, linguists trained in transformational-generative grammar proceed the other way around, from the sentence to its various constituents. Let us consider the following pair of sentences: "Father is eager to please" and "Father is easy to please." The structure of both sentences appears to be the same, and in an analysis concerned with listing morphemes and their arrangements the two would be considered very much alike. Yet they are fundamentally different: In the first one, it is Father who is doing the pleasing and is the subject of the sentence, whereas in the second Father is the person being pleased and therefore the underlying object. If one changes the sentences from active to passive voice, "Father is easily pleased" is acceptable as grammatical and meaningful, but "Father is eagerly pleased" is clearly not. Although the superficial, or surface, structure of the two original sentences is much the same, there is a basic difference between them, and it can only result from differences in their deep structure. It appears, then, that the mere listing of morphemes and their arrangement in sentences is not enough to account for the differences that may obtain between them.

To write the generative grammar of a language is to develop a finite device capable of generating an infinite number of grammatical sentences of that language. The phrase-structure rules that make this possible are referred to as the syntactic component. This component assigns to each sentence an abstract deep structure that reveals the logical relationships among the individual sentence elements and a concrete surface structure that determines the phonetic character of the sentence—the way it is spo-

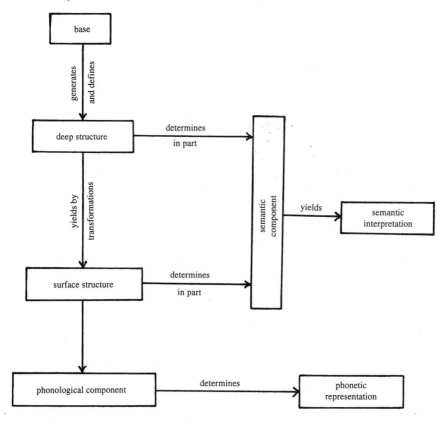

FIGURE 5.1   The Transformational-generative Approach

ken and heard. For example, the sentence "The children were spanked" derives from a deep structure that in some important ways resembles some such sentence as "Someone spanked the children." At the same time, the surface structures of these two sentences differ because the words and their arrangements are not identical.

In addition to the syntactic component of a sentence, there are the phonological component and the semantic component. The former assigns to the surface structure of a sentence a phonetic representation; the latter determines the meaning of a sentence. If one takes as a point of departure for a language its base—that is, the lexicon and the phrase-structure rules applicable to the language—one may then diagram the relationship among the various aspects of grammar as shown in Figure 5.1.

Linguists who follow the transformational-generative approach have little use for the autonomous phonemes of the earlier structural and descriptive approach. They view speech sounds as complexes of distinctive phonetic features (such as + or – syllabic, voiced, continuant, nasal, and so on). The semantic component has not yet been fully charted, but future

---

BOX 5.1   Contrasting the Descriptivist and Generative Approaches

Consider the operation of a gas-powered automobile. Like a language, a car that runs is a complex functioning whole. Like a language, too, it consists of many different parts that make up various systems (the drive train, the electric system, the cooling system, and others), each of which operates according to specific principles. Applying the view of Chomsky and his followers to this example, one can liken the descriptivist approach to the skills and operations of a mechanic who is well acquainted with the various automobile parts and their functions but who is not seriously concerned with *how* and *why* a car runs. Very much like the descriptivist linguist, who restricts his or her analysis to surface structures, the mechanic is familiar with the car only superficially, although capable of maintaining it in good running condition.

According to Chomsky, such an approach is not truly scientific because it makes no effort to explain. A real understanding of what makes a car run comes from the comprehension of such fundamental principles as those of combustion, friction, application of force, and the like. Not until these principles are grasped can one say significant things not only about a particular make of car but about cars in general, and about other conveyances that utilize these principles (for example, snowmobiles). Consequently, the fundamental principles, like the rules of grammar, are prior; and the parts and their arrangements, like the linguistic units and their arrangements, assume secondary importance. ... Nevertheless, for the anthropological field worker, who is mainly concerned with recording native terms in a serviceable phonemic transcription and who rarely possesses intuitive knowledge of the language he or she is dealing with, the descriptivist approach continues to be useful.

from Oriol Pi-Sunyer and Zdenek Salzmann,
Humanity and Culture (1978), 356–357

---

research in semantics will be of special interest to linguistic anthropologists if lexical semantic structure can be significantly related to the structure of the corresponding culture.

How would one compare the merits of descriptive and structural linguistics with those of generative grammar, and in linguistic anthropology to what extent has transformational-generative grammar replaced the earlier approaches? One way of answering the question is presented in Box 5.1.

Summary and Conclusions

Morphology is the study and description of word formation. The principal unit of morphology is the morpheme, the smallest meaningful part of language. There are thousands of morphemes in any language: Those that may be used by themselves are termed free; those that occur only attached to other morphemes are termed bound. Many morphemes have more than one phonemic shape; the variant forms of a morpheme are its allomorphs. Grammar—the various rules that govern the workings of a language and the processes that implement these rules—varies from one language to the next. Some languages are characterized by many inflectional forms (for example, Latin), others by relatively few (for example, English). The complexity of grammar, however, does not add to the prestige of a language. The study of the phonemic differences among allomorphs of the same morpheme is referred to as morphophonemics. The plural morpheme of English nouns has a variety of allomorphs; one may therefore speak of the morphophonemic rules of English noun pluralization.

Sentences are the largest structural units of a language, and their study in the traditional conception is called syntax. In transformational-generative grammar, syntax refers not only to sentence structure but to word structure as well. In this approach, the syntactic component is one of three major organizational units of a grammar, the others being the phonological and the semantic components. Having to do with the structure of meaning, the semantic component has been the last to be studied in modern linguistics and the one worked out in least detail.

The interest of structuralists and descriptivists in linguistic variety the world over has long been shared by linguistic anthropologists, many of whom deal with unwritten languages of little-known peoples. Before the introduction of transformational grammar, the approach to the study of language was somewhat mechanical because it was concerned primarily with items (units) and their arrangement. Chomsky, the founder of transformational-generative grammar, has both posed and attempted to answer new questions concerning language, many of which are of great importance. For example, how is it possible that already at an early age individuals know as much about their native languages as they do without any formal learning? According to Chomsky, one must assume that children are born with a knowledge of what can be termed universal grammar, in other words, that universal grammar is part of our human biological endowment. What the speakers of a particular language must learn, of course, are the specifics of the language they are acquiring (for example, the lexicon).

Linguistic anthropologists are primarily interested in understanding language within the overall matrix of culture, and speech as an inseparable link to social behavior. But even though they are not so much concerned with linguistic structure as such, they are obviously influenced by the latest developments in linguistic theories and methods because of their interest in the speech of those whose cultures they study.

Notes and Suggestions for Further Reading

References to textbooks of linguistics may be found in the Notes to Chapter 4.

The Chontal examples are from Waterhouse 1962, the Isthmus Nahuat examples from Law 1958, and the summary of the rules of Turkish vowel harmony from Gleason 1961.

For an excellent, but demanding, introduction to semantics, see Lyons 1995.

The publication by Chomsky that proved to be a turning point in modern linguistics is *Syntactic Structures* (1957). Other writings by Chomsky include *Aspects of the Theory of Syntax* (1965) and *Language and Mind* (1972). A good introduction to Chomsky's contributions to linguistics is Lyons 1978.

Problems

Again, in order to make it possible for the reader to apply some of the discussions of this chapter to linguistic data, five simple problems are included below. Solutions can be found following the bibliography at the end of the book.

Problem 1

Based on Langacker 1972, this problem is taken from Luiseño, a Uto-Aztecan language spoken in southwestern California. [ʔ] is the glottal stop; [q] is a postvelar voiceless stop (similar to [k] but articulated farther back in the mouth); long vowels are written as a sequence of two vowel symbols; the stress, ['], is marked only on the first of two adjacent vowels. From the data below—to be taken as representative of the language—isolate Luiseño morphemes and provide each with an English gloss (a brief translation to indicate meaning).

1. nóo wukálaq	'I am walking'
2. nóo páaʔiq	'I am drinking'
3. nóo páaʔin	'I will drink'
4. temét čáami páaʔivičunin	'The sun will make us want to drink'
5. nóo póy wukálavičuniq	'I am making him want to walk'
6. nóo páaʔivičuq	'I want to drink'
7. temét póy wukálavičuniq	'The sun is making him want to walk'

Problem 2

Based on Zepeda 1983, this problem is from Tohono O'odham (formerly referred to as Papago), a Uto-Aztecan language spoken in southern Arizona and northwestern Mexico. [ʔ] is the glottal stop and [ñ] is pronounced like the ñ in the English word *piñon*, also spelled *pinyon*. On the basis of the third-person singular verb forms in Column A and the plural forms in Column B, how would you describe in general terms the process of pluralization of these verb forms in Column A?

A	B
1. ñeok 'speaks'	ñeñeok
2. ʔul 'sticks out'	ʔuʔul
3. helwuin 'is sliding'	hehelwuin
4. him 'walks'	hihim
5. dagkon 'wipes'	dadagkon

Problem 3

The regular English past-tense morpheme has three allomorphs: /-d/ as in *begged*, /-t/ as in *chirped*, and /-əd/ as in *guided*. The third-person singular morpheme also has three allomorphs: /-z/ as in *goes* or *begs*, /-s/ as in *chirps*, and /-əz/ as in *houses*. Describe the environments in which the allomorphs of each of the two morphemes occur.

Problem 4

Based on Merrifield and others 1967, this problem is taken from Sierra Popoluca, a Mixe-Zoque language spoken in about two dozen villages and settlements in the state of Veracruz, Mexico. The raised dot after a vowel marks vowel length; [ʌ] is a central unrounded vowel; [ʔ] is the glottal stop; [ŋ] is a velar nasal (similar to *ng* in *sing* or *king*); and [tʸ], [č], [š], [ñ], and [y] are palato-alveolars—a voiceless stop, an affricate, a fricative, a nasal, and a semivowel, respectively. From the data below, list the allomorphs of the morpheme marking what corresponds to the English gloss "my" and then state the rules that govern the morphophonemics of this prefix.

1. co·goy	'liver'		21. anco·goy	'my liver'
2. čikši	'itch'		22. añčikši	'my itch'
3. ha·ya	'husband'		23. anha·ya	'my husband'
4. he·pe	'cup'		24. anhe·pe	'my cup'
5. kawah	'horse'		25. aŋkawah	'my horse'
6. kʌ·pi	'firewood'		26. aŋkʌ·pi	'my firewood'
7. me·me	'butterfly'		27. amme·me	'my butterfly'
8. me·sah	'table'		28. amme·sah	'my table'
9. nʌc	'armadillo'		29. annʌc	'my armadillo'
10. nʌ·yi	'name'		30. annʌ·yi	'my name'
11. petkuy	'broom'		31. ampetkuy	'my broom'
12. piyu	'hen'		32. ampiyu	'my hen'
13. suskuy	'whistle'		33. ansuskuy	'my whistle'
14. suuŋ	'cooking pot'		34. ansuuŋ	'my cooking pot'
15. šapun	'soap'		35. añšapun	'my soap'
16. ši?mpa	'bamboo'		36. añši?mpa	'my bamboo'
17. tʌk	'house'		37. antʌk	'my house'
18. tʸaka	'chick'		38. añtʸaka	'my chick'
19. wʌčo·mo	'wife'		39. aŋwʌčo·mo	'my wife'
20. yemkuy	'fan'		40. añyemkuy	'my fan'

Problem 5

The tree diagrams below are incomplete because the words of the sentences that would fit them have been omitted. For each diagram, supply an appropriate sentence by filling in each blank at the bottom of the diagram with a word. *Poss* stands for Possessive phrase, *Comp* for Complementizer, and *S'* for the complete sentence preceded by the Complementizer, in this case, *that*.

(A)

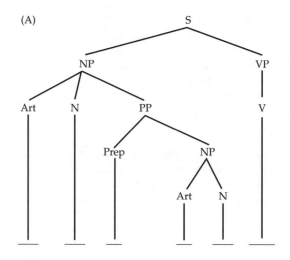

(B)

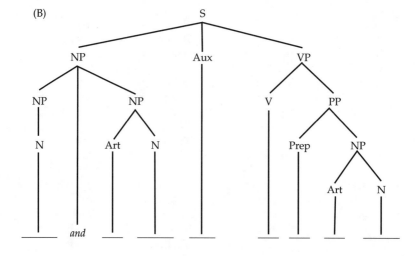

(C)

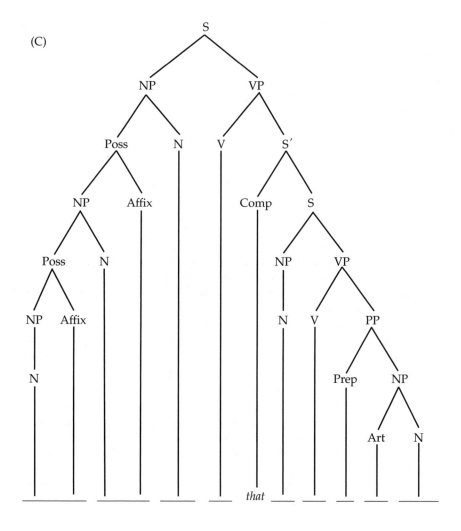

that

6
Language Origins

Because language is such a fundamental attribute of the human species and speech is so inseparably tied to social behavior, illuminating the nature of language should bring us closer to an understanding of the roots of our humanity. This is why the question concerning the origin of speech must have intrigued humans for thousands of years. The available record amply supports this claim.

According to the Book of Genesis, God created the first words. Later, God created the first man, spoke to him, and subsequently let him name the various animals that God had created (2:7, 19–20). Many generations later, after the Flood, "the whole earth had one language and few words"; Genesis attributes the differentiation of the original language into numerous mutually unintelligible forms of speech to God's chastisement of those who sought to erect a tower in Babel for the purpose of reaching to heaven: "And the Lord said, '. . . let us go down, and there confuse their language, that they may not understand one another's speech'" (11:1–7). The implication of these biblical passages is that human speech is a gift from God to humans and the subsequent diversity among languages the result of divine intervention.

Herodotus, the Greek historian of the fifth century B.C. whom the Romans called "the father of history," recorded a story about an Egyptian ruler who resorted to an unusual experiment to determine which was the most ancient people in the world. The experiment involved raising two children from birth in isolation from all speech. When two years later the first word uttered by these children turned out to be the Phrygian word for bread, the priority was assigned to the Phrygians.

Early Theories

Although numerous grammatical treatises, both theoretical and practical, were written throughout the Middle Ages and the Renaissance, it was

112

not until the Enlightenment of the eighteenth century that significant contributions were made to the question of language origin. According to the French philosopher Étienne Bonnot de Condillac (1714–1780), "the [early] humans had acquired the habit of linking certain ideas with arbitrary signs [and] natural cries served them as a model for producing a new language. They articulated new sounds, and by repeating them several times and accompanying them with some gesture which pointed out such objects as they wanted to indicate, they became accustomed to giving names to things" (Condillac 1947:1:61). Jean-Jacques Rousseau (1712–1778) agreed in the main with the theory put forth by Condillac but attributed the transition from gestures to sounds to some sort of agreement comparable to his idea of the social contract among members of a society.

Probably the most famous essay on the subject was published in 1772 by the German philosopher Johann Gottfried von Herder (1744–1803), writing in response to a contest announced by the Prussian Academy of Sciences in Berlin. For Herder, language was not of divine origin, as some others before him had attempted to prove, because it lacked perfection; rather, it sprang from humanity's innermost nature, developing together with thought, from which it is inseparable. Although Herder believed that all languages descended from a common source, he was convinced that individual languages faithfully reflect the thought patterns and the spirit of those who speak them.

From the end of the eighteenth century onward, speculations concerning the origin of language grew so numerous and were occasionally so bizarre that the constitution of the Linguistic Society of Paris, founded in 1865, stipulated that no communication dealing with the subject would be accepted at its meetings. It was at about this time that the various attempts to explain the origin of language received the names by which they would come to be known and referred to for more than a century.

Among the dozens of such ingenious but unprovable accounts of how language may have come about were the bowwow theory, according to which the first words of the early humans were uttered in an effort to imitate natural sounds, particularly those made by animals; the pooh-pooh theory, which sought the origin of speech in the sounds spontaneously emitted to register pain and other strong sensations or feelings; and the dingdong theory, according to which the peculiar ring each substance in nature possesses came to be vocally represented in the first human words.

Although the question of language origins will likely never be authoritatively settled, the probings of recent years have proceeded from sounder positions both because many new finds have increased our understanding of the fossil record and because the problem is now viewed in the broad context of human biocultural evolution.

When Does a Communication System Become Language?

The question, When did language originate? is altogether too vague unless one first specifies what is meant by the term **language.** If it stands for a set of discrete vocal sounds, meaningless by themselves, that can be strung together to produce higher-order units ("words") endowed with conventional but arbitrary meanings, and, further, if such a system makes it possible for its users to generate an unlimited number of unprecedented comments about events removed in time as well as space, then most of the several million years of hominid existence would have been languageless.

Members of all animal species have a way of transmitting information among themselves, and before the hominids branched off from other hominoids—the gorillas and chimpanzees in particular—5 to 8 million years ago, they undoubtedly possessed a means of communicating similar to that of their closest primate relatives. Judging from what is now known about the behavior of the great apes in the wild, the communication system of the earliest hominids is likely to have employed signals that were both visual and acoustic (or auditory) as well as olfactory (connected with the sense of smell) and tactile (especially grooming).

The visual signals, or gestures, would have been made by various parts of the body, including the face; the auditory signals no doubt consisted of a variety of vocalizations—grunts, roars, barks, moans, hoots, howls, and the like—but also of such nonvocal sounds as chest beating or ground stamping. The overall repertory, however, must have been rather modest, with the signals employed only when the stimuli that provoked them were present. The significance, or meaning, of these signals would have been limited to very basic "comments" concerning the immediate environment (for example, sudden danger or the discovery of food) or the individual's emotional state (annoyance, surprise, distress, assertion of dominance, fear, and the like).

It is clear that a vast distance had to be bridged between some such limited means of communication—a mere call system—and full-blown language that modern humans have been making use of for thousands of years. One may refer to the communication system that preceded full-fledged language as **prelanguage.** But even this differentiation into language and prelanguage is extremely rough because it suggests an evolutionary leap from one stage to the next rather than a long series of countless incremental changes that would have been imperceptible to the evolving hominids as they were occurring. Some anthropologists have attempted to reconstruct the evolution of human communication in some detail. For example, Roger W. Wescott (1974) postulates hand waving and vocal synchronization among the members of a group for the australo-pithecines, finger-pointing and vocal imitation for *Homo erectus*, and manual signing and unintelligible "speech" involving the use of meaningless syllables for the Neanderthals; writing and fully developed language he reserves for later *Homo sapiens*. Most anthropologists would probably find this scheme too conservative; its virtue is in its attempt to correlate the development of two communicative channels, the visual and the acoustic.

Milestones in Human Evolution

The emergence of the order of primates, to which humans belong, dates to some 60 to 70 million years ago, only a small fraction of the 3 to 4 billion years since life on earth began. Most of the early primates were arboreal, but in the course of time, as a result of changes in the natural environment, some of them became adapted to existence on the ground (see Figure 6.1).

One of the subdivisions of primates is the superfamily of **hominoids** (Hominoidea), which in turn comprises three families: the lesser apes (siamangs and gibbons), the great apes (gorillas, orangutans, and chimpanzees), and the **hominids** (Hominidae)—humans and their immediate ancestors. Current evidence suggests that the earliest hominids came from East African sites in Tanzania, Kenya, and Ethiopia and go back about 3 to 4 million years. The best-known specimen among them, referred to as Lucy, and fossil bones of a similar type have been assigned to the genus *Australopithecus* (southern [African] ape) and the species *afarensis*, named for the Afar badlands in Ethiopia, where the discovery was made in 1974. Small-brained, with cranial capacity estimated at about 1 pint (473 cubic centimeters), these early hominids were bipedal, that is, they used only their lower limbs for locomotion.

There is not complete agreement on the intermediate link between *Australopithecus afarensis* and the first representatives of the human genus, although most experts would probably choose another **australopithecine** species, *Australopithecus africanus*. This man ape, whose fossil remains in South Africa date back to about 3 million years ago, was quite likely an ancestral form of ***Homo habilis,*** with whom it may have shared parts of Africa for several hundred thousand years. As the term suggests, *Homo habilis* is considered to be the first human, though still far removed from the modern species. The remains of *Homo habilis,* found in Tanzania and Kenya and dated between 1.9 and 1.6 million years old, came from individuals with a braincase capacity equal to about one half that of modern humans. These early humans were correspondingly shorter in stature but more capable of making and using simple tools than the australopithecines may have been before them. Members of this species undoubt-

Years Before the Present	Stages of Hominid Evolution	Prehistoric Periods		Landmarks in Cultural Evolution	Hypothetical Stages in the Evolution of Language
		Neolithic		Farming	(Proto-Indo-European)
_10,000					
	Mesolithic				
			Upper	Carvings and wall paintings	
_40,000	Cro-Magnons (*H. s. sapiens*)				Full-fledged language
			Middle	Ritual activities	
_100,000					Duality of
	Neanderthals *Homo sapiens*	Paleolithic		Stone tools from prepared cores Organized hunting	patterning
_500,000					
			Lower	Use of fire	
					Blending
_1 million					
	Homo erectus *Homo habilis*			Hunting	
_2 million					
				First tools made and used	
_3 million	*Australopithecus africanus*				Adaptations for language
_4 million	*Australopithecus afarensis*				Multimodal communincation
_5 million	Hominids branch off from other hominoids Monkeys and apes diverge				
_50 million					
	Primates emerge				
_100 million					

FIGURE 6.1 Main Stages of Human Evolution. A simplified time chart linking the hypothetical stages in the evolution of language with stages of hominid evolution, prehistoric periods, and landmarks in cultural evolution. Note that in order to accommodate the chart to a page, the time scale changes several times (at dotted lines).

edly began to depend to an ever-increasing degree on group activity and a culturally patterned means of subsistence rather than on behavior governed solely by instinct.

With the appearance of *Homo habilis*, the pace of human evolution accelerated, producing a new species, ***Homo erectus***, close to 2 million years ago. Members of this species spread from Africa to Asia and Europe, enduring for well over 1 million years until some 400,000 to 300,000 years ago. The tool kit of *Homo erectus*, best known for the multipurpose hand ax, included a variety of other implements used for cutting, piercing, chopping, and scraping. Evidence indicates that these ancestors of modern humans possessed the skills needed to become proficient hunters of large game. They also learned to make use of fire to keep warm, to prepare food, and to drive animals to locations where they could more easily be dispatched. The greater complexity of their culture was associated with an increased size of the brain, the average volume of which in *Homo erectus* approached about 1 quart (1,000 cubic centimeters).

The last major stage in human evolution took place about 300,000 years ago with the transition from *Homo erectus* to ***Homo sapiens***, the species to which all contemporary humans belong. It is not yet possible to determine with assurance what course the transition took from one species to the next. One hypothesis is that *Homo erectus* in Africa evolved first into an archaic form of *Homo sapiens* and subsequently into the fully modern subspecies *Homo sapiens sapiens*. In Europe these modern humans replaced the Neanderthals (*Homo sapiens neanderthalensis*), who, according to some anthropologists, did not complete the full transition. According to the recent mitochondrial DNA analysis by Rebecca L. Cann and others, modern humans can be traced back 150,000 to 200,000 years, to a single population in Africa—in fact, to a single female dubbed Eve. But other scientists argue that both fossil and genetic evidence support a theory of multiregional evolution of modern humans.

At this point, a cautionary note is in order. The use of taxons (formal names referring to taxonomic groups), particularly in such an abbreviated account of hominid evolution as that presented above, may be mistakenly taken to suggest a straightforward unilinear process toward anatomically modern forms. Nothing could be further from what the bulk of evidence indicates. At each stage of human evolution there must have existed considerable variation, with generalized hominid forms changing to more specialized ones as a result of adaptation—a process known as adaptive radiation. In other words, the branches of the "tree" of human evolution must have been tangled indeed. Amidst all the differentiation, however, there is a relatively narrow thread of continuity from population to population that has led to contemporary humans, and it is along this line that the various changes resulting in language must have taken place.

The evolution from *Homo erectus* to *Homo sapiens* was marked by a significant increase in cultural complexity. The Neanderthals, who persisted in Europe until the appearance of the Cro-Magnons of the *Homo sapiens sapiens* variety, appear to have been the first to bury at least some of their dead with deliberate care, furnishing them with tools and food, decorating them with red ocher, and even surrounding them with wildflowers. Several finds, taken to represent some sort of bear cult, consist of a number of bear skulls, some neatly arranged in a rock chest, others carefully placed in wall niches. These and other activities of the Neanderthals are considered by some as evidence of ritual behavior and possibly even belief in an afterlife. The material culture of the Neanderthals also became more complex. Their characteristic method of producing a variety of specialized implements made use of flakes struck off stone cores that had been carefully shaped in advance (see Figure 6.2).

The Old Stone Age, referred to technically as the Paleolithic, lasted over 2 million years, terminating only about 10,000 to 12,000 years ago. The most recent subdivision of the Paleolithic, extending from about 37,000 to 11,000 years before the present, is referred to as Upper Paleolithic. From the Oldowan tradition through to the Mousterian culture, a span of about 2 million years, progress in toolmaking was very slow. But an explosion of creative activity occurred during the Upper Paleolithic, when the Cro-Magnons began to fashion elaborate objects—burins, barbed harpoons, spear-throwers, bone needles, but above all exquisite art. Working with paints as well as in stone, clay, bone, ivory, and antler, they created art both delicate and monumental (one frieze portraying animals of the hunt is about 40 feet long) in styles ranging from abstract and geometric to naturalistic or daringly stylized. The rather sudden and rapid advances in the manufacture of a large variety of material items no doubt parallel similar advances in cognitive processes and indicate that full-fledged language would have been in place.

Today no one would question the assumption that language was well established at the time of the relatively brief Mesolithic period that followed the Upper Paleolithic and ushered in the Neolithic. Most certainly, the revolutionary changes that human culture underwent during the Neolithic as a consequence of the domestication of plants and animals are unthinkable without full-fledged language.

Blending and Duality of Patterning

Among those anthropologists who have significantly contributed to the modern theory of language origins, C. F. Hockett deserves special credit. It is to him that we owe a realistic scenario that would lead from a closed call system—one consisting of a finite and relatively small repertory of

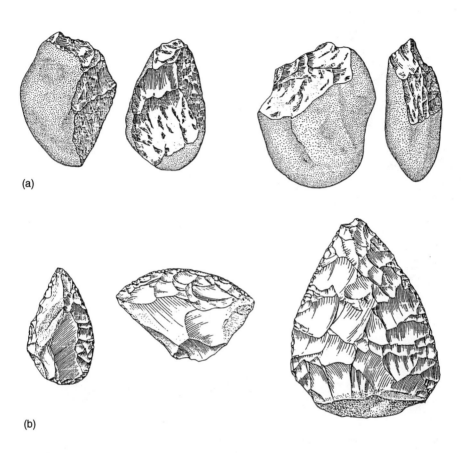

(a)

(b)

FIGURE 6.2 Cultural Evolution During the Paleolithic Period (for chronology, see Figure 6.1)

(a) Lower Paleolithic chopping tools, front and side views (Olduvai Gorge, Tanzania). *Source:* From Brian M. Fagan, *People of the Earth*, 6th ed. (Glenview, IL: Scott, Foresman and Company, 1989), 114. Adapted by permission from M. D. Leakey, *Olduvai Gorge: Excavations in Beds I and II* (Cambridge, UK: Cambridge University Press, 1971).

(b) Middle Paleolithic scrapers and hand ax (France). *Source:* From François Bordes, *The Old Stone Age* (New York: McGraw-Hill, 1968), 99, 100, 104. Reprinted by permission of McGraw-Hill.

(*continues*)

FIGURE 6.2   (*continued*)

(c) Upper Paleolithic art: carving of a leaping horse at the end of an implement or ceremonial object (France); "leaping cow" from the cave wall of Lascaux (France). *Sources:* Musée des Antiquités Nationales, Saint-Germain-en-Laye; Musée de l'Homme, Paris.

(c)

BOX 6.1 Hockett on Blending

Suppose a gibbon finds himself in a situation characterized by both the presence of food and the imminence of danger. The factors, we shall say, are closely balanced. The normal consequence among gibbons is that one or the other factor prevails and just one call is given. This time we imagine our gibbon atypical. Instead of emitting either the food call or the danger call, he utters a cry that has some of the characteristics of each: he produces a *blend* of the two.

This is beyond the experience of the other gibbons in his band. Depending on acoustic conditions, some of them may hear the actual cry as the food call, others as the danger call, and others as nonsense. It is unlikely that any hear it as a new signal, conveying two kinds of information at once. The consequences are thus negligible.

But now suppose that the early hominids had a somewhat richer call system (though closed) functioning in a somewhat more complex social order. Then we may also assume that this type of event occasionally happened, and that sooner or later the other members of a band responded appropriately, thus handling an unusually complex situation more efficiently than otherwise. With this reinforcement, the habit of blending two calls to produce a new one would gain ground.

We have to assume that this is what happened, because blending is the only way in which a closed system can move towards openness of the kind characteristic of language.

from Charles F. Hockett, *Man's Place in Nature* (1973), 381

---

unitary calls, or signals—to full-fledged language. According to Hockett (1973), two major breakthroughs must be assumed for this to have happened. He considers the first of these essential conditions to be blending, that is, producing a new call from two old ones. (A modern analogy, and therefore not altogether appropriate, would be the coining of the word *brunch* from *breakfast* and *lunch*.) Blending could not have greatly multiplied the number of available calls because if the "vocabulary" had grown too large, the calls would have become too much alike and therefore not easily distinguishable. What blending did do, however, and with revolutionary consequences, was to open a closed system, bringing the development to the prelanguage stage (see Box 6.1).

The second breakthrough, one which would have eliminated the increasing congestion of calls, was duality of patterning—the process by which the units of a limited set of signals on one level were combined to form a very large number of arrangements on another level. (To continue with the previous analogy, the sounds, not letters, that make up the words *breakfast* and *lunch* would also be used to generate *bench, bunch, chest, fun, less, lust, nest, rest, rough, run, rust, stench, wrench,* and many other combinations of the dozen or so sounds.) Once our hominid ancestors made the "discovery" that unitary blends are actually made up of different clusters of discrete sounds, duality of patterning was established and prelanguage could advance to language. As far as we know, no other species of animals possesses a system of communication that makes use of this feature. What we do know is that the flexibility of human language is unmatched in the rest of the animal kingdom.

Monogenesis Versus Polygenesis

Did the potentialities and traits requisite for the development of language originate in separate places at different or approximately the same times (polygenesis), or did they come into being just once (monogenesis)? Although one cannot ever expect a conclusive answer to this question, a reasoned discussion of the alternatives is in order.

The theory of polygenesis, with its implication that languages spoken today ultimately derive from several unrelated sources in the remote past, is not easy to defend. For one thing, the process leading to prelanguage and language must have consisted of a long chain of transformations, both structural and functional. That two or more parallel developments of such complexity took place independently of each other cannot be taken for granted. (In a recent work, Derek Bickerton [1990] supposes that the transition from "protolanguage" [referred to here as prelanguage] to true language was abrupt and the result of a single crucial mutation. However, it is difficult to accept that a system of communication as unique and complex as human language could have been the consequence of a single mutation.) Then, too, the capacity of all normal children, regardless of ethnic background, to acquire any one of the several thousand natural languages with the same degree of mastery and according to approximately the same timetable is a strong indication that speech is innate throughout the human species and that all languages are simply variations on a common basic structural theme.

The theory of monogenesis may take two forms: radical (or straight-line) and, to use Hockett's term, fuzzy. Of the two, the fuzzy version of monogenesis appears more realistic. Although it presupposes a single origin of traits essential for language, it allows for the further development of the incipient capacity for speech to take place in separate groups of hominids within an area. The resulting differentiation could have been bridged by gene flow among the groups or brought to an end by the eventual dominance and survival of that early human population whose communicative system was most efficient (see Figure 6.3). If instead several varieties of

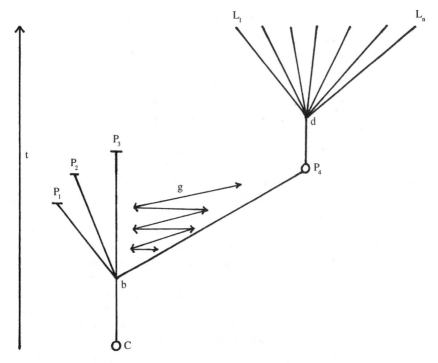

FIGURE 6.3   A Simplified Representation of the "Fuzzy" Version of the Monogenetic Theory. The time scale (t) is several million years, and the starting point is a closed call system (C). The acquisition of traits essential for the development of language culminates in the introduction of blending (b), which gives rise to several prelanguages (P_1 ... P_4). Of these, P_1, P_2, and P_3 become extinct; gene flow (g) occurs between the speakers of prelanguages P_3 and P_4, of which P_4 survives in the long run and after the introduction of duality of patterning (d) becomes the source of all extant languages (L_1 ... L_n).

prelanguage managed to persist, then there would be more than one "dialect" ancestral to all those languages that developed subsequently.

Estimating the Age of Language: Linguistic Considerations

Anthropologists do not expect to find a firm and unequivocal answer to the question of the age of language, but they do hope that various strands of indirect evidence will help them assign the main stages of linguistic development to approximate ranges along the time chart of human evolution. Some clues come from linguistics, others from the archaeological record, and still others can be derived from the study of primate anatomy.

Although scholars active in comparative and historical linguistics have developed a reliable method of reconstructing unwritten languages that were spoken in the distant past, evidence from linguistic prehistory can make only a limited contribution. To be sure, reconstructions have revealed, in considerable detail, many structural features of languages ancestral to present-day language families. The best example is **Proto-Indo-European,** the parent of a large number of languages that first spread throughout Europe and many parts of southern Asia and later, during modern times, to every other part of the world as well. The consensus among linguists is that the speakers of Proto-Indo-European were most likely to be found somewhere in eastern Europe, possibly in the steppes of southern Russia, during the fourth millennium B.C. Despite its early date, Proto-Indo-European matched in grammatical patterns the complexity of its various descendants: It distinguished among three genders (masculine, feminine, and neuter), three numbers (singular, dual, and plural), and perhaps as many as eight cases, and also possessed a comparably rich inflectional verb system. One can take Proto-Indo-European and other such reconstructed parent languages (**protolanguages**)—for example, those of the Uralic and Afro-Asiatic language families—and attempt further reconstructing, as some linguists have in fact done.

In his posthumously published work on the subject, Morris Swadesh (1909–1967) appears to be convinced that protolanguages of language families are more similar in structure than the languages that descended from them because "human languages were then appreciably closer to their common origin than they are today" (Swadesh 1971:116). But despite the pioneering efforts of Swadesh and others, the majority of those who work in comparative and historical linguistics today have doubts about the effectiveness and reliability of the comparative method beyond a certain time depth. In the words of Paul Kiparsky (1976:97), "the time span over which we can hope to reconstruct anything at all about protolanguages, however generously we set it at, say, 10,000, or even 20,000 years, is still a very small fraction of the period during which language has presumably been spoken by man. Therefore, protolanguages as reconstructed cannot possibly be identified with any original stage of language." That the assumed Proto-Indo-European language was grammatically more complex than many of its modern descendants cannot be taken to mean that the older a language is, the more complex structure it must possess. If this were so, one would have to conclude that the earliest language was the most highly complex, a presumption that runs counter to what we know about long-term evolutionary process. In short, fully developed language must have preceded by many thousands of years any of the protolanguages linguists have been able to reconstruct to date, though contrary to Kiparsky's estimate, 10,000 to 20,000 years may not have been a "very small fraction" of the period during which true language has been in existence, but a sizable one.

Estimating the Age of Language:
View from Cultural Prehistory

Approaching the question of language origins from a different vantage point, some anthropologists look for clues in cultural prehistory. It is generally agreed that the development of the various aspects of culture, both material and nonmaterial, must have been paralleled by developments in communicative behavior, and that a positive feedback must have existed between the two. In other words, the more complex the culture of the early hominids grew, the more elaborate the system of communication had to become to accommodate it, and the more the communication system was able to handle, the more elaborate culture could become. During the initial stages of hominid evolution, advancement was slow. The cultural takeoff dates back to the period of transition from the Neanderthals to the Cro-Magnons. Hockett refers to this relatively recent acceleration when he writes (1973:413), "True language is such a powerful instrument for technological and social change [that] if our ancestors had it five hundred thousand or a million years ago, why did it take us so long to get where we are?"

Although no one would argue in principle against the linkage between the degree of cultural elaboration and the complexity of a communication system, interpretations of evidence from prehistory vary a great deal. Ashley Montagu argues (1976:270) that some of the stone-tool assemblages found at Olduvai Gorge in Tanzania and dated to be nearly 2 million years old (Figure 6.2) required so much skill and forethought that in all likelihood "speech was already well established among the makers of those tools, so that for the origins of language and speech we shall have to look to earlier horizons, and perhaps to even earlier forms of man [than *Homo habilis*]." Many anthropologists find the reference to "well established speech" in *Homo habilis* overdrawn but would readily agree to the presence of some of the traits that were to contribute to prelanguage.

The possession of prelanguage would, however, probably be granted to the more recent representatives of *Homo erectus*. The first hominid able to adapt successfully to regions of the world having cold winters, *Homo erectus* must have been an efficient hunter of large game. This claim has been particularly well substantiated by excavations at Torralba and Ambrona in northeastern Spain. These two sites revealed large quantities of bones from a variety of animals as well as a large assortment of tools, widely distributed bits of charcoal, and such an intriguing find as the end-to-end arrangement of an elephant tusk and leg bones, probably laid out by those who had butchered the animals. It appears that at one time the site locations lay along a trail between the seasonal grazing areas of animal herds. According to a widely accepted scenario, a band or bands of *Homo erectus* hunters of 200,000 to 400,000 years ago managed by either brandishing torches or setting grass afire to stampede elephants into a swampy area in order to render them defenseless for the kill. In the context of our discussion, however, it is not so much the hunting prowess of these people that is important as the planning and coordination that would have been required to bring a potentially dangerous hunt to a successful conclusion—a feat that could not have been accomplished without some sort of prelanguage.

The Neanderthals, far from being the fierce-looking or dim-witted creatures portrayed in earlier reconstructions, adapted the stoneworking techniques of their predecessors to produce far more varied and carefully finished tools and became even more proficient hunters. Of greater importance, however, are the already mentioned finds that are strongly suggestive of ritual activities. If indeed these early humans believed in life after death, and if their treatment of the remains of cave bears can be associated with mythmaking or taken as an act of worship or the practice of hunting magic, the Neanderthals would have had to make references to other times and places, thus moving a significant distance from prelanguage to language.

The nature of Neanderthal communication continues to be subject to debate, but the presence of language among the Cro-Magnons cannot be disputed. With brains as large as the average for modern humans, they were able to adapt to the climatic and ecological extremes of the Americas, Australia, and even the arctic regions. The concrete evidence of their imagination and dexterity is no less astounding: Many of the elaborately embellished items of their material culture that they bequeathed to posterity compare favorably with some of the best art that has been created since (Figure 6.2 [c]). Their cultural achievements are unthinkable without the aid of language as fully developed, or very nearly so, as that of recent and contemporary times.

Evidence from Anatomy

That all normal humans acquire command of at least one particular language is the result of learning; that all humans possess and make use of the capacity for speech is part and parcel of a biological endowment unique to our species. Any inquiry into language origins should therefore give consideration to the biological foundations of language—in particular those parts of the human anatomy that facilitate it, the brain and the vocal apparatus, and the receiving organ, the ear.

Among the primates, humans have brains that are relatively large in comparison to total body mass. In the course of human physical evolution, the size of the braincase apparently expanded quite rapidly twice: first during the period of transition between *Homo habilis* and *Homo erectus*, the second time coincidentally with the rise of *Homo sapiens*. These expansions made it possible for the braincase to hold a substantially larger number of brain cells and to achieve a greater density of pathways among them, but it is not certain that of itself expansion was the direct result of a selection for greater mental capacity.

Despite much recent research, we still lack adequate knowledge of the structures in that part of the human brain to which the control of speech production is attributed. One variable feature of the neural basis for speech is the lateralization of language functions in the left cerebral hemisphere in nearly 99 percent of right-handed adults. Right-handedness appears to have been prevalent since the times of *Homo erectus* and according to some scholars may have been in evidence as far back as the australopithecines. Handedness and the associated lateralization even appear to be established in the great apes, if not also among the other primates, despite their total incapacity for speech.

The general configuration of the brain is similar in hominids, apes, and monkeys except for the more extensive and deeper folding of the outer layer of gray matter, the cortex, and the relatively small size of the limbic region in humans. The limbic system, which in mammals acts as the "emotional brain," is responsible for vocalizations associated with emotional and motivational factors and transmits signals of low informational content, such as cries. The several regions of the brain that appear to be closely associated with speech production (especially Broca's area, Wernicke's area, and the angular gyrus) are located in the more recent outer part of the human brain, which is developed more fully and complexly than the corresponding structure of our closest primate relatives. It is unfortunate that casts made of fossil cranial cavities showing the approximate shape of the brain do not reveal its internal structure.

In short, the differences in the brain structures between humans and the other primates are sufficiently apparent to indicate why the otherwise highly teachable apes cannot be taught to speak, but prehistoric evidence concerning the internal evolution of the human brain is either spotty or controversial.

The evolution of the vocal apparatus has been studied by Philip Lieberman together with several coworkers. Comparing the skulls of modern human adults with those of newborn infants, the Neanderthals, and contemporary apes, Lieberman and his associates found that the modern adult skull varies from the others in certain important respects. The significant difference seems to be in the position of the larynx and the size of the pharynx that lies directly above it (see Figure 4.1). In modern human

adults the larynx is located farther down in the throat, and as a consequence the supralaryngeal area is much larger than in infants, Neanderthals, and apes. Consequently, the sounds emitted from such an area
can be modified to a greater degree and encompass the three extreme
vowels—[i], [u], and [a] as in *be, boo,* and *bah.* The reconstruction of the
supralaryngeal vocal tract of the Neanderthals indicates that these hominids were not capable of producing the three critical vowels and certain
consonants, at least not very effectively and consistently, and that they
therefore lacked the special characteristics of modern human speech,
though not by much. As Lieberman concludes (1984:323),

> The evidence of Neanderthal culture indicates a highly developed tool-
> making and using culture, the use of fire, burial rituals, and a social order
> that cared for the elderly and infirm. . . . I therefore find it hard to believe
> that Neanderthal hominids did not also have a well-developed language. . . .
> Though it is . . . impossible to state with certainty all the factors that might
> have differentiated the linguistic and cognitive ability of classic Neanderthal
> hominids from their anatomically modern human contemporaries, their
> speech ability was inferior.

Also during the 1980s, Jeffrey T. Laitman and his colleagues noticed
that the shape of the base of the skull is related to the position of the larynx. A detailed analysis of the skull base for many species of mammals
revealed that either the skull base is fairly flat and the position of the larynx high or the skull is arched and the position of the larynx low. The first
configuration is characteristic of all mammals except humans older than
two years. The second configuration is found only in humans past in-
fancy. Laitman's next step was to evaluate the skull bases of various fossil
hominid remains and then judge from their shape what the position of
the larynx would have been. Laitman reports that "the australopithecines
probably had vocal tracts much like those of living monkeys or apes."
Furthermore, according to preliminary data on the skulls of *Homo erectus,*
Laitman's group discovered "the first examples of incipient basicranial
flexion away from the nonflexed apelike condition of the australopithecines and toward that shown by modern humans. This indicates to
us that the larynx in *Homo erectus* may have begun to descend into the
neck, increasing the area available to modify laryngeal sounds." Fossil
data Laitman and his colleagues obtained further suggest that a full arch-
ing of the skull base comparable to that in contemporary humans coin-
cides with "the arrival of *Homo sapiens* some 300,000 to 400,000 years ago.
It may have been then that a modern vocal tract appeared and our ancestors began to produce fully articulate speech" (Laitman 1984:26–27).

Other experiments have involved making casts of the cranial cavity
showing the approximate shape of the brain (Falk 1984). Brains of apes

have a particular groove that runs from the side of the frontal lobe to its surface; human brains display instead a particular pattern of convolutions. The endocast of a *Homo habilis* specimen has been interpreted as having belonged to a hominid probably capable of some form of speech. But an endocast of a hominid specimen dated about half a million years later, probably an australopithecine, appears to have apelike features. The supposition that specimens of both genera (*Homo* and *Australopithecus*) coexisted at one time in eastern Africa poses no problem.

In summary, the anatomical changes requisite for the development of full-fledged language must have involved crucial restructurings of not only the hominid brain but the vocal apparatus as well. The general outline of these transformations has by now been fairly well identified, but many of the finer points needed to complete the picture are still missing.

The Gestural Theory of Language Origin

The notion that hominids were making effective use of gestures before they developed speech has a distinguished scholarly pedigree; it has recently received fresh support from Gordon W. Hewes (1917–1997). According to him, "a preexisting gestural language system would have provided an easier pathway to vocal language than a direct outgrowth of the 'emotional' use of vocalization characteristic of nonhuman primates" (1973:12). What sorts of evidence can be adduced in support of the gestural theory?

Recent experimental work with chimpanzees and gorillas has shown that these primates are capable of acquiring a "vocabulary" of gestural signs that is larger than the repertory of their vocalizations and that on occasion they use these signs with a degree of originality. It is not unreasonable to suppose that early hominoids had the capacity to use gestures for communication and that the earliest hominids (for example, the australopithecines) in fact did. Because gestural signs tend to be **iconic**—that is, resembling what they are supposed to convey rather than arbitrary— the assignment of evolutionary priority to gestures over speech is generally acceptable. A noiseless form of communication would have been of distinct advantage to the early hunters stalking game, as it also would have been to members of small groups hiding from predators.

Yet communication by speech requires less energy, the potential for vocabulary expansion is virtually unlimited, and the vocal-auditory channel is clear unless the mouth is occupied with chewing or the ears happen to be blocked. (By contrast, making, carrying, or using tools interferes with effective gestural communication.) The main problem with the gestural theory is how to account convincingly for the change from a visual-gestural mode to a vocal-auditory one—a process involving not only a behavioral shift from pointing and showing to talking but also the requisite anatomical changes in the brain and the vocal tract. Hewes suggests that the transition might have been facilitated through the unconscious imitation of manual gestures by the movements of the lips and the tongue, but this hypothesis goes only a short distance to bridge the gap. In a sense, then, the gestural theory does not contribute satisfactorily to answering the question of how spoken language evolved.

Summary and Conclusions

The abiding interest in language origins and the enormous amount of scholarship focused on the subject over the centuries are best attested to by the bibliography of over 11,000 entries Hewes published in 1975. As of the early 1990s, at least 2,000 more items would have to be added. And yet even the latest attempts to throw light on the evolution of speech are no more than speculations, some more solidly grounded than others. The opaqueness of the problem is reflected in the carefully qualified statements found in almost every paragraph of this chapter. The following brief summary of the major stages in the development of language must be considered tentative and hypothetical; a consensus on this subject may never be reached.

Communication among early hominids such as the australopithecines undoubtedly involved several modes, with a combination of the visual channel (manual gestures or facial expressions) and the vocal-auditory channel (simple vocalizations) predominating over touch and smell. Adaptations that made speech possible very likely coincided with the initial stages of hominization—the evolutionary development of human characteristics—some 2 to 3 million years ago. The process was exceedingly slow, but in the course of time the early hominids came to rely primarily on the vocal-auditory channel, probably as a result of the increasing employment of hands for making and using tools. The steadily expanding repertory of calls eventually led to blending, which may have had its beginnings with *Homo habilis* and reached the limits of serviceable complexity (prelanguage) in late *Homo erectus* times. At that point the stage was set for the development of duality of patterning, which could have been accomplished in principle among the late Neanderthals but did not attain the efficiency of full-fledged language until the complete sapientization of humans some 50,000 to 70,000 years ago.

Of necessity, this has been a very brief and oversimplified account of how language may have come about; the reader should bear in mind the length of time the process took and the countless changes, both behavioral and anatomical (and hence genetic), required for the attainment of full humanness (see Figure 6.4).

Years Before the Present	Stages of Hominid Evolution	Available Indirect Evidence	Presumed Stages in Language Evolution
_10,000			
_40,000	Cro-Magnons	Spectacular portable and cave-wall art	
			Earliest stage of full-fledged language
_100,000	*Homo sapiens sapiens*	Size of supralaryngeal area Earliest burials; caring for the dead	Duality of patterning
_200,000		Ritual behavior? Belief in afterlife?	
_300,000	Neanderthals		
_400,000	*Homo sapiens*	Earliest shelters Full arching of skull base Organized hunting	Beginnings of articulate speech
_500,000	Archaic *Homo sapiens*		
_1 million	*Homo erectus*	Control of fire	Early stage of prelanguage Blending
_2 million	*Homo habilis* / Australopithecines		Presence of traits contributing later to prelanguage
		First tools made and used	Adaptations for prelanguage
_3 million			
_4 million			Simple multimodal communication

FIGURE 6.4 Presumed Stages of Language Evolution (supplementing Figure 6.1). A simplified time chart linking the stages of hominid evolution with the available indirect evidence for the presumed stages of language evolution. The time scale changes at dotted lines. The reader is reminded that the stages of language evolution and their time assignments are conjectural but reasonable, given the present state of our knowledge.

Notes and Suggestions for Further Reading

The biblical quotations are from *The New Oxford Annotated Bible with the Apocrypha* (Revised Standard Version), edited by Herbert G. May and Bruce M. Metzger (New York: Oxford University Press, 1977). The translation of the passage from Condillac's "Essai sur l'origine des connoissances humaines" (1746) is based on Georges Le Roy's 1947 edition of Condillac's philosophical writings (vol. 1, p. 61, sec. 6). Herder's essay (1772) is available in an English translation under the title *On the Origin of Language* (1966). For excerpts from Rousseau's "Essay on the Origin of Languages," see Salus 1969.

An excellent critical evaluation of and guide to recent works concerning language origins was published by Hockett (1978), who also generously commented on the first draft of this chapter. A detailed bibliography of books and articles on the subject was compiled by Hewes (1975).

Of the many books, book chapters, and articles dealing with the evolution of speech, the following may be of interest to readers who seek less technical treatment: Campbell 1979, Hockett and Ascher 1964, Stross 1976, and Time-Life Books 1973. More technical accounts may be found in de Grolier 1983; Harnad, Steklis, and Lancaster 1976; and Wescott 1974.

The recent book by Bickerton (1990) is full of stimulating ideas and interesting speculations, but reviewers tend to consider many of Bickerton's specific claims indefensible and even contradictory (see Pinker 1992 and Burling 1992). For contrary views concerning the evolution of modern humans, see Wilson and Cann 1992 and Thorne and Wolpoff 1992.

A richly illustrated and well-written series titled "The Dawn of Humans" began appearing in the January 1996 issue of *National Geographic* and continued in several subsequent issues throughout 1997.

7

Language
Through Time

The structure of a language may be analyzed and described as it exists at some point in time (which in practice means during a short period) either in the present or the past (for example, the English of Chaucer's *Canterbury Tales* from the 1380s). Collecting data for the study of a spoken language that has not yet been described and then analyzing the material takes time, usually at least a year, but languages do not change appreciably within such a relatively short period and what few changes may have occurred can generally be disregarded. The approach that considers a language as though it had been sliced through time, ignoring historical antecedents, is referred to as **synchronic**. But it is also possible to study the historical development of a language, giving attention to the changes that occurred in the language over a period of time. Such an analysis or approach is termed **diachronic**. Diachronic linguistics is commonly referred to as **historical linguistics**. The purpose of this chapter is to take a long-term view of languages and indicate how such a view can benefit anthropologists.

Language Changes: English a Thousand Years Ago

Living languages change through time, and these changes affect all aspects of a language. Some have to do with pronunciation. An example of such a phonetic change is the replacement in most dialects of English of the earlier trilled initial *r* (as is typical of Spanish) by a retroflex alveolar liquid *r* (as is usually heard in American English, for example, in the initial consonant of *red*). Other changes have been phonological, affecting the distribution of English phonemes. In the following examples, contrast is made between Modern English and Old English (or Anglo-Saxon, in use until about 1100). Old English *ā* (which sounded very much like the fairly long *a* of *father*) corresponds in many contemporary dialects of English to the sound heard when one pronounces the letter *o*. Accordingly, Old English words *āgan, bān, hām, rāp,* and *stān* have changed to Modern

English words (*to*) *own, bone, home, rope,* and *stone.* Among Shakespeare's rhymes (from either side of 1600) we find such pairs of words as *groin* and *swine, spear* and *there, ear* and *hair, bushes* and *rushes,* and *proved* and *loved.* As a result of sound changes, these pairs no longer rhyme.

Still other changes have been morphological. For example, the Old English adjective *gōd* 'good' had in the singular of the strong declension (used with nouns not preceded by the definite article or similar word) the same form for all three genders. For the objective case, however, the forms were *gōdne, gōde,* and *gōd* for the masculine, feminine, and neuter gender, respectively. In the singular of the weak declension (when preceded by the definite article or similar word), the masculine form was *gōda* whereas both the feminine and neuter forms were the same, *gōde.* But for the objective case, both the masculine and feminine forms were *gōdan* whereas the neuter form was *gōde* (for the full set of forms of *gōd,* see Table 7.1). These and other inflectional forms of Old English were greatly simplified in the subsequent development of English. Today the same form, *good,* is used in all such phrases as *good man, the good man, I saw a good man* (with the adjective modifying a direct object), *good men, good woman, good word,* and so on.

Changes of meaning over the past centuries have also been numerous. When in *King Lear* Shakespeare has Edgar say, "But mice and rats, and such small deer, / Have been Tom's food for seven long year" (act 3, scene 4), the reference to Tom's diet is not exactly appetizing, referring as it does to any small quadruped. Old English *dēor* 'beast, usually a four-footed animal' is the word from which Modern English *deer* was derived. Because *deer* refers only to members of the family Cervidae, distinguished by the possession of hooves and antlers, the modern meaning is much more specialized than the earlier one. The converse may also occur: The noun *box* referred originally to a container made of boxwood and used for the safekeeping of precious items such as jewelry or ointment. Today the word refers to a container made from any of a variety of materials and used to hold things that are not usually of any special worth. In addition, the word has acquired several new senses: It may refer to any six spaces on a baseball diamond, a guitar (slang), a tape player (slang), or a television set (slang). The meaning of the old word *box,* then, has undergone generalization. The Old English word *sǣlig* 'blessed, happy,' in its modern form *silly,* has come to refer since the beginning of the seventeenth century to a less complimentary trait meaning "foolish" or "frivolous."

The extent of the changes that English has undergone since the Old English period can best be illustrated by citing the first three lines of the long epic poem *Beowulf* in their original version and supplementing them with word-for-word (parenthetically) and free Modern English translations.

TABLE 7.1   The Strong and Weak Declensions of the Old English Adjective *gōd* 'good'

Number/Case	Masculine	Feminine	Neuter
Strong Declension			
Singular			
N	gōd	gōd	gōd
G	gōdes	gōdre	gōdes
D	gōdum	gōdre	gōdum
A	gōdne	gōde	gōd
I	gōde	gōdre	gōde
Plural			
N, A	gōde	gōda, gōde	gōd, gōde
G	gōdra	gōdra	gōdra
D, I	gōdum	gōdum	gōdum
Weak Declension			
Singular			
N	gōda	gōde	gōde
G, D, I	gōdan	gōdan	gōdan
A	gōdan	gōdan	gōde
Plural			
N, A	gōdan	gōdan	gōdan
G	gōdra, gōdena	gōdra, gōdena	gōdra, gōdena
D, I	gōdum	gōdum	gōdum

The traditional names of cases are used here, as is customary in grammatical descriptions of Old English. Typically, cases identify syntactic relationships between words of a sentence. In this table, the nominative case (N) marks the subject of a verb; the genitive (G) marks a possessive relationship; the dative (D) marks the indirect object of a verb, in Modern English introduced frequently by the preposition *to*; the accusative (A), or objective case, marks the direct object of a verb; and the instrumental (I) expresses the notion of "by means of."

Original:
Hwæt,   wē Gārdena   in gēardagum
(Behold, we of spear[-armed] Danes   in former days

þēodcyninga   þrym gefrūnon,
of people's kings' glory we have heard

hū þā   æðelingas   ellen   fremedon!
how those princes [with] courage performed!)

Free translation:
*Yes, we have heard of the glory of the kings of the people of
the spear-armed Danes in the old days, how those princes
performed brave action!*

A few orthographic and grammatical comments are in order here. In contrast to Modern English, the pronunciation of Old English was correlated closely with orthography. The runic letter þ stood for the initial sound of *thin* and ð for the initial sound of *this*. The letter *g* before *e* was pronounced like the letter *y* in *yes;* the letter *c* (as in *þēodcyninga*) was pronounced like the letter *k* in *keg;* double consonants were pronounced long; the vowel *y* sounded like the German *ü;* the ligature *æ* had the same sound as the *a* in *hat;* and long vowels were marked by a horizontal sign above them, as in *ē, ā,* and *ū.*

Gārdena is a compound consisting of the masculine noun *gār* 'spear' and *dena* 'Danes,' the genitive plural of a masculine noun; in the compound *gēardagum* 'former days,' *gēar* is from *gēara* 'of yore, formerly,' the genitive plural of the neuter noun *gēar* 'year,' and *dagum* is the dative plural of the masculine noun *dæg* 'day'; *þēodcyninga* is a compound consisting of the feminine noun *þēod* 'people, nation' and *cyninga,* the genitive plural of the masculine noun *cyning* 'king'; *gefrūnon* is the indicative plural form of the preterite (past tense) of *gefrignan* 'to hear of,' made up of the prefix *ge-* and *frignan* 'to inquire'; *þā* is the nominative plural of the demonstrative pronoun *sē* (*sēo, þæt*) 'that'; *æðelingas* derives from the adjective *æðele* 'noble' suffixed by *-ing* (also present in *cyning*) 'one belonging to,' the full form being a nominative plural masculine meaning 'princes'; *ellen* 'courage, zeal' is a neuter noun; and *fremedon* is the indicative plural form of the preterite of *fremman* 'to perform, accomplish.'

Probably composed during the first half of the eighth century, *Beowulf* has been preserved in a manuscript from the late tenth century. Today the Old English of *Beowulf* looks, and would sound, like a foreign language.

Internal and External Changes

Languages change not only from within but also as a result of influences from without. These changes are referred to as internal and external. Those that have taken place in English over the centuries are language-internal changes. The reasons for such changes vary; here we will illustrate them by discussing sound changes known as assimilation, dissimilation, and metathesis, and a grammatical change by means of which certain irregular forms become regularized.

Assimilation is the influence of a sound on a neighboring sound so that the two become similar or the same. For example, the Latin prefix *in-* 'not, non-, un-' appears in English as *il-, im-,* and *ir-* in the words *illegal, immoral, impossible* (both *m* and *p* are bilabial consonants), and *irresponsible* as well as the unassimilated original form *in-* in *indecent* and *incompetent.* Although the assimilation of the *n* of *in-* to the following consonant in the preceding examples was inherited from Latin, English examples that would be considered native are also plentiful: In rapid speech native speakers of English tend to pronounce *ten bucks* as though it were written **tembucks,* and in anticipation of the voiceless *s* in *son* the final consonant of *his* in *his son* is not as fully voiced as the *s* in *his daughter,* where it clearly is [z].

Another process of this type is dissimilation, which works the other way around: One of two identical or very similar neighboring sounds of a word is changed or omitted because a speaker may find the repetition of the same articulatory movement difficult in rapid speech. This is why it is so common to hear *February* pronounced as if it were written *Febyuary,* with the substitution of [y] for the first [r] in anticipation of the [r] toward the end of the word. People are asked to repeat a tongue twister (for example, "The sixth sheik's sixth sheep's sick") in order to test their ability to pronounce similar neighboring sounds rapidly without making any errors. Still another process producing sound change is metathesis, the transposition of sounds or larger units; for example, the antecedent of Modern English *bird* is Old English *bridd* 'young bird.' A spoonerism, involving the transposition of the initial sounds of several words, is a slip of the tongue based on metathesis, as when *the dear old queen* becomes *the queer old dean.*

An example of a grammatical change is the regularization of a number of strong (irregular) Anglo-Saxon verbs: Old English *fealdan* 'to fold' and *helpan* 'to help' had the first-person singular past-tense (preterite) forms *feold* and *healp* and the past-participle forms *fealden* and *holpen.* In Modern English these verbs are regular: *fold, folded* and *help, helped.* As for semantic change, Old English *mete* referred to food in general (usually solid), not just to animal flesh, as does Modern English *meat.*

As long as they are being used, all languages change. Today no members of any society and no speakers of any language are completely isolated from speakers of other languages and dialects, and these contacts between speakers of different languages cause external language changes. The most common instances of external language change are borrowings, which can be of various types. The letter *b* in the word *debt* apparently has been borrowed for the sake of prestige from Latin (*dēbitum* 'debt') even though the Middle English antecedent of the word was *dette,* without a *b,* from Old French *dette* 'something owed.'

Much more common than orthographic borrowings are lexical borrowings, known as **loanwords.** Not all languages adopt foreign words to the same extent. Even though Icelandic serves a modern industrial society, for two centuries now Icelanders have resisted borrowing words from other languages and instead coin new words from their native linguistic resources for the many things and concepts that come to Iceland from other cultures. In grammar, too, Icelandic is highly conservative, having changed only a very little since the Old Norse period. In contrast, Japanese vocabulary reflects quite clearly the historical contacts between the Japanese and European peoples that began in the middle of the sixteenth century. It has loanwords from Portuguese (for example, *konhisan* 'confession' from *confissão*, and *shabon* 'soap' from *sabão*), Dutch (*biiru* 'beer' from *bier*, and *garasu* 'glass' from *glas*), and most recently from English (*masukomi* 'mass communication,' *suupaa[-maaketto]* 'supermarket,' *insutanto fuudo* 'instant food,' and *kabā-gāru* 'cover girl').

English has always been very hospitable to words of foreign origin. The vocabularies of the Angles, Jutes, and Saxons were enriched by words from Celtic (for example, the word ancestral to Modern English *bin*), Latin (*pipe* and *angel*), Old Norse of the Vikings (*take*), and Anglo-Norman French (*journey*). From the sixteenth century forward, during the Modern English period, the English lexicon borrowed from a great many of the world's languages, ranging from Afrikaans (for example, *aardvark*) to Czech (*robot*) to Yiddish (*chutzpa[h]*) to Japanese (*kamikaze*) to Dakota (*tepee*) to one of the native Australian languages (*boomerang*) to one of the native languages of Africa, probably related to Twi (*okra*). The many thousands of loanwords that have been incorporated into English since earliest times would not recommend English to misguided purists who think a language should be protected from the use of foreignisms, but such borrowings have certainly made the English vocabulary one of the richest in the world.

Some languages borrow selectively. In one of his studies of Native American languages of California, William Bright investigated the origin of words for those domestic animals introduced by white settlers. Borrowing from Spanish was considerable, but there appears to have been a resistance toward borrowing from English. In Bright's opinion, this disparity may well have been due to the benevolent (if condescending) treatment of Native American peoples in California under the Spanish mission system and, by contrast, the inhuman treatment they received from Anglo-Americans (Bright 1960:233–234). In this case, then, the nature of the sociocultural contact between the native peoples and the newcomers was reflected in the vocabularies of the Native American languages.

In addition to borrowing, languages enrich their vocabularies in two other ways. One way is to coin new words from native resources. Newly coined words are added to English (and many other languages) every year: Among thousands of such coinages are *brunch* (from *breakfast* and *lunch*), for a late-morning meal usually combining menu items from both breakfast and lunch; *vaporware*, for new software that has been announced but is not yet available; and *wanna-be* (from the phrase *want to be*), for a person who aspires to be or tries to act or look like someone else.

Vocabularies also adjust to new inventions or ideas and objects introduced through intercultural contact by extending the meaning of existing words to include a new referent. For example, during the 1930s when the Western Apache in east central Arizona began using automobiles and pickup trucks and needed terms in their language for the various parts of these vehicles, they chose to extend many anatomical terms referring to the human body to the "corresponding" parts of the automobile: The meaning of the word *biyedaaʔ* 'chin and jaw' was extended to mean 'front bumper,' *bigan* 'hand and arm' to 'front wheel,' *bizéʔ* 'mouth' to 'gas pipe opening,' *bidááʔ* 'eye' to 'headlight,' *bitaʔ* 'forehead' to 'windshield,' *bizig* 'liver' to 'battery,' *'bijíí* 'heart' to 'distributor,' and so on (Basso 1990: 20–21). Which sense of the word applies is invariably clear from the context. That no confusion results from the use of words that have several senses—unless one indulges in punning—should be evident from the example of the English word *horse*, which has designated the quadruped *Equus caballus* from Old English (before the twelfth century) to the present but later gained additional senses: 'trestle' or 'sawhorse,' 'pommel horse' or 'vaulting horse,' 'horsepower,' and 'heroin' (in slang).

How and Why Sound Changes Occur

Characteristically, sound changes are gradual. Only some speakers of a dialect or language adopt a particular speech innovation to begin with; others do so later, and ultimately all or most speakers accept the change. To put it differently, a particular sound change initially affects words that are frequently used, and only later is the change extended to other words. The modern view concerning how sound changes operate—namely, that they gradually spread, or diffuse, through the words (the lexicon) of a language—is referred to as lexical diffusion. Pioneered by William Labov and others during the 1960s, this view differs from the neogrammarian hypothesis of the 1870s, according to which sound laws admit no real exceptions, operating across the board within any given language.

An example of linguistic change proceeding from above (that is, from speakers enjoying higher prestige) is provided by Labov (1966) in his study of English used by salespeople in three New York City department stores. According to this study (discussed in more detail in Chapter 9), the use of [r] after a vowel in such words as *car, card, four*, and *fourth* tended to characterize careful lower-class speech once the usage had become associated with higher prestige. For an example of linguistic change proceeding from below, one may refer to Labov's study of the speech of Martha's Vineyard, an island several miles south of Cape Cod, Massachusetts. This study deals with the progressive change in the quality of the first vowel of the diphthongs /ay/ and /aw/ in such words as *firefly* and *outhouse*. During the 1930s, when data for the *Linguistic Atlas of New England* were being collected, and for a long time prior to that, the diphthong /aw/ was not centralized whereas /ay/ was (that is, its pronunciation resembled [əɪ]). During Labov's fieldwork in the early 1960s, the centralization of both diphthongs was most noticeable in the speech of thirty-one- to forty-five-year-old fishermen in the rural parts of the island, especially the Chilmark area in the west. According to Labov (1963:297, 304–305),

> [the] high centralization [of the two diphthongs] is closely correlated with expressions of strong resistance to the incursions of the summer people [who at the time outnumbered the native Vineyarders by a ratio of seven to one]. . . . It is apparent that the immediate meaning of [centralization] is 'Vineyarder.' When a man [uses the centralized diphthongs], he is unconsciously establishing the fact that he belongs to the island. . . . [The] younger members of the English descent group [of Vineyarders] . . . recognize that the Chilmark fishermen are independent, skillful with many kinds of tools and equipment, quick-spoken, courageous and physically strong. Most importantly, they carry with them the ever-present conviction that the island belongs to them. If someone intends to stay on the island, this model will be ever present to his mind.

Sound changes, then, are clearly neither random nor do they operate without exception. Careful studies of the conditions under which sound changes take place reveal not only the direction and rate of linguistic change but the motivation behind it as well.

And why do languages change? One reason is a •trong tendency in languages to maintain a definite pattern of organization. Analogy is another factor: Regular forms tend to influence less regular forms. Many Latin loanwords, for example, are now made plural almost exclusively by using the suffix -*s* (as in *auditoriums*) rather than their original Latin plural ending (as in *auditoria*). At least in some cases, more easily articulated sound sequences replace those that require greater effort (the principle of least effort). Not only have short words (*prof, exam, dorm, math,* and the like) been coined to supplement the original longer ones, but sometimes the simplification has been phonetic, as in the word *clothes,* which is usually pronounced as if it did not contain the sound represented by *th*.

Changes even occur when a language is passed on from parents to children and when children's speech habits are influenced by those of their peers. Though typically small, especially in phonology and morphology, such changes are cumulative and are noticeable when the speech of grandparents is compared with that of their grandchildren.

As we have already seen, sociocultural factors also promote language change. Some individuals like to imitate the sounds, grammar, and words used by those who have social prestige. When such imitations are overdone, hypercorrection results. Someone who has learned that *it is I* is correct rather than *it is me* may then say *between you and I* instead of the correct *between you and me*. On the phonetic level, hypercorrection occurs when *singer* is made to rhyme with *finger* because the two words are orthographically similar. Speakers of any language coin new words continually in order to give names to new inventions or new concepts. By the same token, those words that stand for items or ideas that are going out of use become obsolescent and eventually obsolete. The vocabulary of any living language, then, is constantly changing. In the case of written languages, new editions of dictionaries need to be published every ten years or so to record the changes that have come about.

The comparative method in phonology rests on the assumption that sound changes are regular and predictable (this is why these changes have been referred to as "sound laws"). But their regularity is not absolute because the conditions under which sound changes take place are not identical. For example, Latin *t* corresponds to the sound written as *th* in English words cognate with Latin words (a **cognate** is a word related to another by descent from the same ancestral language): Compare Latin *tenuis* and English *thin*, Latin *tongēre* 'to know' and English *think*, Latin *trēs* and English *three*, and Latin *trāns* 'across' and English *through*. But English words have retained *t* when it is preceded by *s* in the Latin cognate: Latin *stāre* 'to stand' corresponds to English *stand*, Latin *stēlla* to English *star*, Latin *stīpāre* 'to compress, cram' to English *stiff*, Latin *stringere* 'to clasp, tighten' to English *strain*, and so forth.

Or to give an example of a so-called regular sound correspondence from the historical development of English, consider Old English *ā* (that is, long *a*) as in *bāt, gān, māwan, sāwan, slāw,* and *stān* changing in Modern English to the respective vowel sound in the words *boat, (to) go, (to) mow, (to) sow, slow,* and *stone;* but in words in which Old English *ā* occurred after a cluster containing *w,* the sound correspondence was different: Thus *hwā* and *twā* changed in Modern English to *who* and *two,* respectively.

Sometimes an expected correspondence is not found because the words that are being compared are not cognate despite their having similar forms. For example, this is why Latin *d,* which in English cognates corresponds to *t* (as in *two, duo* in Latin, and *ten, decem* in Latin), does not appear as *t* in *day* because the words *day* and *diēs* 'day' are not related. Another example: The first consonant of the word *tooth* shows the expected correspondence to Latin *d* in *dēns (dentis)* 'tooth,' but the word *dental* does not because it was borrowed from medieval Latin at the end of the sixteenth century, too late to be subject to the regular change of Latin *d* to English *t.*

The force of analogy may also interfere with the regularity of sound changes. The inflection of the strong Old English verb *helpan* 'to help,' which had among its various forms *hilpst* (second-person singular), *healp* (the first- and third-person singular of the preterite), *hulpe* (the second-person singular of the preterite), *hulpon* (the plural form of the preterite), and *holpen* (the past participle), was simplified by analogy with weak verbs to Modern English forms *help* and *helped*.

In short, then, sound changes are regular provided they occur in like circumstances, but given the complexity of languages and the many different influences on them (regional, social, and others) as they are spoken century after century, it seems more appropriate to refer to such so-called laws as tendencies. Speaking of the conflict between "phonetic laws" and analogy, one of the most outstanding American comparative linguists, Edgar H. Sturtevant (1875–1952), wrote: "Phonetic laws are regular but produce irregularities. Analogic creation is irregular but produces regularity" (1947:109).

Reconstructing Protolanguages

It is generally accepted that the beginning of modern linguistics, historical linguistics in particular, dates back to 1786. It was then that Sir William Jones (1746–1794) observed in his presidential address to the Royal Asiatick Society of Bengal that Sanskrit, Greek, and Latin "have sprung from some common source, which, perhaps, no longer exists [and that] there is a similar reason . . . for supposing that both the *Gothick* and the *Celtick* . . . had the same origin with the *Sanscrit* [and] the old *Persian* might be added to the same family" (Salus 1969). As early as the sixteenth century it had been suspected that many European languages were related and that their parent language might be Sanskrit, an ancient language of India. Jones, however, went still further; according to him, Sanskrit, ancient Greek, Latin, and other European languages were the descendants of a language spoken in prehistoric times. During the first half of the nineteenth century a number of major works were published to demonstrate in some detail that relationships existed not only among the several ancient languages that were no longer spoken but also between them and Germanic, Slavic, Romance, Baltic, and other languages spoken in Europe and southwestern Asia. During the same period reconstructions were begun of words of the ancestral language, assumed to have been spoken before the invention of writing and therefore never documented. These reconstructions proceeded so rapidly that in 1868 the German philologist August Schleicher (1821–1868) was able to "translate" into the prehistoric ancestral language a short fable about a sheep and three horses.

What can be reconstructed, and how are such reconstructions accomplished? It is possible to reconstruct the sounds and meanings of words as well as the grammar and syntax of an earlier undocumented state of a language, but usually the ultimate goal of linguistic reconstruction is the assumed ancestral language, or protolanguage, of all those languages derived from the same source. Reconstruction of a protolanguage requires thorough knowledge of historical grammar and good acquaintance with the daughter languages. The procedure is intricate, but the two main assumptions underlying it are not difficult to explain. The first assumption is that recurring similarities between words from different languages or dialects indicate that these languages or dialects are related to each other and must therefore have descended from a common ancestral language. The second assumption is that, as discussed above, sound changes are regular under like circumstances.

For example, we know from written records what the forms of the word meaning cloud were in the three ancient languages assumed to be related: *nábhas* in Sanskrit, *néphos* in ancient Greek, and *nebo* in Old Church Slavonic. There is a similarity among the three words, and the sound correspondences may be represented as follows:

Sanskrit	Ancient Greek	Old Church Slavonic
n	n	n
a	e	e
bh	ph	b
a	o	o
s	s	

If these three words for cloud are found in the daughter languages of the protolanguage, in this case Proto-Indo-European (PIE), what would the PIE word most likely have been? The first sound, the nasal consonant *n*, presents no problem; one would reconstruct a PIE **n* (the asterisk marks a reconstructed form, one that has not been attested or is unattestable). An alternative reconstruction, using the nasal **m*, is much less probable because the presumption would then be that all three daughter languages independently made the same change, from **m* to *n*. The second sound, a vowel, was *a* in Sanskrit and *e* in both ancient Greek and Old Church Slavonic. Here one would reconstruct the PIE sound as **e* because it is more logical to assume that only one of the daughter languages innovated while the other two kept the original sound than to assume that two of the daughter languages independently effected the same change. The medial consonant, which is different in each of the three words, is reconstructed as **bh* because the reconstructed sound has something in common with each of the three sounds derived from the earlier one—bilabial articulation in all three cases, a voiced sound with Sanskrit and Old

Church Slavonic, and aspiration (*h*) with Sanskrit and ancient Greek. The second vowel and the final consonant pose no new questions. Consequently, the reconstructed PIE word for cloud is **nebhos*. This is not to assert, however, that this very word must actually have existed in proto-Indo-European times but rather that there must have been such a word, or a very similar one, to have given rise later to the three words attested for Sanskrit, ancient Greek, and Old Church Slavonic.

Historical linguists have further established that Proto-Indo-European was a highly inflected language. For example, its nouns had three genders (masculine, feminine, and neuter), three numbers (singular, plural, and dual for objects occurring in pairs), and eight cases, and its verbs had three persons, three numbers, and a variety of tenses, moods, and other features. Those who assume that the grammatical systems of prehistoric languages must have been rather simple (primitive) could scarcely be further from the truth. The grammatical system of Modern English is an example of simplicity when compared with that of Proto-Indo-European.

For several Indo-European languages, written records (some on clay tablets) exist from as far back as the second millennium B.C., and for many others the earliest records are on the order of 1,000 years old. Documentation of such time depth provides invaluable information about the changes that occur over time and aids historical linguists in their efforts to make reliable reconstructions. But for most other groups of related languages, such documentation is the rare exception rather than the rule. Some scholars were convinced, in fact, that comparative reconstruction was feasible only in the case of related languages whose history was known at least to some extent. That the comparative method is just as applicable to unwritten languages, provided that some reliable sketches of their contemporary structures are available, was demonstrated in 1946 by Leonard Bloomfield (1887–1949), a well-known American linguist. His reconstruction of the sounds and grammar of the ancestral language of Native Americans speaking Algonquian languages was based on four of the so-called Central Algonquian languages—Fox, Cree, Menomini, and Ojibwa. Through his fieldwork begun in the early 1920s, Bloomfield was well acquainted with three of them. Basing his judgment on his knowledge of Algonquian languages, Bloomfield believed that the "reconstructions will, in the main, fit all the [Algonquian] languages [including the divergent Blackfoot, Cheyenne, and Arapaho in the West] and can accordingly be viewed as Proto-Algonquian" (1946:85). Research by others during subsequent decades has shown that except for some details, Bloomfield was correct. The reconstruction of protolanguages on the basis of their modern descendants is now a fairly common linguistic undertaking. Some of the protolanguages reconstructed for North and Central America are Proto-Athapaskan, Proto-Mixtecan, Proto-Otomian, Proto-

Popolocan, Proto-Salishan, Proto-Siouan, Proto-Uto-Aztecan, and Proto-Zapotecan.

Reconstructing the Ancestral Homeland

People—individuals, families, bands, and still larger groups—have always migrated to new places from localities in which they were born and raised, frequently as far away as to another continent. The main reason for such migrations has been population pressure: Whenever the natural resources of an area have become insufficient to support the local population, some of its members have had little choice but to move away. Moving from one locality to another was already true of early humans, who were hunters and gatherers—foragers for game, wild plants, and water. But once animals and plants were domesticated in the Middle East about 10,000 years ago, the need for hunting and gathering diminished in many parts of the world as permanent settlements became established. In modern times new situations caused people to migrate. The institution of slavery was responsible for the forced removal of large numbers of people not only from region to region but even from one continent to another (by the middle of the nineteenth century, the slave population in America had surpassed 4 million). Others migrated voluntarily, attracted to a particular area or country by the news of better living conditions as reported by acquaintances or relatives who had already resettled there (chain migration). Many of the 17 million or so people from various European countries who entered the United States between 1880 and 1910 were following compatriots who had pioneered the transatlantic migration. During the twentieth century, much migration occurred for political reasons. Immediately following World War II, over 10 million Germans were either transferred to a reduced German territory from countries that had suffered under the Nazi regime or chose to resettle there on their own initiative. At about the same time (in 1947), the Indian subcontinent was partitioned between India and Pakistan, and a total of more than 15 million Hindus from Pakistan and Muslims from India moved from one of the two new countries to the other in order to live among peoples of the same religion. As recently as August 1990, the global refugee population was estimated at 15 million, about 2 million more than in the preceding year.

For those time periods and parts of the world long characterized by the use of writing, information is available in more or less detail concerning the historical migrations that took place. However, such information is very shallow where written language has been in use for only several centuries, the Americas and Australia in particular. For example, in North America speakers of over two dozen languages and major dialects of the Algonquian language family (along with enclaves of other language families, of course) extended from Tennessee and eastern North Carolina in the Southeast, to northeastern Newfoundland and the southern coast of Hudson Bay in the North, and to Colorado, Wyoming, Montana, Saskatchewan, and southeastern Alberta in the West. In the absence of historical records extending several thousand years into the past, is it possible to discover where the speakers of Proto-Algonquian, the language that must have been ancestral to the present Algonquian languages, originally lived? It is, and the method of investigation involves the careful use of linguistic data as well as information pertaining to the natural history of the North American continent. This method of reconstruction was illustrated by Frank T. Siebert, Jr., in his well-known article "The Original Home of the Proto-Algonquian People" (1967).

Let us summarize the working assumptions on which reconstructions of this kind are based. First, the territory occupied at some time in the past by speakers of an ancestral language would have been rather limited in extent when compared with the area in which the daughter languages are (or were) spoken. The fairly large part of North America that the Algonquian-speaking peoples inhabited at the time of their initial contact with the European immigrants was the result of many centuries of movements by their ancestors away from wherever their ancestral home may have been. Second, the vocabulary of the ancestral group must have included words designating the main features of the surrounding natural environment—among them the words for the various kinds of mammals, fish, birds, trees, and the like. To be able to refer fairly specifically to such features of the environment would have been essential for their survival. The families and groups that wandered off from the population in the ancestral homeland began their independent existence using the speech of the parent group. In the course of time, however, the speech habits of those who moved away began to show the inevitable changes to which all living languages are subject. The method for locating the ancestral homeland of linguistically related peoples is based on the justifiable assumption that one can reconstruct from certain cognates in the descendant languages the portion of the ancestral vocabulary that reveals the original location of the parent population.

Drawing on over a dozen available vocabularies of modern Algonquian languages and their dialects, Siebert reconstructed fifty-three Proto-Algonquian (PA) words referring to particular features of the natural environment. Of these words, eighteen are bird names, nineteen mammalian names, twelve tree names, and four fish names. All these reconstructed words of the ancestral vocabulary are regularly derivable from the corresponding words of the modern Algonquian languages. For example, PA *a·skikwa '(harbor) seal' (*Phoca vitulina concolor*), one of the fifty-three words, is reconstructible from the Swampy or Woodland dialect of the Cree word *a·hkik*, the Lake St. John dialect of Montagnais *a·hčok*, Ojibwa *a·skik*, and the Penobscot dialect of Abnaki *àhkikᵂ*; PA **aʔšikanwa* 'smallmouth black bass' (*Micropterus dolomieu*) is reconstructible from the Fox word *ašikanwa*, Menomini word *aʔsekan*, Ojibwa word *aššikan*, Shawnee word *aʔšika*, and the Penobscot dialect of the Abnaki word *ásikan;* and PA **a·kema·xkwa* 'white ash' (*Fraxinus americana*), a compound of PA **a·kem-* 'snowshoe' and PA **-a·xkw-* '(hard)wood,' from the modern cognates obtained from Swampy or Woodland dialect of Cree, the Lake St. John dialect of Montagnais, Ojibwa, and the Penobscot dialect of Abnaki. (In Ojibwa and Penobscot the original meaning has been preserved, whereas in the Cree and Montagnais dialects the name came to be applied to the black ash after the speakers of these two dialects migrated north of the white-ash range.) Of the approximately fifty reconstructible species terms, about a score contributed significantly to the solution of the problem.

The data Siebert used consist of the reconstructed Proto-Algonquian words designating the following natural features: for mammals, bear, beaver, bison or buffalo, buck (male of moose, deer, elk, caribou), fawn, flying squirrel, fox, lynx or bobcat, mink, moose, muskrat, porcupine, raccoon, (harbor) seal, skunk, squirrel, weasel, woodchuck or groundhog, and woodland caribou; for birds, blue jay, bobwhite or quail, common loon, golden eagle, great horned owl (two terms), greater yellowlegs, gull, hawk, heron or crane, kingfisher, merganser, nighthawk, old-squaw, pileated woodpecker or logcock, raven, ruffed grouse or partridge, and large edible game bird; for fish, brown bullhead, lake trout, northern pike, and smallmouth black bass; and for trees, (speckled) alder, basswood, American beech, conifer or evergreen, elm, quaking aspen, sugar maple, tamarack, white ash, white spruce, willow, and a kind of tree whose species could not be determined.

Because all these animals and trees—the names for which are reconstructible for the Proto-Algonquian language—must have been present in the environment surrounding the speakers of the ancestral language, the task that next confronted Siebert was to locate the corresponding area on this continent. But finding it was not as easy as it might seem. The distribution of individual animal and plant species had changed considerably over the past several centuries as a result of the rapid settlement of the continent by immigrants from the Old World. Some forestlands had been converted to fields and pastures, some species of fish had been eliminated by pollution while other fish species may have been introduced into streams and lakes in which they were not native, and some species of mammals had been greatly reduced or virtually exterminated by indiscriminate hunting (for example, the buffalo) or urbanization. What Siebert therefore had to establish was the earliest possible ranges of the fifty-odd species. He consulted nearly 100 sources containing information about the natural history of North America, some dating as far back as 1625. Trees served as particularly reliable guides because they are fixed and their ranges are governed by soil, moisture, and long-term climatic patterns. Bird species contributed much less to the investigation because seasonal migrations tend to make their geographic ranges quite extensive. Once the geographic distributions had been established, Siebert plotted the ranges on a map of the continent (for examples of the original ranges, see Figures 7.1 and 7.2). The earliest homeland of speakers of Proto-Algonquian would have had to be in the area that all of the significant species shared in common or at least touched. For Siebert's ingenious reconstruction of the location of the original home of the proto-Algonquian people, we can refer to the author's own discussion and conclusion (here abbreviated in Box 7.1 and supplemented by the map in Figure 7.3).

Reconstructing a Protoculture

Reconstruction of words of a protolanguage and their meanings is likely to throw light on some aspects of the prehistoric culture of those who spoke the protolanguage. A good way to illustrate this statement is to consider those Indo-European kinship terms that are reconstructible for Proto-Indo-European. They include ancestral words (protowords) for individuals related by blood, such as *father, mother, brother, sister, son, daughter*; protowords for a woman's relatives by marriage, such as *husband's brother, husband's sister, husband's mother, husband's father*; and protowords referring to women related by marriage, such as *daughter-in-law*. To give an example, there are cognate words in a number of Indo-European languages for the kinship term *daughter-in-law*; among these words are Sanskrit *snuṣā́*, Greek *nuós*, Latin *nurus*, Russian *snokhá*, Old English *snoru*, German *Schnur*, and others. On the basis of numerous known sound correspondences, it is possible to reconstruct the PIE form *snusós* 'daughter-in-law.' Because the word referring to son-in-law is not reconstructible, the assumption can be made that there was no such word in proto-Indo-European times. The existence of *snusós* 'daughter-in-law' but not of the corresponding male term (son-in-law) strongly indicates that a young wife would have been brought to live with or near her husband's family and then referred to by a special term to distinguish her from the blood-related females of the household. If the custom had been for a young man to live with his wife's parents, one would expect to find cognate terms for son-in-law rather than for daughter-in-law. The linguistic evidence based on the protolanguage points to patrilocal residence among the ancient Indo-Europeans, that is, a young couple habitually living with or near the

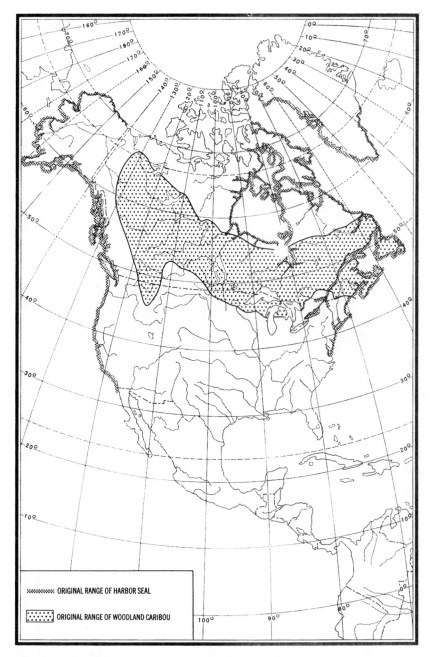

FIGURE 7.1 Original Ranges of Harbor Seal and Woodland Caribou. *Source:* From Frank T. Siebert, Jr., *The Original Home of the Proto-Algonquian People,* National Museum of Canada, bulletin 214 (Ottawa, 1967), 20. Reproduced by permission of the Canadian Museum of Civilization.

150

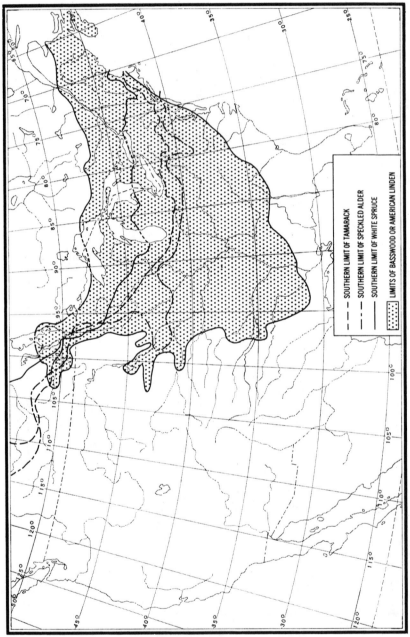

FIGURE 7.2 Original Southern Limits of Three Tree Species and the Original Distribution of Basswood. *Source:* From Frank T. Siebert, Jr., *The Original Home of the Proto-Algonquian People,* National Museum of Canada, bulletin 214 (Ottawa, 1967), 28. Reproduced by permission of the Canadian Museum of Civilization.

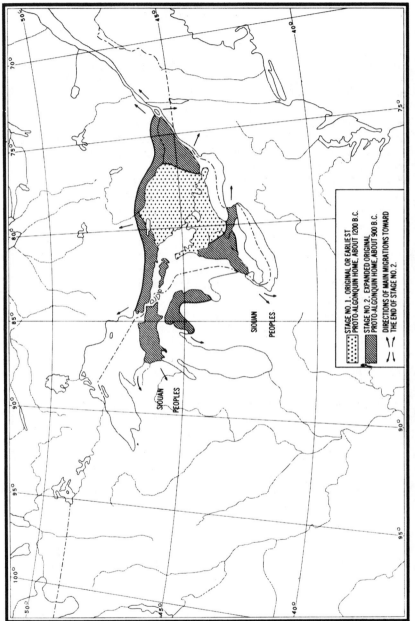

FIGURE 7.3   The Two Assumed Stages of the Proto-Algonquian Home and Their Locations. *Source:* From Frank T. Siebert, Jr., *The Original Home of the Proto-Algonquian People,* National Museum of Canada, bulletin 214 (Ottawa, 1967), 35. Reproduced by permission of the Canadian Museum of Civilization.

BOX 7.1 Siebert on the Original Home of the Proto-Algonquian People

The primeval home was a region abounding in lakes and was well supplied with a large variety of fish, waterfowl, and game animals. It lay between the almost strictly coniferous forests to the north and the deciduous woodlands to the south. That the Proto-Algonquians lived in a mixed-forest zone is evident from the frequent use of the two contrasting noun-finals in many tree names, PA *-a·ntakw- 'evergreen tree, conifer' and *-a·xkw- 'wood; hardwood or deciduous tree.' The relatively southern species of deciduous trees, like the white ash, sugar maple, basswood, and beech, extend more or less only slightly farther north than the Algonquian homeland, whereas northern conifers, like the white spruce and tamarack, were found commonly only to the southern borders of the original home or slightly beyond.

The original home lay at the southern limit of the woodland caribou. …

… The harbour seal is the only seal that is common on the eastern coast of the United States … [but] in aboriginal times its ascent penetrated … into the interior along the upper St. Lawrence River and affluent streams. …

… The distributions of [the four species of fish] provide additional reasons for pinpointing the earliest Algonquian residence to southern Ontario rather than to a more western portion of the Great Lakes region. …

In order to allow for possible undetermined changes in the distribution of fauna and flora in the prehistoric period, and partly in order to account for alternative interpretations of the linguistic facts themselves, the earliest original home is diagrammatically represented as Stage Number 1 … and an expanded area of occupancy of slightly later date, which certainly includes the entire Algonquian homeland, is characterized as Stage Number 2. To these the tentative dates of 1200 B.C. and 900 B.C., respectively, are assigned as suppositions to serve as a basis for further discussion. …

The earliest residence of the speakers of Proto-Algonquian is ascertained by the multiple intersections of the distributional lines of significant species. The original home of the Algonquian peoples lay in the region between Lake Huron and Georgian Bay and the middle course of the Ottawa River, bounded on the north by Lake Nipissing and the Mattawa River and on the south by the northern shore of Lake Ontario, the headwaters of the Grand River, and the Saugeen River.

from Frank T. Siebert, Jr., "The Original Home of the Proto-Algonquian People" (1967), 36–40 husband's father's family. Such information could not be obtained from archaeological evidence.

Linguistic reconstructions tell us much more about the ancient Indo-Europeans: that they used yokes and probably wheeled vehicles of some kind and depended on or kept horses, cows, dogs, sheep, pigs, and goats; furthermore, that they lived in an environment in which they encountered wolves, bears, foxes, eagles, salmon (probably a type of trout resembling salmon), otters, beavers, and other animals, as well as alder, aspen, beech, birch, oak, and yew among the flora. They practiced agriculture and cultivated cereals, which they ground into flour. The ancient Indo-Europeans used numerals at least through 100 and employed a decimal system. They were led by tribal chiefs or kings and, judging from the reconstructible vocabulary, developed rather elaborate religious practices. The wide distribution of words for snow and the easy reconstructibility of *sneigwh- '(to) snow' appears to exclude as the probable ancestral Indo-European homeland those warm southern parts of Europe and southwestern Asia where snow is not seen.

The reconstructions of protoculture have not been limited to prehistoric Indo-European society but have been extended to other parts of the world, for example, sub-Saharan Africa. Some linguistic inferences about early Bantu history are reproduced in Box. 7.2 (the Bantu languages form a large subgroup of the Niger-Congo language family).

Dating the Past: Glottochronology

A modern attempt to determine statistically the length of time during which a language or a group of genetically related languages has been undergoing independent development was made by Swadesh in his article concerning the internal relationships within the Salishan language family of the American Northwest (Swadesh 1950). The method, which Swadesh and others subsequently elaborated, merits the designation lexicostatistical glottochronology because it studies time relationships among related languages by statistical comparison of samples of their vocabularies. For the sake of brevity, I refer to it here as glottochronology. The method became controversial soon after its introduction, but because it has been repeatedly applied to linguistic data and frequent references to it appear in the literature, it deserves to be briefly examined.

When first introduced, glottochronological analysis yielded relative dates not unlike those archaeologists obtain from the stratigraphic record. The method was later revised so that absolute dates could be determined much like those archaeologists obtain by using carbon 14 to date ancient organic materials recovered from archaeological sites. Glottochronological dating is based on the assumption that in all languages there are cer-

---

BOX 7.2   Linguistic Inferences About Early Bantu History

The oldest Bantu subsistence vocabulary so far reconstructible accords with postulation of a high-rainfall, tropical environment for the proto-Bantu homeland. No grain terms can be reconstructed, but there is instead a word for yam. Two or three possible root words dealing with the oil palm may also date to proto-Bantu, and the reconstructible proto-Bantu name for alcoholic drink apparently referred specifically to palm wine. At least one cucurbit, probably the bottle gourd, a pulse (the cowpea?), and probably the *Voandzeia* groundnut were also known to the proto-Bantu. ... These three crops would all have been domesticated elsewhere than in the proto-Bantu homeland, but apparently they could be effectively grown in high-rainfall savanna and/or rain forest. ...

A second indication of a high-rainfall environment is provided by the reconstructibility of fishing and boating vocabulary. ... Apparently the proto-Bantu made considerable use of riverine resources and lived where large perennial streams were commonplace.

Knowledge of two domestic animals, cattle and goats, can be reconstructed. ... Whatever the cause of proto-Bantu knowledge of cattle, it was lost by those who expanded into the equatorial rain forest, for the proto-Bantu root *nyaka is found no farther south than some of the forest languages in which it was reapplied, in the absence of cattle, to the buffalo. ...

Contrary to a widely held view, knowledge of ironworking cannot be linguistically reconstructed for proto-Bantu. ... By the beginnings, however, of Bantu expansion into eastern Africa, on linguistic grounds most probably during the last millennium B.C., metallurgical terms had come into use among at least the ancestral Eastern Bantu communities.

from Christopher Ehret, "Linguistic Inferences
About Early Bantu History" (1982), 61–62

---

tain words that tend to be replaced at a constant rate over long periods of time. This basic core vocabulary consists of words that designate things, qualities, and activities most likely to be named in all languages of the world. Among these words are body parts, natural objects and phenomena, plants and plant parts, animals, colors, numerals, bodily sensations and activities, and words belonging to several other semantic domains, among them positions and movements, persons, and common qualities. On the basis of tests made with 200-word lists from languages whose history is known, the rate of replacement, or loss, of the basic core vocabulary appears to average nearly 20 percent per 1,000 years, amounting to a word retention rate of just over 80 percent. For the smaller and more concentrated 100-word list developed by Swadesh in 1955 (see Table 7.2), the

TABLE 7.2 The 100-Word Core Vocabulary

I	dog	nose	die	smoke
you	louse	mouth	kill	fire
we	tree	tooth	swim	ash
this	seed	tongue	fly	burn
that	leaf	claw	walk	path
who	root	foot	come	mountain
what	bark	knee	lie	red
not	skin	hand	sit	green
all	flesh	belly	stand	yellow
many	blood	neck	give	white
one	bone	breasts	say	black
two	grease	heart	sun	night
big	egg	liver	moon	hot
long	horn	drink	star	cold
small	tail	eat	water	full
woman	feather	bite	rain	new
man	hair	see	stone	good
person	head	hear	sand	round
fish	ear	know	earth	dry
bird	eye	sleep	cloud	name

It should be noted that the large majority of these words can be traced to Old English—that is, they are very old English words. Because of the universal nature and occurrence of the referents for which these words stand, equivalents in other languages are available and may also be expected to be old.

comparable rates are 14 and 86 percent. According to the proponents of glottochronology, the length of time required for two languages to diverge from a single language can be calculated by using the formula $t = (\log C)/(2 \log r)$, where t is the time depth in millennia, C is the percentage of cognates, and r is the constant, that is, the percentage of cognates assumed to remain after 1,000 years of divergence (81 percent for the 200-word list and 86 percent for the 100-word list).

In applying the method, one first translates the basic core vocabulary into the colloquial equivalents of the two related languages and then determines which pairs are cognate by virtue of similarity. For example, the English words *blood, cloud, hair, sand, tree,* and *black* would translate into German as *Blut, Wolke, Haar, Sand, Baum,* and *schwarz.* Of the six pairs, only three would be considered cognate (*blood, hair,* and *sand* and their German equivalents). In contrast *deer* and German *Tier* 'animal' are cognate but no longer equivalent. Other pairs of words are cognate but may not be recognized as such, for example, the English word *toe* and the German cognate *Zehe* 'toe,' English *beam* and German *Baum* 'tree,' and English *swart(hy)* and German *schwarz* 'black.'

Almost since the development of glottochronology, its basic assumptions have been controversial. Some of the problems were aptly summarized by Dwight Bolinger: "We cannot be sure that the social and historical forces of change have not been stronger in one epoch than in another, or that many items of supposedly basic vocabulary have not actually been borrowed rather than inherited." And he continued, referring to a study by Labov, "A survey of the speech of the year-round inhabitants of Martha's Vineyard found that their desire to be different from the detested mainlanders is leading them to speed up certain changes in the pronunciation of their vowels. Social pressures create variable rates of change in phonetics as well as in vocabulary" (Bolinger 1968:132–133). It is also known, for example, that the retention of cognates between Old Norse and Modern Icelandic is much higher than the formula would indicate. Another problem is the assumption that the basic core vocabulary list is equally applicable to all cultures, that is, that it has no cultural bias. Harry Hoijer (1904–1976) has shown, for example, that one would have to choose from among five Navajo forms for the English *this* and *that*, from among four for *who* and *what*, from among two for *black*, and so on (Hoijer 1956).

To eliminate the objection that the acceptance of absolute time references is untenable, the suggestion was made to adopt a relative unit of time depth that would be less misleading. This unit is referred to as *dip* (for "*d*egree of lexical relationsh*ip*"). To arrive at dips, the absolute time depth (in millennia) is multiplied by fourteen. Accordingly, two related languages, each of which has gone its own way for 2,000 years, would be separated by twenty-eight dips.

In summary, if applied to related languages whose history is not known and for which written records do not exist, glottochronology may provide some preliminary estimates of their closeness. But careful linguistic anthropologists would look for supporting evidence from archaeology, comparative ethnology, and linguistic reconstruction using the comparative method before accepting glottochronological results as valid.

Time Perspective in Culture

How linguistic data can aid the reconstruction of cultural history was discussed at length and exemplified in one of the early works of Edward Sapir, a brilliant American linguist and anthropologist of German origin. The work, *Time Perspective in Aboriginal American Culture: A Study in Method* (1916), was his longest monograph in ethnology and is testimony to his methodological prowess. The few examples that follow illustrate Sapir's discussion of inferential linguistic evidence for time perspective.

The relative age of a culture element can be determined with some reliability from the form of the native (not borrowed) word that refers to the element. Such simple and not further analyzable words as *bow, plow, spear,* and *wheel* are as a rule much older than words that can be broken down into smaller constituent parts—for example, *airplane, battleship, railroad,* and *spaceship.* Irregular grammatical forms also indicate the great age of those words with which they are associated and, by implication, of those entities to which they refer; hence the plurals *geese, kine* (archaic plural of *cow*), *lice, oxen,* and *sheep* on the one hand, but *elephants, lions, parrots,* and *tigers* on the other.

Loanwords, which usually designate elements of foreign cultures, can frequently be identified by their different phonetic structure (we would now say "phonemic"). Thus, although /z/ and /ʃ/ occur in old words of the native English vocabulary in medial or final position (as in *frozen, rise, bridges,* and *ridge*), initially these two sounds are found only in loanwords, for example, in *zeal* (adapted from Late Latin but ultimately from Greek) or *just* (adapted from Middle French but ultimately from Latin). Similarly, some combinations of sounds betray the foreign origin of words in which they occur, as /ps/ does in *apse* and *lapse* (both from Latin) and *rhapsody* (from Greek via Latin); but the final /-ps/ in *lips, sleeps, ship's,* and other such words is not comparable because the /-s/ represents other morphemes—the plural, the third-person singular, or the possessive. For societies with a long tradition of writing, inferential linguistic evidence may add little if anything to what is already known about their cultural history. This is not the case, however, with nonliterate societies.

The assignment of related languages to a language family implies the earlier existence of an ancestral language from which all modern languages of the family have descended. The more differentiated these descendant languages are, the longer the period of time one must allow for their development to have taken place; the time depth has important consequences for culture history.

Linguistic scholars have known for some time that phonetic (or phonemic) and morphological similarities sometimes exist among unrelated neighboring languages to an extent that could scarcely be due to chance. Such similarities are indicative of an extensive period of cultural contact between the respective societies, a circumstance the ethnologist must take into account.

In the concluding remarks of his monograph, Sapir makes the point that although direct evidence is much to be preferred to inferential evidence in the study of culture history and the establishment of culture sequences, anthropologists frequently face situations where direct evidence is either insufficient or completely lacking. In such cases inferential evidence, linguistic in particular, becomes invaluable.

How Languages Are Classified

It is difficult to give the exact number of languages spoken in the world at present, but the total undoubtedly approaches 6,000 (Krauss 1992:5–6). What is impossible even to guess at is how many languages must have become extinct in prehistoric times and how many have survived in a different form. We do know, of course, that during the historical period for which we have written records a great many languages have died out. Today, some languages of very small societies in large industrial countries are spoken only by the older men and women. Their grandchildren speak the language of the larger society around them, which is also the language of school instruction, and are not able to speak the native language of grandparents. The parents of these children may have some passive knowledge of the native language, but the language of the larger society is used in the home. In such situations the native languages live on borrowed time—their demise appears to be a matter of only one or two generations.

In many cases a language quite vigorous several thousand years ago—for example, Proto-Indo-European, believed to have been spoken over five millennia ago probably somewhere in the steppes north of the Black Sea—is no longer spoken today because in the course of time it evolved from a single protolanguage into a number of descendant languages. Some of these languages are now mutually unintelligible, as are English and Russian or Albanian and French, but they are genetically related because they go back to the same source, their common ancestral language.

When it comes to classifying the several thousand languages of the world, genetic classification predominates. The most common term used in language classification is **language family** (or language stock). The term refers to all languages that have descended from one common ancestral language and are therefore related. The concept of the language family is somewhat conservative: It is generally employed only if the relationship and the correspondences among the languages have been firmly established by careful comparative work and a convincing number of cognates. Subdivisions of a language family are usually referred to as branches. The Indo-European language family consists of about a dozen branches. The branches still represented by spoken languages include Albanian (a single language), Armenian (a single language), Balto-Slavic (more than a dozen languages belonging to the Baltic and Slavic subbranches), Germanic (about a dozen languages, including English), Celtic (four languages), Hellenic or Greek (a single language), Italic (about a dozen languages, including French and Spanish), and Indo-Iranian (with

Indic and Iranian subbranches consisting of several hundred languages and dialects spoken mostly in southwestern Asia). Each of the spoken languages has several or even many dialects. Some branches of Indo-European, for example, the Tocharian and Anatolian branches, are no longer represented by spoken languages.

The number of languages that make up a language family varies greatly. The largest African family, Niger-Congo, is estimated to consist of about 1,000 languages and several times as many dialects. Yet there are many languages that do not appear to be related to any other. These single-member language families are referred to as **language isolates.** The Americas have been more linguistically diversified than other continents; the number of Native American language families in North America has been judged to be more than seventy, including more than thirty isolates. The numbers for South America have been even larger, but they are only estimates because our knowledge of the languages of South America is still incomplete. Many Native American languages are isolates, and even the families with many members (for example, the Algonquian family) have not been spoken by large populations.

Several attempts have been made to simplify the apparent linguistic diversity of the New World. In 1929 Sapir proposed a major reduction in the number of language families, assigning all Native American languages north of Mexico to only six "major linguistic groups" (superfamilies), later referred to as phyla. Consequently, a phylum in linguistic classification is a grouping that encompasses all those languages judged to have more remote relationships than do languages assigned to a family. Except for the Eskimo-Aleut "group," which is considered to be one family, each of the other five groups of Sapir's proposed classification included several families and one or more language isolates. A similar simplification of South American language families was proposed in 1960 by Joseph H. Greenberg, who subsumed the hundreds of native South American languages under three "families" (using the term not in the older conservative sense but more in the sense of superphylum or macrophylum). In a recent classification Greenberg (1987) assigns all native languages of the New World to only three "families," of which the Amerind "family" covers all native languages of the two continents except for those belonging to the Na-dene and Eskimo-Aleut groups (spoken for the most part in the northern half of North America). Most specialists in Native American languages are not ready to accept the validity of Greenberg's huge Amerind genetic unit, or family. In any case, a family of this size has little in common with the earlier conservative concept of language family. (Most of the objections to this classification are discussed in the lengthy review of Greenberg's work by Campbell [1988].) In 1964 two comparative linguists in the Soviet Union produced evidence that six major language families of the Old World—Indo-European, Afro-Asiatic, Altaic, Dravidian, Uralic, and Kartvelian (South Caucasian)—were remotely related. To this macrofamily, referred to as Nostratic, some scholars have subsequently added other language families and languages, among them Eskimo-Aleut, Nilo-Saharan, and Sumerian (Kaiser and Shevoroshkin 1988). And still another proposed macrofamily links together many languages from both the Old and the New World (one of the names of this macrofamily is Dene-Caucasian).

The ten largest conventional language families, ranging from well over 2 billion speakers to about 60 million, are Indo-European, Sino-Tibetan, Niger-Congo, Afro-Asiatic, Austronesian, Dravidian, Japanese, Altaic, Austroasiatic, and Korean (Japanese and Korean are frequently considered language isolates but may be distantly related to each other and to the Altaic family).

Less frequently used are typological classifications, based on structural similarities of languages regardless of their history—that is, regardless of genetic relationship. Typological classifications take various structural features into consideration. For example, some scholars have classified languages according to their sound systems, basing their grouping on how many and which distinctive vowels and consonants are used and whether tones are employed. Others have classified languages according to word order, that is, the sequence of subject (S), verb (V), and object (O) in simple declarative sentences (in English the typical arrangement is SVO, as in "The dog bit the thief"). Recently, semantic typology has been proposed; its proponents compare languages, for example, according to how much specificity relating to meaning a language requires. The best-known language classifications are based on morphological characteristics; the most widely used assigns languages to one of four types—isolating, inflecting, agglutinative, and polysynthetic, although frequently a language combines features of more than one type.

Any one of the several Chinese languages or dialects may be given as an example of an isolating (or analytic) language—a language in which there are no (or very few) affixes and in which grammatical relations are shown by word order. For example, the English sentence "I like Linda" would be *Wǒ xǐhuan Linda* in Beijing Mandarin, and "Linda likes me" would be *Linda xǐhuan wǒ*. The forms of the words in the two sentences are identical, but the order is different to indicate who likes whom.

As we have already seen, English has only a few inflectional suffixes, such as the *-s* in *speaks*, *-ed* in *called*, *-s* in *son's*, and *-s* in *cups*, but some sentences are of the isolating type because the words in them are single morphemes, as in "The girl will take the book to school soon." In contrast, an excellent example of an inflecting language—one in which words display grammatical relationships by means of bound morphemes—is Latin.

What is more, Latin endings express several grammatical meanings at the same time: The *-ō* in *laudō* 'I praise' stands for first-person singular, active voice (where the grammatical subject is typically the actor), present tense, and indicative mood (expressing a statement). How the relationship between the subject and the object of a sentence is conveyed may be illustrated by the Latin sentences *Magister discipulum vocat* 'The teacher calls the pupil' and *Magistrum discipulus vocat* 'The pupil calls the teacher' (or more exactly, 'It is the teacher whom the pupil calls'). The order of the words in the two sentences is the same, but the adding of the suffix *-um* to one or the other noun makes it clear who is calling whom.

In agglutinative languages each grammatical meaning is expressed by a separate piece of structure (morpheme). In the Turkish word *yazmalïymišïm* 'I should have written,' the stem *yaz* 'write' is followed by three suffixes here taking the forms of *malïy-miš-ïm* meaning, respectively, 'obligative' (expressing obligation), 'perfective' (implying completion), and 'I.' Turkish, Finnish, Swahili, and Japanese are among languages that are agglutinative.

The last type, polysynthetic, is considered by many linguists to be a combination of agglutinative and inflectional features. The words in polysynthetic languages are long and morphologically complex, such as the single Eskimo word *a:wlisa-ut-iss?ar-si-niarpu-ŋa*, which translates 'I am looking for something suitable for a fishing line' (the hyphens in the Eskimo word are used to indicate morpheme boundaries).

Typological classifications are not used as often as genetic classifications because they require good knowledge of the grammatical systems of languages. Such knowledge is still unavailable for many unwritten languages of New Guinea, the tropical rain forests of South America, and several regions on other continents. One more comment should be made here: No relationship exists between a group's language type and the nature of its culture. That is nothing new, of course. In his classic book *Language*, Edward Sapir put it very cogently (today, one would phrase the last sentence somewhat differently): "All attempts to connect particular types of linguistic morphology with certain correlated stages of cultural development are vain . . . [and] rubbish. . . . When it comes to linguistic form, Plato walks with the Macedonian swineherd, Confucius with the head-hunting savage of Assam" (1921:234).

Summary and Conclusions

Living languages change slowly but constantly. The Old English poem *Beowulf* is no longer intelligible to speakers of Modern English. Words that rhymed in Shakespeare's time do not always rhyme today, and what Shakespeare had Marcus Antonius say to Roman citizens in the forum after Caesar's murder, "This was the most unkindest cut of all" (*Julius Caesar*, act 3, scene 2), is no longer grammatical. But even dead languages may continue to change. Latin, which for many centuries has not been the native language of any society, can serve as an example. Its vocabulary continues to grow because Latin is the official language of the Roman Catholic church, and the pope uses it in his occasional encyclicals commenting on contemporary problems.

The tendency of sound changes to be regular makes it possible to reconstruct the assumed ancestral language of all those languages related to each other. Reconstructible words having to do with the natural environment of a prehistoric society facilitate determining the location of its ancestral homeland. Furthermore, the reconstruction of protowords may also throw light on features of a prehistoric culture not discoverable by other means. For example, the reconstructibility of certain kinship terms, such as those for in-laws, may provide clues to postmarital residence practices of the people who used them.

Reconstruction of an ancestral homeland location and other protocultural features on the basis of linguistic data is not a standard procedure, but when the archaeological record is insufficient or lacking, it may be the only means of probing the prehistoric past.

When languages are classified genetically, those that are related by virtue of a common origin are assigned to one language family. The original concept of a language family was conservative, requiring the relationships among the member languages of a family to be close and well documented. The tendency since the 1960s has been to group together languages that are considered to be much more remotely related. Such languages are said to constitute a phylum or even a superphylum (or macrophylum). The difference between the older conservative unit of language family and the newer phylum can best be illustrated by comparing numbers: The several hundred language families of the New World are reducible to only three superphyla.

Linguistic typology is based on similarities among languages other than those due to a common origin. Scholars engaged in finding common features or attributes in cross-linguistic diversity have taken various approaches as they attempt to assign to a relatively few basic types the many languages of the world.

Notes and Suggestions for Further Reading

For an up-to-date but technical introduction to and survey of historical linguistics, see Anttila 1989. Several thematic sections on the subject of this chapter are included in Crystal 1991a. Most of the Japanese examples come from Inoue 1979.

The reconstruction of the PIE word for cloud is based on Jeffers and Lehiste 1979. The example of the reconstruction of *snusós* has been abbreviated from the discussion by Calvert Watkins of the Indo-European lexicon and culture appended to *The American Heritage Dictionary of the English Language* (1992).

Sapir 1916 is not easily available, but the entire monograph is reprinted in Sapir 1949:389–462.

The number of North American language families and isolates is based on Voegelin and Voegelin 1966. Sapir's reduction of North American Indian language families to six "major linguistic groups" was published in 1929 in the *Encyclopaedia Britannica* (14th ed.) and reprinted in Sapir 1949:169–178.

8
Language Variation

People whose mother tongue is English have a great advantage over speakers of other languages. Not only is English the official or unofficial language in some eighty countries, but it is also favored as the language of international congresses, commercial negotiations, science journals, popular music, sports, civil aviation, diplomacy, technology and industry, and other undertakings or activities involving worldwide participation. Americans traveling abroad have become so accustomed to having foreigners communicate with them in English that they are surprised and even annoyed (unjustifiably) when these expectations are not met. In short, English has become the world's number one second language, even though resistance to it is growing in some parts of the Third World.

The primacy of English is of relatively recent date, deriving from the political, economic, scientific, and technological role the United States has come to play in the decades following World War II. During the Middle Ages, Latin served as the language of intellectual discourse in most countries of Europe even though it was no longer the first language of any speech community. French functioned as the "universal" language from the seventeenth through the nineteenth centuries by virtue of French political and intellectual influence, and it remained the preferred language of diplomacy until World War II.

Americans find it both flattering and convenient that so many people the world over have at least a working knowledge of English but give the matter little further thought—after all, they are used to traveling for thousands of miles in their own country and throughout much of Canada without a change in language. (Canada has two official languages, English and French. About one-fourth of Canadians, primarily natives of the province of Quebec, claim French as their mother tongue, and over 10 percent of Canadians speak a mother tongue that is neither English nor French.) In Europe the situation is strikingly different; there, traveling a mere 100 miles may involve crossing two or even three language boundaries. It is therefore not surprising that many young Europeans begin serious study of foreign languages, including English, in primary or secondary schools. (It should be noted that German is regaining some of the prestige it lost after World War II.)

According to a well-known Czech proverb, the number of languages a person knows, that many times is he or she a human being. Significant benefit indeed accrues to those who learn to speak more than just their mother tongue. They are not only made more aware of the workings of their own language but are far better able to appreciate and understand other cultures. The lack of skills in other languages on the part of young English-speaking Americans was recognized by the President's Commission on Foreign Language and International Studies, which in its final report stated that "Americans' scandalous incompetence in foreign languages also explains our dangerously inadequate understanding of world affairs" (1979:7).

As for cultural and linguistic anthropologists, any attempt on their part to conduct serious fieldwork in a foreign setting would be inconceivable without at least some knowledge of the language of those whom they study.

Idiolects, Dialects, and Styles

Strictly speaking, the speech pattern of one individual is somewhat different from the speech pattern of the next, even though the two speak the same language. This is why it is possible to identify over the telephone people we know well without their having to say who they are; similarly, we recognize familiar television newscasters even when we cannot see the screen. The recognition of individuals by voice alone is possible because of their idiosyncratic combination of voice quality, pronunciation, grammatical usage, and choice of words. Voice quality, or timbre, is determined by the anatomy of the vocal tract (the tongue, the nasal and oral cavities, the vocal cords, the larynx, and other parts), over which the speaker has little or no control. Other voice features—for example, tempo, loudness, and to some extent even pitch range—can be controlled fairly simply. But none of these features of an individual's speech pattern is constant. Voice quality changes with age as muscles and tissues deteriorate and the dentition undergoes modification. Over a lifetime changes tend to occur in the choice of words, grammar, and pronunciation as well.

An individual's speech variety is referred to as **idiolect**. Almost all speakers make use of several idiolects, depending on the circumstances of communication. For example, when family members talk to each other, their speech habits typically differ from those any one of them would use in, say, an interview with a prospective employer. The concept of idiolect refers to a very specific phenomenon—the speech variety, or linguistic system, used by a particular individual. All those idiolects that have enough in common to appear at least superficially alike belong to a dialect. The term **dialect,** then, is an abstraction: It refers to a form of language or speech used by members of a regional, ethnic, or social group. Dialects that are mutually intelligible belong to the same language. All languages spoken by more than one small homogeneous community are found to consist of two or more dialects.

Mutual intelligibility, of course, can vary as to degree. In the early 1950s, a number of men and women from eight reservations in New York and Ontario were tested in an experiment designed to determine which of their local dialects were mutually intelligible and therefore dialects of one language and which were not and therefore could be classified as individual languages of the Iroquoian language family. Even though the investigators arrived at percentages of intelligibility between any two of the Iroquoian speech communities, the question where the boundaries lay between intelligibility and unintelligibility remained unresolved. If the boundaries between language and dialect had been drawn at 25 percent of mutual intelligibility, there would have been four different languages, of which one would have consisted of two dialects and another of three. If set at 75 percent, there would have been five languages, two of which would have consisted of two dialects each.

Because it is spoken in so many different areas the world over, English is particularly diversified dialectally. Speakers' home countries may be guessed from their pronunciation and from the use of certain words that are characteristic of specific varieties of English. For example, included in the vocabulary of Australians is *bludger* 'loafer, shirker'; of Canadians *to book off* 'to notify an employer that one is not reporting for work'; of the Irish *spalpeen* 'rascal'; of the Scots *cutty sark* 'short (under)garment'; and of the British *to knock up* 'to wake up (someone), as by knocking on the window.' A speaker of any dialect of American English is likely to find it quite difficult to understand a cab driver in London who speaks cockney, the dialect of London's East End, even though both speak dialects of the same language.

English was brought to North America during the seventeenth century by colonists from England who settled along the Atlantic coast from Maine to Georgia. The language of these colonists consisted of dialects reflecting the social stratification and geographic division of their former home country. Today, despite regional differences (especially along the East Coast and in the South), American English exhibits a remarkable degree of uniformity. Historically this uniformity resulted from the mingling of settlers from various parts of the East as they pushed westward; since World War II it has been due to the ever-increasing mobility of Americans. Today very few people live in the communities in which they were born; most move from one place to another when they change jobs, marry, or retire. Nevertheless, certain regional dialects in the United States are well known and readily recognizable when heard—for example, those of Boston, Virginia, or Texas. Vocabulary may be just as helpful in identifying where older speakers from rural areas have come from. For example, the dragonfly is referred to in most of Virginia as *snake doctor*, in southwestern Pennsylvania as *snake feeder*, in eastern North Carolina as *mosquito hawk*, in New England as *(devil's) darning needle*, in coastal New Jersey as *spindle*, in northern California as *ear sewer*, and so on.

The way individuals speak varies not only according to their regional and social dialects but also according to context. The distinctive manner in which people express themselves in a particular situation is referred to as style. Speech styles are thus comparable to styles of dress. One would feel out of place and uncomfortable going on a hiking trip in formal attire or attending a traditional wedding reception in sneakers, jeans, and a sweatshirt. Similarly, a person who might use the vulgar expression "I'm pissed" when talking with former schoolmates would probably substitute the colloquial phrase "I'm mad" under other circumstances and use such words as "angry" or "aggravated" under more formal conditions.

Stylistic variations are not only lexical, as in the examples above, but also phonological (for instance, the casual pronunciation of *butter* with the flap [ɾ] rather than the dental [t]), morphological (as in the casually styled "Who are you taking to lunch?" as against the formal "Whom are you taking to lunch?"), and syntactic (as in "Wanna eat now?" as against "Do you want to eat now?"). A stylistic or dialectal variety of speech that does not call forth negative reaction, is used on formal occasions, and carries social prestige is considered **standard;** varieties that do not measure up to these norms are referred to as nonstandard or substandard. Standard British English, referred to as Received Standard (and its pronunciation as Received Pronunciation), is used at English public schools (private secondary boarding schools), heard during radio and television newscasts, and used when circumstances call for a serious, formal attitude (sermons, lectures, and the like). In less formal situations there has been an increasing tendency to use a style that deviates from or falls short of the standard. Informality in dress, behavior, and speech is a sign of the times both in the United States and elsewhere.

How many different styles do speakers of English use? According to Martin Joos (1907–1978), five clearly distinguishable styles were characteristic of his dialect of American English (spoken in the east central United States); he termed them frozen, formal, consultative, casual, and intimate (Joos 1962). Today, very few speakers of American English ever use the frozen style except perhaps occasionally in formal writing. The assumption that the exact number of speech styles can be determined for a language serving millions of speakers does not seem to be warranted. No two native speakers of English talk alike, and just exactly what use each person makes of the various stylistic features, ranging all the way from a pompous formality to an intimate or even vulgar informality, is up to the individual speaker.

Multilingualism, Diglossia, and Code-switching

A particular people is as a rule linked with a particular language, and it is this language more than anything else that serves as the people's badge of ethnic identity and uniqueness. As an example, the Plains Indian societies were similar in culture but quite distinct by virtue of the languages they spoke, some of which were as different from each other as English is from Russian or Japanese.

It used to be assumed that peoples who speak different languages have different cultures and therefore the boundaries between different societies coincide with lines separating mutually unintelligible languages; it was also widely accepted that any given language is the medium of communication for members of the corresponding society and that the relationship among language, culture, and communication tends to persist in time. Such assumptions greatly oversimplify matters, as has been shown by Dell Hymes (1968). According to Hymes, the world of human societies is divisible not so much according to the languages their members speak but rather according to communicative units "composed of repertoires of codes and rules of code-use," and it must further be recognized that these units overlap, that the criterion of mutual intelligibility is only one of several factors to be taken into account, and that the nature of the association between a particular code and particular cultural features must be considered on a case-by-case basis (Hymes 1968:42).

The following example is taken from an article by Hans Wolff (1967) and concerns the relationship of language, ethnic identity, and social change in southern Nigeria. In one part of the eastern Niger Delta live, from east to west, two coastal peoples—the Kalabari and the Nembe—and three hinterland peoples—the Abua, the Odual, and the Ogbia—five ethnic groups altogether. This five-unit ethnic division does not coincide with the language situation. The two coastal peoples speak closely related dialects of the Ijo branch of the Niger-Congo language family. The hinterland peoples speak related dialects of another language group. The Abua and Odual speak divergent dialects of the same language, with poor mutual intelligibility. However, four ethnically Odual villages speak a closely related but different language, Kugbo. To complicate matters further, the eastern dialects of Ogbia are not mutually intelligible with the western dialects but are intelligible with Kugbo. Although the three hinterland groups are aware of their close linguistic relationship, little communication takes place among them because of long-standing feuds over fishing rights and farmlands and because of different trading contacts in the past. Until recently, a great many of the Abua and Odual, especially the males, spoke Kalabari as their second language, whereas a large percentage of the western Ogbia spoke Nembe as a second language. Coastal languages were used in the interior on such important occasions as village gatherings and during Christian church services conducted by African clergy drawn from the coastal peoples. Yet the bilingualism found among the hinterland peoples was nonreciprocal: The coastal peoples did not learn or use the languages spoken by the Ogbia, Odual, or Abua. At the time of Wolff's visit to the area during the mid-1960s, the linguistic situation was undergoing change. Bilingualism continued to be present, with Igbo becoming the second language among the Abua. Another language increasingly used by those with formal education was English. At the same time, there was a concerted effort on the part of the hinterland peoples to use the local vernacular as the main, if not the only, medium of communication in order to achieve political recognition as distinct ethnic units.

Even from this simplified account of the situation it is evident that the existence of mutual intelligibility among some of the languages or dialects spoken by members of these ethnic groups had little significance with respect to their ethnic affiliation or the nature and volume of communication among them.

The second example is drawn from central Europe. The forefathers of contemporary Czechs and Slovaks were members of one political entity during the Great Moravian Empire. After the empire fell at the beginning of the tenth century, its Czech-speaking western part began a thousand-year-long separate historical development, whereas present-day Slovakia became an integral part of the Hungarian state. The Czechs and Slovaks were not again joined together politically until after World War I, when the Czechoslovak Republic was established in 1918. One of the reasons for assigning these two peoples to a common country was linguistic: Czechs and Slovaks speak mutually intelligible languages. In the new state, however, the attitude of the Czechs toward the much less urbanized Slovaks was patronizing, and the relationship between the two peoples remained asymmetrical until 1969, when the federalization of the republic helped to bring about some measure of balance.

During the course of the twentieth century, nationalist movements in Europe lost much of their force. The subsiding of nationalism was due to the increasing economic interdependence of one region on another; in Eastern Europe it was also the consequence of the internationalist character of Communist rule. After the collapse of Soviet control over Eastern Europe at the end of the 1980s, ethnic tensions in Czechoslovakia resurfaced and the Slovaks began to strive for either autonomy in a joint country with the Czechs or for complete independence. That Czechs and Slovaks are able to converse with one another using their two languages had little if any restraining effect on the desire of the numerically smaller Slovak people to emphasize their different historical experience and distinct ethnicity, more than seventy years of coexistence in a common state notwithstanding. The result was that the two peoples peacefully separated as of January 1, 1993, the former Czechoslovakia becoming two countries—the Czech Republic and Slovakia. And to the southeast of what was Czechoslovakia, in former Yugoslavia, peoples who for the most part speak the same or mutually intelligible languages or dialects but are of different cultural and religious backgrounds have gone so far as to resort to armed conflict costing many thousands of lives and causing wholesale migration of families from communities in which their ancestors had lived for centuries. (There are only a few minor vocabulary differences between what the Serbs and Croats speak. The major difference is the alphabet: The Serbs use the Cyrillic, the Croats the Latin.)

The identification between a sociopolitical unit and language does not hold for the state, a form of politically centralized society that usually encompasses within its boundaries several or even many ethnic groups, each with its own speech. The multilingual nature of both historic and modern states has been obscured because a state is ordinarily associated with the official or quasi-official language used by the majority of its citizens. In the former Soviet Union, for instance, Russian increasingly served as the common language throughout the country's vast area even though the number of its distinct nationalities was around 100 and most of their languages were actively used. In India, nearly three times as populous as the former Soviet Union but occupying an area only one-seventh as large, the number of different languages is reported to be almost 200. In the United Kingdom the number of minority languages presently in routine use exceeds 100, and in the United States close to 8 percent of the population regularly speak a language other than English. In several African countries that have a single official language, as many as nine out of every ten people are estimated to make regular use of more than one language.

If members of different ethnic groups live side by side and interact frequently, at least some of them learn to speak a language or languages other than their own mother tongue and thereby become multilingual. Multilingualism refers to the use or the ability to use two or more languages. The most common instance of multilingualism is bilingualism, characterized by the ability to speak two languages. Not everyone agrees on the definition of this term. Strictly speaking, bilinguals are individuals who have complete and equal command of two languages in all situations—in other words, those who are ambilingual, who pass for native speakers in either language. In practice, however, the term is applied more loosely, extending to those who can spontaneously produce meaningful utterances in a language other than their first.

Relatively stable bilingualism characterizes the situation in Switzerland, which accords national status to four languages—German, French, Italian, and Romansh—and where bilingualism is common and trilingualism far from rare. At the same time, none of the four languages thrives at the expense of the others despite the widely different percentages of their habitual speakers (German with over 65 percent, Romansh with less than 1 percent). In Canada, which in 1969 granted official status to both French and English, most bilingual Canadians live in the province of Quebec, where a large majority (over 81 percent in 1986) consider themselves French Canadians and are on guard against the spread of English at the expense of French, even though a great many of them (about 38 percent) speak both languages. A particularly interesting case of multilingualism exists among the Native Americans of northwestern Brazil and the adjacent part of Colombia (Sorensen 1967). Almost every member of at least twenty different tribes in a culturally homogeneous area is fluent in three, four, or more regional languages. The source of this phenomenon is strict tribal exogamy, a custom requiring marriage partners to be from different tribes, making multilingualism the cultural norm rather than the exception. Children first learn their parents' languages, acquire two or more additional ones during adolescence, and often learn still others in adulthood.

More commonly, though, multilingualism is a transitional and asymmetrical phenomenon. During the latter part of the nineteenth century, few working-class immigrants from continental Europe to the Americas learned to speak the language of their newly adopted country to any extent, if at all. Although many of their children used the language learned at school only as a second language, they nevertheless became bilingual or nearly so. By subsequent generations, however, only a few retained even limited passive acquaintance with the speech of their forebears. Much the same has been true of many Native Americans in the United States: The transition from their native languages to English through the intermediate stage of bilingualism has in many cases been accomplished in the course of this century, with only the oldest tribal members still possessing today a serviceable knowledge of their original speech. Where the concentration of immigrants maintains itself at a high level, bilingualism tends to persist longer. Many Latinos in the United States speak Spanish in the home and with compatriots but use English as the medium for contact with the larger society.

For some years now, efforts have been made to establish English as the official language of the United States (thus far, about half of the fifty states have done so, but these laws are largely symbolic). It has been suggested that a constitutional amendment be adopted to the effect that English is the official language of the United States, that laws mandating multilingual ballots and voting materials be repealed, and that funding for bilingual education be restricted to short-term transitional programs. Those who favor English as the official language maintain that they are not trying to discourage the use of languages other than English in the homes of recent immigrants or unacculturated adults of other ethnic backgrounds; they simply believe that the bond of a common language helps to promote unity in a country made up of people from every corner of the world.

On the other side of the argument are those who point to the First Amendment to the Constitution guaranteeing freedom of speech. They maintain that citizens of the United States should have the right to use the language in which they are most proficient. From an anthropological viewpoint, the value of diversity and gradual voluntary assimilation is preferable to the imposition of inflexible language laws that would try to produce a common culture by decree.

The range of languages or language varieties available to members of a sociopolitical unit varies from near uniformity in small, well-integrated societies to sizable repertoires in such multilingual nations as India, the former Soviet Union, or the United States. Between the two extremes lie those speech communities that have two markedly divergent forms of a language at their disposal, one colloquial (low) and the other formal (high). Such use of two varieties of a language by members of a speech community for two distinct sets of functions is referred to as **diglossia.** Of the two varieties, the colloquial typically is learned first and is used for ordinary conversation with relatives and friends or servants and workingpersons, in cartoons, popular radio and television programs, jokes, traditional narratives, and the like. The formal variety, which carries prestige, is taught in schools and assumes most of the literary, administrative, legal, and religious functions.

Instances of diglossia are fairly common. Those Swiss who use Standard German as their formal variety are fluent in the Swiss German dialect (Schwyzertütsch), the low variety, in addition to the other national languages they may have learned. Similarly, Classical Arabic, based on the standards of the Quran (Koran), complements in many countries the local or regional dialects of colloquial Arabic; and in Greece colloquial Greek is in use side by side with the literary form derived in large part from its classical ancestor. In actual speech, however, neither the two diglossic varieties nor the languages of a bilingual community are always kept strictly apart. Two Czechs in the United States conversing in Czech may use English words, phrases, or sentences whenever they feel more comfortable doing so—as in "Víš co? Popovídáme si pěkně u mě doma u piva. Ale než si vlezeme do subwaye, let's buy some pastrami and potato chips! [Here's an idea! Let's talk over beer at my place. But before we get on the subway, let's buy some pastrami and potato chips!]" Such changing from one language or language variety to another is termed **code-switching.**

Pidgins

Speakers of mutually unintelligible languages who wish to communicate with each other have a variety of means available to them. A widespread method of bridging the linguistic gap is to use a **lingua franca,** a language agreed upon as a medium of communication by people who speak different first languages. In present-day India, the English that spread with British imperialism frequently serves as a lingua franca among speakers of the many different languages native to the subcontinent. In the United States the language used for communication with members of the many different Native American tribes has been English, the speech of the dominant society. And in Kupwar, a southern Indian village with speakers of four separate languages—Marathi, Urdu, Kannada, and Telugu—where almost all male villagers are bilingual or multilingual, the speakers of the first three languages have been switching among them for so long that the structures of the local varieties of these languages have been brought very close together, making it easier for their speakers to communicate (Gumperz and Wilson 1971).

Yet another way in which individuals and groups interact across language boundaries is by means of a pidgin language, or **pidgin.** Typically, a pidgin originates when speakers of two or more mutually unintelligible languages develop a need to communicate with each other for certain limited or specialized purposes, especially trade. Because pidgins have a much narrower range of functions than the languages for which they substitute, they possess a limited vocabulary, and because they need to be learned rapidly for the sake of efficiency, they have a substantially reduced grammatical structure. From a sociocultural perspective, an important characteristic of a pidgin is that it does not serve as the native, or first, language of any particular group.

A pidgin is not the result of the same kind of development true languages are subject to: It tends to come about suddenly, as the need arises, and ceases to exist when no longer called upon to perform its original function. It may last as little as a dozen or so years; only infrequently does it outlast a century. In its phonology and morphology, a pidgin is invariably simpler than the first languages of those who use it, and the bulk of its lexicon is based on, or derived from, one of the languages in contact.

Although customarily associated with European colonialism, pidgins have developed whenever speakers of different languages have been in regular but limited contact. Among the examples that abound are the English-based China Coast Pidgin that may have originated as early as the seventeenth century but became especially widespread during the course of the nineteenth; the English-based Maori Pidgin current during the early years of British colonization of New Zealand; Trader Navajo, the Navajo-based pidgin used by traders in the Southwest; and the various Congo pidgins that facilitate contacts among the speakers of a variety of African languages used in the Congo River basin. Reflecting the impact of European colonialism during the eighteenth and nineteenth centuries, many of the former pidgins as well as those still in existence are English-, French-, Spanish-, Portuguese-, or Dutch-based.

A good illustration of the origin, succession, and demise of pidgins can be drawn from recent Vietnamese history. When Vietnam was ruled by the French as part of Indochina, a French-based pidgin was used by those French and Vietnamese who lacked command of the other's language. After the defeat of the French at Dien Bien Phu in 1954 and the evacuation of French forces from Vietnam two years later, the pidgin was no longer needed and became almost extinct. With the introduction of U.S. combat forces into the Republic of Vietnam in the early 1960s, an English-based pidgin rapidly developed to assume the role of its French-based predecessor. After the U.S. soldiers were withdrawn in 1973 and political events in 1975 brought the influence of the United States in Vietnam to an abrupt end, the new pidgin, too, all but disappeared.

Although they characteristically lack inflection and possess a limited vocabulary, pidgins have a structure of their own and readily adapt to changing circumstances. The structural simplicity of pidgins is to their advantage, allowing cross-cultural communication with a minimum of effort. The reduction or total elimination of inflectional affixes, the use of morphemic repetition for intensification, and simplified syntactic constructions make geographically separated pidgins look remarkably similar—so much so that some scholars have argued that in their basic structure all modern and recent pidgins may well go back to some such protopidgin as Sabir, the original lingua franca, a medieval pidgin based on Romance languages and used in Mediterranean ports until the beginning of this century. As similar as pidgins may be structurally, though, they differ according to the languages that have lexified them (that is, supplied them with the bulk of their word-stock).

From Pidgins to Creoles

The process of grammatical and lexical reduction of a language such as English or Navajo to a pidgin, referred to as pidginization, reflects a limitation on functions the pidgin is expected to serve. But it would be wrong to assume that the role pidgins are destined to play is invariably humble. In many instances, a pidgin has come to be used by a growing number of people over an increasingly large area, especially when none of the native languages can claim priority by virtue of population size or the prestige of a written tradition. In short, a pidgin may become widely recognized and depended upon as an indispensable means of interethnic communication. Under such circumstances, the growing demands placed on the pidgin cause an expansion of its vocabulary and elaboration of its syntax—a process opposite to pidginization. It may be furnished with a writing system and used in the mass media, it may acquire a semiofficial status, and it may even become the mother tongue of those children in whose families it is habitually used. This process of expansion of a pidgin to other language functions is referred to as creolization, and the end result is termed a **creole**. A creole, then, is a pidgin that has become the first language of a speech community.

Among the many places in the world where this process has taken place is Papua New Guinea. There what once was an English-based pidgin of limited utility has been elevated over the past several decades to one of the official languages of the now independent country (see Figure 8.1). Known as Neo-Melanesian, or Tok Pisin (from *talk pidgin*), it has become the lingua franca of about 1 million people who speak some 700 languages native to Papua New Guinea and the first language of some 20,000 households (Mühlhäusler 1987:178). Tok Pisin has acquired such prestige that more parliamentary debates are now conducted in it than in English, and most recently it has been heard even in the country's university lecture halls.

At least three-fourths of the Tok Pisin vocabulary derives from English, some 15 percent from indigenous New Guinea languages, especially Tolai (Kuanua), and the remainder from various other languages, including German. In the singular, Tok Pisin personal pronouns *mi* 'I, me,' *yu* 'you,' and *em* 'he, him; she, her; it' remain the same whether they serve as subject or object. In the first-person plural, the distinction is made between the inclusive form *yumi* 'we, us (including the hearer)' and the exclusive form *mipela* 'we, us (excluding the hearer),' and in all three persons of the plural the exact number (up to three) is usually indicated, as in *yutupela* 'you two' or *yutripela* 'you three'; the form *ol* for the third-person plural occurs in addition to the expected form. Possession is indicated by *bilong*, the predicate is commonly marked by the particle *i*, and transitive verbs have the suffix *-im*, which also converts adjectives into causative verb forms. Accordingly, "Mi kukim kaikai bilong mi" translates as "I cook my food," "Wanpela lek bilong mi i bruk" as "One of my legs is broken," "Em i krosim mi" as "He scolded me," and "Ol i kapsaitim bensin" as "They spilled the gasoline."

Namaliu tok orait long ol opisa go bek wok

OL SENIA pablik sevan na ol plis opisa husat i gat nem long ripot bilong piksa nogut bai kisim bek wok bilong ol.

Praim Minista Rabbie Namaliu i em moa gutpela nau bikos mejistret i askim pinis long kirapim wanpela wok painimaut long dispela ol muvi.

Em i tok dispela wok painimaut em bai nupela wok. Em i no wankain olsem ol plisman i wokim. Ministabilong Jastis, Bernard Narakobi i wok long skelim yet ripot. Mista Narakobi i

lukim pinis ripot orait bai tokim Praim Minista long wanem kain ol samting ol i ken mekim.

Mista Namaliu i tok ol wokman bai wok inap dispela wok painim i redi bai ol i kamap gen long kot.

FIGURE 8.1 Tok Pisin of Papua New Guinea. *Wantok,* the weekly newspaper of Papua New Guinea, is published almost exclusively in Tok Pisin.

A New Guinea road safety handbook (*Rot Sefti Long Niugini*), which instructs readers in three languages, contains the following English paragraph and the Tok Pisin equivalent:

> If you have an accident, get the other driver's number, if possible, get his name and address too, and report it to the police. Don't fight or abuse him.

> Sapos yu kisim bagarap, kisim namba bilong narapela draiva, sapos yu ken, kisim naim bilong em na adres tu, na tokim polis long em. Noken paitim em o tok nogut long em.

Even though creoles are languages in their own right and have in some instances found their way into the mass media as well as into primary school instruction, they nevertheless tend to carry less prestige than the standard European languages beside which they are used and from which they derive the bulk of their vocabulary. Consequently, some speakers of creoles, especially those who live in cities and hold semiprofessional jobs, try to "improve" their speech by using the standard language as a model. When this happens, creoles undergo a change, moving in the direction of the standard language in a process known as decreolization. Such a change is currently taking place, for example, in English-based Jamaican Creole, giving rise to a continuum ranging from the basilect, the variety most differentiated from the standard and used by members of the rural working class, to the acrolect, an urban variety approaching the standard and therefore seen as more prestigious.

The great majority of pidgins and creoles are found in coastal areas of the equatorial belt where contacts between speakers of different languages, including those of former European colonialist nations, have been a common occurrence because of trade. Some recent pidgins, however, have been developing under different circumstances—for example, the Gastarbeiter Deutsch spoken in the Federal Republic of Germany by several million guest workers from southern and southeastern Europe.

Pidgins and creoles have received the serious attention they deserve only during the past quarter of a century. Some of the most stimulating (but also controversial) contributions to their study have been made by Bickerton. One important concept based on the study of creoles is Bickerton's bioprogram hypothesis (1981), that is, the assumption that the human species must have a biologically innate capacity for language. (This hypothesis is very similar to the earlier innatist theory discussed in Chapter 2.) In support of this hypothesis, Bickerton links pidgins and creoles with children's language acquisition and language origins. Because the syntax of Hawaiian Creole English, with which Bickerton is well acquainted, shares many features in common with other creole languages, the cognitive strategies for deriving creoles from pidgins are so much alike as to be part of the human species-specific endowment. Furthermore, the innate capacities that enable children to learn a native language are also helpful to children as they expand a pidgin into a creole. According to Bickerton, some basic cognitive distinctions (such as specific vs. general and state vs. process) must have been established prior to the hominization process (development of human characteristics), and these distinctions are evident in the structure of creoles as well as in the earliest stages of language acquisition.

Some of the recent research concerning pidgins and creoles has resulted in the "blurring" of these two types of speech (Jourdan 1991). It is now accepted that both pidgin and creole varieties of a particular language can exist side by side and that a creole can become the main language of a speech community without becoming its native language. In other respects, however, our understanding of pidgins and creoles has improved because greater attention is being paid to the historical and socioeconomic contexts in which pidgins and creoles come into being (see Box. 8.1).

African-American English: Its Use and Characteristics

African-American English (AAE) is characterized by pronunciations, syntactic structures, and vocabulary associated with and used by a fairly large number of North American African-Americans. Some of those who speak AAE use it habitually and exclusively; others use it in certain situations, Standard English in others. As the speech of a sizable portion of a population living in a continent-sized area, AAE is no more uniform than the English spoken by other Americans: It exhibits a wide range of pronunciations and forms varying in the degree to which they differ from each other and from Standard English. Some AAE pronunciations charac-

---

BOX 8.1   Creolization of Tok Pisin

World War II greatly accelerated the spread of Tok Pisin within New Guinea. New Guinean males who were pressed into service by the various foreign armies had only Tok Pisin as a common language. In addition, there were extensive movements of indigenous populations during the war and Tok Pisin spread with them. Following the war, the traditional state of warfare or hostility between indigenous groups in Papua New Guinea was almost completely eliminated as a result of the continuous efforts of missionaries and the pacification programs of various foreign governments. This has enabled people to leave their native groups without the fear of being killed. Mobility is increasing considerably as transportation improves, and many people are leaving their home villages to seek employment and excitement in urban areas. When groups mix in this way, Tok Pisin is usually the only means of communication, except where Hiri Motu or English is spoken, and thus Tok Pisin is commonly used in public urban life in New Guinea. There are an increasing number of marriages between men and women from different linguistic groups. When such couples live in towns away from the home group of either partner they generally speak only Tok Pisin in the home, and their children acquire Tok Pisin as a native language. Such young native speakers now number in the thousands.

from Ellen B. Woolford, *Aspects of Tok Pisin Grammar* (1979), 3

---

terize southern speech in general, both black and white, although they are likely to occur in AAE with greater frequency or to a larger degree.

Spoken rather than written (with the exception of those writers who try to represent faithfully the AAE of their characters), AAE is used with great effect by African-Americans ranging from religious and civil rights leaders to school dropouts spending most of their time in the streets of black ghettos. Studies made of their speech have repeatedly established the importance assigned to verbal skills. Far from limited to ordinary communicative functions, AAE ranges from the narrative poetry of so-called toasts to the accommodating style of "shucking (it)" and "jiving" on the one hand and the aggressive verbal behavior referred to as "signifying" on the other.

Because of the dialectal variation that exists in AAE, only some of its most prominent and common characteristics are discussed below. One should not expect to find these features in the speech of all African-Americans, particularly some of those who have lived in the North for several generations. For the most part these features characterize the nonstandard variety of English spoken by lower-income African-Americans in urban ghettos of the northern United States and elsewhere, a variety referred to as **African-American Vernacular English** (AAVE).

In pronunciation, the vowels of AAVE tend to be much more variable than consonants. The most common vowel contrasts of Standard English that are likely to be lost are in such pairs as *pride* and *prod* or *find* and *fond* as well as *pride* and *proud* or *find* and *found*, which in AAVE tend to be pronounced alike. The loss of contrast in these and similar word pairs is usually limited to the position before the consonants *b, d, g, m, n, r,* and *l.* The words *oil* and *all* and similar word pairs also frequently sound alike in AAVE, in particular when vowels are followed by the consonant *l.* The vowels of *pin* and *pen* and of similar word pairs lose their contrast especially before the nasal consonant *n.* Finally, such word pairs as *fear* and *fair* and *sure* and *shore* may be pronounced alike; in all of these and like cases, the loss of vowel contrast is conditioned by the consonant *r* that follows the vowels.

The least stable consonants of AAVE are those found at the end of words. The sound written as *th* may be heard in the final position as *f*, making the words *both* and *with* rhyme with *loaf* and *sniff*, respectively. The consonants *r* and *l* tend to be weakened or are completely lost. Following a vowel, the weakened *r* makes such words as *sure, shoe,* and *show* or *your* and *you* sound alike or nearly so; *r* between vowels may be lost completely, leading to such pronunciations as *inte'estin', pass,* and *tess* for *interesting, Paris,* and *terrace*, respectively. A weakened *l* before a consonant may be heard in such words as *help* or *wolf;* when it is completely lost, such word pairs as *fooled* and *food, toll* and *toe,* or *bolt* and *boat* come to sound alike.

The stops *t* and *d* are quite commonly lost or modified after another consonant: Thus *last* may come to sound like *lass, mend* like *men, rift* like *riff,* and *told* like *toll.* Other final consonant clusters are frequently subject to similar simplification, resulting in the pronunciation *dess* for *desk* or *liss* for *lisp.* Other differences from Standard English are less generalizable: Speakers of AAVE, for example, say *axe* instead of *ask* and *'lectric* instead of *electric.*

Grammatical differences are usually more noticeable than differences in pronunciation or vocabulary. This is so because it is the use of "proper" grammar that is associated with a style of speaking considered prestigious and worthy of emulating. From the perspective of linguistic anthropology, the grammar used by the native speakers of any language variety cannot be termed incorrect, different though it may be from other dialects or the standard itself. Some of the features that differentiate the grammar of AAE from Standard English are to be found in the speech of non–African-Americans as well.

When compared to other European languages, English has very few inflectional suffixes; the tendency in AAVE is for even these few to be weakened or lost. The *-s* of the third-person singular is frequently lacking in AAVE verbs, as in "Johnny run" or "He eat meat." (Such occasional usages as "I hates this" represent an attempt to include mistakenly the *-s* where it does not belong—a hypercorrection.) The *-s* marking the possessive (spelled *'s*) may be lost, as in "Hand me that man coat"; in "They come back in they car," the possessive pronoun of the third-person plural has suffered the loss of a postvocalic *r*. The *-s* in the plural of nouns is retained, as in *desses* for *desks* after the simplification of the word-final consonant cluster *-sk* in the singular, but there is a tendency toward regularizing irregular plurals, that is, making use of such forms as *foots, mens,* and *childrens* for *feet, men,* and *children.*

The past tense of verbs is either retained, as in *gave* or *brung* (instead of *brought*); weakened, as in *kep* (instead of *kept*) or *toll* (instead of *told*); or lost altogether, as in "He pay me yesterday." When there is an option in Standard English to use a contraction, for example, "He is going" to "He's going," AAVE offers the additional option of full deletion of the form of *be,* resulting in "He going." When the option to contract does *not* exist in Standard English, as in the latter part of the sentence "That's the way it is here" (one would never say "That's the way it's here"), the option to delete the form of *be* likewise does not occur in AAVE, which would use "That the way it is [*or* be] here." The phrase *there is* that introduces a sentence or clause is replaced in AAVE by *it is* or the contractions *it's* or just *'s.*

In comparison with Standard English, AAVE is characterized by multiple negation, as in the following sentences that are to be understood as statements rather than questions: "Didn't nobody see it"; "Wasn't nobody home"; "Ain't nobody complainin' but you, man"; and "I don't got none."

The verb form *be,* as in "She be busy," contrasts in AAVE with its absence, as in the corresponding "She busy." The latter, "She busy," means that the person referred to is busy at the time the statement is made. "She be busy" denotes a habitual or repeated state of busyness, what in Standard English would be expressed as "She is always busy," "She keeps busy," or "She is often busy."

As for optional tenses, the situation of one particular variety of AAVE has been described as follows:

> *I do see him* is just anterior to the present and intrudes upon it, and is therefore the *past inceptive tense. I did see him* is slightly longer ago, or the *pre-present tense. I done seen him* is still further ago, or the *recent past. I been seen him* is even farther ago and designated as the *pre-recent past.* Moving ahead from the present, if someone says *I'm a-do it,* he will do it in approximately 30 seconds, or in the *immediate future.* If someone says *I'm a-gonna do it,* he will do it soon, that is, in the *post-immediate future.* If he says *I gonna do it,* however, the execution may be indefinitely delayed. (Fickett 1972:19)

AAVE further differs from Standard English in specialized vocabulary, variant stress patterns on certain words, and the like. Despite these and other features that set the two Englishes apart, however, the adjustment a nonspeaker of AAVE has to make in order to comprehend it is no more than the effort needed to understand cockney.

Scholars disagree on the current developmental tendencies in AAVE. Some believe that the long-standing but slow decreolization is continuing, that is, that the speech of African-Americans is converging with the English spoken by non–African-Americans. Others, including Labov, have reported that as a result of the increasing segregation and isolation of urban African-Americans from the rest of the society, and despite the homogenizing influence of the media on language, AAVE appears to be steadily diverging not only from Standard English but from regional and local white dialects as well. If this is so, children who speak it will encounter even more difficulties when at age six they enter an environment that uses a strikingly different code.

How African-American English Came About

This question is closely tied to the question, How do varieties of AAE relate to American English in general? Scholarly opinions on the subject vary. Some have argued that AAE is just another dialect of American English. They attempt to justify this interpretation by pointing out that none of the features of AAE departs significantly from those found in other dialects of English or from the historical development of English as a whole. For example, multiple negation, commonly referred to as the double negative, which today is frowned upon as one of the main sins against "good English grammar," was widely used in Elizabethan times; its retention in AAE can be interpreted as a conservative feature. By contrast, the loss of -s in the third-person singular can be viewed as the continuation of a tendency toward simplification that has characterized the English verb throughout its history. What AAE has done is to eliminate the last remaining suffix of the present-tense verb paradigm, something that may well happen in Standard English in the next few hundred years. (Simplification of Standard English continues unabated, as can be seen from the ever more frequent substitution of *I* for the object form of this pronoun, *me*, as in "between you and I," that can now be heard even from major network television anchors and U.S. congresspeople.)

Opposed to the dialectal interpretation is the contention that AAE is sufficiently distinct from and independent of Standard English to merit assignment to English-based creoles, where it would join company with Jamaican Creole and Gullah, the creole surviving in the Sea Islands off the coast of South Carolina and Georgia. Although AAE is today less divergent from Standard English than either Jamaican Creole or Gullah, a number of similarities between it and the two creoles are worth noting, for example, certain patterns of pronunciation, the loss of the third-person singular -*s* and the possessive '*s*, multiple negation, the zero copula (loss of inflected forms of *be*, as in "He rich"), some residual Africanisms, and others. Consequently, a real possibility exists that the process of creolization contributed to the formation of AAE.

The making of AAE dates back to the seventeenth century, when slave ships sailed from Bristol, Liverpool, and other English ports with cheap goods to be exchanged along the West African coast for Africans who in turn were sold as slaves in the Caribbean and the North American South for work on plantations. The ships would then return to England loaded with sugar, tobacco, cotton, and other commodities, and the cycle would be repeated. To minimize the risk of organized uprisings, the cargoes of future slaves were assembled from a variety of tribes speaking different languages. According to the revealing testimony of one Capt. William Smith in 1744,

> As for the Languages of *Gambia,* they are so many and so different, that the Natives, on either Side the River, cannot understand each other; which, if rightly consider'd, is no small Happiness to the *Europeans* who go thither to trade for Slaves; . . . the safest Way is to trade with the different Nations, . . . and having some of every Sort on board, there will be no more Likelihood of their succeeding in a Plot, than of finishing the Tower of *Babel.* (1744:28)

It is understandable that the need for a pidgin, or pidgins, developed even before the ships left the African coast: The captives had to find a means of communicating, at least about the most vital matters, not only with each other but with their captors and overseers as well. Even after the captives had been sold into slavery in the New World, the need for pidgins continued for reasons similar to those that gave rise to them in the first place. In the Louisiana area, the pidgin was French-based; elsewhere in the South, it was English-based. According to J. L. Dillard, one of the exponents of the creole hypothesis, "When new generations grew up which used only the pidgin, the pidgin became creolized . . . [to] Plantation Creole" (1972:22).

Which of the two interpretations is the more plausible, the dialectal or the creolist? According to Burling (1973), the evidence appears to support both in that AAE shares some features with Standard English and others with creoles such as Gullah and Jamaican. Figure 8.2 shows the complex interrelationships that Burling believes existed among the various forms of speech that are likely to have contributed to AAE.

African-American English: Myths and Facts

Without question, AAE is a much-stigmatized language variety. A great many people, regardless of ethnic background, consider it a badly corrupted, deficient form of English. If the various dialects of English are accorded different degrees of social prestige, Standard English ranks the

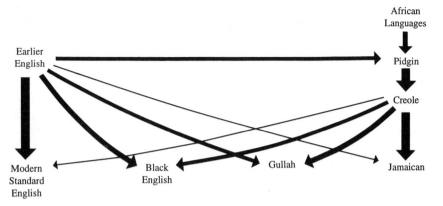

FIGURE 8.2 Languages That Shaped African-American (Black) English. In this diagram the four degrees of thickness of the arrows suggest the differential weight of influences that earlier forms of various languages have had upon later ones. *Source:* From Robbins Burling, *English in Black and White,* 122. Copyright © 1973 by Holt, Rinehart and Winston, Inc. Reprinted by permission of Holt, Rinehart and Winston.

highest, and AAE is among those that are least esteemed. The negative attitude toward AAE in U.S. society is in part reinforced by the low socioeconomic status of many African-Americans resulting from a longstanding pattern of racial discrimination.

Many people believe, and even some educators and educational psychologists have claimed, that African-American children from urban ghettos in particular are verbally deprived. These children are said to mispronounce words, slur endings, and mumble; to answer in monosyllables or incomplete sentences replete with grammatical errors; to make use of a very limited vocabulary; and in general to use English sloppily and illogically. There is further a widespread belief that the use of the nonstandard vernacular is a serious obstacle to learning, with a few members of the academic profession going so far as to use the verbal performance of ghetto pupils in testing situations as evidence of genetic inferiority. But is there in fact anything wrong with AAE? Let us briefly review the evidence.

Rather than being simply a random and corrupted version of Standard English, AAE is just as rule-governed as other forms of English, but the rules that characterize its usage are, as may be expected, somewhat different. We have already seen that, for example, it uses multiple negatives and dispenses with the third-person singular marker -s in verbs, and yet the meaning of what is being said is never in question. The absence of a linking verb between subject and predicate, as in "He tired," is not a sign of corrupted speech or laziness on the part of AAE speakers; the same grammatical construction is found in many other languages of the world, Russian among them.

Careless diction and slurring of word endings are not, of course, limited to speakers of any particular dialect or language but are largely a function of speech tempo and sociocultural setting. Similarly, to fault children for answering such questions as "Where is the squirrel?" with "In the tree" rather than the full "The squirrel is in the tree" is nothing short of pedantry (Labov 1970:5). The vocabulary of a habitual speaker of AAE cannot be expected to coincide with that of a speaker of Standard English, but not to acknowledge the expressiveness that characterizes African-American verbal performances is to display prejudice or ignorance.

In a widely known and frequently reprinted article, Labov (1970) has convincingly identified the main sources of misconceptions concerning the nature of AAE. African-American children indeed respond defensively to a strange white interviewer (even when he or she is friendly), giving monosyllabic answers if they find the setting or experience unfamiliar or intimidating. Once the sociolinguistic factors operating in this inherently asymmetrical situation have been removed, though, these same children produce a steady stream of speech, effectively using the various stylistic devices AAE has to offer.

In the same article Labov quotes an interview conducted with Larry H., a fifteen-year-old African-American youth from Harlem. For someone who was put back from the eleventh grade to the ninth and who has also been threatened with disciplinary action, Larry displays a remarkable ability to think acutely and argue logically (see Box 8.2).

It is one thing to say that AAE enjoys little prestige among the great majority of Americans and that under certain circumstances those who use it are at a disadvantage compared with those who use a dialect of English that is socially more acceptable. It is another thing, however, to claim that AAE is a form of speech deficient in structure as well as lexically and stylistically impoverished. That is simply not true.

Nevertheless, the social and educational implications of the existence and use of AAE will be receiving national as well as local attention for years to come, and these implications are likely to generate controversies. The most recent case in point was the Oakland (California) School Board resolution unanimously passed on December 18, 1996.

The "whereases" of the resolution included statements that "numerous validated scholarly studies demonstrate that African-American students as a part of their culture and history [as] an African people possess and utilize a language described in various scholarly approaches as 'Ebonics' (literally 'Black sounds')" and that "these studies have also demonstrated that African Language Systems are genetically based and not a dialect of English"; and it was therefore resolved (among other things) that "the Superintendent in conjunction with her staff shall immediately devise and implement the best possible academic program for imparting instruction to African-American students in their primary language for the combined

**BOX 8.2   African-American English in Action:
A Fifteen-year-old Speaks**

INTERVIEWER: What happens to you after you die? Do you know?
LARRY: Yeah, I know.
I: What?
LARRY: After they put you in the ground, your body turns into—ah—
bones, an' shit.
I: What happens to your spirit?
LARRY: Your spirit—soon as you die, your spirit leaves you.
I: And where does the spirit go?
LARRY: Well, it all depends …
I: On what?
LARRY: You know, like some people say if you're good an' shit, your
spirit goin' t'heaven … 'n' if you bad, your spirit goin' to hell. Well, bull-
shit! Your spirit goin' to hell anyway, good or bad.
I: Why?
LARRY: Why? I'll tell you why. 'Cause, you see, doesn' nobody really
know that it's a God, y'know, 'cause I mean I have seen black gods,
pink gods, white gods, all color gods, and don't nobody know it's really a
God. An' when they be sayin' if you good, you goin' t'heaven, tha's bull-
shit, 'cause you ain't goin' to no heaven, 'cause it ain't no heaven for
you to go to.
I: Well, if there's no heaven, how could there be a hell?
LARRY: I mean—ye-eah. Well, let me tell you, it ain't no hell, 'cause
this is hell right here, y'know!
I: This is hell?
LARRY: Yeah, this is hell right here!
I: … But, just say that there is a God, what color is he? White or
black?
LARRY: Well, if it is a God … I wouldn' know what color, I couldn'
say,—couldn' nobody say what color he is or really *would* be.
I: But now, jus' suppose there was a God—
LARRY: Unless'n they say …
I: No, I was jus' sayin' jus' suppose there is a God, would he be white
or black?
LARRY: … He'd be white, man.
I: Why?
LARRY: Why? I'll tell you why. 'Cause the average whitey out here got
everything, you dig? And the nigger ain't got shit, y'know? Y'understan'?
So—um—for—in order for *that* to happen, you know it ain't no black
God that's doin' that bullshit.

from William Labov, "The Logic of Nonstandard English"
(1970), 12–15

purposes of maintaining the legitimacy and richness of such language whether it is known as 'Ebonics' [or] 'African Language Systems' . . . and to facilitate their acquisition and mastery of English language skills. . . ."

Some of the phrasing of the resolution was false (that language systems are genetically based), and some could easily be misunderstood (that the schools of the Oakland Unified School District could [or should?] implement a program of instructing African-American students in various subjects by using Ebonics as the language of instruction). The dean of the Graduate School of Arts and Sciences at Howard University, himself an African-American, was quoted as saying that "it is criminal to graduate African American students who cannot speak and write standard English."

Presentation of the Ebonics controversy is of necessity greatly abbreviated here, but at least the following points would seem to merit emphasizing: (1) There is no question that so-called Ebonics is one among many variations of English and, more specifically, of AAE; (2) not helping African-American students to become proficient in Standard American English will do them socioeconomic disservice; (3) it might be helpful to use Ebonics in some manner with students who speak it if doing so would aid them in learning Standard English; and (4) competence in more than one language or dialect is an asset.

Men-of-words

Public speaking and the tradition of eloquence among African-Americans are of long standing, but appreciative studies of their verbal art and the various genres to which it has been applied are of relatively recent date. One scholar who has written a number of insightful essays on the art of speaking among African-Americans is Roger D. Abrahams. Some of the street performers whom Abrahams remembers from the late 1950s were such good talkers that he felt they deserved a term that would recognize their skills (see Box 8.3 for the source of this section's title).

Abrahams originally believed that men-of-words were to be found only in the urban areas of the United States. His subsequent fieldwork during the 1960s and 1970s in communities of the southern United States and on the islands of Nevis, St. Kitts, St. Vincent, and Tobago in the West Indies convinced him that men-of-words can be found in most African-American communities. Some of Abrahams's best essays on the subject were republished in 1983 under the title *The Man-of-Words in the West Indies* and subtitled *Performance and the Emergence of Creole Culture*.

Among the genres and styles of African-American verbal art Abrahams discusses and exemplifies are "playing the dozens" or "sounding" (commonly referred to in the West Indies as "rhyming"), "good talking" or "talking sweet," "broad talking" or "talking bad," "rapping" or "signifying" ("giving rag," "making mock," or "giving fatigue" in the West Indies),

---

BOX 8.3 Men-of-words

In 1958 and 1959, while living in a predominantly black neighborhood in South Philadelphia, I observed a number of traditional performances and began to perceive a pattern of traits in the roles played by the performer, his relation to his material and his audience, and in the audience's attitude toward the performer and his enactment. This pattern centered upon the acclaim given those individuals who were good at using words—individuals I came to call "men-of-words." Significant in their performances was the way in which these artful narrators became closely identified with the style and action of the heroes they described. The audience seemed almost as fully involved, physically and verbally, in the enactment as the speaker. My examination of how this situation was structured centered upon the relative lack of psychic distance between the performer and his performance and between the audience and the described actions. A further trait inducing this strong sense of sympathetic involvement and vicarious identification was the repeated and insistent use of the first-person singular pronouns by the man-of-words. ... Finally, it became clear that these performances almost always arose in contests with other men-of-words, and that such contests were a community-accepted manner of establishing and maintaining a public (or *street*) reputation.

from Roger D. Abrahams, *The Man-of-words*
in the West Indies (1983), 2

---

storytelling, and gossiping. The occasions on which these and other genres are used include Christmas, carnival, wakes, courtship, send-offs, weddings, christenings, tea meetings (a combination of variety show and church social), and church services. The West Indians use two basic codes—high and low—and consider each appropriate for different types of situations. The high ("talking good" or "sweet") is an approximation of formal Standard English and is decorous and ornamental. The low ("talking broken," "bad," or "broad") makes use of West Indian Creole; abounds in ambiguity, puns, derision, and wit; and is characterized by very fast delivery.

The World of Languages

It may come as a surprise to learn that no one knows exactly how many languages are spoken in the world today. As mentioned in Chapter 7, a good rough estimate sets the total somewhere between 5,000 and 6,000. This number includes creole languages but excludes pidgins, as well as the thousands of languages in the course of history and prehistory that must have disappeared without a trace. There are several reasons for the lack of precision in gauging the world's linguistic diversity. A few languages are likely to be discovered in those regions of the world still only partly explored, especially the equatorial rain forests of South America, Africa, and New Guinea. Some languages are on the very verge of extinction, currently used by as few as a handful of speakers and not even habitually at that. Then, too, it is not always easy to determine whether two dialects are sufficiently divergent to become mutually unintelligible and therefore merit the status of two separate languages. In this respect, sociocultural considerations sometimes override the linguistic criterion of mutual intelligibility. For example, Czechs and Slovaks communicate with one another in their respective languages without the slightest hindrance, although Czech and Slovak have separate standards and literary traditions as well as dictionaries and textbooks. If these two languages were to be spoken in nearby villages somewhere in New Guinea, they would unquestionably be classified as two dialects of one language. As for the number of dialects of the languages currently spoken in the world, the total would reach tens of thousands if anyone were interested in making such a count.

The figure of 5,000 (or more) languages amounts to an impressive number when one considers that each represents a distinct means of communication with its own elaborate structure and unique way of describing the cultural universe of its speakers. However, in terms of the numbers of speakers, the great bulk of today's world population makes use of relatively few languages. It is obvious that at this point in human history, speakers of some languages have been more successful than speakers of others, whether by conquest, historical accident, or some other circumstance. The greatly uneven distribution of speakers of the world's languages is graphically represented in Figure 8.3.

This rapid global survey, which has included only natural languages, would be somewhat incomplete if we were to neglect the existence of artificial, or auxiliary, languages invented to facilitate international communication. Although several hundred are known to have been devised over the past several centuries, only a few have achieved any measure of acceptance and use, with Esperanto, already over 100 years old, the most widespread. Despite efforts to make Esperanto the official international language, however, English, the mother tongue of some 350 million speakers and the official or semiofficial language serving an additional billion people in the world, appears today to have little if any serious competition.

Summary and Conclusions

Although about 5,000 to 6,000 languages, assignable to several hundred language groups (families), are currently spoken, the overwhelming majority of people speak languages that belong to only a dozen or so

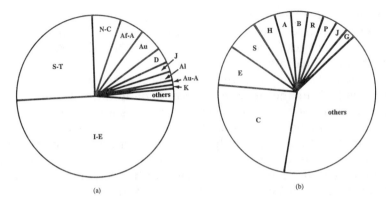

FIGURE 8.3 The World's Languages and Their Speakers. The estimated relative numbers of speakers belonging to the top ten language groups (families) are graphically represented in (a). The following abbreviations are used:

I-E	Indo-European: most of the languages spoken in Europe, several of which have spread to other parts of the world, as well as some languages spoken in India and southwestern Asia
S-T	Sino-Tibetan: various Tibetan, Burmese, and Chinese languages spoken in southeastern Asia
N-C	Niger-Congo: most of the languages spoken in western, central, and southern Africa, including the Bantu languages
Af-A	Afro-Asiatic: various Semitic, Berber, Cushitic, and Chadic languages spoken in northern Africa and southwestern Asia, as well as extinct (Ancient) Egyptian
Au	Austronesian: languages spoken in the vast area extending from Madagascar eastward through the Malay Peninsula to Hawaii and Easter Island
D	Dravidian: languages spoken primarily in southern India and parts of Sri Lanka
J	Japanese: the language of Japan, considered by some scholars to be distantly related to the Altaic family
Al	Altaic: languages spoken from Turkey in the west across central Asia into Siberia
Au-A	Austroasiatic: languages spoken for the most part in southeastern Asia (Laos, Vietnam, and Cambodia) but also in some parts of India
K	Korean: the language of the two Koreas, considered by some scholars to be distantly related to Japanese or the Altaic family
Others:	a great variety of languages belonging to numerous language groups and spoken in Eurasia, Africa, and Australia as well as all native languages of the New World—altogether nearly 3,000 languages, or half of the world's total

The estimated relative numbers of speakers of the top ten mother tongues are graphically represented in descending order in (b). The following abbreviations are used: C = Chinese (languages or dialects); E = English; S = Spanish; H = Hindi; A = Arabic; B = Bengali; R = Russian; P = Portuguese; J = Japanese; G = German; the others include the remaining 5,000 to 6,000 languages of the world.

The top ten official or semiofficial languages serving the largest number of speakers are, in descending order: English, Chinese, Hindi, Spanish, Russian, French, Arabic, Portuguese, Malay (including Indonesian), and Bengali.

Based on data provided in David Crystal, *The Cambridge Encyclopedia of Language* (Cambridge, UK: Cambridge University Press, 1991).

language families, with Indo-European at the top of the list for most speakers. The worldwide spread of English and various other European languages dates back to the beginning of the Age of Discovery in the middle of the fifteenth century.

Competency in one language only, typical of most Americans with English as their mother tongue, is uncommon in the rest of the world, where hundreds of millions of people are able to speak several languages or language varieties—that is, are multilingual or diglossic. Among the great variety of languages, pidgins occupy a special place: Although structured and efficient as a means of communication, their vocabularies are limited because pidgins are not called upon to perform the broad range of functions that characterize full-fledged languages.

Even though many people speak only one language, they are actively or at least passively acquainted with several dialects and speech styles of that language. Their own speech patterns differ from those of others, even if slightly. All speakers have their individual idiolects. One distinctive variety of English, spoken in the United States is African-American Vernacular English, used primarily by African-Americans in ghettos of large urban centers. Far from being deficient and its speakers verbally deprived, AAVE has its own structure, related to but distinct from other varieties of English, and a range of very expressive styles. The stigma attached to it is misplaced because it confuses the low socioeconomic status of the African-Americans who use it with their speech—a good example of ignorance breeding prejudice, which is only one step from discrimination.

Notes and Suggestions for Further Reading

The procedures used to measure the mutual intelligibility among Iroquoian languages are described in an article by Hickerson, Turner, and Hickerson 1952. The term *diglossia* was coined by Ferguson (1959).

The origin of the word *pidgin* is not known for certain, although it is usually considered to be a Chinese mispronunciation of the English word *business*. A recent survey has identified well over 100 pidgins and creoles the world over, including some that are now extinct. This figure should be viewed as a conservative estimate, as many pidgins must have ceased to exist without any record and some of the creoles of the past are no longer identifiable as such.

An excellent recent guide to the study of pidgin and creole languages is Romaine 1988; a shorter and more popular introduction to pidgins is Hall 1959; the theory and structure of pidgins and creoles is the subject of Holm 1988. For a survey of pidgin and creole studies through the mid-1970s, with a bibliography, see Bickerton 1976, and for an update, see Jourdan 1991. For a brief and more popularly written article on creole languages, see Bickerton 1983. A critical, partly negative evaluation of Bickerton's bioprogram hypothesis is to be found in Mühlhäusler 1986 and Romaine 1988.

The Tok Pisin examples are from Woolford 1979; the short text is taken from Todd 1984:65.

The sections concerning African-American English draw heavily on Burling 1973. In comparing African-American Vernacular English with Standard English, linguists use such expressions as *loss of* and *weakened* in their technical linguistic senses; they are not to be construed as carrying negative connotations. Weakening and losses have characterized the history of English inflections from Old English to the present, and no one has ever claimed that Modern English is the worse for it. For a survey of literature concerning the features of African-American English, theories of its origin, and several related topics, see Morgan 1994, and for a discussion of the Ebonics issue, see Fields 1997.

9

Language in Its Social Context

The degree of variation that characterizes the speech of a people differs from one society to another. The speech of members of a small, well-integrated tribal group residing in a highly circumscribed area is likely to be much less differentiated than the speech of citizens of a populous society inhabiting a large territory. But it is not simply regional differences that are reflected in speech; varieties of speech may also be due to differences in religion, socioeconomic background, education, sex (gender), or other factors. In this chapter the emphasis is on the relationship between speech or language on the one hand and society on the other. We are not concerned here with the relationship between language and culture—more specifically, the worldview and common values of a people—but with language and society—that is, the links and networks that join or separate individuals or groups within a common societal framework. The branch of linguistics that studies the many aspects of the relationship between society and language is **sociolinguistics.** Susan Philips has defined sociolinguistics briefly but aptly as the "study of the ways in which a person's speech conveys social information" (Philips 1980:523).

Because speech is an essential lubricant for the functioning of a society, speech differences are good indicators and sometimes even causes of social distinctness. Social distinctness tends to be especially pronounced in such multiethnic nations as India or Nigeria, in which a variety of different languages are spoken. Writing about the social structure of the Kachins of highland Myanmar (formerly Burma), E. R. Leach (1954:49) observes that "for a man to speak one language rather than another is a ritual act, it is a statement about one's personal status; to speak the same language as one's neighbours expresses solidarity with those neighbours, to speak a different language from one's neighbours expresses social distance or even hostility." In short, languages and styles of speech are prominent badges of ethnic and social identity, and anthropologists and other social scientists must take them into careful consideration.

Taboo Words, Politeness, and Deference

The word *taboo* (also spelled *tabu*) was first used by Captain James Cook in 1777 in his journal; he had heard the word from speakers of Tongan, a Polynesian language. It referred originally to persons, activities (including speech), or things under prohibition. After it was borrowed into English, it acquired in addition to 'dangerous' or 'sacred' the sense 'avoided or banned by social custom on grounds of morality or taste.' Our concern here is with examples of what are referred to as word taboos.

The subject matter to which verbal references are taboo varies from culture to culture. It has been quite common in societies around the world and in North America in particular, to avoid or forbid the use of the names of the dead. Among some Northern Paiutes (a Native American people of eastern Oregon, western Nevada, and northeastern California), such use was permanently forbidden; among the Carriers (in southwestern Canada) it was forbidden for a generation; among the Maidu (in northeastern California) for about a year; and among the Pawnees (who now live in Oklahoma) for the period of mourning. According to informants, the taboo on these names was (and may still be) due to respect for the bereaved or fear of the dead. Consequently, any violation of the restrictions on the use of names of the dead was considered a punishable offense. In some cases the matter of name avoidance was taken so seriously that a living person who happened to have the same name as the deceased was expected to change his or her name (this was so among the Walapai, Washoe, Bella Bella, and others). And for some Native American tribes (Nootka, Wishram, Hupa, Mescalero Apache, and others), even common words that were the same as or similar to the names of deceased persons were banned from ordinary use.

In Slavic languages the word for bear is a euphemistic substitute for what would have developed from the ancient Indo-European word for the animal, reconstructed as *$r̥$tko- (regular development took place in Greek [*arktos*] and Latin [*ursus*]). In Czech, for example, the word for bear is *medvěd* 'honey eater,' as it also is in Russian (*medved'*) and other Slavic languages. Apparently the ancient speakers of Slavic languages were afraid to utter aloud the bear's true name for fear its magical powers would be summoned. In English and German, the words for bear were derived from an old word meaning 'brown.' Germanic peoples must also have spoken of the bear indirectly—out of respect and fear—calling him "the brown one."

Over time, the vocabulary of any language undergoes changes. Those words that become subject to taboo disappear either permanently or for a period of time, and euphemisms replace them. Instances of this kind sometimes provide anthropologists with information about beliefs that were of some importance to people in prehistoric times—the word 'bear' is a case in point. But tabooing of words still exists today, primarily to avoid the use of expletives: 'Rooster' is substituted for 'cock,' 'donkey' for 'ass,' 'heck' for 'hell,' and 'shoot' for 'shit.'

Then there are swearwords—the irreverent use of sacred names and obscene language, the so-called four-letter words in English. In modern complex societies such words are not usually considered taboo by all members and under all circumstances. Most members of the U.S. middle class, for example, have tended to avoid them, especially in public or in mixed company, but all inhibitions tend to disappear for such an event as an all-male camping trip or a bachelor party. In general, the number of words considered obscene and therefore taboo in English has been rapidly decreasing. It took almost thirty years for D. H. Lawrence's notorious *Lady Chatterley's Lover,* originally published in Florence in 1928, to become available in the United States. In the past several decades, however, the offensive words used in that novel have become part of every person's passive vocabulary as well as part of the active vocabulary of millions, and they have now found their way into every comprehensive dictionary of the English language. First the occasional and later the frequent use of taboo words reduces their tabooness. Once these words are no longer censured, their use becomes merely a matter of taste or style.

In the past two decades a number of studies have focused on how politeness is expressed in language and who is polite to whom and why. The several studies undertaken thus far indicate that women are more polite than men, but of course there are exceptions: Among the Malagasy of Madagascar, for example, women's speech is characterized by abruptness and directness, breaking the cultural norms of nonconfrontation and playing down self; men, by contrast, endeavor to speak with care and gentleness, and their oratorical and poetic skills are highly prized.

That there is a good reason for research interest in politeness was summed up by John J. Gumperz in his foreword to a work devoted to politeness: "Politeness . . . is basic to the production of social order, and a precondition of human cooperation, so that any theory which provides an understanding of this phenomenon at the same time goes to the foundation of human social life" (Brown and Levinson 1987:xiii). What is or is not considered polite in any given context and what verbal form politeness takes vary from society to society and from one language to another. Some cultures value directness ("Would you please close the door?"); others prefer roundabout speech ("It seems to be getting a bit cold in here, don't you think?"). The main contribution of Penelope Brown and Stephen C. Levinson has been to look for cross-linguistic and cross-cultural universal features. For instance, they have attempted to show how certain counterparts in usage in different languages derive from assumptions about self-esteem or dignity (face, as in "he is afraid he will lose face"), and they distinguish among three main strategies of politeness: positive politeness, to express solidarity; negative politeness, to express restraint; and off-record politeness, to express ambiguity and allow negotiation (including denial). Each of these sets of strategies is tied to the relationship between the speaker and the addressee. Among examples of positive politeness is the use of an in-group identity marker ("Help me with this bag, will you, pal?") or the expression of optimism ("Look, I'm sure you won't mind if I borrow your typewriter"). Negative politeness may be exemplified by questions or hedges ("Do me a favor, will you?") or an apology ("I don't want to bother you, but . . .")—requests worded in these ways make it easier for the addressee to avoid cooperating. An off-record polite remark can use irony or vagueness (as in "Looks like someone may have had too much to drink") to make a point. To present corresponding examples in other languages, the authors use Tzeltal (spoken in Chiapas, Mexico) and Tamil (spoken in southeastern India and Sri Lanka).

Questions have been raised as to whether the "face-saving approach" is as universally applicable as Brown and Levinson had hoped. If it were so, then the meaning of politeness and self (face) would have to be fairly uniform across cultures and the relationship between the two much less complex than it has been found to be. It certainly has been recognized that such factors as age and gender do not weigh equally in all societies, and sometimes not even among members of the same society. For example, age matters more in Asian countries than in the United States, and in the United States older individuals accord more deference and courtesy to women than do younger ones. And, finally, the examples given by Brown and Levinson are isolated utterances divorced from the discourse (context) in which they are embedded, and the authors' theory is therefore a list of devices rather than strategies to be used in concrete situations.

Politeness—that is, consideration, courtesy, and tact—is expected among all members of many societies regardless of age or position. The term *deference* is more circumscribed: It refers to the respect accorded persons because of age or superior status. And the term *honorific* refers to a linguistic form used to express deference toward an addressee or a person spoken of. An honorific is therefore a respectful term of address or reference that is culturally required. Honorifics are not used in all languages but are highly developed in Asian languages—for example, in Thai, Japanese, and Korean. The most basic and widespread forms of honorifics occur in salutations. In English they include *Mr., Mrs., Ms., Doctor, Your Eminence* (to cardinals), *Reverend Father* (to priests), *Your Honor* (to judges), *Madame Ambassador* (to foreign woman ambassadors), and many others.

Japanese serves as a good example of a language in which deferential language is very highly developed. When addressing individuals by their proper names, one adds -*san*, as in *Suzuki-san* or *Suzuki Jiroo-san* (when *Jiroo* is the first name). A formal expression of respect is indicated by the suffix -*sama*, and an expression of affection frequently added to children's first names is -*chan*; teachers, doctors, politicians, and members of some other professions are addressed by adding -*sensei* 'teacher' to their names.

A wide range of personal pronoun forms is used in Japanese, some by both men and women, others only by men. For example, the second-person forms ("you") include *anata* (standard, polite, not used to address an individual of higher status), *anta* (informal), *sochira* (very formal and polite), *kimi* (mostly by a man to another man of equal or lower status), *kisama* (derogatory), and others. To honor someone in Japanese, one may choose not only the most appropriate honoring expression but also a humble expression, by means of which the speaker elevates another person by professing his or her own insignificance.

What has just been described is a highly simplified account of the honorific grammar of Japanese. The full system of deferential expressions is so complex that even native speakers of Japanese sometimes find it difficult to use the most appropriate form. In part this is so because the speaker is not always prepared to evaluate his or her relation to others at a moment's notice; then, too, a speaker's status changes during his or her lifetime, as does the status of the addressee or the person spoken of. And, finally, it should be noted that the style of young people is much less deferential than that of their parents and grandparents. Today, young people tend to be informal everywhere.

After this brief general discussion of how awe and respect are reflected in speech, let us look in more detail at forms of address and greeting and the many factors speakers of Javanese have to take into consideration before they utter even a simple sentence.

Forms of Address and Greeting

As we have seen, in some languages an individual's social position with respect to others is conveyed by the choice of the personal pronoun, the corresponding verb form, or both. However, in some languages a person's social position is indicated instead, or in addition, by the form of address or greeting used when that person communicates directly with another.

The term *form of address* designates the word or words used to refer to someone who is spoken or written to. In most cases, speakers of American English address each other by first name, title (or rank) and last name, or kin term. "Come on over and join us, Bill" is an example of form of address by first name; "When should I have my next physical examination, Dr. Smith?" or "Did anyone call while I was gone, Mrs. Brown?" by title and last name; and "What are we having for dinner, Mother?" by kin term.

Forms of address are often omitted, especially among close friends or relatives (as in "Quit nagging me, will you?") or when addressing a stranger (as when saying to an airline passenger in the adjacent seat, "Would you mind if I had a look at that magazine when you are finished with it?").

In general, the first-name address form is used reciprocally by speakers of American English when two individuals are of similar age and social status. The reciprocal title-and-last-name pattern is characteristic only of formal exchanges. The nonreciprocal pattern—when someone addresses another person by first name but is addressed in return by title and last name—is used in exchanges between individuals who differ significantly either in age or social and occupational status. But departures from these general rules are commonly found in individual practice as well as regionally. For example, either reciprocity or nonreciprocity in address forms may be heard between a cleaning woman and her woman employer.

Even in those countries where all citizens are said to be equal because of the presumed classlessness of their societies, forms of address that include titles have managed to keep their importance. The term *comrade,* which commonly applies not only to members of the Communist party but also to members of labor unions and certain other organizations, is frequently followed by a title that acknowledges the position of the addressee in the bureaucratic hierarchy ("Comrade Chairman," "Comrade Director"). In some countries a man's title is ordinarily extended to the form of address used for his wife (but not the other way around). In Czech, for example, a physician's or director's wife is commonly addressed as *paní doktorová* 'Mrs. Doctor' or *paní ředitelová* 'Mrs. Director.' This general custom has persisted even though it was ridiculed some years ago by the humorous address form *paní vrchní krotitelová lvovová* 'Mrs. Chief Lion Tamer,' which in theory could be used to refer to a chief lion tamer's wife.

In a country as large and ethnically heterogeneous as the United States, no single system of forms of address applies across the board, and one must therefore specify what segment of population is being referred to and under what circumstances certain forms of address are to be expected. According to Susan Ervin-Tripp (1969), the form of address system valid (in the late 1960s) for "a competent adult member of a western American academic community" may be represented as a series of choices in a flowchart (see Figure 9.1).

The form of address system diagramed in the flowchart is not to be taken as representing the thought process of someone addressing another person. What the diagram shows is the relevant information a speaker needs to take into account in order to address members of a given speech community in a proper or at least acceptable manner. The same flowchart updated for the 1990s would include a box among those farthest to the

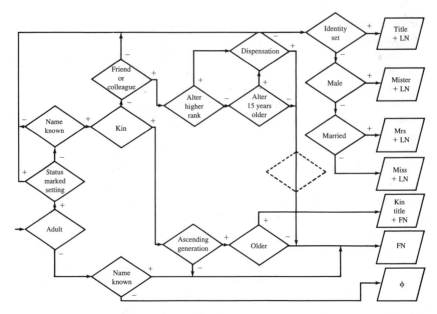

FIGURE 9.1   Form of Address System as Used by a Competent Adult Member of
an Academic Community in the Western United States. The entry point of the
flowchart is indicated by the arrow at bottom left. The diamond-shaped areas are
selectors, each with a + or − exit depending on whether the condition indicated is
or is not met. For example, a faculty member in this community would be expected to address an adult in formal circumstances where the use of titles is appropriate (status-marked setting) by using an occupational title or conventional
title of courtesy plus last name (LN), for example, "Dean Black," "Mr. White,"
"Ms. Brown," and the like. *Source:* From Susan Ervin-Tripp, "Sociolinguistics," in
Advances in Experimental Social Psychology, vol. 4, ed. Leonard Berkowitz (New
York: Academic Press, 1969), 95.

right with Ms + LN, the form used to address a woman whose marital
status is unknown or irrelevant. As a rule, members of a speech community are well acquainted with the address forms they need to know, and
they use them unconsciously just as they use their native language without having to think about its lexicon and grammar. Despite the rather
routine fashion with which forms of address are applied in spoken exchanges, however, they may also be used creatively or destructively. For
example, if a man wishes to remind a much younger friend that he
prefers to be addressed by his first name, he may do so indirectly by un-
expectedly addressing the younger person with a title and last name
(meaning, "If you insist on addressing me formally, then I will do the
same when talking to you"). And when the African-American psychia-
trist Dr. Alvin Poussaint was addressed by a white policeman as "boy"

and subsequently, after having fully identified himself, by his first name, the inappropriate form of address was not only a clear expression of racism but was employed as a deliberate insult.

Although the gender of the speaker and of the addressee is not a prominent feature in Figure 9.1, it is frequently a factor in the choice of form of address. Women speakers of American English tend to make use of a smaller variety of address forms than do men. In contrast, terms of endearment in service encounters ("hon[ey]," "dear"), heard a generation ago in some parts of the country, were used only by females to address another female, and had no parallels among forms of address applied to males. Similarly, "Mac" is an informal form of address occasionally used by men in urban areas in the East to refer to another male whose name is not known. In general, asymmetry in social position between men and women tends to be reflected in the system of address forms applied to the two genders, and the study of how people address each other in a given society can be quite revealing of its social structure (Wolfson and Manes 1979; Kramer 1975).

Just as forms of address depend to a great extent on how those who address each other evaluate their relative social positions, so do greetings. The following abbreviated description of how Wolof villagers greet each other is based on an account by Judith T. Irvine of her fieldwork in Senegal in 1970 and 1971. Whenever two villagers catch sight of each other (even at some distance), they must exchange greetings, even if to do so requires one or the other to deviate from a direct route. Although gestures and eye contact are important aspects of greeting, verbal exchanges are the necessary components. A person of higher status—his or her ranking depending on age, gender, caste, and achieved prestige—first receives a greeting, which is then responded to. The greeting process is considered to be so important that it must be repeated if someone who temporarily leaves an evening social gathering finds upon return that the topic of conversation has significantly changed. This new round of greetings may take some time to complete because each person must be greeted individually rather than the assembled group as a whole.

A typical Wolof greeting exchange consists of salutation; giving one's name if the persons are not already acquainted; asking at least one question concerning the state of the other person and, optionally, additional questions concerning the whereabouts and health of the other person's family and friends; and ending with the praising of God. The person of lower status initiates the process and asks the questions, the other responds.

There are situations, however, when some of the criteria that determine one's relative rank cancel rather than reinforce each other—for example, when a younger man meets an old woman (Wolof males have higher status than women, but old persons rank higher than young people). Then, too, people are not always anxious to claim higher status because it carries a potential financial burden inasmuch as the person of high rank can be requested to provide a gift or some sort of support to a person of low rank. When the two persons encountering one another are not certain about their relative social position or wish for some reason to claim a particular rank, they may choose one of two available strategies for manipulating status: self-lowering or self-elevating. The self-lowering strategy is accomplished by assuming the role of the initiator and questioner in the greeting exchange. But the responder, who may have initially missed the opportunity to claim the lower status, can correct the situation by putting the standard questions to the initiator as soon as the praising-God stage has been reached.

It is not a common occurrence for each of the two greeting parties to attempt to claim a higher status. The difficulty in such a case would be that although neither would want to initiate the greeting process, greeting must take place because remaining silent during an encounter would be unthinkable. A way to manipulate such a situation is for one of the persons to greet the other as briefly as possible and then ask, "Why didn't you greet me?"

In addition to choosing the role of the initiator and questioner, or accepting the opposite role of responder, vocal effects may be applied to utterances to reinforce the chosen role: A low-pitched, quiet, slow, and concise style of speaking is characteristic of Wolof nobles, and the opposite style characterizes the speech of people of lower castes. To sum up, greeting among the Wolof is closely linked with the speakers' social identities, or as a Wolof proverb puts it, "When two persons greet each other, one has shame, the other has glory" (Irvine 1974:175).

Linguistic Etiquette of the Javanese People

In some languages the nature of the social relationship between individuals who are talking to each other is signaled still more comprehensively than simply by using the appropriate personal pronoun, verb form, or form of address. One such language is Javanese, in which age, gender, kinship, family background, wealth, education, occupation, familiarity, and other characteristics of both the speaker and the listener determine the choice of the dialect and of the particular words in it to be used. Although not many words differ according to the status and degree of familiarity they imply, these few words occur quite frequently in actual speech.

For a good illustration of Javanese "linguistic etiquette" we are indebted to a chapter in Clifford Geertz's account of the religion of Java (1960). According to Geertz, the equivalent of the English sentence "Are you going to eat rice and cassava now?" as spoken by the Javanese of Modjokuto (a town in east central Java) may be heard at six different speech levels, depending on the social relationship and other factors concerning those who take part in the dialog. Whereas at the highest level—considered to be the model of correct speech—the Javanese sentence is "Menapa pandjenengan badé dahar sekul kalijan kaspé samenika?" at the lowest level it is quite different: "Apa kowé arep mangan sega lan kaspé saiki?" Although the two sentences mean the same thing, they share only one word: *kaspé* 'cassava.' Using the middle level, the sentence would be "Napa sampéjan adjeng neda sekul lan kaspé saniki?" Of the three levels, the highest and the lowest have sublevels, altogether yielding six different sentences with the same denotation but different connotations. In addition to the lexical variation in these sentences, their presentation differs as well: The higher the level, the slower, softer, and more even the speech. Among the factors that further contribute to the selection of a particular level are the social setting (a wedding calls for higher levels than a street encounter), the subject matter (discussion of religion or aesthetics calls for higher levels than a commercial transaction), and audience (the presence of others listening calls for higher levels).

It is of course true that any request in English can also be expressed in widely differing terms and made to range from rudeness to exaggerated deference of manner, as in "Shut the door!" as compared to "Would you mind if I asked you to please shut the door?" However, one should note that the action requested—shutting the door—is conveyed by the same words in both cases ("shut the door"). The former version, the briefest possible, is meant and understood as a command; the latter, augmented by nine additional words, is couched in very polite terms.

In Javanese, in contrast, the equivalent of the English word *going* in the sentence discussed earlier is *badé* at the highest level (referred to by the Javanese as *krama*), *adjeng* at the middle level (*madya*), and *arep* at the lowest level (*ngoko*). Only the word *kaspé* 'cassava' is the same at all levels and sublevels. For the other referents—corresponding to the English "are, you, to eat, rice, and, now"—the Javanese must choose from at least two lexical alternatives in order to indicate the nature of the relationship between the speaker and the addressee in terms of status and familiarity. The speech level referred to as *ngoko* is basic. It is used when a person feels unrestrained; one thinks in it, speaks in it to intimate friends and those of low rank, and uses it to express anger.

Speech and Gender

The term *gender* refers in linguistics to a grammatical category according to which certain word classes (parts of speech) are formally classified. In

Latin, for example, the gender of nouns is for the most part grammatical, that is, it has nothing to do with distinguishing between male and female: The gender of *pēs* 'foot' is masculine, of *manus* 'hand' feminine, and of *caput* 'head' neuter. By contrast, gender in English is on the whole natural: A male is referred to by the pronoun *he*, a female by *she*, and almost everything else by *it*. Exceptions are very few: Some people use the feminine pronoun to refer to ships and cars, and the neuter pronoun *it* to refer to an animal of either sex. In some languages, nouns are classified according to gender as either animate (possessing life) or inanimate (not endowed with life). Such a distinction is not as obvious as one might suppose. In Arapaho, *hinén* 'man,' *hísei* 'woman,' *wox* 'bear,' and *hééni?* 'ant' are of animate gender as one would expect, but so are *hokóóx* 'tepee pole,' *hííí* 'snow,' *hotíí* 'wheel,' and others. Animate nouns in Arapaho and other Algonquian languages are subject to different grammatical rules than inanimate nouns (Salzmann 1983).

The purpose of this section, however, is not to discuss gender as a grammatical term but to survey briefly the relationship between language on the one hand and gender in the sense of male/female distinction on the other. To put it differently, how is the natural division between females and males reflected in language and speech?

The most obvious are the physical differences in voice quality that become pronounced during puberty. As a result of the greater lengthening of the vocal cords in boys, the range of the male voice broadens and lowers by about an octave, whereas the female voice becomes louder and changes its timbre, that is, "color" (quality) because of overtones.

Apart from timbre and relative pitch, does women's speech differ from men's? In essence, of course, it does not, because regardless of the differences that may exist between the position of males and females in any particular society, men and women must be able to communicate efficiently. But minor differences between women's and men's speech do exist in most if not all languages. Among the languages in which certain morphemes have a different phonemic shape depending on whether women or men are speaking is Koasati, a Muskogean language spoken in southwestern Louisiana. According to Haas (1994), the speech of middle-aged and older Koasati women in the late 1930s differed from that of men in certain indicative and imperative verb forms. Because in a few instances the speech of women appeared to be older and more basic, Haas described the men's forms as derived from the women's forms. For example, verb forms ending in a nasalized vowel, such as *ą·* in *lakawwą́·* 'he will lift it [woman speaking],' add an *s* after the corresponding oral vowel, yielding *lakawwą́·s* 'he will lift it [man speaking].' Similarly, the women's word *lakawhôl* 'lift it! [addressed to second-person plural]' yields the men's form *lakawhós*. In other instances, a vowel is lengthened and the final *n* becomes an *s*, and in still others the men's form simply adds an *s* to the form occurring in women's speech. One may summarize the changes at the end of certain Koasati verb forms as follows (W = women's form, M = men's form, V = any vowel, Ṿ = nasalized vowel, C = any consonant, and (·) = short or long):

W	M
Ṿ(·)	V(·)s
V̂l	V́s
V̂n	V̂·s
V(·)C	V(·)Cs
V(·)CC	V(·)CCs

Haas further reported that in telling traditional narratives, Koasati women used men's forms when quoting male characters, and conversely.

In North Africa, Arabs who speak French as a second language articulate the French (r) according to the speaker's gender: In men's speech it is an apical consonant (produced with the tip of the tongue serving as the active articulator); in women's speech it is a uvular consonant (made by the back of the tongue with the aid of the uvula). Because both of the (r)s occur and are phonemically distinct in the Arabic dialects native to these people, the two variants are easily pronounceable by both men and women. According to a recent survey of French dialects by Henriette Walter (1988), North African men would now prefer to approach the contemporary French norm, which happens to be the uvular *r*, [R]. What prevents them from doing so is a fairly rigid convention, according to which the uvular articulation of *r* in North African French is a social characteristic of women.

Differences of this kind between the speech of men and women are not at all rare. They have been documented for languages of North and South America as well as Asia and are also found on other continents. In some instances they may not even be noticed by linguistically untrained listeners. For example, in a small sample of children in a semirural New England village studied by John L. Fischer (1958), the girls were more likely to pronounce the present-participle suffix as *-ing* [ɪŋ] rather than *-in'* [ɪn], a form used more frequently among the boys. The choice between *-ing* and *-in'* appeared to be related not only to gender but also to the personality (aggressive vs. cooperative) and mood (tense vs. relaxed) of the speaker, the nature of the conversation (formal vs. informal), the socioeconomic circumstances of the family (above vs. below median), and the verb used (for example, *correcting* vs. *chewin'*).

Douglas Taylor (1951) reports on a more complex situation in Central American Carib, a modern dialect of Island Carib. Two genders, masculine and feminine, are distinguished in this dialect. Gender is in part natural (assigned as a rule in accordance with the sex of a living thing), in part grammatical (for example, the words for *sun, milk, river,* and *maize* are masculine, whereas those for *star, liver, knife,* and *snake* are feminine). However, words denoting qualities, states, actions, and the equivalent of the pronoun *it* in such English sentences as *it is raining* tend to be assigned to the feminine gender by men but to masculine by women. The equivalent of "the other day," for example, is *ligíra buga* when said by women but *tugúra buga* when said by men (*buga* is a past-tense particle).

The choice of words used by men and women varies according to the occasion, the type of audience present, and various other circumstances. Profane or coarse speech is less likely to be heard when children or people held in respect are within earshot, and a job interview calls for a more considered vocabulary than a casual conversation between two close friends. Nevertheless, some lexical differences between the speech of men and women are fairly common and can be illustrated from American English. Certain words are used by women much more frequently than by men. Among such words are expressive adjectives that convey approval or admiration—for example, *adorable, charming, cute, divine, lovely,* and *sweet*—and fashionable color names—for example, *beige, chartreuse, ecru, fuchsia, magenta,* and *mauve.* Men are much more likely to phrase their approval or liking for something by using a neutral adjective, such as *fine, good,* or *great,* and reinforcing it, if necessary, with such an adverb as *damn,* as in "That was a damn good show." Men's color vocabulary as a rule is much less discriminating, and hence poorer, than women's. There is no doubt, however, that in the United States and many other countries the differences between men's and women's word choices are steadily growing smaller. Profanities are now casually used by many young women whose mothers and grandmothers not only would never have uttered them but would probably have been embarrassed even to hear them. On the whole, however, as several authors have noted, in careful speech women are likely to use fewer stigmatized words than are men.

On the sentence level, the trait most frequently cited as characteristic of women's speech is the use of the tag question in certain contexts. The term refers to a question attached to an utterance to obtain the assent of the addressee, as in "That was a stupid thing for them to do, wasn't it?" Seeking confirmation or validation of a statement may indicate the speaker's desire to avoid assertiveness. Another purpose of the tag question is to include the person spoken to in friendly conversation by offering the opportunity to respond, as in "It's a nice day today, isn't it?" Again, younger women appear to use tag questions much less frequently than do older women. On the subject of tag questions, however, some scholars have argued that "a more sophisticated view of the complexity of both linguistic and social behaviour" is needed (Cameron, McAlinden, and O'Leary 1988:92).

Last, some differences in intonational patterns between male and female speakers have also been noted. If one analyzes intonational contours of American English in terms of four relative pitch levels, then men tend to use only three of them, hardly ever reaching the highest one. Women's range frequently includes all four. Among the contours very rarely heard from men is the full downglide from the highest to the lowest pitch level, as in

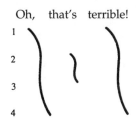

to express surprise, excitement, and the like. In general, women's speech appears to be more dynamic, making greater use of paralinguistic features and extending over a broader pitch range.

To sum up, in American English there are no pronunciations, grammatical forms, words, or sentence constructions that are employed exclusively by men or by women. Rather, what differences there are between male and female speech have to do with the frequency with which some usages are employed by one sex or the other. That these differences are decreasing rather than maintaining themselves or growing is an indication that long-standing social differences between women and men are breaking down.

Sexual Bias in Language

The several illustrations given above have shown how women and men may use the same language somewhat differently. But are there also gender-biased terms and usages in languages that favor either men or women over the other gender? There certainly are, and examples can easily be drawn from English, whose bias is masculine. Even though the ratio of women to men in the United States and many other countries is about 51 to 49 percent, masculine terms in most languages are grammatically basic—that is, feminine forms are usually derived from masculine forms (as *goddess, lioness, aviatrix,* and *usherette* are derived from *god, lion, aviator,* and *usher*). Furthermore, masculine terms are frequently used to include women. The most common is the case of the word *man* (see Box 9.1), frequently found in compound nouns referring to occupations. The

---

BOX 9.1   What Does the Word *Man* Mean?

In the case of the word *man,* as in *man is a primate,* it has been argued that this usage is independent of sex, that it refers to all members of the species, and that it is just an etymological coincidence that the form for the species is the same as that for the male members of the species. Certainly, using the same form for the entire species and for half the species creates the possibility of confusion, as those colonial women discovered who rashly thought that the word *man* in the sentence "All men are created equal" included them. More confusion may come about when we use phrases like *early man.* Although this presumably refers to the species, notice how easy it is to use expressions like *early man and his wife* and how hard it is to say things like *man is the only animal that menstruates* or even *early woman and her husband.* ... The common theme running through these last examples is that the male is taken as the normal, that masculine forms refer both to the sex and the species, while women are the exception, usually absorbed by the masculine, but needing special terms when they become noticeable.

If the above examples have not convinced you that *man* as a generic is at best ambiguous, consider the following quote from Alma Graham ...:

> If a woman is swept off a ship into the water, the cry is "Man overboard!" If she is killed by a hit-and-run driver, the charge is "manslaughter." If she is injured on the job, the coverage is "workmen's compensation." But if she arrives at a threshold marked "Men Only," she knows the admonition is not intended to bar animals or plants or inanimate objects. It is meant for her.

from Francine Frank and Frank Anshen,
Language and the Sexes (1983), 71–72

---

word originally designated a human being of either sex, but in Modern English it refers especially to an adult human male. During much of this century anthropology was briefly defined as the study of man(kind); today, it is customary to define it as the study of humankind or the study of human beings (*human* does not derive from *man* but from the Latin *hūmānus*). Words referring to males but used to include both women and men are now being replaced by gender-neutral words or phrases. Thus, *manpower, man-made, to man (a boat), mailman, fireman,* and *men of goodwill* have been giving way to *human energy, manufactured, to operate, mail carrier, fire fighter,* and *people of goodwill,* respectively.

Similarly, one should avoid the use of a masculine or feminine pronoun when reference may be to members of both sexes. Such sentences as "Each applicant must include a vita with his application" or "A full-time secretary is entitled to her own desk" are easily rephrased as "All applicants must include vitas with their applications" or "Each applicant must submit a vita," and "A full-time secretary should be given a separate desk."

Since the nineteenth century, a number of attempts have been made to coin gender-neutral personal and possessive pronouns in the singular corresponding to the plural forms *they, them,* and *their,* which apply to either sex or to both. None of these attempts has been successful, including the recently suggested forms (*s*)*he* and *his/her* for written English. Even without gender-neutral pronoun forms, though, eliminating linguistic sexisms is not particularly difficult. Publishers and thoughtful writers alike have made strong efforts in recent years to eliminate linguistic sexisms as well as to avoid stereotyping members of ethnic minorities. A number of handbooks are currently available to help those who wish to phrase their ideas free of sexual and other stereotyping.

Linguistic Variation in a Plural Society

The Republic of India is an excellent example of a plural society. Occupying an area only one-third as large as the United States but with a population of close to a billion, India is one of the most multilingual countries of the world. According to the 1961 Indian census, the 1,019 mother tongues reported by the country's citizens are assignable to 199 languages belonging to four language families. Affiliation could not be determined for 530 more mother tongues, and over 100 additional languages were of foreign origin. The country's constitution recognizes fourteen languages plus ancient classical Sanskrit as national languages and three more as additional administrative languages, English among them.

How does the federal republic of India deal administratively with such a variety of languages, many spoken by millions of people? On a regional basis, eastern India is dominated by three Indo-European languages (Bengali, Oriya, and Assamese), western India by two (Marathi and Gujarati), northern India by four (Hindi and Urdu, Panjabi, and Kashmiri), and southern India by four languages of the Dravidian language family (Telugu, Tamil, Kannada, and Malayalam). The principal official language in six of the twenty-five states of the republic as well as of the country at the federal level is Hindi. However, as long as many non-Hindi-speaking citizens are reluctant to accept Hindi, English—the language of those who governed most of India as a British crown colony for nearly a century—serves as the associate national language and as a lingua franca acceptable in both the Hindi-speaking north and the Dravidian-speaking south.

In a country where many languages are spoken but not all enjoy the same degree of prestige, bilingualism, multilingualism, and diglossia are of common occurrence. For interethnic oral communication of an informal nature, Hindi or Urdu is used to a varying degree throughout the country (the two are very similar in their colloquial forms, but Hindi is written in the Devanagari script, Urdu in a modified form of Arabic script). For reasons of cultural prestige, there has been some resistance to the use of Hindi as a contact language in the Dravidian-speaking part of the country and in Bengal. For formal and written communication, English (its South Asian variety) is used to a great extent. The importance of English can readily be seen: In 1977, although newspapers and periodicals in India were available in about seventy languages, Hindi- and English-language newspapers and periodicals accounted for, respectively, 26 and 20 percent of the total published, and those in English had the highest circulation. When India became independent in 1947, the official use of English was intended to be only temporary. But the need for English continues and in some respects has even increased. For example, to translate technical and scientific works into Hindi would be a nearly impossible task. Today, almost half a century after India gained independence, knowledge of English is still considered indispensable for high government positions, and although only a very small percentage of the population speaks and reads English, Indians with a knowledge of English tend to be the cultural, economic, and political leaders.

According to Lachman Khubchandani (1983:26), "Indian society as a whole . . . shows variation in speech related to identity and purpose of interaction." Among his examples are the following: In many communities of Bihar, a state in northeastern India, certain vernaculars (dialects) are used in speaking with elders, whereas a particular subdialect of Western Hindi is used with peers and younger persons. Brahmin (the highest caste) and non-Brahmin speech varieties are commonly used in Dravidian languages, depending on the caste affiliation of the speakers. High forms of Hindi and Urdu are employed under formal circumstances, but so-called bazaar Hindustani is heard in informal settings. In Sanskrit plays, royal male characters make use of cultivated speech; royal females speak the natural, colloquial standard; and commoners use "contaminated" speech.

John Gumperz (1964) reports on the speech varieties of Khalapur, a village located about 80 miles north of Delhi. Although only a small agricultural community of several thousand inhabitants at the time of Gumperz's fieldwork in the 1950s, Khalapur was divided into thirty-one endogamous castes or extended kin groups of unequal status. In addition to using several dialectal varieties of Khalapur, many villagers used Hindi as the high variety of speech and Khalapur, the local dialect, as the low variety. Each of the two varieties was further subdivided into high and low: Hindi was spoken in either the oratorical (high) or conversational (low) style; Khalapur was styled either as "clean speech," which was employed with more

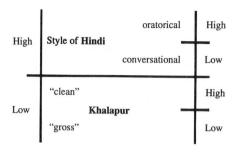

FIGURE 9.2   The Double-nested Diglossia of Khalapur, India

distant acquaintances and elders, or "gross speech," which was used with close relatives, children, untouchable servants, and animals. This quadripartite division was subsequently termed "double-nested diglossia" (Fasold 1984:46–48) and is diagramed in Figure 9.2.

Such a large linguistic variety (in both languages and dialects) as exists in India poses a number of questions. Although it might be expected that one official language would tend to promote unity in a multiethnic nation, such unity would be achieved at a considerable loss of prestige to other native languages spoken by many millions of people. This is why the most widely used second language in India, Hindi, has encountered resistance in many parts of the country. And this is also why a nonindigenous and formerly colonial language, English, has maintained itself surprisingly well as an associate official language since India's independence and will undoubtedly continue to do so in the future. A second language for many Indians, English does not give an advantage to speakers of one particular native language, as does Hindi. Another question has to do with determining the languages to be taught and used for instruction in Indian schools. What eventually became known as the three-language formula has resulted in secondary students' being taught the regional language, Hindi, and English (and in many instances their mother tongue is yet a fourth language or local dialect).

Throughout much of the world, dialectal differences have tended to diminish rapidly in recent decades as a result of the mass media, education, and mobility. This has not been the case in India, where caste differences are effectively symbolized by speech differences. As long as the old and well-established social hierarchy persists, linguistic differences serve a useful function and are likely to be retained.

Sociolinguistic Change

Contemporary scholars tend to consider linguistic change as **sociolinguistic change,** that is, as change to be understood in the context of the society in which it occurs. Among the best studies of this kind have been those Labov conducted from the mid-1960s. One of Labov's pioneering works concerns the relationship between the social status of speakers from New York City and their pronunciation of (r). (Linguistic variables are commonly enclosed in parentheses.) The study was conducted in some of the department stores of the city in 1962. The variation of the phonetic feature under consideration ranged from the absence of (r) altogether to its presence in postvocalic position, as in the words *car, card, four,* and *fourth.*

On the basis of exploratory interviews, Labov decided to test the following hypothesis: "If any two subgroups of New York City speakers are ranked in a scale of social stratification, then they will be ranked in the same order by their differential use of (r)" (Labov 1972:44). Rather than simply comparing the pronunciations of occupational groups representing the city's social stratification, Labov chose to try to find out to what extent stratification is identifiable within a single occupational group. The population he selected for his study consisted of salespeople in the stores of Saks Fifth Avenue (at Fiftieth Street), Macy's at Herald Square (Thirty-fourth Street and Sixth Avenue), and S. Klein at Union Square (Fourteenth Street and Broadway). These three stores represented, respectively, three status rankings—high, middle, and low—confirmed not only by virtue of the socioeconomic status of their customers but also by the newspapers in which the stores advertised, the prices of the merchandise they offered, the physical appearance of their premises, and so on.

Assuming that salespeople in large department stores are likely to "borrow prestige" from their customers, Labov further hypothesized that "salespeople in the highest-ranked store will have the highest values of (r); those in the middle-ranked store will have intermediate values of (r); and those in the lowest-ranked store will show the lowest values" (Labov 1972:45). In order to elicit the relevant linguistic data, Labov asked a question that was best answered "[On the] fourth floor"; pretending not to understand, he then elicited the answer once more in an emphatic style of speech. On the fourth floor he asked another question to elicit the same answer. As soon as he was out of view of his informants, Labov recorded the two words phonetically, also noting the store in which the data were obtained and the gender, function, race, and approximate age of the informant.

The results of the study were in agreement with the hypothesis. At Saks, 30 percent of the salespeople interviewed always pronounced both (r)s of the test phrase "fourth floor" whereas 32 percent pronounced them sometimes and sometimes not (as though "fourth floor" were written "fawth floah"); the comparable figures for Macy's were 20 and 31, and for Klein's 4 and 17. Furthermore, at Saks the difference between casual and emphatic pronunciation was insignificant, whereas at the other two stores the difference was considerable. Careful, emphatic speech appeared to call for the final (r) of "floor"; casual speech did not.

Although prior to World War II certain (r)s were "dropped" (except before a vowel) in the more prestigious pronunciation of New York City, in the years since then this consonant has become one of the markers of social prestige and its occurrence has increased, particularly in formal speech. In fact, some New Yorkers pronounce an (r) even where it does not occur in spelling, as in the words *idea, Cuba,* and *saw* when the following word begins with a vowel. (As we saw in Chapter 8, such a pronunciation, or usage in general, that in an attempt to approach a presumed standard goes too far and produces a nonstandard form, is hypercorrection.) In short, as Labov's study shows, the pronunciation of (r) in the dialect of New York City is variable: The variation depends on social factors and speech context (for example, casual vs. emphatic).

Collecting authentic sociolinguistic data is not a simple matter because speakers are likely to adjust their manner of speaking if they are aware of being carefully observed or recorded. One way for the investigator to divert speakers' attention from their own speech is to lead informants into a relaxed dialog. Natural speech also tends to characterize topics that help to re-create emotions, as when one asks an informant, "Have you ever been in a situation where you were in serious danger of being killed? . . . What happened?" The answer to such a question is likely to be spontaneous, that is, given in an unaffected manner (Labov 1972:209–210). Tape-recording data has a great advantage over writing out a phonetic transcription of speech. Recording conversation between two or more speakers, or recording one speaker long enough or often enough for the person to become unconcerned, is preferable to recording a more or less formal interview that may well keep the informant from relaxing into the **vernacular**—the casual, normal spoken form of the language or dialect of the person's speech community.

In early sociolinguistic studies scholars sought to identify language varieties and relate them to social differences among speakers. Since the mid-1960s, largely because of the stimulus of Labov's work, linguists have emphasized the use of the quantitative method in order to be able to describe with some accuracy the relationship between social differences and linguistic varieties (see Figure 9.3). From the incidence and distribution of language variables in different social groups, scholars expect to learn not only the rate and direction of linguistic change but also to obtain valuable clues concerning the motivations that lead to such change.

In this connection, it may be appropriate to introduce the recent concept of social network. Each speaker has a social network that includes all those people with whom a speaker interacts. A high-density network

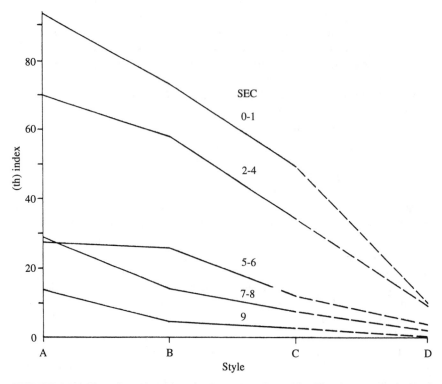

FIGURE 9.3 Class Stratification of a Linguistic Variable. The data were derived from a sample of adult respondents raised in New York City: (th) in *think, through, fourth*, etc., The vertical axis is the scale of average (th) index scores. The prestige form is the interdental fricative [θ]; the most strongly stigmatized variant is usually the lenis dental stop [t], making *think* sound much like *tink;* an intermediate form is the affricate [tθ].

The horizontal axis represents four contextual styles: A, casual speech; B, careful speech; C, reading style; and D, pronouncing words in isolation, as in word lists.

The ten-point socioeconomic class scale (SEC) is based on the occupation of the breadwinner, the education of the respondent, and family income, and it may be informally described as follows: 0–1, lower class; 2–4, working class; 5–8, lower middle class; and 9, upper middle class.

The linguistic variable (th) is sharply stratified and has had a stable social significance for at least seventy-five years. *Source:* Adapted from William Labov, *Sociolinguistic Patterns* (Philadelphia: University of Pennsylvania Press, 1972), 112–115.

refers to a group of individuals who are in frequent contact and are therefore familiar with each other. A multiplex social network is one in which interacting parties share more than one role, often reciprocal—for example, employer/employee as well as father-in-law/son-in-law. The denser and more multiplex the network, the stronger it is (perhaps the father-in-law and son-in-law are also members of a chess club and a choral society). Members of a strong network tend to make use of what is referred to as *restricted code*—informal speech lacking in stylistic range because the speakers share enough assumptions that some of the meaning of their messages is derived from context and gestures. By contrast, *elaborated code* refers to the variety of language use characteristic of relatively formal speech situations. In such situations little if any reliance is placed on extralinguistic context to make the message fully meaningful.

Summary and Conclusions

A thorough description of the various elements that make up a language and of the relations that hold among them is a prerequisite for understanding the structure of a language, but there is much more to be considered. Any given language, regardless of the time and place it may have been spoken, is above all a social institution, one without which human societies are unthinkable. When it comes to studying how languages work, anthropologists are therefore interested in answers to such questions as, What are the linguistic varieties used in a speech community, and how are they related to social differences? What are a community's attitudes toward speech and its varieties? and What is the function of language and speech in the exercise of social control? The anthropologist's concern is not with language in isolation, abstracted from those who speak it, but with the use of speech in actual life and the meaning it has for the members of a community or society. Sociolinguistic studies must therefore draw on the findings of sociology and cultural anthropology, and because language acquisition is the result of a socialization process, they must also take into account psychological factors. In acquiring a language, children (and those who study a second language) are learning not only to produce grammatical and meaningful sentences but sentences and utterances appropriate to the occasion and audience. For example, in the United States it is quite common to use a humorous reference or tell a short joke at the beginning of a public speech, but it would not be appropriate to do so when speaking at a funeral; similarly, among close friends almost any question is acceptable, but to say to a person one has just met, "What a great apartment! How much rent do you pay?" would be in bad taste.

Because some of the social difficulties people experience can be traced
to the way they speak or at least are reinforced by their speech, sociolinguistic research and findings can be usefully applied to social problems.
Such applications have been primarily in language arts—reading and
writing—and language testing. For example, the question has been
asked whether a child's mother tongue (the language a child acquires at
home, which normally becomes the adult's natural instrument of
thought and communication) should be tolerated during the early school
years if it is different from the national language or its standard form.
Many sociolinguists would agree that some role should be assigned to
the vernacular of minority-group children, who would otherwise be
forced to begin learning about the world in a language or dialect that is
not their own. Another question concerns language testing. To minimize
the disadvantage of speakers of a vernacular compared to those who
speak either the standard language or a dialect close to it, test preparers
should consider their methods of measuring how well students identify
and code fundamental semantic concepts and relationships rather than
how well they recognize merely the surface linguistic forms that represent concepts and relationships. For example, in African-American Vernacular English the relationship between a possessor and what is possessed is not overtly marked (as in *man coat*), whereas in Standard
English it is (as in *man's coat*). To take off points for not using or recogniz-
ing the possessive suffix (-'s) from young students whose dialect does
not overtly mark possession but who have no problem with the concept
of possession amounts to judging them on the basis of mechanical criteria and making no allowance for their mother tongue, which differs on
this particular point of grammar.

If sociolinguistics is to be taken as "socially constituted linguistics,"
then the field can be characterized by the following themes (adapted from
Hymes 1974:205–206):

1. Theory of language entails the organization of speech, not just of
   grammar.
2. Foundations of theory and methodology entail questions of function, not just of structure.
3. Speech communities are organizations of ways of speaking and are
   not definable according to the distribution of grammatical features
   alone.
4. Competence is a personal ability to communicate appropriately in
   a given context, not simply grammatical knowledge.
5. Languages are what their users have made of them, not just what
   human nature has given their users.

Notes and Suggestions for Further Reading

Chapter 2 of Labov 1972 is a revision of chapters 3 and 9 of Labov 1966. Labov 1981 provides useful methodological insights for those engaged in sociolinguistic research. For a discussion of the social network concept, with examples, see Milroy and Margrain 1980. The terms *elaborated code* and *restricted code* have created controversy when employed in connection with social-class background and educational settings. An article by Basil Bernstein, who coined the terms, and comments by others can be found in Gumperz and Hymes 1972 (and 1986).

For a survey of books and articles dealing with address forms, politeness, honorific registers, and related matters, see Agha 1994. For studies of address systems in American English, see Brown and Ford 1961 and Blocker 1976. The chapter in Geertz 1960 dealing with the sociolinguistic variation in Javanese is quite appropriately entitled "Linguistic Etiquette" (Geertz 1960:248–260). The description given here is based on Geertz's account but has been simplified. For the latest, more technical discussion of Javanese linguistic etiquette, see Errington 1988.

Some additions and corrections pertaining to Haas's report on gender-specific speech among the Koasati are the subject of Kimball 1987. The entire example from North African French has been drawn from Walter 1988. There are a number of articles and books concerned with the speech of women and men. Noteworthy among them are Coates 1986; Coates and Cameron 1988; Kramarae 1981; Lakoff 1975; Philips, Steele, and Tanz 1987; Silverstein 1985; and Thorne, Kramarae, and Henley 1983. The last book includes an extensive annotated bibliography (pp. 151–342). The literature on sex differences and language is reviewed in Philips 1980, McConnell-Ginet 1988, and Eckert and McConnell-Ginet 1992. For a reader on the feminist critique of language, see Cameron 1990. The section on India is based on Khubchandani 1983 and Gumperz 1964, but for use here their accounts have been simplified.

In addition to Labov 1972, a number of books deal with sociolinguistics in some detail. Among the more recent ones are Fasold 1984 and 1990, Hudson 1980, Hymes 1974, Peñalosa 1981, Trudgill 1983, and Wardhaugh 1986. Sociolinguistic readers include Gumperz and Hymes 1986 and Pride and Holmes 1972.

For popular and best-selling accounts of the complexities of communication between men and women, see Tannen 1986 and 1990.

10
Ethnography of Communication

In an article written in 1966, Hymes observed that it used to be customary to consider languages as different from each other but the uses to which they are put as closely similar if not essentially the same. Hymes then noted that the opposite view was beginning to prevail: Languages are seen as fundamentally very much alike but the social uses of speech as quite different from one culture to the next. In the earlier period, distinct division of labor existed between linguists and cultural anthropologists. With few exceptions, linguists studied languages to discover the structural differences between them and to learn about their historical development, whereas anthropologists studied human societies in order to understand the workings of their cultures. But of course culture and the use of language are not easily separable. People must use language to accomplish a wide variety of culture-specific goals. In order for societies to function smoothly, their members must have not only linguistic competence (the knowledge of the grammatical rules of their mother tongue, acquired well before adulthood) but also **communicative competence**—the knowledge of what is and what is not appropriate to say in any specific cultural context. As Hymes puts it, "A child from whom any and all of the grammatical sentences of a language might come with equal likelihood would be . . . a social monster" (Hymes 1974:75). Some parents occasionally learn this from their own experience when a child who is not yet fully communicatively competent makes an embarrassing comment in front of guests, such as saying to a guest who praises the coffee cake being offered, "My mom said it was lousy, but it was good enough to give to you."

The nature and function of communicative behavior in the context of culture is the subject of **ethnography of communication.** In its modern form, ethnography of communication dates back to Hymes's article "The Ethnography of Speaking," published in 1962. Inasmuch as this relatively new field focuses on those aspects of human behavior in which communication meets culture, research in ethnography of communication contributes to the interdisciplinary studies that are proving to be of increasing value in modern scholarship. Some scholars consider ethnography of communication as one of the several fields of inquiry within the scope of sociolinguistics. Others argue that ethnography of communication, as the study of communicative behavior in relation to the sociocultural variables associated with human interaction, is broader and more encompassing than sociolinguistics. Be that as it may, both sociolinguistics and ethnography of communication are fields of inquiry that have been gaining in importance and attracting significant research.

Speech Community and Related Concepts

The terms *society* and *culture* in anthropology are useful as general concepts, but no society's culture is uniform for all its members. Any complex of learned patterns of behavior and thought that distinguishes various segments of a society (minorities, castes, and the like) is referred to as a subculture. By extension, this term is also used to refer collectively to all those who exhibit the characteristics of a particular subculture (for example, the homeless as well as the so-called beautiful people). Language and speech, too, are characterized by lack of uniformity. In general, any particular society is associated with a specific language and, in the case of multinational societies, with several languages. But no language is ever uniform for all speakers of a society (people, community, tribe). As we have already seen, certain ways of speaking the same language may differentiate men from women, the young from the old, the poor from the rich, and the like. All those who share specific rules for speaking and interpreting speech and at least one speech variety belong to a **speech community.** However, it is important to remember that people who speak the same language are not always members of the same speech community. On the one hand, speakers of South Asian English in India and Pakistan share a language with citizens of the United States, but the respective varieties of English and the rules for speaking them are sufficiently distinct to assign the two populations to different speech communities. On the other hand, Muriel Saville-Troike (1982:20) considers even monolingual speakers of either Spanish (the official language) or Guarani (the national language) as belonging to the same speech community in Paraguay because the social roles of the speakers of the two languages are complementary—both groups are mutually dependent for services or employment.

Most members of a society, even if they happen to live in the same town, belong to several speech communities. For example, an elderly person may have considerable difficulty following the monotonous chant of an auctioneer or comprehending what students talk about among themselves. But both the auctioneer and a college student can easily make the adjustment necessary to engage in a conversation with the elderly person and be fully understood; all they have to do is to share enough characteristic patterns of pronunciation, grammar, vocabulary, and manner of speaking to belong to the same speech community.

It may also be the case that peoples live in different countries and speak different languages but share some rules for speaking, as do the Czechs and the Austrians (and for that matter some of the other peoples who until World War I were part of the Austro-Hungarian Empire or lived in adjacent areas). As an example, the commonly used phrase for greeting or taking leave of a woman who is economically and socially well situated was (and to some extent still is) "Rukulíbám, milostivá paní!" in Czech and "Küss' die Hand, gnädige Frau!" in German. The English translation, "I kiss your hand, gracious lady," clearly indicates how different such rules of speaking are from those used, say, in Britain or the United States. Linguists refer to an area in which speakers of different languages share speaking rules as a speech area.

Less frequently employed terms for related concepts include *language field, speech field,* and *speech network* (Hymes 1972:55). The first of these (language field) refers to all those communities in which an individual is able to communicate adequately by virtue of knowing the languages and language varieties serving the communities. The concept of speech field parallels that of language field but involves the knowledge of rules for speaking rather than knowledge of languages. The last term (speech network) refers to linkages between persons from different communities who share language varieties as well as rules for speaking. To give an example, in addition to her mother tongue, a woman knows four languages well enough to read books and newspapers published in them; a total of five languages make up her language field. However, the same woman is able to communicate easily in only one foreign language in addition to her native language; the speech communities within which she functions effectively in the two languages make up her speech field. Within that speech field the woman has special rapport with those persons, regardless of where they may come from, who share with her the two languages, rules for speech, and a professional interest in, say, archaeology; the linkages with these people make up her speech network.

Units of Speech Behavior

To distinguish among different levels of speech activity Hymes makes use of three terms for the ethnographic analysis and description of speech behavior—speech situation, speech event, and speech act (Hymes 1972: 56–57). (If one were to include nonverbal communication as well, these three terms would need to be broadened and the word *speech* replaced by *communicative;* after all, a hand gesture or the wink of an eye can be just as effective as a whole sentence.)

A speech situation is the context within which speaking occurs—that is, any particular set of circumstances typically associated with speech behavior (or absence of it). A speech situation may be a family meal, birthday party, baby shower, seminar meeting, campus beer party, auction, fishing trip, Quaker meeting, or any one of a large number of situations that take place in a society and are definable in terms of participants and goals and are therefore distinguishable from other speech situations.

The minimal unit of speech for purposes of an ethnographic analysis is the speech act. A speech act may be a greeting, apology, question, compliment, self-introduction, or the like. Although normally attributable to a single speaker, collective speech acts also exist as, for example, the "Amen" said by a congregation or the reciting of the Pledge of Allegiance by young pupils. In size, a speech act may range from a single word ("Scram!" or "Thanks") to a five-minute shaggy-dog story or a long harangue on conduct. Speech acts that follow each other in a recognized sequence and are governed by social rules for the use of speech combine to form a speech event, the basic unit of verbal interaction. Examples of speech events include conversation, confession to a priest, interview, dialog with a salesperson, telephone inquiry, and so on. Boundaries between successive speech events are marked by a change of major participants, a noticeable silence, or some remark designed to introduce another topic of conversation, for example, "If I can change the subject . . ." or "By the way, have you heard that. . . ." Under special circumstances, a speech act may become a speech event, as when someone shouts "Fire!" in a crowded movie theater.

An alumni reunion can be used to illustrate the three units of speech behavior. The gathering itself is an example of a speech situation: It has a beginning and an end and lasts usually only part of one day; the participants are restricted to former members of a class and their spouses or partners. Within such a speech situation, a number of speech events invariably take place: For example, one group may be reminiscing about favorite teachers and classroom antics; those in another group may be giving brief accounts of what they have been doing since graduation or the last reunion; and still others may be simply swapping jokes and stories. Within these speech events, the telling of a single joke or personal experience is a speech act.

Just as native speakers of any language are expected to produce sentences that are grammatically acceptable and meaningful, speech acts are judged according to how appropriate they are to any specific speech situation or speech event. It would be considered odd if one were to say to a stranger in the street, "My name is John Smith; what time do you have?"

Similarly, at a baby shower it would be out of place to bring up the increasing infant mortality rate. When inappropriate speech acts do occur, participants in the speech event or situation are later likely to comment on them: "Did you hear what she said? How inconsiderate!" or "What a crazy thing for Bill to say. Has he lost his mind?"

Components of Communication: Participants and Setting

Describing a language with emphasis on its function as the primary means of communication requires more than simply describing its sounds (phonology) and grammatical structure (morphology and syntax). Careful field research is necessary to discover how members of a society use their language under differing circumstances to satisfy the goals they set for themselves.

Traditionally, speech behavior was said to involve a speaker and a hearer and include the message transmitted between them. Modern ethnographic descriptions and analyses have shown that many more components need to be taken into account if any particular instance of communicative behavior is to be fully understood. Which of these components assume a crucial role depends on a given speech situation and the particular community in which it takes place.

The component termed *participants* includes not only the sender of a message (also referred to as the speaker or addresser) and the intended receiver (hearer, addressee) but anyone who may be interested in or happens to perceive (hear, see) the message—the audience. The number of participants can vary from only one to many thousands. For example, a person who has a job interview scheduled may practice for it by posing potential questions and then answering them, thus assuming the role of both sender and receiver. But at an outdoor political rally one or more charismatic leaders may not only address but succeed in mobilizing several hundred thousand followers.

In some cultures, the ability to communicate is not perceived as limited to ordinary humans. Among the Ashanti, a West African people on the Gulf of Guinea, a midwife may direct a question to a fetus concerning its father's identity, and recently deceased persons are believed to be able to inform their surviving relatives as to who or what was responsible for their death. The Ashanti also believe that forest fairies and monsters are able to instruct young men in medicine; these beings are said to communicate in a whistle language but are able to understand Twi, the language in which humans pray to them.

As indicated earlier in the discussion of language in its social context, a thorough ethnographic account of communicative behavior must carefully note the characteristics of the participants. Age, gender, ethnic affiliation, relationship (kinship) among participants, their relative social status, the degree to which they are acquainted, and other factors can influence how communication proceeds. Who talks to whom and in whose presence not only tends to determine how one talks (casually or respectfully) but also whether or not one can interrupt the other participant, how long speech acts should be, what additional channels one should use to enhance the presentation, and so on.

Any communicative act or event happens at a particular time and place and under particular physical circumstances—that is, it is characterized by a particular setting. Settings are likely to vary somewhat from one instance to the next even if the events are of the same kind, but the variation has culturally recognized limits. Small college classes normally meet in classrooms, but on warm spring or autumn days they may be conducted in the shade of a tree outside the classroom building; to meet in a nearby tavern or the lobby of the administrative building would be considered inappropriate. On April Fools' Day practical jokes are found acceptable by people who would consider them presumptuous on any other day. Hymes makes a distinction between setting and scene, the latter designating the "psychological setting." It is of course true that the mood pervading a given setting may invite or inhibit certain communicative acts or events, and in this sense the scene contributes to the definition of setting. One can easily imagine the identical setting and participants but completely different scenes: Compare, for example, the atmosphere surrounding the announcement of across-the-board wage increases with the announcement of the company's going out of business.

Components of Communication: Purpose, Channels, Codes, and Message Content and Form

The purpose of speaking is not always to transmit information or to exchange ideas. Sometimes it is to establish an atmosphere of sociability and is the equivalent of a hug or a hearty handshake. Speech behavior with the goal of bringing about such an emotional effect is referred to as phatic communion.

The motivation for communicative behavior varies from one occasion to the next: An individual may make an offer or a request, threaten or plead, praise or blame, invite or prohibit some action, reveal or try to conceal something, and so on. One's goal or purpose quite frequently determines the manner in which one speaks or acts. Even an aggressive person may speak meekly and deferentially when stopped for speeding by a police officer, hoping that polite and apologetic speech behavior will influence the officer to issue a warning instead of a fine.

Although the acoustic channel, best exemplified by spoken words, is the one most commonly employed, other channels of communication should not be overlooked. To do so would be to ignore that communicative behavior that makes primary use of one channel frequently depends on other channels for reinforcement. To hear a play read aloud or to see it professionally performed can mean the difference between experiencing boredom or enjoyment. Quite commonly, too, one channel offers an effective substitute for another: The military salute, using the optical channel, substitutes a visual expression of respect or honor for what could otherwise be orally recited, and photojournalists strive to present news events pictorially because "a picture is worth a thousand words."

The most common form of the acoustic channel is oral, as in singing, whistling, and of course speaking. If human language is to be considered as a general language code, then it is manifested in several thousand specific codes, of which English, Russian, Navajo, and Japanese are examples. Each of these codes subsumes a number of subcodes. English has not only the several national varieties such as American, British, and Australian, but also regional dialects such as those of New England, the English Midlands, and South Australia, and a number of slangs peculiar to particular groups.

Among the Ashanti, the acoustic channel is quite diversified. The principal verbal code is Twi, a language characterized by five distinctive tones. The ceremonial language priests and priestesses use is a subcode; it is identified as an earlier form of Twi that Ashanti laypeople apparently cannot understand. The so-called language of the ghosts, consisting of cooing noises and said to be intelligible only to unborn babies and toothless infants, is an example of an oral but nonverbal form of the acoustic channel. Other nonverbal codes of the Ashanti include the drum code to convey messages and signals; the horn code, used for similar purposes; the gong code, employed for public summonses; and whistling, used not by the Ashanti themselves but by the forest fairies and monsters who instruct their medicine men. Some parts of the ceremony at which ancestral spirits are propitiated are conducted in complete silence; other parts permit the chief to communicate only by gestures.

Message form and message content are closely related, or as Hymes (1972:59) puts it, "It is a truism . . . that *how* something is said is part of *what* is said." A paraphrase may be sufficient to indicate the message content, but only the quoting of the exact words can represent adequately the message form of a speech act. To paraphrase the statement "Like hell I'm kidding; I've warned you—now get out, fast!" as "I told him in no uncertain terms that he was no longer welcome" does away with so much color and feeling that the changed form no longer has much in common with the original content.

Here it is appropriate to mention the term *register,* referring to a variety of language that serves a particular social situation. In American linguistics the term is used to differentiate between broad varieties of a language—for example, between the vernacular (everyday, casual spoken form) and the standard (prestige form) in English. In Great Britain *register* is used for any of a number of specifically defined varieties, such as legal, scientific, religious, intimate, and so on.

Components of Communication: Genres, Key, Rules of Interaction, and Norms of Interpretation

The term *genre* refers to speech acts or events associated with a particular communicative situation and characterized by a particular style, form, and content. Ritual or religious occasions, for example, regularly call for such special genres as prayers and sermons. Both sermons and prayers make use of a ceremonial style of speech with special attention to form. This is why *thou, thee, thy,* and *thine* for 'you,' 'your,' and 'yours' have survived to the present in prayers and the language of the Friends (Quakers).

A good storyteller of Old World fairy or wonder tales would customarily begin the telling by some such phrase as "Once upon a time" and signal the end of the tale by the formula "And they lived happily ever after" or, more elaborately, "The festivities lasted nine days and nine nights. There were 900 fiddlers, 900 fluters, and 900 pipers, and the last day and night of the wedding were better than the first." Important incidents in Old World tales usually take place three times (that is, the formulistic or magic number is three) whereas in Native American tales things happen four times.

Myths represent another genre, one found in the traditions of all of the world's societies. Arapaho stories concerning *nihʔóóθoo* 'Whiteman,' a popular character of Arapaho trickster tales, almost invariably have him walking down (or up) the river in the initial sentence of the story. The end is signaled by the formula, "This is the end of the story." In Upper Chinook, a Native American language spoken in Oregon, myths are characterized by features not found elsewhere in the language (Hymes 1958). The diagnostic features of Upper Chinook myths are phonological (for example, the doubling of a consonant word-finally to indicate stuttering from fright or excitement), morphological (limiting the use of certain noun prefixes to the speech of characters appearing in myths), lexical (reserving the use of certain names for myths only), and syntactic. Other linguistic features of Upper Chinook are limited to casual speech.

A "war talk" genre was employed among the Navajo (Hill 1936) and other Native Americans. Upon entering enemy territory, the leader of a Navajo war party would instruct the group to use words different from the ones commonly used to refer to the livestock, captives, and whatever else they hoped to bring back; members of the war party spoke this warpath language until they turned toward home.

Perhaps more than genre or other components, key varies widely among cultures. By the term *key*, Hymes refers to the "tone, manner, or spirit in which an act is done" and adds that "acts otherwise the same as regards setting, participants, message form, and the like may differ in key, as, e.g., between *mock* [and] *serious* or *perfunctory* [and] *painstaking*" (Hymes 1972:62). Key may even override another component, as when a speaker who is presumably praising someone becomes slowly but increasingly so sarcastic that the person spoken of feels hurt or ridiculed. A particular key may be used so frequently by members of a group that it loses much of its effect, whereas another key may be so rarely employed that it may require some effort on the part of hearers to identify it and comprehend its social meaning.

Communicative activity is guided by rules of interaction: Under normal circumstances, members of a speech community know what is and what is not appropriate. Among members of the middle class in the United States, for example, interruptions are not considered appropriate except among close friends or family members, but if someone monopolizes a conversation, there are acceptable ways of breaking in. A compliment addressed to another person is usually gratefully acknowledged or some remark is made to the effect that the compliment may not be fully deserved. When rules of interaction are broken or completely neglected, embarrassment results, and unless an apology is offered, future contacts between the parties may be strained or even avoided.

The judgment as to what constitutes proper interaction is of course subject to interpretation. The norms of interpretation (just as the rules of interaction) vary from culture to culture, sometimes only subtly but usually quite distinctly or even profoundly. And within a single society, if that society is socially or ethnically diversified, not all members are likely to use the same rules of interaction and the same norms of interpretation. For example, U.S. citizens of Mexican origin may well have different norms of interpreting communicative behavior than their fellow citizens of Japanese ancestry. Awareness of these differences and a need for understanding and adjustment is particularly crucial in intercultural communication. In a study conducted at the University of Colorado among male students from Arabic-speaking countries and male students from the United States, Michael Watson and Theodore Graves (1966:976–979) found, much as they had hypothesized, that "Arabs confronted each other more directly than Americans when conversing. . . . They sat closer to each other . . . [and] were more likely to touch each other. . . . They looked each other more squarely in the eye . . . and . . . conversed more loudly than Americans. . . .

Persons from the various Arab countries [appear to] be more similar to each other than to any regional group of Americans." Interpretation of American communicative behavior by foreign visitors to the United States according to their own norms, and vice versa, can only result in misunderstanding rather than the appreciation of different cultures.

In discussing the various components of speech, Hymes used as a mnenonic device the word S P E A K I N G, whose letters stand for *s*ettings, *p*articipants, *e*nds (discussed above as "purpose"), *a*ct sequences (the arrangement of components), *k*eys, *i*nstrumentalities (discussed above as "channels," "codes," and "message form"), *n*orms (of interaction and interpretation), and *g*enres.

Subanun Drinking Talk

A good example of an ethnography-of-speaking account of a speech situation is the paper "How to Ask for a Drink in Subanun" (Frake 1964). The Subanun are swidden agriculturists who live in the mountainous interior of a peninsula on the Philippine island of Mindanao. Frake's article deals only with the drinking of *gasi*, a fermented beverage usually made of rice, manioc, and maize, that Frake labels "beer." The drinking of beer is a required activity limited to festive gatherings occasioned by some specific event and characterized by the participation of several families. The beer is drunk with bamboo straws from a Chinese jar containing the fermented mash. Just before the drinking begins, the jar is filled with water. The resulting beer, which contains a fair amount of alcohol, is sucked up by straw from the bottom of the jar by each participant in turn.

The first stage of the drinking encounter consists of tasting. During this stage the person who provides the jar invites the participant who enjoys the highest respect to drink. This person must then ask each of the other participants to permit him to drink, expressing role distances and authority relations between himself and the others by the order in which he asks their permission and the terms of address he uses. Several rounds of tasting are succeeded by competitive drinking. During this stage the talk centers on the quality of the beer and the performance of the participants. The drinkers must consume no less than the amount drunk by the person initiating the round. During the competition the number of participants as a rule is reduced to less than half a dozen. Competitive drinking then continues with a discussion—beginning with trivial gossip and proceeding to subjects of current concern. It culminates in what Frake terms "game drinking," which features a display of verbal art. (Frake's description of the last two discourse stages, discussion and display of verbal art, appears in Box 10.1.)

In short, among the Subanun, speaking in the context of festive drinking can be used to extend, define, and manipulate a person's social rela-

---

BOX 10.1   Festive Drinking and Talking Among the Subanun

As the size and role-structure of the gathering becomes defined, discourse changes in topic to removed referents, usually beginning with relatively trivial gossip, proceeding to more important subjects of current interest, and, finally, in many cases arriving at litigation. ... Success in effecting legal decisions depends on achieving a commanding role in the encounter and on debating effectively from that position. Since there are no sanctions of force legally applicable to back up a decision, the payment of a fine in compliance with a decision is final testimony to the prowess in verbal combat of the person who made the decision.

... If drinking continues long enough, the focus of messages shifts from their topics to play with message forms themselves, following stylized patterns of song and verse composition. Songs and verses are composed on the spot to carry on discussions in an operetta-like setting. Even unsettled litigation may be continued in this manner, the basis for decision being shifted from cogent argument to verbal artistry. The most prestigious kinds of drinking songs require the mastery of an esoteric vocabulary by means of which each line is repeated with a semantically equivalent but formally different line. Game drinking is a frequent accompaniment to these displays of verbal art. Together they help assure that the festivity will end with good feelings among all participants, a goal which is explicitly stated by the Subanun. Participants who had displayed marked hostility toward each other during the course of drinking talk may be singled out for special ritual treatment designed to restore good feelings.

from Charles O. Frake, "How to Ask for a Drink in Subanun"
(1964), 130–131

---

tionships. To speak Subanun grammatically and sensibly is not enough. In order to become respected and achieve a position of leadership in Subanun society, a person must have the skill to "talk from the straw," that is, one must know what to say to whom and when, and in addition be able to use the language creatively.

Attitudes Toward the Use of Speech

The bulk of information in all communities is transmitted by speech, but members of some communities engage in speaking more readily than do members of others. In his *Laws*, Plato has an elderly Athenian comment that in Greece it is widely believed that Athenians not only take delight in talking but talk a great deal, Lacedaemonians (Spartans) are inclined to be taciturn, and Cretans have versatile minds but prefer to be concise in speech (Plato 1961:1242:641e). In other societies talking is encouraged and appreciated by some members but discouraged or negatively valued by others. According to Inez Hilger (1957:44–45, 81–83), among the Araucanians of south central Chile and neighboring parts of Argentina, men are expected to talk a great deal, and those who do and speak well are highly respected. By contrast, Araucanian women are brought up to say little and speak quietly in public and to keep silent in the company of their husbands (although they speak freely when in the company of women). Among Mongolian nomads, daughters-in-law have such a low status that they are severely restricted in the use of language. For example, they are forbidden to use not only the names of their husbands' male relatives but any words or syllables that sound like these names.

In the United States almost everyone knows some individuals who talk incessantly or at least a great deal (talkers, gabbers, chatterboxes, jabberers, chatterers) and others who say very little (they are said to be tight-lipped, close-mouthed, reticent, taciturn, and so on). Those who talk freely are generally preferred because they appear more self-confident and are easier to get to know than those who say very little. The saying "Still waters run deep" suggests that a quiet demeanor may conceal some unexpected characteristics. On the whole, keeping silent is not looked upon favorably in the United States: Even ten seconds of no one's saying anything during a party can cause such embarrassment that several people are likely to begin speaking at the same time to break the silence. But under some circumstances speech is virtually proscribed: During the meetings of the Society of Friends (Quakers), for example, communion with God is sought through silent waiting for the Inner Light rather than through praying aloud or singing.

In some societies, refraining from speaking is expected under a variety of circumstances and provides an interesting contrast with the general attitudes toward speech in the United States. For a description of situations in which the Western Apache of Cibecue in east central Arizona "give up on words," we are indebted to Keith H. Basso (1970). Basso discusses six types of situations in which Western Apaches are expected to refrain from speaking. Three of these are of particular interest. One concerns meeting strangers, whether Apaches or others. Such a situation usually takes place at large gatherings such as rodeos but is reported to have occurred even when two strangers happened to work together on a four-man roundup crew. They did not begin to speak to each other until the night of the fourth day. In Western Apache culture a stranger who is quick to talk to others is suspected of wanting something from them or of having had too much to drink. Another situation in which no speaking occurs has to do with the initial stages of courtship. At public gatherings young couples may be holding hands but saying nothing to each other for as much as an hour, and they are generally just as silent when they are alone. Their silence, especially that of the girls, is attributed to shyness, self-consciousness, and modesty.

Complete silence is also maintained for as long as a quarter of an hour when Western Apache parents meet children who are returning from boarding schools. While the children become comfortable enough to talk soon after their arrival, it may take several days before the parents engage in normal conversation with them. The reason for the initial restraint on the part of the parents is their belief that the attitudes and behavior of their children are likely to have changed as a result of exposure to new ideas and that it is therefore wise to wait and see "how they would like . . . being [at] home [again]." Basso hypothesizes that in Western Apache culture "the absence of verbal communication is associated with social situations in which the status of [the main] participants is ambiguous . . . [and constitutes] a response to uncertainty and unpredictability in social relations" (Basso 1970:227).

That speaking is a cultural focus for the Tenejapa Tzeltal, who live in the central highlands of the state of Chiapas in Mexico, is evident from their elaborate terminology for ways of speaking. Among the 416 terms recorded by Brian Stross (1974) are those referring to talk occurring in a grassy area, nighttime talk, speech coming from a person who is lying on his (her) side, the announcement by a woman that she is pregnant, talk among several people who are sitting down, speech of a person who is hungry or fasting, and so on. Malicious gossip, insults, mockery, threats, and ungrammatical or incoherent speech are considered of little worth; songs, prayers, eloquent speech, and deliberate utterances using careful pronunciation are highly valued.

The ability to speak well, especially in public, is valued in all societies. But definition of what "speaking well" means would not be the same in all cultures. The sacred vocabulary of Zuñi prayers, songs, myths, and ceremonial conversations carries prestige and is considered dignified; the rapidly changing slang words of young Zuñis are considered foolish and of little value but are not condemned (Newman 1955). The tendency of the Kwakiutl of Vancouver Island, British Columbia, to go beyond the literal meaning of words is documented by Boas (1940) in his discussion of metaphorical expressions in Kwakiutl. They range (in English translation) from "to nettle" for "to ridicule" to "post of our world" for "chief" to "having a sweet taste" in reference to a good speech. And for the Navajo, words are "things of power. Some words attract good; others drive away evil [and] certain words are dangerous—they may be uttered only by special persons under specially defined conditions" (Kluckhohn and Leighton 1962:260).

As a rule, people consider their native language to be the most natural and efficient means of communication, and one can easily understand why they would think so. But it is also true that many peoples view other languages (and their speakers) with less respect. The Czechs believe their language to be very rich and expressive (which it is), and many Czech writers and poets have celebrated their language in their writings. At the same time, some Czechs tend to view the very closely related and mutually intelligible Slovak language, which is spoken to the east of the Czech Republic, as a caricature of Czech. Slovak expressions that are not identical or nearly identical with Czech ones seem to Czechs to possess a measure of grotesqueness, and Slovak words or phrases they cannot understand at first hearing strike Czechs not simply as foreign but as monstrous. Unintelligible languages fare no better. The Czech word for a German, *Němec*, was derived centuries ago from the adjective *němý* 'mute' because, it was thought, someone who uttered inarticulate and unintelligible foreign sounds might as well be mute.

To sum up, those who study the attitudes of members of a society toward the use of speech and communicative behavior in general should ask the following: Do particular ways of speaking (or communicating with others) help to define people held in respect or disrespect? Does the use of speech (or manner of communicating) help to define a particular sociocultural role (for example, that of grandfather, chief, or medicine man), and if so, how? What does it mean to speak well (or communicate effectively), and what kind of speech (communicative) behavior is viewed with dislike? Is speaking encouraged or discouraged, and by whom and under what circumstances? How do people view dialects and other varieties of their own language? and How do they look at languages spoken by neighboring peoples, whether friends or enemies?

Recent Trends in the Ethnography of Speaking

The methods of the ethnography of speaking are increasingly applied even in what is essentially linguistic (rather than linguistically anthropological) inquiry. When field-workers so apply these methods, they make use of recorded narratives, monologs, or dialogs to show, for example, how the syntactic patterns of a language are adjusted to principles of culture-specific discourse. Jeffrey Heath discusses this approach in his article concerned with clause structure in Ngandi, a language now spoken by only a very few aborigines in southeastern Arnhem Land (northern Australia). For his analysis, rather than using a text corrected and refined with the help of an informant after a more or less spontaneous first recording has been made, Heath prefers "the original text, warts and all" or at least keeps "editorial emendations . . . to a minimum" (Heath

1985:90). Furthermore, he likes to obtain texts that are stylistically diverse rather than uniform. Having such texts makes it easier to match different styles with corresponding grammatical (or even "ungrammatical") forms.

To cite (in a simplified form) one of the several examples with which Heath illustrates his discussion: Among many speakers of English such fillers as *er, uh, um* used to fill pauses or gaps in discourse carry a stigma. Not so among speakers of Ngandi. The most common of what Heath terms a "whatchamacallit" element in Ngandi, the noun *jara*, is fully acceptable in all styles, and its syntactic prominence is attested by its having derivational forms (as in *man-jara* 'group associated with whatchamacallit' and *bicara* 'whatchamacallit [place-name]') and a full set of noun-class prefixes and suffixes. The word *jara*, usually heard after a pause, is used while a speaker searches his or her memory for a specific noun, and when a second such element is used in the same utterance, *ŋuni* is added to express impatience and self-irritation, as in *buluki? bicara ba-ga-ŋ-i:, bicara ŋuni* 'they also sat (lived) at whatchamacallit place—what the hell was the name of that place?' (Heath 1985:107). To linguists who would most likely be analyzing unwritten languages spoken by very small out-of-the-way societies, Ngandi discourse structure might well appear as highly fragmented and unpredictable. What strikes Heath in particular "about the differences between English and such Australian languages as Ngandi . . . is that most of them relate closely to 'psycholinguistic' aspects of speech production" and that the underlying clear-cut grammar and the psycholinguistic component concerned with memory limitations, surface ambiguities, and the like "are far more tightly welded to each other than it seems at first" (Heath 1985:108). To make some sort of sense of this connection, the investigator must attach due significance to language as it is used. Here we have a good example of the recognition of the contribution that ethnography of speaking can make to linguistics.

In papers dealing with language use, the term *context* has been commonly employed to denote the interrelated conditions under which speech and other forms of communicative behavior occur. There has recently been a tendency to employ the term *contextualization* instead. Many linguistic anthropologists believe that it is preferable, at least in some instances, to view context as a process—as something that develops and perhaps even changes significantly while two or more individuals are interacting rather than as something that is given, or fixed. Those features of the settings that are used at particular stages of the interaction to aid in the interpretation of the content are signaled by contextualization cues.

To put it differently: When two (or more) individuals interact for even a relatively short period of time, the nature and purpose of their verbal exchange may abruptly change as well as the message content and form, rules of interaction, and so forth. Such a situation is easy to imagine. For example, two neighbors are chatting casually about the weather and their gardens until one happens to make a remark about the other's child and the remark is taken as a criticism of parenting skills. The casual atmosphere surrounding the conversation changes instantly. The tone of the person whose child's behavior has been found wanting may suddenly turn cool, indicating that the conversation is about to end, and on a very different note from the way it began; or the tone may become angry, with a countercharge launched against the child of the one making the original criticism. In the latter case, the contextualization cue could well be some such remark as "My child is fine—why don't you concentrate on your own, who is always leading our boy astray!"

Summary and Conclusions

Ethnography of communication is an important recent development supplementing the already well-established study of cultures by anthropologists and languages by linguists. The goals of this new field are first to give as complete an account as possible of the social uses of speech in different societies and then to produce historical and comparative studies on the subject (ethnology of communication). Thus far the scope of ethnography of communication has been almost exclusively descriptive and synchronic, but cross-cultural comparisons of the social uses of speech as well as studies of how speech uses change over time should soon be forthcoming.

Because their purpose is to discover how humans interact under the many different circumstances of the real world, anthropologists who specialize in the ethnography of communication obtain their data from direct observation of communicative performances. The social unit to which studies in ethnography of communication refer is the speech community—that is, all those people who share at least one speech variety as well as specific rules for the social uses of speaking and for interpreting what is being communicated.

An understanding of the diversity in the ways of communicating is of course of great interest to linguistic anthropologists, but we need to look beyond the merely intellectual satisfaction derived from the study of the subject. There is reason to hope that the application of the growing body of information in the field of ethnography of communication may contribute to the solution of some of the social problems of societies in which many peoples live side by side but do not always share the same ways of speaking.

Notes and Suggestions for Further Reading

The information concerning the Ashanti has been drawn from a study by Helen Marie Hogan (n.d.), who based her account on a thorough review of published data. Because most of her sources appeared between the 1920s and 1960s, some of the information may no longer conform to the current communicative behavior of the Ashanti. The examination of the essential components of communicative behavior draws on Hymes 1972 and Saville-Troike 1982. The regional labels of American dialects have been selected from among thirty-seven regional labels used in the *Dictionary of American Regional English* (Cassidy 1985).

Boas's article on the use of the metaphor in Kwakiutl was originally published in 1929 in the Netherlands; it was reprinted in Boas 1940.

Articles and books dealing with the ethnography of speaking include Bauman and Sherzer 1974 (or 1989); Gumperz and Hymes 1964, 1972, and 1986; Hymes 1974; Saville-Troike 1982 and 1989; Sherzer 1977; and Sherzer and Darnell 1972. For a survey of literature on the subject, see Bauman and Sherzer 1975 and 1989, and Duranti 1988, and for a bibliography, see Philipsen and Carbaugh 1986.

11

Nonverbal Communication and Writing

Spoken language—speech—is by far the most common and important means by which humans communicate with one another, but it is not the only one. The many different writing systems used throughout the world are of tremendous importance for communication, having in some respects an advantage over spoken language, especially their relative permanence.

The term **nonverbal communication,** taken literally, refers to any transmission of signals accomplished by means other than spoken or written words. Not everyone agrees on what the term encompasses, and some even question whether nonverbal communication is definable. Used broadly, the term includes bodily gestures, facial expressions, spacing, touch, and smell as well as whistle, smoke-signal, and drum "languages" and such optional vocal effects as those that accompany spoken utterances and can be considered apart from actual words.

Nonverbal systems of communication may be divided into those that are derived from spoken language and those that are independent of it. With only a few exceptions, writing systems belong to the first category, representing as they do the sounds of speech. In turn, writing systems may serve as the source of other systems. The English word written as *tree* can be transmitted in the International Morse Code by audible or visual signals as – ·—· · ·, with –, ·—·, and · representing respectively the letters *t, r,* and *e.* Similarly, the braille alphabet, a system of writing for the blind, makes use of raised dots within a 2 × 3 matrix. The different arrangements of raised dots (•) represent the letters of the alphabet, as in

$$
\begin{matrix}
\circ\bullet & \bullet\circ & \bullet\circ & \bullet\circ \\
\bullet\bullet & \bullet\bullet & \circ\bullet & \circ\bullet \\
\bullet\circ & \bullet\circ & \circ\circ & \circ\circ
\end{matrix} \quad ,
$$

corresponding to *t, r, e, e.*

Other systems of communication that are based on speech are drum and whistle "languages," which imitate some of the reproducible distinctive features of the spoken languages along with which they are used.

Sign language, such as that widely used in earlier times by the Plains Indians, is independent of speech. It could not have been otherwise because it had to serve as a means of communication transcending the many language boundaries of the polyglot Great Plains.

Another way of classifying nonverbal communicative systems is according to channel, or the medium by which signals are conveyed. The channel employed in drum "language" is acoustic, whereas sign language or smoke signals use the optical channel. Individuals who are blind make use of touch as they feel the raised dots of the braille system, and those who are both blind and deaf may learn to monitor articulatory movements by placing a hand on the speaker's face and neck (Tadoma method). The olfactory channel is not used in the highly structured manner of the channels just mentioned but should not be underestimated: As a rule, Americans do not indulge in eating fresh garlic before a social occasion or an important business engagement for fear of sending the wrong signals.

For the most part, human communication is a multichannel affair operating on both verbal and nonverbal levels. Regardless of the society, it is not only how people talk and what they say but also how they present themselves to others that seems to make a difference as to how they are perceived. The study of the properties of signs and symbols and their functions in communication is referred to as semiotics. Because of the increasing attention given to all modes of communication in both humans and other animals, the field of semiotics has been steadily growing in volume and popularity.

Paralinguistics, Kinesics, and Proxemics

Characteristics of vocal communication considered marginal or optional and therefore excludable from the customary linguistic analysis are referred to as **paralanguage.** The most common paralinguistic features have to do with the tone of voice and pacing of speech and are marked by noticeable variations in pitch, tempo, rhythm, articulation, or intensity. For example, highly controlled articulation produces the crisp, precise pronunciation expected of formal pronouncements addressed to large audiences; by contrast, speech so relaxed as to become slurred is heard from those who are very tired, sleepy, or under the influence of alcohol or other drugs. Speakers of English and other languages tend to associate extreme pitch variation with happiness and surprise; high pitch level or fast tempo with fear, surprise, or anger; and low pitch level or slow tempo with boredom and sadness. The rounding of lips imparts to the voice the cooing quality that is frequently used by adults when talking to a baby.

Besides these and other voice qualifiers, there are various vocal characterizers that accompany speech or, more precisely, through which we talk.

These range from laughing to crying and from whispering to shouting, and include such other vocalizations as moaning and yawning. Then there are the so-called vocal segregates represented for the most part by such extralinguistic sounds as the ones graphically rendered in English as *uh-huh* to indicate agreement or gratification, *ah* to express a variety of emotions from delight to regret, and *tut-tut* or *tsk-tsk* to show mild disapproval. These optional vocal effects may not carry the same meaning from one language to the next. The breathy or husky tone of voice that in some languages is associated with intense emotion or sexual desire conveys respect or a submissive attitude in Japanese.

Just as any speech that is not completely neutral tends to be accompanied by one or more paralinguistic features, that is, by vocal gestures, it is also likely to be supplemented by visual gestures—facial expressions and other body motions. These are the subject of kinesics.

There is no question that bodily gestures serve as important means of communication. Comedians are notably adept at slanting, canceling, or completely turning around the meaning of their spoken lines with a well-chosen grimace or gesture of different communicative content, and professional mimes know how to move their audiences to tears or laughter without uttering a single word. But speech-related body motions are by no means limited to performers—they are an integral part of everyone's daily communicative activity.

The basic assumptions that underlie kinesics are that no body movement or facial expression lacks meaning in the context in which it occurs and that like other aspects of voluntary human behavior, body movements, posture, and facial expressions are patterned. Influenced by structural linguistics, Ray L. Birdwhistell (1918–1997) in the 1950s developed a method of studying and describing the body-motion aspects of human communicative behavior by means of units that parallel those employed in linguistic analysis. One such unit, the kineme (analogous to the phoneme), has been defined as the smallest discriminable contrastive unit of body motion. A variant of the kineme is an allokine (analogous to the allophone). Kinemes are said to occur in combinations, termed kinemorphs, and these in turn in larger constructions. For example, the rapid closing and reopening of an eyelid may be communicatively significant if it is not involuntary; the meaning of such a wink may range from teasing to conspiratorial, and the action would be considered a kineme. A combination of a wink with the raising of an eyebrow and a corner of the mouth produces a facial kinemorph, which in turn may be linked to head or hand movements, and so on.

Observant travelers noticed centuries ago that members of societies along the Mediterranean Sea used many more bodily gestures and facial expressions than, say, those living in Scandinavia or Japan. However, not all Italians, for example, use the same "body language," just as they do not all speak the same dialect of Italian. Birdwhistell offers an interesting example in support of the expectation that kinesic behavior is bound to be just as culture-specific as the corresponding language. He reports that even when the sound is removed from films of the speeches of the late politician and mayor of New York City Fiorello La Guardia, it is possible to tell whether he is speaking English, Yiddish, or Italian, as characteristic body motions are associated with each language (Birdwhistell 1970:102). Although the holistic and contextual approach to communication that Birdwhistell advocated has been uniformly accepted, the extent to which "body language" can be analyzed in terms of his units remains controversial, in part because the detailed transcription he designed is far too complicated and time-consuming.

In the early 1960s the interdependence between communication and culture stimulated Edward T. Hall to develop proxemics, the study of the cultural patterning of the spatial separation individuals maintain in face-to-face encounters. The term has subsequently come to embrace studies concerned with privacy, crowding, territoriality, and the designing of buildings, private as well as public, with the view of meeting the different cultural expectations of their prospective users.

According to Hall, the distances individuals maintain from one another depend on the nature of their mutual involvement and are culture-specific. For example, under normal circumstances middle-class American adults of North European heritage make regular use of four proxemic zones, or distances, ranging from intimate to public, each of the zones consisting of a close and a far phase (see Table 11.1). In the close phase of the intimate distance, the individuals are close enough to be encircled by each other's arms. All senses are engaged: Each individual receives the body heat as well as any odor or scent emanating from the other individual, and the other person's breath is felt; because of the closeness, vision may be blurred or distorted and speaking is at a minimum. As is obvious, this narrowest of all interpersonal distances is suited to lovemaking, protecting, or comforting.

By contrast, business is transacted at the social-consultative distance: The close phase is characteristic of contact among people who work together or are participants at casual social gatherings; the far phase characterizes more formal business transactions, such as interviews or situations where two or more people find themselves in the same space and do not want to appear rude by not communicating. For instance, receptionists who are also expected to type and manage a switchboard must have enough space between them and the visitors to permit them to work rather than to feel they must engage in polite conversation with those waiting to be seen.

TABLE 11.1   The Four Distance Zones of Informal Interpersonal Space Among Middle-Class Americans of North European Heritage

Distance Zone	Physical Distance (approx., in feet)	Acoustic-Auditory Channel	Olfactory Channel
Intimate			
Close	0–.5	grunts, groans	
Far	.5–1.5	whispers or very low voice	
Personal			
Close	1.5–2.5	soft voice	almost all odors
Far	2.5–4	moderate voice	disapproved of
Social-consultative			
Close	4–7	normal voice	almost all odors
Far	7–12	louder voice	disapproved of
Public			
Close	12–25	loud voice	almost all odors
Far	25+	full-volume voice	disapproved of

SOURCE: Adapted from *The Hidden Dimension* by Edward T. Hall. Copyright © 1966, 1982 by Edward T. Hall. Used by permission of Doubleday, a division of Bantam Doubleday Dell Publishing Group, Inc.

The manner in which members of different societies space themselves in each other's presence varies along a contact-noncontact continuum. For example, Arabs, other Mediterranean peoples, and Latin Americans prefer spatially close interactions; northern Europeans prefer to keep their distance, both literally and figuratively (see Box 11.1).

Whistle and Drum "Languages"

Among the various systems of nonverbal communication, of particular interest are those speech surrogates that depend on and are derived directly from spoken language. Some of these "languages" are produced in the vocal tract—for example, so-called whistle speech—whereas others make use of resonating objects, especially musical instruments.

Whistling as a means of serviceable communication is not very common but is known to occur in such widely separated areas of the world as Myanmar (formerly Burma), Mexico, the Canary Islands, the French Pyrenees, Cameroon, and New Guinea. One of the better-known cases of whistle speech concerns the Mazateco Indians of northern Oaxaca, Mexico. The language of the Mazateco is a tone language, one in which relative variations in pitch are used to distinguish words of different meanings that otherwise would sound alike. There are four distinctive pitch levels, or tonemes, in Mazateco, ranging from high, 1, to low, 4, with two

BOX 11.1   Hall on Proxemics in a Cross-cultural Context

In Latin America the interaction distance is much less than it is in the United States. Indeed, people cannot talk comfortably with one another unless they are very close to the distance that evokes either sexual or hostile feelings in the North American. The result is that when they move close, we withdraw and back away. As a consequence, they think we are distant or cold, withdrawn and unfriendly. We, on the other hand, are constantly accusing them of breathing down our necks, crowding us, and spraying our faces.

Americans who have spent some time in Latin America without learning these space considerations make other adaptations, like barricading themselves behind their desks, using chairs and typewriter tables to keep the Latin American at what is to us a comfortable distance. The result is that the Latin American may even climb over the obstacles until he has achieved a distance at which he can comfortably talk.

from Edward T. Hall, *The Silent Language* (1959), 209

Many Americans feel that Germans are overly rigid in their behavior, unbending and formal. Some of this impression is created by differences in the handling of chairs while seated. The American doesn't seem to mind if people hitch their chairs up to adjust the distance to the situation—those that do mind would not think of saying anything, for to comment on the manners of others would be impolite. In Germany, however, it is a violation of the mores to change the position of your chair. An added deterrent for those who don't know better is the weight of most German furniture. ... To a German, light furniture is anathema, not only because it seems flimsy but because people move it and thereby destroy the order of things, including intrusions on the "private sphere." In one instance reported to me, a German newspaper editor who had moved to the United States had his visitor's chair bolted to the floor "at the proper distance" because he couldn't tolerate the American habit of adjusting the chair to the situation.

from Edward T. Hall, *The Hidden Dimension* (1966), 129

intermediate tonemes, 2 and 3; when two different tones are associated with one syllabic nucleus, they form a glide. Accordingly, the speakers of Mazateco distinguish between te^1 'he will dance,' te^2 'he dances,' te^{2-3} 'I dance,' te^{4-3} 'wide,' te^3 'ten,' ni^3nto^2 'slippery,' ni^4nto^{3-4} 'pimple,' ni^3nto^3 'mountain,' and so on (Pike and Pike 1947:88).

Under special circumstances, as when the distance between two Mazateco men is too great for them to shout, they use whistle speech. By reproducing, with a few modifications, the four tonemes and other whistleable features (glides, different types of syllabic units, and pauses), they are able to carry on an effective conversation concerning a variety of topics. The following exchange was observed by George M. Cowan (1948), to whom we are indebted for the description of Mazateco whistle speech: A Mazateco standing in front of his hut whistled to another man a considerable distance away on a trail below. After several exchanges in whistle talk, the man on the trail turned around and walked up to the hut with the load of corn leaves he had been carrying to market. At the hut, he dumped his load on the ground and received some money from the first man. The entire transaction, including the customary bargaining over price, had been carried on exclusively through whistling.

Although Mazateco women do not whistle, they understand whistle talk. In addition to overcoming distance in the hilly terrain in which these people live, whistling is used to attract the attention of another person by sounding his name or to exchange information without interfering with a simultaneous oral conversation carried on by elders. Even though there are no limitations in principle on what can be signaled by whistling, identical tonal patterns can give rise to ambiguities or confusion. However, the subject that is communicated by whistling is usually easily identifiable from the context.

Whereas Mazateco whistle speech makes use of the prosodic features of the language from which it derives, the whistle speech employed on La Gomera, one of the Canary Islands, is based on articulations. The reason for the development of the *silbo* (Spanish for whistle), as it is called, is apparently the island's rugged terrain, alternating between mountains and gorges. According to André Classe (1957), accomplished users of the *silbo* can be heard and understood over a distance of 3 miles and perhaps even more.

The native language of the inhabitants of La Gomera is a dialect of Spanish. Many members of the island's peasant class, both men and women, are proficient in the *silbo* by the time they have reached their teens. The whistled sounds approximate the sounds of the spoken language, making the *silbo* in effect whistled Spanish. Whether or not the whistler uses one or two fingers in the mouth, the dorsal part of the tongue is the only active articulatory organ. Because Spanish is not a tone language, whistled vowels can be differentiated by varying pitches, and most of the consonants of the relatively simple sound system of the spoken language are heard as modifications of the whistled vowels that come before or after them.

Instrumental signaling is more common than whistling, with wind instruments (such as horns and whistles), stringed instruments (especially the lute and musical bow), and percussion instruments (drums, gongs, xylophones, and others) employed in various parts of the world. Use of the so-called talking drums has been especially frequent and elaborate along the West African coast between Guinea and Zaire. One of the best descriptions of drum signaling was provided by George Herzog (1901–1983), who did research among the Jabo of eastern Liberia in 1930.

According to Herzog (1945), the signaling drums of the Jabo are of two kinds: those hollowed out from the trunk of a tree and provided with a longitudinal slit (from a technical standpoint, these slit-drums are bells) and single-headed skin-covered drums. Only a very limited number of signals are sent on true drums. The slit-drums are used to call meetings to order or dismiss them, to summon specific tribespeople who may be working in the fields, or to introduce warriors or other persons of eminence by their laudatory titles. Just as in the case of the Mazateco whistle speech, Jabo drum signaling is made possible by the character of the spoken language, whose four distinctive pitch levels and various glides resulting from their combination are imitated by the drummers.

In some regions of Africa the drum "language" has become elaborated enough to permit fairly unrestricted, though somewhat stereotypical, conversations. To minimize the potential ambiguity resulting from several words having identical tonal patterns, drummers resort to paraphrasing short words with stock phrases consisting of many syllables: *Leopard* may be signaled by the phrase "he who tears up the roof," *moon* as "the moon that looks down upon the earth," and the like. In addition to distinctive tones, drummers also reproduce prosodic features such as stress, the duration and structure of syllables, and the rhythm and speed of an utterance.

That whistling and drumming are as effective as they are is excellent proof of the high redundancy that characterizes all natural languages: Even when some features are eliminated from the code, as may occur, for example, when one is using an old telephone, there is no appreciable loss of essential information.

Sign Languages

Signing, that is, communicating manually by **sign language** of some kind, is undoubtedly at least as old as speech. From the writings of ancient Greeks and Romans, we know that their deaf made use of signs. It is, however, reasonable to assume that even among the earliest humans those who were not able to communicate orally would have used their hands to make themselves understood. Sign languages used to the exclusion of spoken language—for example, by people born deaf—are referred to as primary. Sign languages found in communities of speaker-hearers as regular or occasional substitutes for speech are termed alternate sign languages.

Abbé Charles Michel de l'Épée (1712–1789), who founded the first free public educational institution for the deaf in Paris in the early 1770s, developed a sign language for the use of his students. De l'Épée's system, further elaborated by his successor, Abbé Roch A. C. Sicard (1742–1822), had direct influence on the development of sign languages in a number of countries throughout the world. American Sign Language (ASL), or Ameslan for short, is one of its derivatives. For many years scholars neglected the study of sign languages, considering them as little more than crude substitutes for speech. Serious attention to sign languages dates back to the late 1950s; it was accompanied by renewed interest in the sign language of the Indians of the Great Plains.

In the United States, the hearing-impaired use a combination of two signing systems. One is the manual alphabet, which is made up of signs representing the twenty-six letters of the English alphabet and the ampersand (&). It is fingerspelled, using one hand only, and both the sender and receiver must be acquainted with the orthography of the language. (By contrast, the signs of the manual alphabet used in Great Britain and Northern Ireland are made with both hands.) In the other signing system, sign language proper, a particular sign stands for a concept, or, to put it in terms of spoken language, a word or a morpheme. There are a number of sign languages in use in English-speaking countries, most involving some modification of either Ameslan or British Sign Language (BSL). Ameslan offers its users some 5,000 signs, with new ones coined as needed. It makes use of three-dimensional sign space that forms a "bubble" about the signer extending roughly from the waist to the top of the head and outward from the extreme left to the extreme right as far as the signer can reach. Within the sign space, the user can specify time relationships, distinguish among several persons that are being signed about, signal questions and embedded clauses, and express a variety of grammatical categories such as plurality and degree (as in *good, better, best*) as well as aspectual differences of a verbal action such as habituality, repetition, intensity, and continuity. Head tilt, eyebrow and lip configuration, and other body motions are frequently used to add to the expressive capacity of manual gestures.

Fluent use of signs can match the speed of an unhurried conversation, as can be seen from television programs in which speech is being translated into ASL for viewers who are hearing-impaired. Fingerspelling is considerably slower, but it is indispensable for proper names or concepts for which there are no signs (for example, chemical substances).

There are many different manual alphabets just as there are many different writing systems, and sign languages proper vary internally and among themselves just as do the dialects of a spoken language and as one spoken language differs from another. Regardless of the particular sign language used, the majority of signs are not transparently iconic, that is, they cannot be interpreted by those who have not first learned their meanings.

If primary sign languages function much like spoken languages, do they also have duality of patterning, that is, are they analyzable in terms of two levels of structural units comparable to phonemes and morphemes? According to William C. Stokoe, Jr. (1960), who has devoted many years of study to the sign language of the American deaf, Ameslan grammar has the same general form as grammars of spoken languages. It is characterized by a small set of contrastive units meaningless in themselves (cheremes, on the analogy with phonemes) that combine to form meaningful sign units, the morphemes. Chereme refers to a set of positions, configurations, or motions that function identically in a given sign language. The three classes of cheremes Stokoe identifies are the tab (from *tabula*), the location of the sign in the sign space; the dez (from *designator*), the configuration of the hand(s) making a sign; and the sig (from *signation*), the motion component of the signing hand(s). More specifically, each morpheme of a sign language may be defined in terms of handshape, orientation of the palm and fingers, place of formation, movement and its direction, point of contact, and other spatial and dynamic features. Users of Ameslan and other natural sign languages are no more aware of cheremes than users of spoken English are of phonemes.

To sum up, contrary to popular misconceptions, primary sign languages used by the deaf are highly structured, complete, and independent communicative systems, comparable in complexity to spoken and written languages; otherwise they could not substitute for spoken languages as effectively as they do. Furthermore, they are natural languages in the sense that their acquisition is the automatic result of interaction with others who depend upon signing.

Alternate sign languages take a variety of forms, ranging from occupational sign languages such as the one developed by sawmill workers in the northwestern United States and western Canada to the performance sign language employed in the classical Hindu dance tradition to monastic sign languages that make it possible for members of orders that use them to observe the self-imposed rule of silence. The best-known sign languages of this type, however, are those used by the aborigines of various parts of Australia and especially the system of signing developed by the tribes of the North American Plains, the most elaborate in the New World.

For the earliest mention of sign language in North America we are indebted to Pedro de Castañeda de Nájera, the most widely read chronicler of the Coronado expedition in 1540–1542 to what is today the U.S. Southwest. His report concerns an encounter of the Spaniards with what probably was a band of Apaches (he refers to them as Querechos) along the present-day New Mexico–Texas border:

> These people were so skillful in the use of signs that it seemed as if they spoke. They made everything so clear that an interpreter was not necessary. They said that by going down in the direction in which the sun rises there was a very large river, that the army could travel along its bank through continuous settlements for ninety days, going from one settlement to another. They said that the first settlement was called Haxa, that the river was more than one league wide, and that there were many canoes. (Hammond and Rey 1940:235–236)

Although frequently mentioned in the travel accounts of the early explorers west of the Mississippi, Plains Indian sign language has not yet received the attention it deserves, particularly as there remain only a very few individuals who are still proficient in it.

For a score of nomadic tribes whose spoken languages were either completely unrelated or related but mutually unintelligible, Plains Indian sign language is known to have been an effective means of intertribal communication in trade and other negotiations. Moreover, it was commonplace for members of a tribe to recount their war exploits or to "narrate" a long traditional tale exclusively by means of manual signs, and it is a matter of record that the Kiowa Indians gave Gen. Hugh Lenox Scott a detailed account of their sun dance ceremony by using signs. Plains Indian sign language consisted of a large repertory of conventionalized gestures performed with one or both hands. The hands were either held stationary in various configurations or moved between the levels of just above the ground to over the signer's head. For example, to sign *snow* or *snowing*, both hands were extended in front of the face with all ten fingers pointing downward, and then lowered in whirling motions. Abstract concepts were conveyed with equal facility. The concept of cold or winter was conveyed by clenched hands with forearms crossed in front of the chest, accompanied by shivering movements. The idea of badness was indicated by a motion suggesting something being thrown away: The right fist held in front of the chest was swung out and down to the right as the hand was opening up.

Although the bulk of the signs must have been shared by the tribes of the north central Plains, there were no doubt "dialectal" differences similar to those found in widely extended spoken languages. Unlike the whistle or drum "languages," however, sign languages are independent of speech even though they have occasionally been used in combination with it. Only in the case of manual alphabets is there a connection: A manual alphabet represents the elements of a writing system that in turn derives from speech (see Figure 11.1).

244

FIGURE 11.1 Fingerspelling and Signing: A Comparison. (a) The word *tree* spelled in the American manual alphabet; (b) the same word spelled in the British manual alphabet. The word *tree* signed in (c) Chinese Sign Language, (d) Danish Sign Language, (e) American Sign Language, and (f) Plains Indian sign language.

Although all four signs strive to be iconic—to resemble physically that to which they refer—they differ: In Chinese Sign Language, the two hands symmetrically form a circle about the shape of the tree trunk and then move upward to indicate growth; in Danish Sign Language, the two hands outline the rounded shape of the tree crown and then the vertical trunk below it; in ASL, the elbow of the upright right forearm rests on the palm of the left hand, with all five fingers of the right hand spread wide and moving to represent the motion of branches and leaves above the trunk rising from the ground; in the Plains Indian sign language, the open left hand held about ten inches in front of the shoulder, with its back outward and all five fingers spread to represent branches, moves slowly upward to indicate growth. Evidently, the salient features of treehood vary from one group of people to another. *Sources:* (a, b) David Crystal, *The Cambridge Encyclopedia of Language* (Cambridge: Cambridge University Press, 1991), 225; (c–e) Reprinted by permission of the publisher from *The Signs of Language* by Edward S. Klima and Ursula Bellugi (Cambridge, MA: Harvard University Press), 21. Copyright © 1979 by the President and Fellows of Harvard College; (f) William Tomkins, *Indian Sign Language* (New York: Dover, 1969), 56–57.

The Origins of Writing

Viewed in the context of human cultural evolution, writing is a recent invention, apparently going back no more than 5,000 to 6,000 years. But if one includes under the term *writing* any attempt to transmit messages by visible signs that are expected to endure, then writing is undoubtedly much older. To use an example, members of the Abnaki tribe in the American Northeast used to indicate the direction of a journey, its distance, and the expected number of days of travel by means of sticks placed in the ground in a particular manner. Other visual signs must have been used in many parts of the world over many thousands of years. There are two main reasons why these methods of communicating are not usually considered to be true writing: (1) Individuals who use such signs enjoy a great deal of freedom in choosing and executing them but as a rule can represent only some of the features of spoken language, and (2) the interpretation of these signs is independent of any particular language. This is why the road sign portraying a silhouette of a leaping deer, warning drivers of the possibility of a collision between a fast-moving vehicle and a deer crossing the road, is not considered an instance of writing—it can be understood by drivers regardless of the language they speak, provided, of course, that they know what a deer is. To limit the concept of writing in this fashion is not to minimize the importance of pictorial records or messages (for example, the chronicles, or winter counts, that Native Americans at one time painted on buffalo hide). It is useful, though, to limit the discussion to true writing if one is to describe its origins and development on the basis of available evidence.

A system of writing was used as early as the late fourth or early third millennium B.C. by the Sumerians of Mesopotamia (today's southern Iraq). Originally pictographic in character, Sumerian writing gradually became simplified and conventionalized, changing to cuneiform (from Latin *cuneus* 'wedge'). Cuneiform writing takes its name from the wedge-shaped marks made by a stylus in tablets of soft clay, which were then either baked or allowed to dry in the sun to harden.

A number of other systems of writing developed in the Old World at about the same time or somewhat later. Among the earliest and best known were those employed by the Babylonians, Assyrians, and Hittites, all of whom made use of cuneiform writing. In Egypt a pictographic system that developed about 3000 B.C. came to be referred to as hieroglyphic writing. All of these and other ancient Old World writing systems were eventually abandoned and replaced by others by the time of the present era. The one exception has been the Chinese writing system, which has survived from about 1500 B.C. to the present, although in modified form.

It appears that in the New World the earliest system of writing was invented by the Mayas just before the beginning of our era in what today is southern Mexico and Guatemala. Many elaborate glyphs, or characters, of the Mayan writing system have been preserved either in several manuscript books (codices) or in stone carvings. The Mayas were not the only New World society that made use of writing in pre-Columbian times. The Aztecs, who were flourishing at the time of the Spanish conquest in the first half of the sixteenth century, used a system of writing that was largely pictographic, and there is evidence that other pre-Columbian societies (the Zapotec and Mixtec of what today is Mexico) also knew of ways to record information.

Until recently, most scholars believed that although writing in the New World originated independently, Old World writing systems did not develop independently of each other but were the result of diffusion from Mesopotamian Sumer. The only possible exception was thought to be Chinese writing, which was considered likely to be a case of idea diffusion (or stimulus diffusion)—the borrowing, as a result of stimulation, of a general idea rather than of a specific technique, such as a particular writing system. Most studies of the last two decades, however, favor the possibility of several independent inventions of writing systems in the Old World. As for the New World, the independent invention of writing has not been seriously challenged, with most scholars believing that the Mayan system stimulated writing among the later Mesoamerican high cultures.

Types of Writing Systems

Today a great many different writing systems are in use throughout the world, and in the course of history scores of others must have become extinct or have been discarded and replaced. To discuss the origins of and the differences among these various systems, or among simply the ones considered important, would not only fill a sizable book but greatly tax most readers' patience. Fortunately, it is possible to outline the general trends in the development of writing in rather simple terms.

A true writing system represents by means of conventionally accepted visible marks certain elements of the corresponding spoken language. For the purposes of writing, the basic elements of speech come in various sizes that range from words to morphemes to the significant sounds that make them up. For example, the single English word *riskiness* is made up of three morphemes (spelled *risk-i-ness*) and nine phonemes, including one of stress.

The oldest method of transmitting messages by "writing" must have made use of pictograms, signs of a pictorial graphic system. In such a system, a drawing of the sun, for example, would have stood for the sun. A more elaborate use of pictograms occurred once signs stood also or primarily for ideas associated with what was pictorially represented: A drawing of the sun in such a case would have referred also or especially to warmth or light. Signs used in this manner are known as ideograms.

The crucial innovation that changed picture writing to true writing took place when a pictorial sign came to be associated primarily or exclusively with the particular word it represented rather than with its meaning. Graphic signs of this type are referred to as logograms or, emphasizing the sounds they are to evoke, phonograms. In this system, to use an English example, the combination of

'eye' and 'sickle' would read *icicle*, though

alone may stand for *I* as well as *eye*, the two pronounced alike. Now to write a message of some length by means of logograms or phonograms would obviously not only be time-consuming and require a fair amount of drawing skills but in some cases might be impossible to accomplish—how would one represent phonographically, for example, the English words *cousin, enough,* or *if*? A way to simplify matters was to represent the different syllables occurring in the spoken language rather than attempting to find a sign for each of its many words. In such a system, which considerably reduces the repertory of signs, a sign representing, for example, the sounds of the one-syllable English word *mass* would also be used in writing the first syllable of such other words as *mascot, masculine, masker, massive, master, mastic, mastiff,* and so on. A writing system making use of signs representing syllables is referred to as a syllabary.

The logical next step was to simplify syllabic writing systems by the invention of **alphabetic writing,** in which each different distinctive sound of a language tends to be represented by a separate sign, or letter. The advantage of such a system is obvious: Despite the spelling inconsistencies in English, any one of its many thousand words can be written down by means of no more than the twenty-six letters of the English alphabet.

Even though the developmental stages of writing appear to have occurred in the sequence presented above, the presence of one particular system did not necessarily exclude others, with the result that in a number of writing systems several methods were combined. The oldest systems—those used in Mesopotamia, Egypt, China, the Indus River valley, and elsewhere, including the New World—were essentially pictographic but before long incorporated ideographic signs. For example, in early Sumerian writing the picture of a starry sky came to refer to darkness, blackness, or night. Egyptian hieroglyphics were largely pictographic and ideographic but included some phonograms as well as signs specifying which of several possible meanings of a word was intended (see Figure 11.2).

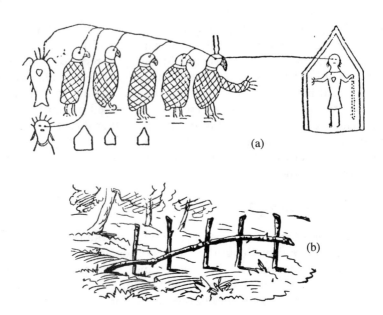

(a)

(b)

FIGURE 11.2 Writing Systems. Only a handful of the many different writing systems are briefly illustrated here. (a) A pictograph independent of spoken language. This is a reproduction of a message from an American Indian chief to the president of the United States. The chief, identified as such by the two lines rising from his head, is followed by five warriors, four of whom belong, together with the chief, to the eagle clan. The fifth warrior belongs to the catfish clan. The additional man, who is unidentified as to clan but appears to be an even more powerful chief, is in agreement with the group. The three dwellings outlined below the group indicate that its members are ready to give up nomadic life and live in houses. The extended arm of the leader symbolizes an offer of peace and friendship, apparently reciprocated by the president. (b) The five sticks placed perpendicular to the ground indicate the expected number of days of travel (five) in the direction pointed out by the raised end of the long stick. (c) Early cuneiform writing on a brick found in an ancient Sumerian city. (d) The development of cuneiform writing from pictographs to true cuneiform writing. The first rectangle of each row contains the original pictograph; the second, the pictograph in the position of later cuneiform; the third, the early Babylonian cuneiform; the fourth, the Assyrian cuneiform; and the last gives the original or derived meaning. (e) Some of the eighty-five signs of the Cherokee syllabary together with a conventional romanization. *Sources:* (a) Henry R. Schoolcraft, *Historical and Statistical Information Respecting the History, Condition and Prospects of the Indian Tribes of the United States,* part 1 (Philadelphia: Lippincott, Grambo, 1851), 418–419; (b) Garrick Mallery, "Picture-writing of the American Indians," in *Tenth Annual Report of the Bureau of Ethnology to the Secretary of the Smithsonian Institution, 1888–89,* by J. W. Powell (Washington: Government Printing Office, 1893), 335; (c) David Diringer, *The Alphabet: A Key to the History of Mankind,* 3rd rev. ed. (New York: Funk and Wagnalls, 1968), vol. 2, 23; (d) *Encyclopaedia Britannica,* 15th ed. (1989), vol. 29, 1056, reprinted courtesy of The Oriental Institute of the University of Chicago; (e) H. A. Gleason, Jr., *An Introduction to Descriptive Linguistics,* rev. ed. (New York: Holt, Rinehart and Winston, 1961), 414.

(c)

⊲ᕗ	◁ᗄ	┼ᗄ	▷⊁⍑	bird
⇁	⑀	⑄	⚏⍑	fish
⚭	⧽⧽⧽⊢	⧉	⚔	grain

(d)

(e)
D a   R e   T i   ᕁ o   Oʻ u   ᒊ ʌ
ꝼ ga   ℎ ge   ꝿ gi   A go   J gu   E gʌ
Oʰ ha   ꝯ he   ꓮ hi   ⊦ ho   Γ hu   ℐ hʌ
W la   ♂ le   Ρ li   G lo   M lu   ꓱ lʌ

A good example of a logographic system is Chinese writing, in which (simplifying matters somewhat) different characters represent different words or morphemes. The Chinese characters also derived from an earlier pictographic and ideographic system. The Japanese system of writing combines characters borrowed from the Chinese with an auxiliary syllabary of over seventy graphemes that comes in two forms, *katakana* and *hiragana*. An interesting example of a syllabary, a result of stimulus diffusion, was the Cherokee syllabary invented in 1821 by the half-Cherokee Sequoya (ca. 1760–1843). In its final version, this syllabary was reduced to eighty-five symbols, some of which were selected or adapted from the capitals of the Latin alphabet used to write English. Because Sequoya apparently did not know how to read English, his selection was completely arbitrary. The Cherokee syllabary was used for a number of years not only by the Cherokee people but also by missionaries working among them.

Alphabetic writing is the easiest and most economical system and has become the means of writing the majority of languages today. The first alphabetic system was probably used by a Semitic-speaking people perhaps as early as 1700 B.C. in ancient Syria, and the earliest preserved alphabetic text, in cuneiform, comes from the site of the ancient city-state of Ugarit on the present-day Syrian coast. With only consonants represented, the early alphabets were designed for the writing of Arabic, Hebrew, and Phoenician. Around 1000 B.C. ancient Greeks came into contact with the Phoenician system and somewhat later used it as a basis for developing their own, adding vowel symbols to adapt the alphabet to the different structure of their language. About two centuries later, the Greek alphabet in turn served as a model for the Etruscans of central Italy, whose alphabet influenced the Romans to develop their own Latin, or Roman, alphabet. Although the so-called Latin alphabet is used today for the writing of the great majority of European languages, the Cyrillic alphabet, current in parts of Eastern Europe and the former Soviet Union, was derived directly from the Greek alphabet, which in many ways it still resembles.

Despite the complicated development of the many writing systems over the past five or six millennia, the main tendencies in the general evolution of writing have been fairly straightforward. One tendency has been toward increasing abstractness (from readily recognizable pictograms to letters—of which Latin *S*, Greek Σ , and Cyrillic *C*, all representing the "s" sound, are examples). The other tendency has been toward simplicity (from a great many pictograms, ideograms, or phonograms to two to three dozen letters that can be easily drawn).

If a simple alphabetic system has such an advantage over a logographic one in which thousands of different morphemes need to be learned and kept apart in their graphic representation, then why have the Chinese not adopted one of the several romanizations (transcriptions using the Latin alphabet) devised over the past several centuries? The answer is simple. A number of different languages are spoken in China, each in several dialects. The present system of characters is used for writing by all Chinese citizens even though they speak mutually unintelligible languages, with the result that the same newspaper, for example, can be read by China's citizens across the length and breadth of the country. If romanization of Chinese writing were to be officially adopted, books and newspapers would have to be published in as many different alphabetic systems as there are different languages spoken in the country.

Writing and Printing

Members of Western cultures customarily think of the materials used for writing and printing in limited terms: Paper is a must, used in combination with pens, typewriters, printing presses, or computer printers. But the world over and throughout prehistory and history the variety of such materials has been surprisingly rich. Among the earliest surfaces on which drawings or engravings were made were cave walls and bones. Specimens of exquisite drawings and carvings have been preserved from as early as the Upper Paleolithic, which began more than 30,000 years ago. Clay tokens, marked with a stylus or a similar object, preceded the clay tablets used for cuneiform writing. Although in ancient Egypt papyrus was most commonly written on, numerous other materials, including limestone, ivory, bone, clay tablets, metal, leather, pottery, parchment, and wax, also came to be used. The principal implement for writing was a rush brush; it was later replaced by the split-reed pen, a development that eventually led in Europe to the quill pen (during the sixth century B.C.) and the steel pen (in the nineteenth century).

Paper was apparently invented in central Asia and began to be produced in its early form in China at the beginning of the second century, adding to such writing materials as bamboo strips, wooden tablets, palm leaves, and silk. The manufacture of paper spread slowly west and south. In the middle of the eighth century at Samarkand in today's Uzbekistan, paper makers incorporated cotton and flax fibers into their product. Paper was increasingly used after the introduction of printing in Europe, but it was only during the nineteenth century that wood pulp became the main raw material in the production of paper.

Ink is a very ancient invention, carbon ink having been used in ancient Egypt before the third millennium B.C. Ink was also known to the Chinese, the Greeks, and the Romans and became especially important in the Middle Ages, when it was produced mainly in the monasteries.

For several millennia the skill of writing was possessed by relatively few individuals, as the vast majority of the world's population was illiterate. By the end of the Middle Ages, however, the demand for copies of the growing number of manuscripts was such that it was not uncommon for well-known booksellers to employ several dozen copyists to satisfy the demand of reader-customers. The time had clearly come for inventing a method of multiplying book pages mechanically. Although block printing was apparently known in Europe by the end of the fourteenth century, it seems not to have threatened the patient work of the copyists. The major innovation, in about 1450, was the printing press and movable type, an invention attributed to the German Johannes Gutenberg (ca. 1390–1468). But even though Gutenberg apparently did invent printing independently, he was not the first to develop it: Movable-type printing was used in China as early as the first half of the eleventh century. Moreover, the earliest known book, which was block-printed, also comes from China and bears a publication date, when converted to our calendar, of May 11, 868.

Both writing and printing have raised communication to great efficacy. Without the permanence of the printed word, civilization could not have grown as rapidly and to the extent that it has. The impersonal messages encoded in writing, though, are generally not as effective as face-to-face communication. For power, the spoken word remains unsurpassed.

Decipherment

Archaeologists have occasionally found material remains of written texts. Because in many cases the script is no longer used and the language no longer spoken, how do we know what system of writing is represented and what the text means? Some of the decipherments already accomplished are among the outstanding achievements of the human mind. The famous Rosetta stone, a black basalt slab found in 1799 by members of Napoleon's Egyptian expedition, can serve as an example.

What made the stone's decipherment possible was that a Greek text of fifty-four lines engraved at the bottom had been translated and engraved in hieroglyphic script (fourteen lines) at the top of the stone, with a version in demotic ("popular") script between the two. The key to the two Egyptian texts was provided by the Greek, which was of course known. References to several royal names gave clues to the sound values of some of the hieroglyphs, and the number of hieroglyphic signs, three times that of the Greek words of the text, suggested the mixed nature of the ancient Egyptian writing (ideographic, phonographic, with additional signs determining the meaning of certain words). The credit for the decipherment goes to the French Egyptologist Jean-François Champollion (1790–1832), who published his findings in 1822.

Ethnography of Writing

Even though the term *communication* also includes writing, accounts of how writing is used in a particular society appear only rarely in ethnographic literature. This is because anthropologists traditionally have been interested in nonliterate societies (that is, societies without written language) and also because anthropological studies of complex industrial societies in which writing is important and widely used tend to concentrate on face-to-face interaction rather than the relatively remote contact established and maintained by writing. Anthropologists have always recognized the invention of true writing about 5,000 years ago as the starting point of a major cultural revolution in human history, and correspondingly their focus has been on the origins and diffusion of writing rather than on the functions of written language in particular societies. As for linguists, most of them have contributed little or nothing to the study of writing because they have given their attention to the older, universal, and in many respects most efficient form of communication—spoken language. However, stimulated by the developing interest in the ethnography of speaking, Basso contributed a programmatic essay urging that attention also be paid to writing. According to him, "the ethnographic study of writing should not be conceived of as an autonomous enterprise . . . but as one element in a more encompassing field of inquiry which embraces the totality of human communication skills" (Basso 1974:426).

The same units and components that are employed in the ethnography of speaking can also be applied to writing. Several related acts of writing (writing a letter, for example, would be one such act) combine to form a writing event (an exchange of letters on a particular subject or for a particular purpose). The sender(s) and the receiver(s) of letters are participants, and the circumstances under which a letter is sent or letters are exchanged provide a setting for an act of writing or a writing event (for example, the exchange of holiday greetings and new year's wishes in December). The reasons for writing a letter vary greatly: Personal letters range from bread-and-butter letters (to thank someone for hospitality) to love letters to letters of condolence, formal letters from letters of commendation to those threatening court action. The channel in the case of writing is optical but the codes vary: Different languages make use of different writing systems, and preschool children sometimes "write" to their grandparents by drawing pictures.

The purpose and message content commonly determine the form of a letter: For example, on the one hand, a letter of application for a position is considered a formal letter and therefore would be carefully composed and typewritten or laser-printed on paper of good quality. On the other hand, a letter to a close friend is usually casual in style and can even be carelessly written, with the possible inclusion of slang or even an obscenity or two. To send someone who has just experienced a death in the family a card expressing wishes for a "Merry Christmas and a Happy New Year" or to type a letter of condolence rather than write it by hand would be considered wholly inappropriate. Spoken utterances judged to be humorous even though somewhat risqué could well be considered insulting when committed to writing. In short, just as speaking is governed by rules of interaction and norms of interpretation, so is writing.

If we extend the term *writing* from true writing to any visual communication accomplished by the use of enduring marks or signs, we can then talk about various genres—road signs, pictorial advertisements, graffiti of various kinds, and many other forms. If studies in the ethnography of writing are to be complete and insightful, they need to include the sociocultural context in which they occur. Basso poses some of the questions to be answered, among them,

> How . . . is the ability to write distributed among the members of a community, and how does the incidence of this ability vary with factors such as age, sex, socioeconomic class and the like? . . . What kinds of information are considered appropriate for transmission through written channels . . . ? Who sends written messages to whom, when, and for what reasons? . . . In short, what position does writing occupy in the total communicative economy of the society under study and what is the range of its cultural meanings? (Basso 1974:431–432)

These questions have not yet been seriously addressed for more than a very few of the world's societies.

Summary and Conclusions

Although spoken language is undoubtedly the oldest and most efficient means of human communication, there are many other ways in which people transmit or exchange information. The most common of these is writing, independently invented in both the Old and the New World several thousand years ago. In the majority of writing systems, visual signs (letters) represent sounds or combinations of sounds of a spoken language.

Nonverbal systems of communication are based on either spoken or written language or are independent of it. The Morse code and braille derive from the written representation of a language; whistle and drum "languages," by contrast, are based on certain acoustic features of speech. When talking, most people accompany speech by facial expressions and other body motions. Hearing-impaired individuals make use of sign systems that are very nearly as efficient and expressive as spoken languages. The Plains Indians of North America used an elaborate sign language to communicate with members of other Plains tribes whose languages they could not understand.

Communication of one kind or another is common in the animal kingdom and characterizes all of its species. Human language, however, is the most complex and expressive means of communication now known. One could easily argue that without language human culture would be impossible—or at best quite limited.

Suggestions for Further Reading

For a discussion of paralanguage and paralinguistics, see Trager 1958 and Crystal 1974; the latter source has an extensive bibliography appended. For a selection of essays concerning kinesics, see Birdwhistell 1970. A very readable introduction to proxemics is Hall 1966; a much shorter account, with comments by a number of scholars and Hall's reply to them, is in Hall 1968. For a discussion of gestures and cultural differences in gestures, see Kendon 1997.

The talking drums of Africa are the subject of a nontechnical article by Carrington (1971). An excellent introduction to American Sign Language can be found in Klima and Bellugi 1979. A nontechnical but reliable source for Plains Indian sign language is Tomkins 1969.

A book of readings concerning nonverbal communication, with commentary, has been edited by Weitz (1974); the topics in the anthology include facial expression, paralanguage, body movements and gestures, and spatial behavior. A survey by specialists of paralinguistics, proxemics, sign languages, drum and whistle "languages," and writing is included in Sebeok 1974. For a research guide and bibliography concerning nonverbal communication, see Key 1977.

A number of books and articles have been written on the origins and development of writing in general or a particular writing system, especially the alphabetic. The most comprehensive source on the subject is Diringer 1968, consisting of one volume of text and one of illustrations. A shorter but informative treatment of the subject (some 130 pages) is Trager 1972. The several aspects of the interface between cultures with and without writing, and between written and oral traditions on the one hand and the use of writing and speech on the other, are dealt with in Goody 1987.

For a review of the relation between written and spoken language and a bibliography on the subject, see Chafe and Tannen 1987.

12

Oral Folklore
and Spoken Art

During its century-and-a-half-long history, the meaning of the term *folklore* has ranged from oral tradition to all traditional practices, including customs, beliefs, and material culture (folklife). This chapter is concerned with some aspects of oral, or verbal, folklore. The definition of oral folklore, too, has been shifting from the earlier emphasis on traditional artifacts, such as folk songs or folktales, to the most recent view of folklore as communicative process, such as a storytelling performance.

There has been a long-standing tendency on the part of many members of complex industrial societies to underestimate the intellectual powers and aesthetic sensibilities of nonliterate peoples, those who do not make use of written language. The findings of anthropologists have demonstrated time and again how false such an assumption is. The frequent reference to traditional narratives as "oral literature" is less a contradiction in terms than the recognition that, for example, the startling imagery and intricate structure of interlocking repetitions in Navajo chants invites comparison with the best in Western poetry, and that many of the origin myths of Native Americans possess the terseness and dramatic quality characteristic of the Book of Genesis. Just as one expects the style of recognized writers in literate societies to rise above the level of everyday speech, it is common to find that demanding standards govern the performances of traditional narratives. And a reminder: Oral folklore is not a product of culture found only in tribal societies or among peasants; it is alive and well in the United States, where it takes the form of tall tales, ballads, jokes, counting-out rhymes, and riddles—to mention only a few genres—and varies from region to region according to occupation, ethnic background, and other characteristics.

Anthropologists have come to depend on oral folklore for clues to a better understanding of cultures; folklorists have recorded and analyzed texts and performances that show the richness of human imagination in spoken art; and linguists have used traditional narratives as a source of valuable data that can be obtained in no other way. For these and other reasons the discussion of oral folklore has a place in the study of linguistic anthropology.

Collecting and Classifying Traditional Narratives

Although the collecting of North American Indian oral traditions was begun by the Jesuit fathers during the second quarter of the seventeenth century, only sporadic contributions to our knowledge of Native American folklore were made during the subsequent two centuries. The pioneer ethnographer who more than anyone else rekindled interest in the original cultures of North America was Henry R. Schoolcraft (1793–1864), who published extensively on the Ojibwa, among whom he lived as an Indian agent.

The beginnings of serious organized scholarly work in the field of Native American languages and oral folklore date back to the last quarter of the nineteenth century. In 1879 John Wesley Powell founded the Anthropological Society of Washington and organized the Bureau of (American) Ethnology as part of the Smithsonian Institution, becoming the bureau's first director. The founding of the American Folklore Society followed in 1888.

Powell, who was trained as a geologist and lost his right arm in the Battle of Shiloh during the Civil War, devoted a major part of his later career to the study of Native American cultures and languages. One of his concerns was that "the myths and folk-lore of the several tribes [be] preserved and recorded in their own languages, with interlinear translation, and without foreign coloring or addition" (Powell 1883:xxx). Inspired by Powell's charge, the contributors to the hundreds of volumes published under the auspices of the Bureau of American Ethnology over a period of nearly a century amassed a wealth of invaluable information, much of it of direct interest to folklorists and linguistic anthropologists.

The most distinguished early leader in the study of Native American languages and traditional narratives was Boas, widely recognized to the present day as the father of American anthropology. In his eighty-page introduction to the first volume of the *Handbook of American Indian Languages*, which marked the beginning of the scientific study of the languages native to North America, Boas put the full weight of his authority behind Powell's earlier injunction:

> Nobody would expect authoritative accounts of the civilization of China or of Japan from a man who does not speak the languages readily, and who has not mastered their literatures. . . . We must insist that a command of the language is an indispensable means of obtaining accurate and thorough knowledge, because much information can be gained by listening to conversations of the natives and by taking part in their daily life, which, to the observer who has no command of the language, will remain entirely inaccessible. (Boas 1911:60)

Despite his wide-ranging research in all subfields of anthropology and his many professional responsibilities—among them a professorship at Columbia University, a curatorship in the American Museum of Natural History, and editorships of scholarly journals—Boas made signal contributions to linguistic anthropology. During his career he undertook thorough investigations of ten languages and partial studies of a dozen others, and on the Northwest Coast tribe of the Kwakiutl alone he published several thousand pages, most of them in both English and Kwakiutl. In addition he trained scores of students, many of whom became dominant figures in American anthropology.

To the extent that traditional narratives of Native American peoples were collected and published in English, they supplemented the standard ethnographic descriptions with important collateral information concerning oral folklore, cultural values, and native theories of origins. Traditional narratives published in the original languages together with translations have become invaluable for the study of Native American languages, in part because they contained words and linguistic forms not commonly encountered in everyday use and in part because by the beginning of the 1900s it had already become clear that the long-term survival of many Indian languages was in danger. The body of Native American tales and other traditional oral genres that were collected in North America alone over the past hundred or so years is vast, but with only few exceptions very little information is on record concerning the culturally genuine settings and characteristics of the performances that gave rise to the texts.

It is inevitable that once a large number of cultural specimens of a particular kind have been assembled, attempts at classification will follow. As early as 1891, in an article dealing with the dissemination of tales among North American Indians, Boas pointed out the recurrence of certain narrative elements and incidents in different traditions and discussed the implications of their distribution for the study of origins (diffusion vs. independent origin). Although a number of Boas's students continued with the analysis of the narrative content of folkloric texts, the taxonomic approach culminated not in the work of an anthropologist but of a literary folklorist, Stith Thompson (1885–1976). Thompson is known throughout the world for his two revisions and expansions (1928 and 1961) of the index of tale types originally published by the Finnish scholar Antti Aarne in 1910, and for his monumental six-volume index of traditional narrative motifs, first published in the 1930s and doubled in content in its second edition some twenty years later.

A motif, according to Thompson, is the smallest element in a tale that has the power to persist in tradition by virtue of having something unusual about it. For the most part, motifs may be assigned to one of three classes. Some refer to actors in the tale—gods, culture heroes, witches, fairies, cruel relatives, mythical animals, animals with human traits, and the like. Others refer to significant items in the background of the action—magic objects such as seven-league boots or the stretching tree, unusual customs such as a taboo on using magic power too often (in Native American folklore, in excess of four times), and the like. The third group of motifs consists of single incidents that, if existing independently, constitute complete short tales—for example, a race won by deception, as when a wood tick rides unnoticed on the back of its competitor, the fox, and jumps off the tip of the fox's nose to win at the finish line. A type, according to Thompson, is a traditional tale that has an independent existence. Some of the best-known tales, such as Cinderella in the Old World tradition or The Star Husband in Native North American tradition, consist of a cluster of motifs that characterize them as specific tale types; others, such as some of the short humorous animal stories popular in both the Old and the New World, consist of one motif only (like the one just cited).

The motif index can be expanded practically without limit as new narrative elements from the oral folklore of all continents are identified and appropriately classified. Because both type and motif indexes are based on narrative materials gathered from all over the world, they are especially suitable for comparative work. But there is more one may wish to study about a particular tale type than just the assortment of its motifs or its geographic distribution. If a folktale has been collected in a great many versions over a large area, folklorists may be tempted to reconstruct its life history, that is, to try to ascertain the assumed original form (archetype) of the tale, discover the most likely place of its origin, and trace the routes of its diffusion. Thompson applied this approach, referred to as the historic-geographic, or Finnish method, to the popular Native American tale type known as The Star Husband, a delightful story of the marriage of two girls to stars, followed by their escape back to earth. By studying the eighty-six published versions of the tale from such widely scattered parts of North America as southwestern Alaska, California, Nova Scotia, and the Southeast, Thompson was able to hypothesize not only about its archetype (the presumed basic tale) but also about its several special regional developments, as well as the most likely place of its origin, the central Plains (Thompson 1953). No doubt it took many centuries for the tale to travel by word of mouth to the four corners of the continent, especially with the hundreds of language barriers in its path.

Oral Folklore: The Functional Approach

The aspect of oral folklore that has been of particular interest to anthropological folklorists is function. In contrast to the taxonomic and comparative approaches, the emphasis in functionalist studies shifts from the text to the cultural context. The important questions are no longer what the different types or motifs are nor where a particular tale may have originated but what folklore does for those who pass it from one generation to the next. Numerous functions of folklore have been identified; in the following discussion only the most important will be taken up.

According to Bronislaw Malinowski, myth serves as "a warrant, a charter, and often even a practical guide to the activities with which it is connected" and "expresses, enhances, and codifies belief; it safeguards and enforces morality; it vouches for the efficiency of ritual and contains practical rules for the guidance of man"; myth acts to "strengthen tradition and endow it with a greater value and prestige by tracing it back to a higher, better, more supernatural reality of initial events" (Malinowski 1926:29, 19, 91–92).

A number of genres play an important role in education, especially among nonliterate peoples. The Arapaho Indians of the Plains used to teach children the danger of wantonness and wastefulness by periodically reminding them of the punishment suffered by Whiteman, one of the tricksters of their many humorous stories. Once in his wanderings Whiteman saw a man whittling his leg to a sharp point. When he had finished, the man jumped and killed a fat buffalo to use for food. Whiteman was impressed by what he saw and begged the man to give him the power to do likewise. After many entreaties the man relented and sharpened Whiteman's leg for him but warned him not to kill with it more than four times. When later Whiteman came to a herd of buffalo and began killing them for sheer pleasure, he received his comeuppance when he pierced the fifth buffalo. With his foot suddenly grown back to his leg, Whiteman couldn't free himself, and the injured animal dragged and crushed him nearly to death.

Teaching by indirection is also characteristic of proverbs, pithy traditional sayings that contain a generally accepted truth—for example, "Marry in haste, repent at leisure" or "Forewarned, forearmed." Few people in the United States today use proverbs, although they were common several generations ago and are still in active use elsewhere in the world. The function of proverbs in culturally genuine situations is to give face-to-face advice not as the proverb user's personal opinion, which could be considered offensive or embarrassing, but as the voice of the age-old authority and collective wisdom of a particular society. In other words, it is not the user of a proverb who speaks but the experience of the many generations that have gone before. The use of proverbs in Africa, especially the Bantu-speaking part of the continent, is widespread, with the various societies having as many as several thousand proverbs at their disposal. The employment of proverbs is particularly elaborate in native judicial systems. The timely use of an appropriate proverb during court proceedings by either the defendant or the plaintiff can be decisive for the outcome of a dispute. Whether in court or in public life, the skillful use of proverbs greatly enhances a person's reputation as an orator.

A traditional narrative may provide a psychological release with respect to behavior that members of a particular society do not condone or regard as shocking. Among the Arapaho, a mother-in-law and son-in-law had to hold each other in high respect but at the same time were obliged never to speak, look at, or be in the same tepee with each other. Because residence with the wife's family was the cultural norm, observing this avoidance behavior must have been particularly stressful for a young married man who found himself living in the camp of his in-laws. This is why the popular story of Whiteman taking his mother-in-law with him on the warpath and seducing her during their first night of camping is astounding and yet easy to understand. Although sexual intercourse with one's mother-in-law was completely unthinkable, joking about it helped to relieve the anxieties imposed upon the Arapaho by the strict avoidance rules of their culture.

Anthropologists have pointed out and documented other functions served by the various traditional oral genres. In the not-too-distant past, storytelling was the main source of entertainment among both the rural folk and tribal peoples on every continent. For example, storytelling kept the children occupied indoors at times when they could not play outside.

Riddles—puzzling questions based on some unexpected connection with a solution that is to be guessed—are not as traditional as proverbs and serve as a good example of oral folklore that is constantly renewing itself. Riddling is widespread in the world, and among the Bantu-speaking peoples of sub-Saharan Africa it is a favorite form of competitive entertainment between teams or individuals, both young and adult. What is more, riddles sharpen the wits of young children, helping them to explore various aspects of the vocabulary and cognitive code of their mother tongue, as in "What has an ear but cannot hear?," "How is a duck like an icicle?" and "A houseful, a hole full; you cannot catch a bowlful!" (the answers: corn, both grow down, smoke).

In Search of Structure

There are different ways in which one can search for structure in specimens of oral folklore. Some scholars look for it among the formal features, others in the content. What all these approaches have in common is an attempt to discover and account for the organization of the significant parts of a particular whole and to probe the nature of the interrelationships of these parts.

One of the earliest practitioners of structural analysis was the Russian Vladimir Propp (1895–1970), who applied it to a body of Russian fairy tales in a work published in 1928. His goal was to arrive at the "morphology" of the folktale, that is, "the description of the folktale according to its component parts and the relationship of these components to each other and to the whole" (1958:18). Despite the variety in the content of Russian fairy tales, the number of units of narrative structure, or functions, according to Propp, is limited to thirty-one; ordinarily not all of them occur in any given tale, but their sequence is always identical.

For example, of special importance is Function 8, which is obligatory and creates the actual movement of the tale. Regardless of what happens in any particular narrative, Function 8 takes the general form of "the villain causes harm or injury to one member of a family" or its morphological equivalent "one member of a family lacks something, he desires to have something" (1958:29, 32). A general characteristic of European fairy tales is that in the end good prevails and evil is punished; accordingly, in Function 19 "the initial misfortune or lack is liquidated" (1958:48). Inasmuch as all the Russian tales Propp examined were analyzable in terms of some of these functions, he concluded that "all fairy tales, by their structure, belong to one and the same type" (1958:21).

Influenced by Propp's work and developments in modern linguistics, Dundes applied the structural approach in his monograph titled *The Morphology of North American Indian Folktales* (1964). Making use of the distinction among the phone, phoneme, and allophone in structural linguistics, Dundes introduced into folklore a parallel terminological set consisting of the motif (a concrete instance of a traditional element in a folktale), motifeme (a distinctive unit of folk narratives, essentially the equivalent of Propp's function), and allomotif (a variety of a motifeme). Much like Propp's functions, Dundes's motifemes tend to occur in pairs. The most common motifemic pairs in American Indian tales are Lack/Lack liquidated, Interdiction/Violation, Consequence/Attempted escape, and Deceit/Deception. For example, one version of The Star Husband (Salzmann 1950) begins with a warning by a girl to her younger sister that it is not appropriate to wish to marry someone who does not belong on the earth (Interdiction). The younger girl does not give up her wish (Violation); her desire for a star husband (Lack) is soon fulfilled and she finds herself in the sky, married to such a husband (Lack liquidated). She is instructed by him not to dig for a certain plant (Interdiction) but disregards the warning (Violation) and opens up a hole in the sky floor through which she can see the camp of her people. She now finds herself lonely, unhappy with her sky home, and desirous of returning to her family on earth (Consequence). She is told by a helpful old woman to fetch 100 sinews, no more, no less (Interdiction), but does not count carefully and secures only ninety-nine (Violation). Using the rope made from the sinews (Attempted escape), she cannot quite reach the ground (Consequence) and is killed by a rock dropped from above by her angry star husband. To illustrate the concept of the allomotif, the second motifemic pair of Interdiction/Violation has a number of variants among those published versions of the tale that contain it: The taboo concerns disturbing the sky floor, digging for roots, moving a large rock, shooting a meadowlark, making a noise or moving before a squirrel and some other animal sing, and the like.

Dundes hoped that "morphological analysis of American Indian folktales [would make] it possible for typological descriptive statements to be made, [that] such statements, in turn, [would make] it possible for folklorists to examine the cultural determination of content, to predict culture change . . . and reveal whether or not certain structural patterns are universal" (1963:129). After more than a quarter of a century, Dundes's hopes have yet to be realized.

In recent years, several linguistic anthropologists have begun studying Native American narratives as works of spoken art. Because the structure of a narrative, including its linguistic patterning and stylistic features, cannot be discovered and fully appreciated without considering the structure of the words that constitute it, the text should be carefully recorded in the original language. The best-known practitioner of ethnopoetics—as this combination of linguistics, ethnography, literary analysis, and folklore has come to be known—is Dell Hymes, who has worked both with texts he himself collected and those Boas and others recorded as early as the end of the nineteenth century. One of the goals of ethnopoetic analysis is to identify the structural levels of a narrative— parts, acts, scenes, stanzas, verses, and lines—and the various means— linguistic, poetic, rhetorical—by which the effectiveness of the message is enhanced. For example, in the myths told by the Takelma Indians of southwestern Oregon, any word spoken by the bear is prefixed by the voiceless palatal lateral ł- to reproduce the coarseness of the bear, and the speech of the coyote is indicated by prefixing words with the sibilant s·- (a sound between the initial sounds of the English *sip* and *ship*).

As a rule, a complete analysis of the structure of a narrative is essential before it can be translated into English (or some other language) in a way that would approximate the poetic qualities of the original. Dennis Tedlock has summarized the argument that Native American spoken narratives are more appropriately considered and translated as dramatic poetry rather than spoken prose fiction:

> The content tends toward the fantastic rather than the prosaic, the emotions of the characters are evoked rather than described, there are patterns of repetition or parallelism ranging from the level of words to that of whole episodes, the narrator's voice shifts constantly in amplitude and tone, and

the flow of that voice is paced by pauses that segment its sounds into what I have chosen to call lines. Of all these realities of oral narrative performance, the plainest and grossest is the sheer alternation of sound and silence; the resultant lines often show an independence from intonation, from syntax, and even from boundaries of plot structure. (1983:55)

The most widely known approach to the study of myth (and human thought), one quite different from those already discussed, is structuralism—epitomized by the French anthropologist Claude Lévi-Strauss, honored in 1973 with membership in the French Academy, the most prestigious intellectual body in the French-speaking world. His entry into the field of anthropology dates back to the 1930s, when he made several trips to the interior of Brazil to gather ethnographic data on several Indian tribes. While in New York during the war years, he became acquainted with structural linguistics and began applying some of its basic concepts first to the study of kinship and later to myths. For Lévi-Strauss, "the mythical value of the myth remains preserved, even through the worst translation. . . . Its substance does not lie in its style, its original music, or its syntax, but in the *story* which it tells" (1955:430).

According to Lévi-Strauss, myths, like other products of culture, vary a great deal from one society to the next, but they all derive from the human mind, which is the same throughout the world. Because the activity of the human mind is unconscious, cultural universals must be sought at the level of structure rather than in manifest ethnographic data. The key to understanding myths is to be found in structures characterized by binary contrasts, that is, pairs of polar opposites, such as nature versus culture, life versus death, male versus female, endogamy versus exogamy, earth versus heaven, and the like. The main task is to identify these oppositions and show how they have been resolved or mediated. To offer a simple example—why is it, asks Lévi-Strauss, that in North American Indian mythology the trickster is most commonly represented by the coyote or the raven? The answer: because each is a mediator, occupying a position midway between two polar opposites (see Box 12.1).

Lévi-Strauss has had many followers and interpreters but also his share of critics. The latter have questioned his selective use of sources, the nonreplicable (nonempirical) nature of his work, and the occasionally cryptic quality of his writing, and they have also wondered whether in fact Lévi-Strauss does not create structure instead of discovering it. Whatever the final judgment, however, there is little doubt that the almost poetic range of associations Lévi-Strauss has been able to marshal as he draws on the vast amount of ethnographic data and mythological texts the world over would be difficult to match both for the volume of his interpretive commentary and the stimulation he has provided for anthropologists everywhere.

BOX 12.1   Trickster as Mediator

The trickster of American mythology has remained so far a problematic figure. Why is that throughout North America his part is assigned practically everywhere to either coyote or raven? If we keep in mind that mythical thought always works from the awareness of oppositions towards their progressive mediation, the reason for these choices becomes clearer. We need only to assume that two opposite terms with no intermediary always tend to be replaced by two equivalent terms which allow a third one as a mediator; then one of the polar terms and the mediator becomes replaced by a new triad and so on. Thus we have [a mediating structure of the following type]:

Initial Pair	*First Triad*	*Second Triad*
Life		
	Agriculture	
		Herbivorous animals
		Carrion-eating animals (raven; coyote)
	Hunting	
		Prey animals
	War	
Death		

... the unformulated argument [is as follows]: carrion-eating animals are like prey animals (they eat animal food), but they are also like food-plant producers (they do not kill what they eat).

... Not only can we account for the ambiguous character of the trickster, but we may also understand another property of mythical figures the world over, namely, that the same god may be endowed with contradictory attributes; for instance, he may be *good* and *bad* at the same time.

from Claude Lévi-Strauss, "The Structural Study of Myth"
(1955), 440, 442

Oral Folklore as Performance

For most of the current century, texts were used as the basis for the study of oral folkloric genres, each text examined for its content, function, or structural features. During the 1960s a number of young American scholars found the existing methods and theories wanting, and they began to develop a strikingly new approach to folklore, one that is performance-oriented. The focus is no longer on the genre, text, structure, comparison, or reconstruction; instead, it is on performance, style, event, and description, verbal art considered primarily as a process inextricably tied to the particular society, individual, and occasion that give rise to it.

The conceptual foundations of this approach are discussed in a theoretical article by Robert A. Georges (1969), according to whom "storytelling events . . . have many different and interrelated aspects, all of which contribute to and are at the same time part of the whole event." The heart of the article is a set of postulates, which are summarized below.

1. "Every storytelling event is a communicative event." The participants in each such event consist of at least a storyteller and an audience member. The communication between them is face-to-face, and the channels employed are both acoustic (speech) and visual (body motions), with continuous feedback in both directions.
2. "Every storytelling event is a social experience." At least one participant assumes the social identity of storyteller and one or more participants that of listener; the social identities of the participants constitute a matching set. By virtue of the social identities deriving from the storytelling event, the participants have certain duties and rights. In brief, the storyteller is obliged to give a culturally appropriate performance and, in turn, expects it to be appropriately received; the listeners' duties and obligations are correlative. Although the social uses of storytelling events can be articulated by the participants, the social functions of such events are inferred by those who study them.
3. "Every storytelling event is unique." A storytelling event occurs only once with a particular set of social interrelationships; its effects on the social environment are likewise unique.
4. "Storytelling events exhibit degrees and kinds of similarities." These similarities make it possible for certain storytelling events to be grouped together according to culture-specific criteria.

This rather abstract account of the nature of storytelling events requires some explanation and concrete examples. Because a storytelling event is above all a communicative event, the teller enhances the message of the narrative not only by appropriate vocal effects (for example, voice imitations, varying volume and tempo) but also by facial expressions, hand motions, and other visual means. The manner in which members of the audience receive a story—their reception may range all the way from undisguised boredom or disgust to wild enthusiasm—derives in large measure from the performance of the storyteller and in turn has a signifi-

---

BOX 12.2   The Verbal Artist Among the Yoruba

The final element in the performance of Yoruba verbal art is the artist himself. He is a man who has gained a mastery of his art through imitation, training, and practice. He is endowed with a sweet voice, a swift tongue, and an efficient control of the Yoruba language. He stands face to face with a particular situation and a given audience, both of which continually influence every aspect of his performance, and both of which he in turn manipulates to suit his art. It is in the midst of all these influences that the verbal artist composes and performs. The variability of the elements governing the performance is the factor that enables him to produce unique verbal art forms at each performance. It is this factor that makes it impossible for a verbal artist to produce a repeat performance of an earlier work, and each performance yields a new work of art. ...

Each artist is free to rearrange and manipulate the content of the subject matter of his genre of oral literature to the full benefit of his art and his audience. But he must never distort or amend the basic facts contained in the content. He is free to interpolate or inject his own free composition of comments on current affairs, jokes, and gossip aimed at educating and amusing members of his audience.

His skill, for which he gets credit and on which his reputation depends, is measured not only by the correctness of the rendering of the stereotyped content forms but also by the appropriateness with which he employs the various verbal formulae and clichés, proverbs and wise sayings, and commentaries. He is also judged by the degree of his competence in the use of the language and his virtuosity with the voice melody.

... Viewed in this context, the Yoruba verbal artist is not only a composer and a performer but also a dramatist. It would require ... the full combination of sound recording and film to reproduce each genre of Yoruba oral literature as it is performed by the different artists.

from Oludare Ọlajubu, "Yoruba Verbal Artists and Their Work"
(1978), 688–689

---

cant effect upon it; storytellers, and indeed performers in general, thrive on positive feedback (see Box 12.2).

A classic example of the importance of audience feedback is the song duel found among the Central and Greenland Eskimo. The song contest was commonly used to dispose of a whole variety of grudges and disputes, more often than not the claim by one man that another had stolen his wife. Each contestant, accompanying himself on a drum, sang in a highly conventionalized style, composing his words in a traditional pattern and making subtle use of language, wit, and sarcasm to elicit support-ive response from the audience. The one who was less successful in this endeavor eventually became discouraged, his performance tended to grow progressively worse, and in the end he lost, regardless of the merits of the case. Among the Arapaho, where most of the storytelling used to take place during long winter nights when it was difficult to maintain vi-sual contact in the darkness of the tepee, children were expected to say *hííí* 'snow' every so often to prove that they were still awake and listening.

Although the storyteller has the freedom to modify a traditional narra-tive by developing or, conversely, condensing parts of the plot to fit the time available, the performance must meet certain expectations. For exam-ple, if a storyteller announces to an audience that the tale to be heard is Hansel and Gretel, or The Star Husband, the narrator must include the salient motifs that define the tale type. The choice of the storytelling reper-toire, however, may be influenced by the audience. Turkish minstrels, tale-singers who narrate the prose parts and sing the verses of folk narratives to the accompaniment of a stringed instrument, select religious songs or texts praising traditional morality and conduct for an audience of older people, love songs for young people, and folk songs for a general audi-ence. The unexpected arrival of a person known to have experienced a re-cent setback or personal tragedy may cause the tale-singer to shift abruptly to more melancholy selections (Başgöz 1975). Among the Arap-aho, some of the traditional narratives involving the sexual exploits of Whiteman were not told in front of women or children; it is important to keep in mind, however, that the definition of what is and what is not ob-scene is culture-specific. Some of the tales obtained from the Arapaho by George A. Dorsey and A. L. Kroeber at the turn of the century and pub-lished in 1903 by the Field Columbian Museum (now Field Museum of Natural History) in Chicago contained passages referring to Whiteman's licentious behavior; these portions were translated into Latin in order for the material to be complete and yet not offend the sensibilities of the reader. The limitation on what can be printed in the United States has changed a great deal in the course of only a few generations.

According to Tedlock (1972, 1983), formal narratives of the Zuñi Indi-ans can be assigned to two classes: *telapnaawe* ('tales'), which are consid-ered to be fictional, and *chimiky'ana'kowa* ('story of origins,' literally "that which was the beginning"), which are regarded as true. The narratives of the former category are identified by special opening and closing formu-las. Zuñi narratives are performed mainly by men over fifty, both at home and in meetings of one of the several medicine societies. The telling of the fictional tales is limited to the months of October through March lest the narrator be bitten by a snake, and to nighttime lest the sun set early. It is further believed that the listener who falls asleep during the tale or who fails to stand up to stretch when the tale has ended may become a hunchback. The story of origins or its individual narrative portions, in contrast, may be told at any time of the day or year, but when used in a ritual context must be chanted.

In addition to giving a careful description of the narrator's performance, the nature of the audience, the setting, and the occasion for the event, the observer must record the narrative itself, as well as any reactions to it from the audience, verbal or otherwise. Keeping detailed account of all these aspects of a folkloric performance is no small task and obviously requires the use of modern recording equipment. The question then arises to what extent a sound recorder or a camera alters the spontaneity of a performance. It goes without saying that the performance-centered approach is a much more complex and ambitious undertaking than the earlier collecting of mere texts, and consequently it will take many years to gather a representative sample of narrative performances from around the world.

Two Recent Studies of Discourse: An Ancient Text and a Contemporary Speech

In the case of ancient oral traditions or historical accounts of which there happens to be a written record, some features of earlier performances can occasionally be reconstructed. The result of Tedlock's efforts to make the Maya epic *Popol Vuh* (Council book) accessible to contemporary readers may serve as a good example (Tedlock 1985).

Popol Vuh was written down during the 1550s in the Quiche language, using the Latin alphabet. Although the original version no longer exists, a friar made a copy of it around 1701. Because this surviving manuscript has few punctuation marks and no capital letters and because some of its vocabulary is archaic, many phrases are now obscure or ambiguous. Tedlock's project to gain full understanding of the narratives of *Popol Vuh* stretched over nine years and received crucial assistance from Andrés Xiloj, a Quiche diviner ("daykeeper") who was able to read the ancient text without much difficulty. Tedlock and his wife were able to apprentice themselves to Xiloj for four and a half months during the mid-1970s, learning from him how to read dreams and omens and to understand the rhythms of the calendar of the ancient Maya.

The narratives of *Popol Vuh* begin when "there is not yet one person, one animal, bird, fish, crab, tree, rock, hollow, canyon, meadow, forest. Only the sky alone is there; the face of the earth is not clear. Only the sea alone is pooled under all the sky. . . . Only the Maker, Modeler alone, Sovereign Plumed Serpent, the Bearers, Begetters are in the water, a glittering light" (Tedlock 1985:72–73). The narratives end with descriptions of the splendor of the Mayan lords who founded the Quiche kingdom (in what is now south central Guatemala).

In order to fully comprehend the ancient text so that a definitive English translation could be made, Tedlock drew on cues found in modern Quiche narratives, speeches, and prayers, as well as announcements made by town criers. He faced the time-consuming task of resolving the solid pages of text into lines, clauses, sentences, and still larger units—that is, of discovering *Popol Vuh*'s original poetic and rhetorical structure. In all, the undertaking required versatility in linguistics, ethnography, archaeology, folklore, and Native American poetics.

The scope of the commentary Tedlock appended is evident from the following figures: His translation, which covers 158 pages (including over twenty illustrations), is preceded by a forty-two-page introduction, a ninety-five-page section of notes and comments, and a forty-seven-page glossary. The notes and the glossary make frequent references to the contributions of Xiloj, who is often quoted directly. How one can use analogies between contemporary Quiché discourse and material dating from the early colonial period to reconstruct the performance features that would have characterized old narratives is the subject of the essay "Hearing a Voice in an Ancient Text: Quiché Maya Poetics in Performance," published by Tedlock in 1987.

Many linguistic anthropologists are aware that those native societies in South and Central America that have remained relatively intact are especially suitable for the study of ethnopoetics. To be sure, discourse among these peoples is rarely poetic for the sake of aesthetic effect alone; the poetic aspects of discourse are almost invariably integrated with ceremonial, ritual, magical, curative, political, or other functions. Sherzer (1986) illustrates the co-occurrence of the aesthetic and pragmatic functions by analyzing a speech made in 1970 on one of the San Blas islands along the northeast coast of Panama.

The occasion for this particular speech was the homecoming of Olowitinappi, one of the outstanding Kuna curing specialists in the village of Mulatuppu. With the help of a scholarship awarded him by the village, Olowitinappi had gone off to study snakebite medicine with a teacher in another part of Kuna territory. On his return, the village community was eager to hear from him what new curing practices he had learned and how the scholarship money had been spent. Olowitinappi's presentation took place in the centrally located gathering house of the village. His report was very effective, mentioning not only how one can prevent snakebite but also what curing chants should be used and what herbal or other medicines should be applied when someone is bitten. Part of his speech was devoted to a financial accounting for the money he had received. In short, the presentation described in some detail his experiences during the study trip. The speech as transcribed by Sherzer (in 455 numbered lines of text) is followed by a line-by-line English translation and several pages of analytical comments.

The information concerning curing methods and the expenses incurred during the trip was only a part of the presentation. Regardless of what practical goals a Kuna public speaker has in mind, he knows that verbal art is greatly valued among his people and that his presentation will be critically evaluated. An analysis of Olowitinappi's speech must therefore also take into account the poetic and rhetorical devices used in its performance. (In Kuna culture, verbal performers are usually men; women express their artistic talents primarily by making colorful appliquéd blouses.)

To begin with, paralinguistic features need to be considered. Olowitinappi stretched out certain words or phrases to emphasize important points; made use of rising pitch, vibrating voice, and pausing for effect; and on several occasions increased or decreased his volume. Direct quotations of others as well as of oneself are a prominent feature of Kuna discourse. Such quotations, identified by the use of *soke* or *soka* ('I say,' 'he says,' or 'they say') and *takken soke* or *soka* ('see I say,' 'see he says,' or 'see they say'), occurred throughout Olowitinappi's speech. At one point during the speech, Olowitinappi quoted his teacher, who was quoting one of the first great leaders of the Kuna, who was quoting a member of a neighboring tribe, who was quoting a spirit-world chief, who was quoting God.

Olowitinappi's speech consisted of a series of narrative episodes, embellished by the use of understatement, irony, and humor as well as parallelisms, allusions, and metaphors (for example, "the golden people" refers to the Kuna and "encountering a vine" refers to being bitten by a snake—a common Kuna euphemism). As Sherzer has noted elsewhere, "There is . . . an intimate relationship between Kuna culture and verbal esthetics. Verbal art and . . . verbal play are at the heart of Kuna culture" (Sherzer 1990:6).

Creative Use of Language

The use of speech is commonly associated with some specific end to be served, usually a tangible one. People talk in order to make friends, to teach or explain something to someone, to transact business, to settle arguments, and for many other reasons; they also make use of language to conduct ceremonies, to declare love, to tell myths, to express sympathy, and so forth. What may be forgotten is that in all societies speech is also used for playful or creative purposes. A good ethnography of communication should include a discussion of the creative aspects of speaking.

A widely known example of a language game is so-called pig latin, a jargon derived by systematic alteration of the everyday version of a language. Most commonly it is used by children as a "secret" language to prevent those not acquainted with it from understanding what is being said. There are usually several versions, or dialects, of pig latin in any particular language, English included. For example, "Put that knife down" would be altered to "Utpay atthay ifeknay ownday" in one version, and "Better late than never" to "Betpetterper latepate thanpan nevpeverper" in another version. The rules for deriving these two dialects of pig latin are easy to state: In the first example the initial consonantal sound(s) of each word is (are) placed at the end of the word and followed by *ay* (*spoon* would be pronounced as though it were written *oonspay*); in the second example each syllable is followed by a rhyming syllable that begins with a *p* instead of the original consonant(s) (*glass of milk* would become *glasspass ofpof milkpilk*). From the point of view of the ethnography of communication, the phonological or other rules by which special speech varieties are derived are only a part of the inquiry. Just as important are the conditions under which the participants use these speech varieties.

The rules for producing play languages also vary from one version to the next. The five play languages (1–5) of the Kuna Indians of San Blas, Panama, described by Sherzer (1976) are derived by means of the following rules: (1) The first syllable of a word is placed at word end (for example, *osi* 'pineapple' becomes *sio*); (2) *pp* followed by the vowel of the preceding syllable is inserted after the initial consonant-vowel sequence of each syllable (*ua* 'fish' becomes *uppuappa*); (3) *r* followed by the vowel of the previous syllable is inserted in the same position as in the previous version (*pe* 'you' becomes *pere*); (4) every vowel changes to *i* (*nuka* 'name' becomes *niki*); and (5) the syllable *ci* is prefixed before every syllable of the source word, each original syllable receiving primary stress (*maceret* 'man' becomes *cimácicécirét*). Children use these play languages not for concealment but for play's sake. They prepare the young Kuna for a culture in which language creativity and playfulness are highly valued.

An interesting example of speech disguise or concealment has been reported by Harold C. Conklin (1959) as taking place among the Hanunóo, jungle farmers on one of the islands in the central Philippines. Marriageable young Hanunóo make use of no less than a dozen methods of modifying their speech during courtship. These include rearranging, substituting, or otherwise modifying the sounds of the original Hanunóo utterances, inverting the meaning of a sentence or using such voice qualifiers as barely audible whispering, clipped pronunciation, or pronouncing words on the inbreath instead of the outbreath. Although the young males and females also use speech disguise for simple amusement (joking and teasing), its primary purpose is to prevent older relatives, younger siblings, and others within earshot from understanding what is being said between the two young people. Sometimes a young man conceals his identity by wearing a blanket over his head and altering his voice. Because Hanunóo music, art, and oral folklore are linked with courtship behavior, a study of the culture that did not consider the use of speech disguise would be incomplete.

Speech play is especially common among children, helping them to acquire both linguistic and communicative competence as well as sensitive awareness of their mother tongue. Children's verbal lore includes such games as counting-out rhymes (for example, "Eeny, meeny, miney, mo, / Catch a tiger by its toe"), jump-rope rhymes ("I love coffee, I love tea, / How many boys are stuck on me? / One, two, three . . ."), ball-bouncing rhymes, tongue twisters ("She sells seashells down by the seashore"), taunts, puns ("If we cantaloupe, lettuce marry; weed make a swell pear"), and riddles ("When is a door not a door? When it is ajar"). In nursery rhymes, adults (usually parents) engage in speech play with little children. They do so, for example, by using tickling rhymes ("Ticklee, ticklee, on the knee, / If you laugh, you don't love me"). In some societies, as we have seen in the example of Hanunóo speech disguise, speech play is reserved for young adults. In other societies, oratorical performances are reserved primarily for adults, but training for them begins in childhood (see Box 12.3 for a short characterization of the oratorical language of the Ilongot of the northern Philippines). But regardless of the age group, there are questions to be asked as one studies this particular aspect of the ethnography of communication—among them, What speech activities does a society define as playful? What age groups, sexes, or classes of a society engage in speech play? Do all adult members of a society approve of, tolerate, or disapprove of speech play? If not, which ones do not? What genres of speech play are especially favored? and What is the social significance of speech play in a society?

Summary and Conclusions

Traditional narratives, such as the fairy tale or myth, have been studied from a variety of perspectives, the main points of departure being content, function, structure, and performance. Among the various approaches, the two that contrast the most are the taxonomic, involving the assigning of a tale to a specific tale type and then defining the type in terms of constituent motifs, and the performance-centered approach. Many contemporary students of oral folklore object to the taxonomic approach because it treats a narrative as though it were a desiccated artifact, much as an old-fashioned curator might mount a butterfly in a museum display case, pinned down among related specimens and labeled as to genus and species. To continue with the comparison, performance-

---

BOX 12.3 The Language of Ilongot Oratory

In play and in oratory, when singing, telling riddles, or conducting a political debate, Ilongots say they are using "crooked language," that they hide behind the wit and beauty of their words. Such language, rich in metaphor and elaborate rhythms, is heard in bursts of anger and of humor, and it is common in focused, public situations, in arguments and playful contests, situations in which an individual's skill, style, and rhetorical genius, have persuasive social force. Skill in witty language is what a young child is thought to learn in repartee with elders; it is what adolescents develop when they answer kinsmen's riddles or match their peers in song; and finally, for adults, and especially for men, a poised command of witty and beautiful ways of talking means that one has "knowledge," the right to leadership, and the political power which comes with an ability to persuade and understand.

from Michelle Rosaldo, "I Have Nothing to Hide" (1973), 193–194

---

oriented folklorists conceive of a traditional narrative above all as a live event, not unlike a butterfly undergoing metamorphosis, fluttering from flower to flower, mating, reacting to its environment, and so on.

The functional approach is especially congenial to anthropologists, who are interested in the context in which a particular item of culture occurs and its integration into the culture as a whole. Structuralism, regardless of type, provides useful insights into the organization of a folkloric text, unless it becomes an end in itself—in which case it reveals little more than a construct that exists in the investigator's mind rather than in the text under study.

The most recent approaches to the study of playful and creative use of language have been greatly influenced by the ethnography of speaking. The pacesetting scholars of today are not given to collecting narratives and other specimens of verbal art and then classifying them, and structuralist studies in the classical sense (à la Lévi-Strauss) draw relatively little attention. The point of departure for many modern linguistic anthropologists is a single (though not necessarily short) discourse collected during actual performance (that is, tape-recorded for sound and, if possible, videotaped). The aim of the subsequent analysis is to determine those features that characterize different forms of discourse, to note how members of audiences respond and evaluate performers and performances, and to relate the structure of discourse to the social and cultural context in which it occurs. Throughout these studies, the language-culture-society linkage is maintained and emphasized.

The various approaches to oral folklore are not mutually exclusive, and even tend to complement each other. Several scholars have subjected individual myths to multiple analyses ranging from the examination of cultural context and function to the determination of formal structure. Because the telling of a traditional narrative is the intersecting of a particular cultural practice, a special use of language, a specific social occasion, and a unique performance, a multifaceted approach is not only warranted but has much to offer.

Notes and Suggestions for Further Reading

I have made no attempt to cover the genres of oral folklore in full or to consider all of the approaches that have been applied to the study of traditional narratives. For example, I have not discussed either folk songs or the psychoanalytic or psychological interpretations of myths inspired by Sigmund Freud, Carl G. Jung, and others, even though some contemporary scholars favor such interpretations.

In Thompson 1961 tales are subdivided into (I) Animal tales, (II) Ordinary folktales (including tales of magic), (III) Jokes and anecdotes, (IV) Formula tales, and (V) Unclassified tales. The arrangement of motifs in Thompson 1955–1958 is as follows: (A) Mythological motifs, (B) Animals, (C) Tabu, (D) Magic, (E) The dead, (F) Marvels, (G) Ogres, (H) Tests, (J) The wise and the foolish, (K) Deceptions, (L) Reversal of fortune, (M) Ordaining the future, (N) Chance and fate, (P) Society, (Q) Rewards and punishments, (R) Captives and fugitives, (S) Unnatural cruelty, (T) Sex, (U) The nature of life, (V) Religion, (W) Traits of character, (X) Humor, and (Z) Miscellaneous groups of motifs.

"Seven-league boots" is Motif D1521.1; "Transformation: stretching tree" is D482.1; and "Tabu: using magic power too often" is C762.1. "The Fox and the Wood Tick" (Salzmann and Salzmann 1952) is a variant of Type 275 consisting of Motif K11.2: "Race won by deception: riding on the back." "Cinderella" is Type 510. "The Man with the Sharpened Leg" and "White Man and His Mother-in-Law," collected both in English and Arapaho, are from Salzmann 1956a and 1956b, respectively; "The sharpened leg" is Motif J2424. "Hansel and Gretel" is Type 327A.

For helpful anthologies dealing with folklore in general, the search for origins, the theories of myth, form and function in folklore, and transmission of folklore, including Thompson's analysis of The Star Husband (1953), see Dundes 1965 and 1984.

Hymes's essays in Native American ethnopoetics are collected in Hymes 1981.

Most of Lévi-Strauss's works have been translated into English. A representative selection of his writings has appeared in two volumes titled *Structural Anthropology* (1963 and 1976), the second of which includes his well-known but controversial analysis of the story of Asdiwal, a Tsimshian Indian myth. Among other works of Lévi-Strauss is the four-volume *Introduction to a Science of Mythology* (Lévi-Strauss 1983a, 1983b, 1990a, and 1990b). For a cultural materialist critique of structuralism in general, and Lévi-Strauss's approach to it in particular, see Harris 1979, which also addresses the case of the coyote as mediator.

On verbal art as performance, see Bauman 1984, 1986, and 1992, Ben-Amos and Goldstein 1975, and Bauman and Briggs 1990; Bauman 1986 and Bauman and Briggs 1990 contain helpful lists of related bibliographic references. On poetics and rhetoric in Native American discourse, see Sherzer and Urban 1986 and Sherzer and Woodbury 1987. And for selected articles on speech play and linguistic creativity, see Kirshenblatt-Gimblett 1976; her book contains an extensive bibliography on the subject (pp. 179–284).

13

Linguistic Anthropology in the Contemporary World

Linguistic anthropology is generally thought to be a field of research understood and practiced only by a relatively few specialists. Although the applications of anthropology to contemporary problems are generally seen as coming from the subfield of cultural rather than linguistic anthropology, many practical uses have been found for socially oriented linguistics, and linguistic expertise is being applied with increasing frequency to problems having their roots in language use.

The most commonly used and best-developed form of applied linguistics (and linguistic anthropology) is language planning. Language planning may be called for when the presence of several competing languages in a country has become divisive or when a particular language or dialect is to be elevated to serve as the official or national language of a multilingual or multidialectal society. The initial step in language planning is to define the nature of the problem. Linguists or linguistic anthropologists are best qualified to assume this task. Because the recommendation that a particular language or dialect be made the official language of a society affects everyone in that society, from elders down to elementary school pupils, such advice must be carefully considered. Once the society's leaders reach a decision, projects to facilitate the implementation of the new language policy must be initiated—for example, preparation of textbooks, grammars, and dictionaries and the development of a teacher training program.

Linguistic expertise is most frequently and extensively applied in the field of education (for example, to enhance literacy), but it also can and does contribute to more effective communication in the fields of law, medicine, and business, and it plays an important role in language maintenance and language disorders. This chapter includes some specific examples of the application of linguistics and linguistic anthropology.

Cross-cultural Communication

Today, when so many people frequently travel far away from home and encounter members of different ethnic groups and societies, interethnic and cross-cultural (intercultural) relations are continually being put to the test. Whether such relations are amicable or hostile, straightforward or confused depends primarily on how individuals or groups with differing cultural backgrounds are able to communicate with each other. Even in languages or dialects that are closely similar or considered to be alike, specific words may have different senses or carry a different emphasis from one language to the other, resulting in occasional misunderstandings. A good illustration of a lack of equivalence between American and British English was provided by Margaret Mead when she pointed out that

> in Britain, the word "compromise" is a good word, and one may speak approvingly of any arrangement which has been a compromise, including, very often, one in which the other side has gained more than fifty per cent of the points at issue. On the other hand, in the United States, the minority position is still the position from which everyone speaks. . . . This is congruent with the American doctrine of checks and balances, but it does not permit the word "compromise" to gain the same ethical halo which it has in Britain. Where, in Britain, to compromise means to work out a good solution, in America it usually means to work out a bad one, a solution in which all the points of importance (to both sides) are lost. (Mead quoted in Kluckhohn 1949:158)

Not always given sufficient attention but frequently of some consequence are differences in communicative styles among ethnic groups of a particular society. A number of research projects have been undertaken to determine the extent of such differences between Anglo-Americans on the one side and Latinos, African-Americans, and members of other ethnic groups that make up the population of the United States on the other. For example, according to one study, the ten- to fifteen-year-old recently arrived Latino pupils of several samples were found to be more interpersonally oriented and more inclined to attribute the feeling of shame to themselves or to others when compared to their Anglo-American peers. If teachers are aware of differences between members of differing ethnic groups that find expression in communicative behavior, they can better understand why under certain circumstances some pupils react differently from others (Albert 1986).

According to another study, black and white students at an eastern college differed in their handling of oral disagreements. The African-American students tended to argue more persistently with each other for their positions and to take more control of the interaction than did white students, who appeared to prefer compromise or solution-oriented strategies in resolving their conflicts. Furthermore, all males in this sample, regardless of ethnicity, were more likely to engage in indirect, nonconfrontational strategies (for example, silence) than females, who tended to use more active strategies (Ting-Toomey 1986).

It is of course necessary to keep in mind that it would be inappropriate to extend the findings pertaining to a sample to an entire ethnic group. Any of a number of circumstances may invalidate such an extension—for example, setting (urban as against rural), the length of interethnic contact (a few years as opposed to decades as opposed to generations), amount of education, geographic location, socioeconomic status, and so on.

If cross-cultural contacts are to be harmonious and productive, it is obvious that communicating with members of a society whose language and culture are very much different from one's own requires great care and in many cases advice from someone knowledgeable about the differences. In a 1970 article, Howard F. Van Zandt discusses a number of characteristics of Japanese behavior and how these might come into play in business negotiations with foreigners. Van Zandt mentions a greater emotional sensitivity on the part of the Japanese, who at the same time make a point of concealing their emotions. Further, they are reluctant to enter into arguments and to say no, they dislike the display of power, and they prefer to have oral presentations supported by written documentation. Van Zandt advises the negotiator to talk slowly and guard against wordiness but to explain major ideas in two or three different ways to be sure they are understood; long sentences and negative constructions are to be avoided, as are slang terms. Even if the interpreter takes much more time than the original speaker, the negotiator must not become impatient, nor should he or she become suspicious when the interpreter covers a five-minute speech in one-fifth of the time.

As anthropologists know, of course, all cultures undergo modification over time, in part as a result of culture contact, but as Van Zandt points out, "the [Japanese] culture is an old one, and, since the Japanese politico-economic system is so successful, there is little likelihood it will be rapidly changed" (Van Zandt 1970:56).

Applications in Legal Proceedings

According to Frake, "The Yakan legal system is manifest almost exclusively through one kind of behavior: talk. Consequently the ethnographer's record of observations of litigation is largely a linguistic record, and the legal system is a code for talking, a linguistic code" (Frake 1969:147; the Yakan are Philippine Muslims inhabiting the island of Basilan southwest of Mindanao). By contrast, the laws of the United States are written down, and legal interpretations and decisions have been recorded in scores of volumes. But the language of the law is just as much spoken as it is read, and its nature may be a source of problems for individuals engaged in litigation. One such problem concerns the understanding of legal terms on the part of those American citizens whose native language is not English; another has to do with comprehending the specialized language of the legal profession, difficult even for native English speakers. Not a few commonly used legal terms are foreign, overly formal, jargonistic, or absent from common speech to such an extent that litigants frequently find it difficult to follow court proceedings. For example, how many college-educated people know the meanings of such legal terms and expressions as *venire, tort, eminent domain, pursuant to, know all men by these presents,* and *(in) flagrante delicto?* Although most citizens may never become litigants, they do encounter legal language in insurance policies and other contractual documents. A humorous quotation from *The Tulsa Tribune* of October 6, 1959, illustrates just how wordy, pompous, and repetitious legal language can appear to be to laypeople: The simple offer expressed by the sentence "Have an orange" might read in legalese as "I hereby give and convey to you, all and singular, my estate and interest, right, title, claim and advantages of and in said orange, together with its rind, skin, juice, pulp, and pips and all rights and advantages therein and full power to bite, suck, or otherwise eat the same or give the same away with or without the rind, skin, juice, pulp and pips" (quoted in Hager 1959:74–75).

The specific phrasing of questions can influence the answers of witnesses. An experiment revealed that the use of the word *smashed* in an inquiry concerning the collision of two cars tended to elicit estimates of higher speed than the use of such words as *collided, bumped, hit,* or *contacted* (in descending order). Further, subjects shown a film of two cars colliding responded to the question "Did you see any broken glass?" more often with a yes if the questioner used the word *smashed* rather than the milder word *hit,* even though the film had shown no broken glass at all (Loftus and Palmer 1974).

In general, *how* things are said in a courtroom—the speech behavior of the prosecuting attorney, the legal counsel for the defendant, the defendant, and witnesses—may carry more weight than *what* is actually being said. For example, what has been characterized as a "powerless" and therefore unconvincing mode of speech includes the use of hedges ("Perhaps . . . ," "Possibly . . . ," or "If I'm not mistaken . . .") on the part of the defendant or a witness. And when lawyers try to manipulate and control witnesses too tightly (by interrupting them, not letting them testify as fully as they would like to), the impression may be created that the lawyers have little confidence in the testimony being given. A juror's negative impression of a lawyer as a result of his or her speech behavior with witnesses may well be transferred to the person the lawyer is representing, with possible consequences for the case (O'Barr and Conley 1996).

If a questioner's use of particular words or constructions can influence the answers without the respondent or jurors being aware of it, or if the highly specialized language used, for example, in contracts or insurance policies is not fully intelligible to the person concerned, some remedy is indicated. In recent years many insurance policies have, in fact, been written in more understandable language or included definitions of the legal terms used. Stylistic changes made to eliminate or at least alleviate incomprehensible legal formulations are examples of applied linguistics.

*   *   *

A concrete example of the application of linguistic findings to social issues is the case of the "Black English trial" in Ann Arbor, so referred to and described by William Labov (1982), one of the most distinguished sociolinguists in the United States. In the 1960s, the city of Ann Arbor, Michigan, decided to distribute low-income housing in various neighborhoods rather than to concentrate it in the downtown area. One of the results of scattered-site housing was that African-American children from the project built on Green Road began attending the Martin Luther King Elementary School, which then came to serve 80 percent white, 13 percent African-American, and 7 percent Asian and Latino pupils.

Several years later the mothers of the African-American pupils from the project became upset that their children were doing quite poorly in school. According to the school staff, the students were either emotionally disturbed or had learning disabilities and in general exhibited behavior problems. Believing their children to be normal, four of the mothers sought out legal assistance, and on July 28, 1977, on behalf of fifteen African-American pupils, charged the King School with failure to take into consideration the cultural and socioeconomic factors that had affected these pupils' progress. The plaintiffs argued that the failure of the school to take appropriate action to overcome the linguistic barrier encountered by the Green Road children—namely, that they spoke a vernacular then referred to as Black English that was quite different from the language spoken by the majority of the pupils—impeded their children's equal participation in the school's instructional program. Witnesses at the trial included linguists known for their work in sociolinguistics, Labov among them. The judge ruled in favor of the plaintiffs on July 12, 1979, and incorporated into his decision a statement that summarized the results of some twenty years of linguistic research concerning the nature of African-American English. The relevant passage reads as follows:

All of the distinguished researchers and professionals testified as to the existence of a language system, which is a part of the English language but different in significant respects from the standard English used in the school setting, the commercial world, the world of the arts and science, among the professions, and in government. It is and has been used at some time by 80 percent of the black people of this country and has as its genesis the transactional or pidgin language of the slaves, which after a generation or two became a Creole language. Since then it has constantly been refined and brought closer to the mainstream of society. It still flourishes in areas where there are concentrations of black people. It contains aspects of Southern dialect and is used largely by black people in their casual conversation and informal talk. (quoted in Labov 1982:194)

In the conclusion of his article, Labov stresses the need for both scientific objectivity and commitment to social action. He further points out that the trial not only took place on the initiative of African-American people but was instrumental in bringing African-American linguists into the field of research concerning African-American English. (Because African-American English is discussed in some detail in Chapter 8, Labov's account of the trial in Ann Arbor is greatly abbreviated here.)

To mention an application of a different type (Gumperz 1982): In 1978 a U.S. Navy doctor of Filipino origin attended an emergency room case. A sixteen-month-old girl was brought to the hospital with burns that her mother and stepfather claimed had been caused by overexposure to the sun. The child was treated and released in the parents' care. Six hours later the child was brought back to the emergency room and examined by another physician then on duty, but she died later that day. It was found that the burns had been intentionally inflicted by her stepfather, who was convicted of second-degree manslaughter and sentenced to a prison term.

Sometime later the first examining doctor was accused of perjury for statements made when he testified for the prosecution at the stepfather's trial, although his testimony had been supported by the hospital personnel who had assisted him in the emergency room. According to a report by the FBI agent charged with investigating the case, the doctor should have suspected child abuse and kept the child in the hospital instead of releasing her to the parents. In the course of the court proceedings, one of the defense attorneys pointed out that on several occasions the doctor had used pronouns in a "funny" way even though his English was good. The doctor's native language was Aklanon, but he was fluent in Tagalog and English, the two official languages of the Philippines. A linguist was brought in as an expert to determine whether a cross-cultural misunderstanding could have occurred. The linguist was able to establish that several passages in the doctor's testimony were ambiguous because he had carried over into English the syntax of his native language, syntax that in Aklanon or Tagalog would not have been ambiguous. To quote from Gumperz's conclusion:

> We have demonstrated that many aspects of [the doctor's] behavior can be explained by his linguistic and cultural background. The features in question are automatic and not readily subject to conscious control. They do not affect his written performance, yet they are likely to recur whenever he is faced with complex oral communicative tasks, so that, in spite of the fact that he speaks English well, he is more likely than native speakers of English to be misunderstood in such situations. (Gumperz 1982:195)

The miscommunication argument was accepted by most of the jurors, and the perjury charges against the doctor were dismissed.

Others who have studied how the use of language can affect legal proceedings have pointed out several instances in which the services of someone with linguistic expertise would be helpful. Such a situation could occur when legal jargon combined with certain features of grammar (for example, passive constructions or the excessive use of nouns where verbs would be clearer or more direct) keeps jurors from understanding the instructions the judge gives to them. Linguistic expertise may also be needed to counter possible listener "contamination," a danger when jurors are left to their own resources to interpret recorded conversations between the defendant and others. The linguist may be able, for example, to indicate that the defendant's silence could have been due to boredom, politeness, or some other factor rather than to tacit agreement with what other speakers may have been saying, or to identify, by their dialectal or idiolectal characteristics, the defendant's utterances among a confusing variety of voices. Another type of situation could occur if statements or questions containing a presupposition create the assumption of truth when such an assumption is not warranted. Such misleading use of language is related to the well-known question, "Have you stopped beating your wife?" to which the person questioned is expected to answer yes or no. Regardless of the choice of answer, the clear implication is that such a misdeed did in fact take place. On a broader scale, the linguist may be of assistance to the court by analyzing recordings for clues relating to the intentions and the conversational strategies of speakers.

There are many aspects to communicative behavior in court that deserve attention if all relevant information is to be available to the judge and the jurors. Among the factors to be considered are the cultural background and communicative competence of the defendant, the plaintiff, and the witnesses; the types of questions asked during a trial (for example, the use of leading questions) and the context in which they are asked; the relative value of narrative testimony as against testimony limited to specific brief answers; the use of interruptions; the relation between body movements and the utterances of litigants and witnesses; the nature of the instructions given by the judge to the jurors; and others. It is clear that linguistic expertise in court proceedings can be of value.

Language Planning

The most common form of applied sociolinguistics is language planning. The term refers to a deliberate attempt, usually at the level of the state, to affect language use in order to prevent or to solve some problem of communication. The need for language planning and the formulation of language policies has been rapidly increasing in the course of the twentieth century. The two main reasons are the dislocation of millions of people as a result of wars and political persecution and the emergence of many new multiethnic states when colonial empires were dissolved after World War II.

In a very broad sense, language planning encompasses even the invention of artificial international languages such as Esperanto or Interlingua. Supranational languages like these are expected to promote understanding and peaceful coexistence among people of different ethnic and linguistic backgrounds. More narrowly, language planning usually takes one of two forms. One form involves a change in the status of a language or a dialect—in other words, a change in language use. The other involves changes in the structure of a language—changes affecting its pronunciation, spelling, grammar, or vocabulary. Frequently, however, the two forms are combined. The following cases illustrate both forms of language planning in practice.

The nationalization of Swahili in Kenya is primarily an example of change in status. In 1974 the first president of independent Kenya, Jomo Kenyatta, decided that the country's national assembly should conduct its business in Swahili. When the members strongly objected, Kenyatta closed the assembly and announced: "Whether some people will like my decision or not KiSwahili will be spoken in our *Bunge* [Parliament], because it is the language of the *wananchi* [citizens, people]. English is not our language and the time will come when we will do everything in Swahili. I know many people will be annoyed but let them" (Hinnebusch 1979:290). There are several dozen languages spoken in Kenya, at least eight of them by more than 1 million speakers each. Kikuyu, the native language of over 5 million people, is the language most frequently heard, whereas Swahili is a native language spoken by very few Kenyans and therefore is relatively neutral. To have selected one of the main languages of Kenya (for example, Kikuyu, Luo, Luhya, or Kamba) would have incited ethnic rivalry and to have chosen English would have given preference to the non-African language of those who ruled Kenya from 1895 until 1963. At present both Swahili and English serve as official languages, but Swahili is the national language. To promote and institutionalize Swahili as the national language of Kenya has called for a variety of government policies ranging from the preparation of instructional materials to seeing to it that the Swahili used in official dealings is "good" Kenyan Swahili. The great variety of languages spoken in Kenya, the use of Swahili as a lingua franca and also as an important instrument of the country's detribalization, and the prestige that English still enjoys all indicate that language planning in Kenya will need to continue into the future.

Language planning of the second type has been fairly common but usually not with the speed and to the extent carried out in Turkey after that country became a republic in 1923. When the Seljuk Turks became Islamized during the ninth and tenth centuries, they adopted Arabic script and borrowed many Arabic words, especially those having to do with religion, law, administration, and commerce. Later, when Persia (now Iran) became a part of the Ottoman (Turkish) Empire, the Turks also adopted Persian loanwords. Arabic and Persian influences affected not only the Turkish vocabulary but phonology and grammar as well. In many cases, then, three words—a native Turkish word and two loanwords, one each from Arabic and Persian—were available for a single referent. Making matters even more complex, the three words were not always subject to the same grammatical rules. Casual spoken Turkish and the literary language (Ottoman Turkish) were in a diglossic relationship, each with a distinct range of social functions. Ottoman Turkish (the high form), with its many loanwords, was virtually unintelligible to peasants and ordinary people, who spoke the low form.

To simplify and modernize written Turkish, Kemal Atatürk, the first president of Turkey, appointed a commission in 1928 to recommend a new system to replace the Arabic script that had been used for centuries even though it had never suited the structure of Turkish. The new writing system—the Latin alphabet with several diacritics—was ready within six weeks and its use became law before the end of the year. The introduction of the Latin alphabet was later followed by a reform designed to rid Turkish of Arabic and Persian loanwords by substituting Turkish words from both the popular language and old Turkish texts or coining new ones; in order to accomplish this demanding task, in 1932 Atatürk founded the Turkish Linguistic Society. The changing of the writing system and the simplification of Turkish grammar and lexicon helped to modernize and Westernize Turkish society, but it also made much of classical Turkish literature in its original form unintelligible to modern Turks.

Language Maintenance and Reinforcement

Since the mid-1960s, increasing efforts by linguists and Native American tribal leaders have been devoted to language maintenance and reinforcement in those communities where the traditional transmission of oral skills from parents to children is no longer functioning effectively. Although perhaps as many as 200 Native American languages are still spoken at least to some extent in the United States and Canada, ever-increasing numbers of them are in danger of being completely replaced by English. Only a relatively few Native American languages (for example, Navajo, some of the Siouan languages of the northern Plains, and Eskimo) continue to play a vital role in Indian community life; they are the languages serving larger populations in the less densely inhabited parts of North America. Language maintenance and reinforcement typically include linguistic analysis (on all levels—phonological, morphological, syntactic, and lexical), a writing system (in most cases the Latin alphabet with a few additional symbols and diacritics if necessary), and the production of instructional materials for the use of Native American pupils.

For the Northern Arapaho of the Wind River Reservation in Wyoming, who are anxious to maintain and even reinforce their ethnic identity and cultural heritage, the present situation is nothing short of critical. Several factors contribute to the gloomy situation:

1. With very few exceptions, the only individuals who have full command of Arapaho—even if they no longer use it habitually and even if English has come to influence it—are members of the oldest generation.
2. Parents no longer teach Arapaho to their children in the home.
3. The numbers of active speakers and of those who have at least some passive knowledge of Arapaho are declining very rapidly.
4. The bulk of the population is for all practical purposes monolingual, with English preferred in essentially all situations, including even some traditional ceremonial contexts.
5. Arapaho is losing its communicative viability—its capability to adapt successfully to new situations.

It is sad that young Arapaho parents can no longer be expected to pass along to their children the rich cultural heritage of the tribe, the Arapaho language in particular. As a result, the task has fallen to the reservation schools.

The most significant step taken to arrest the language decay was to formalize the teaching of spoken Arapaho to the youngest pupils. Thanks to the foresight and energy of the administrators of one of the schools, two week-long workshops were organized in March and September 1984 to experiment with videotaping lessons in spoken Arapaho for use in reservation classrooms. So much was learned from the work of those two weeks that at a January workshop the following year it was possible to approach the task with a greater degree of professional skill and, aided by the administrators of another school, to produce the first formal set of lessons in spoken Arapaho. The Spoken Arapaho Curriculum Development Project team set its goal for the two weeks rather ambitiously at forty lessons, but the enthusiasm of the participants was such that forty-two were completed and are now in classroom use. In order not to burden young pupils with having to learn how to write two languages (Arapaho spelling happens to be much simpler than English spelling because it is phonemic), Arapaho-speaking classroom aides teach the students spoken Arapaho with the help of the videotapes. Forty-odd lessons will not reverse the declining fortunes of the Arapaho language on the reservation, but their completion and use in the lower grades has the great symbolic value of a last-ditch stand and a hope for things to come.

The end of 1983 also saw the completion of the *Dictionary of Contemporary Arapaho Usage,* made possible by a grant from the National Endowment for the Humanities. It was a source of great satisfaction to the Arapaho that the very same government that only a few generations ago prohibited the use of Native American languages in schools has become seriously concerned with their preservation.

While the work on the dictionary and the videotaped lessons was taking place, one of the schools continued to add to the growing series of booklets designed to aid the teaching of Arapaho language and culture in the upper grades. All told, the body of instructional materials produced under various auspices for use with Arapaho students in the reservation schools is quite impressive—more than sixty items, not counting the videotaped lessons. Not to be outdone by the other schools, staff members of a third school came up with an idea to further help revitalize the efforts made on behalf of Arapaho: an annual Arapaho language bowl for the most accomplished students of the reservation schools, with prizes and diplomas to be awarded.

This brief account of one example of language maintenance and reinforcement would not be complete without emphasizing that many additional steps must be taken to expand the program in the future. The following steps are worth mentioning here (the list is meant to be merely suggestive, not complete): workshops designed to develop new Arapaho curricular materials and improve the existing ones; in-service training of current Arapaho studies teachers and teacher aides; an internship program for future teachers of Arapaho studies; tribal scholarships for Arapaho high school students who have shown exceptional intellectual capacity as well as interest and skill in learning Arapaho to allow them to study linguistics and anthropology at the college level; adult education programs featuring elders narrating, in Arapaho or English, traditional tales or life histories and other reminiscences; and an Arapaho-language summer camp for preschoolers and elementary pupils, staffed in part by those

Arapaho elders, both women and men, who have command of the language and a willingness to share it with the young members of the tribe. In the initial stages of any language maintenance programs, linguistic anthropologists provide useful advice and help, but it is preferable and important that, as far as possible, such programs and activities be further developed, organized, and administered by members of the societies concerned.

In a recent article Michael Krauss (1992:7) considers it plausible "that—at the rate things are going—the coming century will see either the death or the doom of 90% of mankind's languages," and he asks, "What are we linguists doing to prepare for this or to prevent this catastrophic destruction of the linguistic world?" Programs for language maintenance or reinforcement, such as the ones used at present in a number of Native American communities, represent one attempt to help.

Ethical Questions and Standards of Conduct

In the introductory chapter I pointed out that "native" consultants make an essential contribution to studies in linguistics, cultural anthropology, and linguistic anthropology and that every effort should be made to enable promising members of small ethnic groups to receive training in these fields. The insight into their cultures such individuals possess would be invaluable. One must realize, however, that it will take some years before members of small societies are reasonably well represented in the fields of linguistics and anthropology, both of which are dominated at present by white males.

Doing fieldwork in a foreign culture almost invariably gives rise to an asymmetrical relationship: On the one hand there is the researcher (the word is used here to mean anyone who is an attentive and systematic observer and makes a study of something) and on the other hand the subjects (that is, those who are being studied) or natives (those who are connected to a particular community or region by birth). The researcher, typically a cultural and linguistic outsider, lives for a number of months with those who are being studied, observes them and asks numerous questions, and now and then accompanies them as they do their chores or even helps with their daily tasks. Because much of the native consultants' time is taken up by the researcher's questions and requests for data concerning language and culture, it is customary to offer them modest but fair compensation (consultant fees usually come out of the grant the researcher has received for fieldwork).

Doing fieldwork in another country or in a foreign culture under physical conditions that are usually less comfortable than those at home, living among and depending on people who at least initially are complete strangers, having to eat unfamiliar foods, and trying to communicate with others who speak a different language require both the will and the ability to make profound adaptations. For these reasons a few anthropologists find fieldwork too taxing, and after their initial experience engage in it only occasionally or not at all. But most anthropologists, both linguistic and cultural, enjoy being in the field and return to fieldwork again and again.

And what about the people who are studied? An extended visit by an anthropologist is bound to have some effect on them, as every researcher needs to be aware. According to the code of professional ethics adopted by the American Anthropological Association, the responsibility of anthropologists to those they study is paramount. The aims of the anthropologists' activities should be communicated as clearly as possible to those among whom they work; consultants (informants) have the right to remain anonymous if they choose to, and their rights, interests, safety, and sensitivities must be safeguarded; consultants are not to be exploited but should receive a fair return for their services; the results of research should be made available to the general public—clandestine research can potentially be used by others against the population under study. In short, prior to commencing research the anthropologist should give serious thought to the possibility that the study of a group or community could at some future time negatively affect the people studied. If such an outcome seems possible, then the research project should be substantively redesigned or abandoned.

A comment should also be made concerning the comportment of researchers in the field. Their expertise, educational background, and material advantages in no way entitle them to any feelings of superiority to those they study, who may live in conditions unaffected by modern technology and may be nonliterate. As guests in a foreign society, community, or home, field-workers should exercise even more sensitivity than they would be expected to use in their home environment. Asking for advice does not necessarily mean accepting it, but there are many instances when advice can be of great value and may even help determine whether a project succeeds or fails. Let us consider, for example, a group's need for educational materials designed to help pupils learn their own language and something about their culture in Western-style schools (such a situation can be encountered in schools in the United States serving primarily Native American students). If there are several adequate ways of writing down a language that has previously only been spoken, which method would be preferable to the potential users? And if an anthology of traditional narratives is to be compiled for the use of students, which of the many stories should be selected?

It occasionally happens, of course, that members of a tribe, a nomadic group, or a peasant village do not want to have their daily lives, religious beliefs, and traditional customs scrutinized by someone they do not know, who comes from another country, and whose intentions they cannot fully comprehend. Reverse the situation: Think of what the attitudes of members of a small community somewhere in the United States might be toward a foreigner of a different skin color, who has different religious beliefs and speaks a foreign language, announcing that he or she will live in the community for half a year or so to study the habits of the "natives."

In a world in which human communities and nations have become interdependent and in which respect for cultural diversity is essential, understanding other cultures is ever more important. This understanding is what anthropologists are committed to promote, and their behavior in societies other than their own must set an example.

Summary and Conclusions

There are many different ways of applying expertise in socially oriented linguistics to the problems of the contemporary world. Knowledge gained from the study of the ethnography of communication can be quite useful when individuals or groups of differing cultural and linguistic backgrounds are attempting to communicate. The informality of Americans (the ease with which they move to a first-name basis, for example) may be regarded by other societies as ill-mannered or even presumptuous; Americans, for their part, are likely to consider the formal behavior characteristic of some other societies as stuffy and inflexible. If individuals or groups involved in intercultural contact know how to interpret each other's behavior, communication will proceed more smoothly. Another area where linguistic applications have been found useful is in legal proceedings. Here the contributions of applied linguistics range from making the technical language of legal documents intelligible to the layperson to helping the judge, jury, witnesses, or litigants resolve problems resulting from misunderstandings caused by differing cultural and linguistic backgrounds.

Language problems in a pluralistic society are commonly due to the uneven status of competing languages or dialects. The question to be answered is not only which language (or languages) is to become the national or official language but what the consequences of a particular choice are likely to be for the whole society. And if an unwritten language spoken by a small population in a pluralistic society is to be maintained by introducing it into the schools as a second language, the linguist may be called upon to devise a writing system and then to help in developing teaching materials.

With cultural differences around the world becoming less distinct as a result of communications media, modernization, and the volume of international travel, the language of a minority population may be the only prominent badge of its ethnic identity and pride. It goes without saying that the language concerns of such a group need to be handled not only with expert knowledge but with understanding and tact.

Notes and Suggestions for Further Reading

Among the publications dealing with applied linguistics are Wardhaugh and Brown 1976, Crystal 1981, and Trudgill 1984. The *Annual Review of Applied Linguistics (ARAL)*, first published in 1981, surveys research and comments on new trends in the field of applied linguistics. With several hundred new citations each year, *ARAL* is a good source of bibliographical references. For a survey of the uses of linguistics in medicine, law, and education, together with an extensive bibliography, see Shuy 1984. Linguistics and education is the subject of a survey article by Heath 1984; for an overview of the language of the law, see O'Barr 1981.

For readers on intercultural communication, see Carbaugh 1990 and Samovar and Porter 1991. Language planning is discussed in Eastman 1983 and Kennedy 1983. A survey of American Indian language maintenance efforts is to be found in Leap 1981 and a guide to issues in Indian language retention in Bauman 1980. Of interest may be the contributions to the symposium "Endangered Languages" by Hale and others 1992; for a contrary view of endangered languages, see Ladefoged 1992; and for a response to Ladefoged, see Dorian 1993.

The discussion of language maintenance and reinforcement among the Northern Arapaho of the Wind River Reservation is based on my personal involvement in such a project during the 1980s.

The discussion of the principles of professional responsibility to those whom anthropologists study is abbreviated from the pamphlet *Professional Ethics*, published by the American Anthropological Association in 1983. Besides discussing relations with those studied, the statements on ethics also cover the anthropologists' responsibilities to the public, to the discipline, to anthropology students, to sponsors, to their own government, and to host governments.

Glossary

A word or phrase with a particular meaning in linguistic anthropology is defined when it first occurs in the text; the pages on which such terms are discussed are indicated in the Index. The Glossary therefore includes only selected terms (bold-faced in the text) that are either of general importance or occur repeatedly in the text. The definitions given here are in their simplest and most general forms.

*　　*　　*

African-American Vernacular English. A nonstandard but expressive variety of English spoken by many African-Americans.

Alphabet (Alphabetic writing). A writing system that represents the different speech sounds by separate letters.

Anthropology. The study of cultural and biological variations in human groups, past and contemporary.

Australopithecines. Members of the genus *Australopithecus*—extinct hominids who flourished in eastern and southern Africa about 2 to 3 million years ago—some species of which are assumed to have been ancestral to humans.

Code-switching. Changing from one language or language variety to another in the course of a spoken interaction.

Cognate. A linguistic form related to another by virtue of descent from an ancestral language; for example, the words *father* in English, *père* in French, and *padre* in Spanish are cognates.

Communication. The transmission of information between individual organisms by means of signs.

Communicative competence. The knowledge of what is and what is not appropriate to say in a specific sociocultural context.

Consonant. Phonetically, a speech sound during the articulation of which the vocal tract is either completely blocked or constricted enough to produce audible friction.

Creole. A pidgin language that has become the first language of a speech community.

Culture. The complex of human learned behavior, knowledge, and beliefs transmitted from one generation to the next. **A culture is** the pattern of learned behavior, knowledge, and beliefs transmitted from generation to generation by members of a particular society.

Diachronic. Dealing with linguistic phenomena as they occur over a period of time, that is, considering their historical development.

293

Dialect. A regional or social variety of language (for example, one of the several varieties of Southern American English or of the socially differentiated varieties of English spoken in New York City).

Diglossia. The use of two distinct varieties of a language for two different sets of functions.

Discourse. The principal analytical unit of communicative behavior, widely varying in length, form, and content.

Emic. Characteristic of an analytical approach that emphasizes units held to be significant and contrastive by members of a society.

Ethnography of communication. The study of the nature and function of communicative behavior among the members of a society with emphasis on linguistic interaction.

Ethnoscience. The study of cultural domains on the basis of how they are lexically encoded by native speakers of a particular society.

Etic. Characteristic of an analytical approach based on data that are verifiable objectively and applicable cross-culturally.

Generative grammar. An analysis that uses formal rules to generate the infinite set of grammatical sentences in a language.

Historical linguistics. A branch of linguistics concerned with the development of language or languages over time.

Holistic. Concerned with a system as an integrated whole rather than with only some of its parts.

Hominids. Members of the family of primates (Hominidae) that includes all extinct and living species of humans and their direct fossil ancestors.

Hominoids. The subdivision of primates that includes all extinct and contemporary humans and apes (but not monkeys and prosimians).

Homo erectus. The extinct species of humans immediately ancestral to modern humans.

Homo habilis. The earliest human species assumed to be directly ancestral to modern humans.

Homo sapiens. The species of humans that includes all contemporary and recent humans (*Homo sapiens sapiens*) as well as members of such extinct subspecies as the Neanderthals (*Homo sapiens neanderthalensis*).

Iconic. Pertaining to a sign that bears a physical resemblance to what it represents.

Idiolect. The speech variety of a single individual; one's personal dialect.

Informant. A person serving as a source of data for the analysis of a language (or culture), usually a native speaker; in recent years the term *consultant* has been frequently used instead.

Language. The complex of potentialities for vocal communication with which all humans are genetically endowed. **A language** is any one of the several thousand systems of vocal communication used by members of different human societies.

Language family. All those languages that are related by virtue of having descended from a single ancestral language.

Language isolate. A language unrelated to any other language.

Lingua franca. A language used as a common means of communication between people who speak different native languages.

Linguistic anthropology. The study of language in both its biological and sociocultural contexts.

Linguistic determinism. The assumption that the way individuals think is determined to a significant degree by the language they speak.

Linguistic relativity. The view that structural differences among languages are reflected in the worldviews held by their speakers.

Linguistics. The scientific study of the various aspects of human speech, including its nature, structure, and changes over time.

Loanword. A word borrowed from another language and at least partly naturalized by the borrowing language.

Morpheme. The smallest meaningful unit of speech (for example, the word *unspeakable* consists of three morphemes: [in conventional spelling] *un-, speak,* and *-able*).

Morphology. The study of the internal structure of words and of the interrelationships of morphemes.

Morphophonemics. The study of the phonemic differences between the various forms of a morpheme.

Nonverbal communication. Transmission of messages by means other than speech or writing.

Paralanguage. Features of vocal communication that are considered marginal or optional, such as tempo or intensity.

Participant observation. The immersion of anthropological field-workers in the day-to-day activities of the people they are studying, usually for an extended period of time.

Phone. The smallest perceptible discrete segment of speech, considered as a physical event.

Phoneme. The smallest distinctive sound unit of a language (for example, the initial consonants of the words *bat, pat, fat,* and *vat* are four different phonemes of English).

Phonetic. Having to do with the description, transcription, and classification of speech sounds.

Phonology. The study of the sound system of a language.

Pidgin. A spoken language with greatly reduced grammatical structure and limited vocabulary that is used by speakers of mutually unintelligible languages to communicate with each other; a pidgin is not the native language of any speaker.

Prelanguage. A stage in the development of speech preceding full-fledged language; an assumed means of communication in early human prehistory.

Proto-Indo-European. The assumed ancestral language of all languages belonging to the Indo-European language family.

Protolanguage. The assumed or reconstructed ancestral language of a language family.

Sign language. A system of hand gestures used as an alternative to speech.

Sociolinguistic change. Linguistic change viewed in the context of the society or community in which it occurs.

Sociolinguistics. The branch of linguistics concerned with the various aspects of the relationship between society and language; the study of ways in which an individual's speech conveys social information.

Speech community. All those who share one speech variety as well as specific rules for speaking and interpreting speech.

Standard. The prestige variety of a language used by a speech community.

Synchronic. Dealing with linguistic phenomena as they exist at a specific point of time, without regard for historical antecedents.

Syntax. Traditionally, the manner in which words of a language are strung together into sentences; in transformational grammar, the study of sentence structure and the relations among sentence components.

Transformational grammar. A grammatical analysis using linguistic operations (transformations) that show a correspondence between two structures.

Vernacular. The casual spoken form of the language or dialect of a speech community.

Voiced. Characteristic of sounds produced while the vocal cords are vibrating.

Voiceless. Characteristic of sounds produced without vibration of the vocal cords.

Vowel. Phonetically, a speech sound articulated with no significant constriction in the breath channel.

Whorf hypothesis. The assumption that structural differences among languages are reflected in the differences in the worldviews of their speakers; the principle of linguistic relativity.

Bibliography

Aarne, Antti
1910   Verzeichnis der Märchentypen. FF Communications, no. 3. Helsinki.
Abrahams, Roger D.
1983   The man-of-words in the West Indies: performance and the emergence
            of creole culture. Baltimore: Johns Hopkins University Press.
Agha, Asif
1994   Honorification. *In* Annual Review of Anthropology, vol. 23. William H.
            Durham and others, eds. Pp. 277–302. Palo Alto, CA: Annual Reviews.
Akmajian, Adrian, Richard A. Demers, Ann K. Farmer, and Robert M. Harnish
1995   Linguistics, an introduction to language and communication. 4th ed.
            Cambridge: MIT Press.
Albert, Rosita Daskal
1986   Communication and attributional differences between Hispanics and
            Anglo-Americans. *In* Interethnic communication: current research, vol.
            10. Young Yun Kim, ed. Pp. 42–59. Newbury Park, CA: Sage.
American Anthropological Association
1983   Professional ethics: statements and procedures of the American Anthro-
            pological Association. Washington: American Anthropological Associa-
            tion.
American Heritage Dictionary of the English Language. 3rd ed.
1992   Boston: Houghton Mifflin.
Anttila, Raimo
1989   Historical and comparative linguistics. 2nd rev. ed. Philadelphia: Ben-
            jamins.
Başgöz, İlhan
1975   The tale-singer and his audience. *In* Folklore: performance and commu-
            nication. Dan Ben-Amos and Kenneth S. Goldstein, eds. Pp. 143–203.
            The Hague: Mouton.
Basso, Keith H.
1970   "To give up on words": silence in Western Apache culture. Southwest-
            ern Journal of Anthropology 26:213–230.
1974   The ethnography of writing. *In* Explorations in the ethnography of
            speaking. Richard Bauman and Joel Sherzer, eds. Pp. 425–432. London:
            Cambridge University Press.
1990   Western Apache language and culture: essays in linguistic anthropol-
            ogy. Tucson: University of Arizona Press.
Bauman, James J.
1980   A guide to issues in Indian language retention. Washington: Center for
            Applied Linguistics.

Bauman, Richard
  1984   Verbal art as performance. Prospect Heights, IL: Waveland.
  1986   Story, performance, and event: contextual studies of oral narrative.
              Cambridge, UK: Cambridge University Press.
  1992   (ed.) Folklore, cultural performances, and popular entertainments: a com-
              munications-centered handbook. New York: Oxford University Press.
Bauman, Richard, and Charles L. Briggs
  1990   Poetics and performance as critical perspectives on language and social
              life. *In* Annual Review of Anthropology, vol. 19. Bernard J. Siegel and
              others, eds. Pp. 59–88. Palo Alto, CA: Annual Reviews.
Bauman, Richard, and Joel Sherzer
  1974   (eds.) Explorations in the ethnography of speaking. London: Cambridge
              University Press.
  1975   The ethnography of speaking. *In* Annual Review of Anthropology, vol.
              4. Bernard J. Siegel and others, eds. Pp. 95–119. Palo Alto, CA: Annual
              Reviews.
  1989   (eds.) Explorations in the ethnography of speaking. 2nd ed. Cambridge,
              UK: Cambridge University Press.
Ben-Amos, Dan, and Kenneth S. Goldstein, eds.
  1975   Folklore: performance and communication. The Hague: Mouton.
Berko Gleason, Jean, ed.
  1989   The development of language. 2nd ed. Columbus, OH: Merrill.
Berlin, Brent
  1976   The concept of rank in ethnobiological classification: some evidence
              from Aguaruna folk botany. American Ethnologist 3:381–399.
Berlin, Brent, and Paul Kay
  1969   Basic color terms: their universality and evolution. Berkeley: University
              of California Press.
Bernstein, Basil
  1972   A sociolinguistic approach to socialization, with some reference to edu-
              cability. *In* Directions in sociolinguistics: the ethnography of communi-
              cation. John J. Gumperz and Dell Hymes, eds. Pp. 465–497. New York:
              Holt, Rinehart and Winston (1972) and Blackwell (1986).
Bickerton, Derek
  1976   Pidgin and creole studies. *In* Annual Review of Anthropology, vol. 5.
              Bernard J. Siegel and others, eds. Pp. 169–193. Palo Alto, CA: Annual Re-
              views.
  1981   Roots of language. Ann Arbor, MI: Karoma.
  1983   Creole languages. Scientific American 249:1:116–122 (July).
  1990   Language and species. Chicago: University of Chicago Press.
Birdwhistell, Ray L.
  1970   Kinesics and context: essays on body motion communication. Philadel-
              phia: University of Pennsylvania Press.
Blocker, Dianne
  1976   And how shall I address you? A study of address systems at Indiana
              University. Working Papers in Sociolinguistics, no. 33. Austin, TX:
              Southwest Educational Development Laboratory.

Bloomfield, Leonard
    1933   Language. New York: Holt.
    1946   Algonquian. *In* Linguistic structures of Native America. Cornelius Os-
              good, ed. Viking Fund Publications in Anthropology, no. 6, pp. 85–129.
              New York: Viking Fund.

Boas, Franz
    1891   Dissemination of tales among the natives of North America. Journal of
              American Folk-Lore 4:13–20.
    1911   (ed.) Handbook of American Indian languages, part 1. Bureau of Ameri-
              can Ethnology, bulletin 40. Washington: Government Printing Office.
    1922   (ed.) Handbook of American Indian languages, part 2. Bureau of Ameri-
              can Ethnology, bulletin 40. Washington: Government Printing Office.
    1933–1938 (ed.) Handbook of American Indian languages, part 3. New York: Au-
              gustin.
    1940   Metaphorical expression in the language of the Kwakiutl Indians. *In*
              Race, language and culture *by* Franz Boas. Pp. 232–239. New York:
              Macmillan.

Bolinger, Dwight
    1968   Aspects of language. New York: Harcourt, Brace and World.

Bright, Michael
    1984   Animal language. Ithaca, NY: Cornell University Press.

Bright, William
    1960   Animals of acculturation in the California Indian languages. University
              of California Publications in Linguistics, vol. 4, no. 4, pp. 215–246.
              Berkeley: University of California Press.
    1992   (ed.) International encyclopedia of linguistics. 4 vols. New York: Oxford
              University Press.

Brown, Penelope, and Stephen C. Levinson
    1987   Politeness: some universals in language usage. Cambridge, UK: Cam-
              bridge University Press.

Brown, Roger, and Marguerite Ford
    1961   Address in American English. Journal of Abnormal and Social Psychol-
              ogy 62:375–385.

Burling, Robbins
    1973   English in black and white. New York: Holt, Rinehart and Winston.
    1992   Review of Derek Bickerton: Language and species. Journal of Linguistic
              Anthropology 2:81–91.

Cameron, Deborah, ed.
    1990   The feminist critique of language: a reader. New York: Routledge.

Cameron, Deborah, Fiona McAlinden, and Kathy O'Leary
    1988   Lakoff in context: the social and linguistic functions of tag questions. *In*
              Women in their speech communities: new perspectives on language and
              sex. Jennifer Coates and Deborah Cameron, eds. Pp. 74–93. New York:
              Longman.

Campbell, Bernard G., ed.
    1979   Humankind emerging. 2nd ed. Boston: Little, Brown.

Campbell, Lyle
  1988   Review of Joseph H. Greenberg: Language in the Americas. Language
              64:591–615.
Carbaugh, Donal, ed.
  1990   Cultural communication and intercultural contact. Hillsdale, NJ: Erl-
              baum.
Carrington, John F.
  1971   The talking drums of Africa. Scientific American 225:6:90–94 (December).
Carroll, John B.
  1963   Linguistic relativity, contrastive linguistics, and language learning. In-
              ternational Review of Applied Linguistics in Language Teaching 1:1–20.
Carroll, John B., and Joseph B. Casagrande
  1958   The function of language classifications in behavior. *In* Readings in so-
              cial psychology. 3rd ed. Eleanor E. Maccoby, Theodore M. Newcomb,
              and Eugene L. Hartley, eds. Pp. 18–31. New York: Holt, Rinehart and
              Winston.
Cassidy, Frederic G., ed.
  1985   Dictionary of American regional English, vol. 1: Introduction and AC.
              Cambridge, MA: Belknap.
Chafe, Wallace, and Deborah Tannen
  1987   The relation between written and spoken language. *In* Annual Review
              of Anthropology, vol. 16. Bernard J. Siegel and others, eds. Pp. 383–407.
              Palo Alto, CA: Annual Reviews.
Chomsky, Noam
  1957   Syntactic structures. The Hague: Mouton.
  1959   Review of B. F. Skinner: Verbal behavior. Language 35:26–58.
  1965   Aspects of the theory of syntax. Cambridge, MA: MIT Press.
  1968   Language and the mind. Psychology Today 1:9:48, 50–51, 66–68.
  1972   Language and mind. Enl. ed. New York: Harcourt Brace Jovanovich.
  1986   Knowledge of language: its nature, origin, and use. New York: Praeger.
Chomsky, Noam, and Morris Halle
  1968   The sound pattern of English. New York: Harper and Row.
Classe, André
  1957   The whistled language of La Gomera. Scientific American 196:4:
              111–112, 114–118, 120 (April).
Coates, Jennifer
  1986   Women, men and language: a sociolinguistic account of sex differences
              in language. New York: Longman.
Coates, Jennifer, and Deborah Cameron, eds.
  1988   Women in their speech communities: new perspectives on language and
              sex. New York: Longman.
Condillac, Étienne Bonnot de
  1947   Oeuvres philosophiques de Condillac. Georges Le Roy, ed. Paris:
              Presses Universitaires de France.
Conklin, Harold C.
  1959   Linguistic play in its cultural context. Language 35:631–636.
Cowan, George M.
  1948   Mazateco whistle speech. Language 24:280–286.

Crystal, David
    1974   Paralinguistics. *In* Current trends in linguistics, vol. 12: Linguistics and adjacent arts and sciences. Thomas A. Sebeok, ed. Pp. 265–295. The Hague: Mouton.
    1981   Directions in applied linguistics. New York: Academic Press.
    1991a   The Cambridge encyclopedia of language. Cambridge, UK: Cambridge University Press.
    1991b   A dictionary of linguistics and phonetics. 3rd ed. Oxford: Blackwell.

Darnell, Regna
    1992   Anthropological linguistics: early history in North America. *In* International encyclopedia of linguistics, vol. 1. William Bright, ed. Pp. 69–71. New York: Oxford University Press.

Deetz, James
    1967   Invitation to archaeology. Garden City, NY: Natural History Press.

de Grolier, Eric, ed.
    1983   Glossogenetics: the origin and evolution of language. Chur, Switzerland: Harwood Academic.

de Laguna, Frederica, ed.
    1960   Selected papers from the American Anthropologist, 1888–1920. Evanston, IL: Row, Peterson.

Dillard, J. L.
    1972   Black English: its history and usage in the United States. New York: Random House.

Diringer, David
    1968   The alphabet: a key to the history of mankind. 3rd rev. ed. 2 vols. New York: Funk and Wagnalls.

Dorian, Nancy C.
    1993   A response to Ladefoged's other view of endangered languages. Language 69:575–579.

Dorsey, George A., and Alfred L. Kroeber, comps.
    1903   Traditions of the Arapaho. Field Columbian Museum Publications, vol. 81, Anthropological Series, vol. 5. Chicago: Field Columbian Museum.

Dundes, Alan
    1962   From etic to emic units in the structural study of folktales. Journal of American Folklore 75:95–105.
    1963   Structural typology in North American Indian folktales. Southwestern Journal of Anthropology 19:121–129.
    1964   The morphology of North American Indian folktales. FF Communications, no. 195. Helsinki.
    1965   (ed.) The study of folklore. Englewood Cliffs, NJ: Prentice-Hall.
    1984   (ed.) Sacred narrative: readings in the theory of myth. Berkeley: University of California Press.

Duranti, Allesandro
    1988   Ethnography of speaking: toward a linguistics of the praxis. *In* Linguistics: the Cambridge survey, vol. 4: Language: the socio-cultural context. Frederick J. Newmeyer, ed. Pp. 210–228. Cambridge, UK: Cambridge University Press.

Eastman, Carol M.
  1983   Language planning: an introduction. San Francisco: Chandler and Sharp.
Echeverría, Max S., and Heles Contreras
  1965   Araucanian phonemics. International Journal of American Linguistics
                31:132–135.
Eckert, Penelope, and Sally McConnell-Ginet
  1992   Think practically and look locally: language and gender as community-
                based practice. *In* Annual Review of Anthropology, vol. 21. Bernard J.
                Siegel and others, eds. Pp. 461–490. Palo Alto, CA: Annual Reviews.
Ehret, Christopher
  1982   Linguistic inferences about early Bantu history. *In* The archaeological and
                linguistic reconstruction of African history. Christopher Ehret and Merrick
                Posnansky, eds. Pp. 57–65. Berkeley: University of California Press.
Errington, J. Joseph
  1988   Structure and style in Javanese: a semiotic view of linguistic etiquette.
                Philadelphia: University of Pennsylvania Press.
Ervin-Tripp, Susan M.
  1969   Sociolinguistics. *In* Advances in experimental social psychology, vol. 4.
                Leonard Berkowitz, ed. Pp. 91–165. New York: Academic Press.
Falk, Dean
  1984   The petrified brain. Natural History 93:9:36, 38–39.
Fasold, Ralph W.
  1984   Introduction to sociolinguistics, vol. 1: The sociolinguistics of society.
                New York: Blackwell.
  1990   Introduction to sociolinguistics, vol. 2: The sociolinguistics of language.
                Cambridge, MA: Blackwell.
Ferguson, Charles A.
  1959   Diglossia. Word 15:325–340.
Fickett, Joan G.
  1972   Tense and aspect in Black English. Journal of English Linguistics
                6:17–19.
Fields, Cheryl D.
  1997   Ebonics 101: What have we learned? Black Issues in Higher Education
                13:24:18–21, 24–28 (January 23, 1997).
Fischer, John L.
  1958   Social influences on the choice of a linguistic variant. Word 14:47–56.
Fishman, Joshua A.
  1960   A systematization of the Whorfian hypothesis. Behavioral Science
                5:323–339.
Fouts, Roger S., and Deborah H. Fouts
  1989   Loulis in conversation with the cross-fostered chimpanzees. *In* Teaching
                sign language to chimpanzees. R. Allen Gardner, Beatrix T. Gardner, and
                Thomas E. Van Cantford, eds. Pp. 293–307. New York: State University
                of New York Press.
Fouts, Roger S., Deborah H. Fouts, and Thomas E. Van Cantford
  1989   The infant Loulis learns signs from cross-fostered chimpanzees. *In*
                Teaching sign language to chimpanzees. R. Allen Gardner, Beatrix T.

Gardner, and Thomas E. Van Cantford, eds. Pp. 280–292. New York: State University of New York Press.

Frake, Charles O.
1961   The diagnosis of disease among the Subanun of Mindanao. American Anthropologist 63:113–132.
1964   How to ask for a drink in Subanun. American Anthropologist 66:6(part 2):127–132.
1969   Struck by speech: the Yakan concept of litigation. *In* Law in culture and society. Laura Nader, ed. Pp. 147–167. Chicago: Aldine.

Frank, Francine, and Frank Anshen
1983   Language and the sexes. Albany: State University of New York Press.

Frisch, Karl von
1967   The dance language and orientation of bees. C. E. Chadwick, trans. Cambridge, MA: Belknap.

Geertz, Clifford
1960   The religion of Java. Glencoe, IL: Free Press.

Georges, Robert A.
1969   Toward an understanding of storytelling events. Journal of American Folklore 82:313–328.

Giglioli, Pier Paolo, ed.
1972   Language and social context: selected readings. Baltimore: Penguin Books.

Gleason, H. A., Jr.
1961   An introduction to descriptive linguistics. Rev. ed. New York: Holt, Rinehart and Winston.

Goodall, Jane
1986   The chimpanzees of Gombe: patterns of behavior. Cambridge, MA: Belknap.

Goodenough, Ward H.
1957   Cultural anthropology and linguistics. *In* Report of the Seventh Annual Round Table Meeting on Linguistics and Language Study. Monograph Series on Languages and Linguistics, no. 9, pp. 167–173. Washington: Georgetown University Press.
1964   Cultural anthropology and linguistics. *In* Language in culture and society: a reader in linguistics and anthropology. Dell Hymes, ed. Pp. 36–39. New York: Harper and Row.

Goody, Jack
1987   The interface between the written and the oral. Cambridge, UK: Cambridge University Press.

Greenberg, Joseph H.
1960   The general classification of Central and South American languages. *In* Men and cultures: selected papers of the Fifth International Congress of Anthropological and Ethnological Sciences. Anthony F. C. Wallace, ed. Pp. 791–794. Philadelphia: University of Pennsylvania Press.
1987   Language in the Americas. Stanford, CA: Stanford University Press.

Gumperz, John J.
1964   Linguistic and social interaction in two communities. American Anthropologist 66:6(part 2):137–153.

1982   Fact and inference in courtroom testimony. *In* Language and social iden-
            tity. John J. Gumperz, ed. Pp. 163–195. Cambridge, UK: Cambridge Uni-
            versity Press.

Gumperz, John J., and Dell Hymes, eds.
1964   The ethnography of communication. American Anthropologist 66:6
            (part 2):1–186 (special publication).
1972   Directions in sociolinguistics: the ethnography of communication. New
            York: Holt, Rinehart and Winston (1972) and Blackwell (rev. ed., 1986).

Gumperz, John J., and Stephen C. Levinson, eds.
1996   Rethinking linguistic relativity. Cambridge, UK: Cambridge University
            Press.

Gumperz, John J., and Robert Wilson
1971   Convergence and creolization: a case from the Indo-Aryan/Dravidian
            border in India. *In* Pidginization and creolization of languages. Dell
            Hymes, ed. Pp. 151–167. Cambridge, UK: Cambridge University Press.

Haas, Mary R.
[1941]   Tunica. *In* Handbook of American Indian languages, part 4, pp. 1–143.
            New York: Augustin.
1944   Men's and women's speech in Koasati. Language 20:142–149.

Hage, Per
1972   Münchner beer categories. *In* Culture and cognition: rules, maps, and
            plans. James P. Spradley, ed. Pp. 263–278. San Francisco: Chandler.

Hager, John W.
1959   Let's simplify legal language. Rocky Mountain Law Review 32:74–86.

Hale, Kenneth
1974   Some questions about anthropological linguistics: the role of native
            knowledge. *In* Reinventing anthropology. Dell Hymes, ed. Pp. 382–397.
            New York: Random House.

Hale, Ken, and others
1992   Endangered languages. Language 68:1–42.

Hall, Edward T.
1959   The silent language. Garden City, NY: Doubleday.
1966   The hidden dimension. Garden City, NY: Doubleday.
1968   Proxemics. Current Anthropology 9:83–108.

Hall, Robert A., Jr.
1959   Pidgin languages. Scientific American 200:2:124–132, 134 (February).

Hallowell, A. Irving
1960   The beginnings of anthropology in America. *In* Selected papers from the
            American Anthropologist, 1888–1920. Frederica de Laguna, ed. Pp. 1–90.
            Evanston, IL: Row, Peterson.

Hammel, E. A., ed.
1965   Formal semantic analysis. American Anthropologist 67:5(part 2) (special
            publication).

Hammond, George P., and Agapito Rey, eds.
1940   Narratives of the Coronado expedition, 1540–1542. Coronado Cuarto
            Centennial Publications, 1540–1940, vol. 2. Albuquerque: University of
            New Mexico Press.

Harnad, Stevan R., Horst D. Steklis, and Jane Lancaster, eds.
1976   Origins and evolution of language and speech. Annals of the New York
        Academy of Sciences, vol. 280. New York: New York Academy of Sci-
        ences.

Harris, Marvin
1979   Cultural materialism: the struggle for a science of culture. New York:
        Random House.
1989   Our kind: who we are, where we came from, where we are going. New
        York: Harper and Row.
1990   Emics and etics revisited. *In* Emics and etics: the insider/outsider de-
        bate. Thomas N. Headland, Kenneth L. Pike, and Marvin Harris, eds.
        Pp. 48–61. Newbury Park, CA: Sage.

Hayes, Alfred S.
1954   Field procedures while working with Diegueño. International Journal of
        American Linguistics 20:185–194.

Headland, Thomas N., Kenneth L. Pike, and Marvin Harris, eds.
1990   Emics and etics: the insider/outsider debate. Newbury Park, CA: Sage.

Heath, Jeffrey
1985   Discourse in the field: clause structure in Ngandi. *In* Grammar inside
        and outside the clause: some approaches to theory from the field. Jo-
        hanna Nichols and Anthony C. Woodbury, eds. Pp. 89–110. Cambridge,
        UK: Cambridge University Press.

Heath, Shirley Brice
1984   Linguistics and education. *In* Annual Review of Anthropology, vol. 13.
        Bernard J. Siegel and others, eds. Pp. 251–274. Palo Alto, CA: Annual Re-
        views.

Herder, Johann Gottfried von
1772   Abhandlung über den Ursprung der Sprache. Berlin: C. F. Voss.
1966   On the origin of language. John H. Moran, ed. and trans. New York: Ungar.

Herzog, George
1945   Drum-signaling in a West African tribe. Word 1:217–238.

Hewes, Gordon W.
1973   Primate communication and the gestural origin of language. Current An-
        thropology 14:5–24 [with comments by others and Hewes's reply].
1975   (comp.) Language origins: a bibliography. 2nd rev. and enl. ed. The
        Hague: Mouton.

Hickerson, Harold, Glen D. Turner, and Nancy P. Hickerson
1952   Testing procedures for estimating transfer of information among Iro-
        quois dialects and languages. International Journal of American Lin-
        guistics 18:1–8.

Hilger, Sister M. Inez
1957   Araucanian child life and its cultural background. Smithsonian Miscella-
        neous Collections, vol. 133. Washington: Smithsonian Institution.

Hill, Jane H.
1978   Apes and language. *In* Annual Review of Anthropology, vol. 7. Bernard
        J. Siegel and others, eds. Pp. 89–112. Palo Alto, CA: Annual Reviews.

Hill, Jane, and Bruce Mannheim
1992   Language and world view. *In* Annual Review of Anthropology, vol. 21.
            Bernard J. Siegel and others, eds. Pp. 381–406. Palo Alto, CA: Annual Re-
            views.
Hill, W. W.
1936   Navaho warfare. Yale University Publications in Anthropology, vol. 5.
            New Haven, CT: Yale University Press.
Hinnebusch, Thomas J.
1979   Swahili. *In* Languages and their status. Timothy Shopen, ed. Pp.
            209–293. Cambridge, MA: Winthrop.
Hockett, Charles F.
1958   A course in modern linguistics. New York: Macmillan.
1960   The origin of speech. Scientific American 203:3:88–96 (September).
1973   Man's place in nature. New York: McGraw-Hill.
1977   The view from language: selected essays, 1948–1974. Athens: University
            of Georgia Press.
1978   In search of Jove's brow. American Speech 53:243–313.
Hockett, Charles F., and Stuart A. Altmann
1968   A note on design features. *In* Animal communication: techniques of
            study and results of research. Thomas A. Sebeok, ed. Pp. 61–72. Bloom-
            ington: Indiana University Press.
Hockett, Charles F., and Robert Ascher
1964   The human revolution. Current Anthropology 5:135–168 [with com-
            ments by others and the authors' reply].
Hogan, Helen Marie
n.d.   An ethnography of communication among the Ashanti. Penn-Texas
            Working Papers in Sociolinguistics, no. 1. [Austin.]
Hoijer, Harry
1954   (ed.) Language in culture: proceedings of a conference on the interrela-
            tions of language and other aspects of culture. American Anthropologi-
            cal Association Memoir, no. 79. Menasha, WI: American Anthropologi-
            cal Association.
1956   Lexicostatistics: a critique. Language 32:49–60.
Holm, John A.
1988   Pidgins and creoles, vol. 1: Theory and structure. Cambridge, UK: Cam-
            bridge University Press.
Householder, Fred W., Jr.
1952   Review of Zellig S. Harris: Methods in structural linguistics. Interna-
            tional Journal of American Linguistics 18:260–268.
Hudson, Richard A.
1980   Sociolinguistics. Cambridge, UK: Cambridge University Press.
1984   Invitation to linguistics. Oxford: Blackwell.
Humboldt, Wilhelm von
1907   Wilhelm von Humboldts Werke, vol. 7. Albert Leitzmann, ed. Berlin:
            Behrs Verlag.

Hymes, Dell H.

1958   Linguistic features peculiar to Chinookan myths. International Journal of American Linguistics 24:253–257.

1961   Functions of speech: an evolutionary approach. *In* Anthropology and education. Frederick C. Gruber, ed. Pp. 55–83. Philadelphia: University of Pennsylvania Press.

1962   The ethnography of speaking. *In* Anthropology and human behavior. Thomas Gladwin and William C. Sturtevant, eds. Pp. 13–53. Washington: Anthropological Society of Washington.

1963   Notes toward a history of linguistic anthropology. Anthropological Linguistics 5:1:59–103.

1964   (ed.) Language in culture and society: a reader in linguistics and anthropology. New York: Harper and Row.

1966   Two types of linguistic relativity (with examples from Amerindian ethnography). *In* Sociolinguistics. William Bright, ed. Pp. 114–167. The Hague: Mouton.

1968   Linguistic problems in defining the concept of "tribe." *In* Essays on the problem of tribe. Proceedings of the 1967 Annual Spring Meeting of the American Ethnological Society. June Helm, ed. Pp. 23–48. Seattle: University of Washington Press.

1971   (ed.) Pidginization and creolization of languages. Cambridge, UK: Cambridge University Press.

1972   Models of the interaction of language and social life. *In* Directions in sociolinguistics: the ethnography of communication. John J. Gumperz and Dell Hymes, eds. Pp. 35–71. New York: Holt, Rinehart and Winston.

1974   Foundations in sociolinguistics: an ethnographic approach. Philadelphia: University of Pennsylvania Press.

1981   "In vain I tried to tell you." Essays in Native American ethnopoetics. Philadelphia: University of Pennsylvania Press.

1983   Essays in the history of linguistic anthropology. Amsterdam Studies in the Theory and History of Linguistic Science, vol. 25. Amsterdam and Philadelphia: Benjamins.

Inoue, Kyoko

1979   Japanese: a story of language and people. *In* Languages and their speakers. Timothy Shopen, ed. Pp. 241–300. Cambridge, MA: Winthrop.

Irvine, Judith T.

1974   Strategies of status manipulation in the Wolof greeting. *In* Explorations in the ethnography of speaking. Richard Bauman and Joel Sherzer, eds. Pp. 167–191. London: Cambridge University Press.

Jakobson, Roman

1968   Child language, aphasia and phonological universals. Allan R. Keiler, trans. The Hague: Mouton.

Jeffers, Robert J., and Ilse Lehiste

1979   Principles and methods for historical linguistics. Cambridge, MA: MIT Press.

Jefferson, Thomas
    1944   The life and selected writings of Thomas Jefferson. Adrienne Koch and
                William Peden, eds. New York: Random House.
Joos, Martin
    1962   The five clocks. Indiana University Research Center in Anthropology,
                Folklore, and Linguistics Publications, no. 22. Bloomington.
Jourdan, C.
    1991   Pidgins and creoles: the blurring of categories. *In* Annual Review of An-
                thropology, vol. 20. Bernard J. Siegel and others, eds. Pp. 187–209. Palo
                Alto, CA: Annual Reviews.
Kaiser, Mark, and V. Shevoroshkin
    1988   Nostratic. *In* Annual Review of Anthropology, vol. 17. Bernard J. Siegel
                and others, eds. Pp. 309–329. Palo Alto, CA: Annual Reviews.
Kendon, Adam
    1997   Gesture. *In* Annual Review of Anthropology, vol. 26. William H.
                Durham and others, eds. Pp. 109–128. Palo Alto, CA: Annual Reviews.
Kennedy, Chris, ed.
    1983   Language planning and language education. London: Allen and Unwin.
Key, Mary Ritchie
    1977   Nonverbal communication: a research guide and bibliography. Metuchen,
                NJ: Scarecrow Press.
Khubchandani, Lachman M.
    1983   Plural languages, plural cultures: communication, identity, and sociopo-
                litical change in contemporary India. Honolulu: University of Hawaii
                Press.
Kimball, Geoffrey
    1987   Men's and women's speech in Koasati: a reappraisal. International Jour-
                nal of American Linguistics 53:30–38.
Kiparsky, Paul
    1976   Historical linguistics and the origin of language. *In* Annals of the New
                York Academy of Sciences, vol. 280: Origins and evolution of language
                and speech. Stevan R. Harnad, Horst D. Steklis, and Jane Lancaster, eds.
                Pp. 97–103. New York: New York Academy of Sciences.
Kirshenblatt-Gimblett, Barbara, ed.
    1976   Speech play: research and resources for studying linguistic creativity.
                Philadelphia: University of Pennsylvania Press.
Klima, Edward S., and Ursula Bellugi
    1979   The signs of language. Cambridge, MA: Harvard University Press.
Kluckhohn, Clyde
    1949   Mirror for man: the relation of anthropology to modern life. New York:
                McGraw-Hill.
Kluckhohn, Clyde, and Dorothea Leighton
    1962   The Navaho. Rev. ed. Garden City, NY, and New York: American Mu-
                seum of Natural History and Doubleday.
Kramarae, Cheris
    1981   Women and men speaking: frameworks for analysis. Rowley, MA: New-
                bury House.

Kramer, Cheris
  1975   Sex-related differences in address systems. Anthropological Linguistics
            17:198–210.
Krauss, Michael
  1992   The world's languages in crisis. Language 68:4–10.
Labov, William
  1963   The social motivation of a sound change. Word 19:273–309.
  1966   The social stratification of English in New York City. Washington: Cen-
            ter for Applied Linguistics.
  1970   The logic of nonstandard English. *In* Report of the Twentieth Annual
            Round Table Meeting on Linguistics and Language Studies. Monograph
            Series on Languages and Linguistics, no. 22, pp. 1–43. Washington:
            Georgetown University Press.
  1972   Sociolinguistic patterns. Philadelphia: University of Pennsylvania Press.
  1981   Field methods of the project on linguistic change and variation. Working
            Papers in Sociolinguistics, no. 81. Austin, TX: Southwest Educational
            Development Laboratory.
  1982   Objectivity and commitment in linguistic science: the case of the Black
            English trial in Ann Arbor. Language in Society 11:165–201.
Ladefoged, Peter
  1982   A course in phonetics. 2nd ed. New York: Harcourt Brace Jovanovich.
  1992   Another view of endangered languages. Language 68:809–811.
Laitman, Jeffrey T.
  1984   The anatomy of human speech. Natural History 93:8:20, 22–24, 26–27.
Lakoff, Robin
  1975   Language and woman's place. New York: Harper and Row.
Langacker, Ronald W.
  1972   Fundamentals of linguistic analysis. New York: Harcourt Brace Jo-
            vanovich.
  1973   Language and its structure: some fundamental linguistic concepts. 2nd
            ed. New York: Harcourt Brace Jovanovich.
Lass, Roger
  1984   Phonology: an introduction to basic concepts. Cambridge, UK: Cam-
            bridge University Press.
Law, Howard W.
  1958   Morphological structure of Isthmus Nahuat. International Journal of
            American Linguistics 24:108–129.
Leach, E. R.
  1954   Political systems of highland Burma: a study of Kachin social structure.
            London: London School of Economics and Political Science.
Leap, William L.
  1981   American Indian language maintenance. *In* Annual Review of Anthro-
            pology, vol. 10. Bernard J. Siegel and others, eds. Pp. 209–236. Palo Alto,
            CA: Annual Reviews.
Lehmann, Winfred P.
  1983   Language: an introduction. New York: Random House.

Lenneberg, Eric H.
1953   Cognition in ethnolinguistics. Language 29:463–471.
1967   Biological foundations of language. New York: Wiley.
Lévi-Strauss, Claude
1955   The structural study of myth. Journal of American Folklore 68:428–444.
1963   Structural anthropology. Claire Jacobson and Brooke Grundfest Schoepf, trans. New York: Basic Books.
1976   Structural anthropology, vol. 2. Monique Layton, trans. New York: Basic Books.
1983a   Introduction to a science of mythology, vol. 1: The raw and the cooked. John Weightman and Doreen Weightman, trans. Chicago: University of Chicago Press.
1983b   Introduction to a science of mythology, vol. 2: From honey to ashes. John Weightman and Doreen Weightman, trans. Chicago: University of Chicago Press.
1990a   Introduction to a science of mythology, vol. 3: The origin of table manners. John Weightman and Doreen Weightman, trans. Chicago: University of Chicago Press.
1990b   Introduction to a science of mythology, vol. 4: The naked man. John Weightman and Doreen Weightman, trans. Chicago: University of Chicago Press.
Lieberman, Philip
1984   The biology and evolution of language. Cambridge: Harvard University Press.
Loftus, Elizabeth F., and John C. Palmer
1974   Reconstruction of automobile destruction: an example of the interaction between language and memory. Journal of Verbal Learning and Verbal Behavior 13:585–589.
Lucy, John A.
1992   Grammatical categories and cognition: a case study of the linguistic relativity hypothesis. Cambridge, UK: Cambridge University Press.
1997   Linguistic relativity. In Annual Review of Anthropology, vol. 26. William H. Durham and others, eds. Pp. 291–312. Palo Alto, CA: Annual Reviews.
Lyons, John
1978   Noam Chomsky. Rev. ed. New York: Penguin Books.
1995   Linguistic semantics: an introduction. Cambridge, UK: Cambridge University Press.
Maddieson, Ian
1984   Patterns of sounds. Cambridge, UK: Cambridge University Press.
Malinowski, Bronislaw
1915   The natives of Mailu: preliminary results of the Robert Mond research work in British New Guinea. Transactions and Proceedings of the Royal Society of South Australia 39:494–706. Adelaide.
1922   Argonauts of the western Pacific: an account of native enterprise and adventure in the archipelagoes of Melanesian New Guinea. London: Routledge and Kegan Paul.
1926   Myth in primitive psychology. New York: Norton.

McConnell-Ginet, Sally
  1988   Language and gender. *In* Linguistics: the Cambridge survey, vol. 4: Language: the socio-cultural context. Frederick J. Newmeyer, ed. Pp. 75–99. Cambridge: Cambridge University Press.

Menyuk, Paula
  1988   Language development: knowledge and use. Glenview, IL: Scott, Foresman.

Merrifield, William R., and others
  1967   Laboratory manual for morphology and syntax. Rev. ed. Santa Ana, CA: Summer Institute of Linguistics.

Milroy, Lesley, and Sue Margrain
  1980   Vernacular language loyalty and social network. Language in Society 9:43–70.

Montagu, Ashley
  1976   Toolmaking, hunting, and the origin of language. *In* Annals of the New York Academy of Sciences, vol. 280: Origins and evolution of language and speech. Stevan R. Harnad, Horst D. Steklis, and Jane Lancaster, eds. Pp. 266–274. New York: New York Academy of Sciences.

Morgan, Marcyliena
  1994   Theories and politics in African American English. *In* Annual Review of Anthropology, vol. 23. William H. Durham and others, eds. Pp. 325–345. Palo Alto, CA: Annual Reviews.

Mühlhäusler, Peter
  1986   Pidgin and creole linguistics. Oxford: Blackwell.
  1987   The history of research into Tok Pisin, 1900–1975. *In* Pidgin and creole languages: essays in memory of John E. Reinecke. Glenn G. Gilbert, ed. Pp. 177–209. Honolulu: University of Hawaii Press.

Newman, Stanley
  1955   Vocabulary levels: Zuñi sacred and slang usage. Southwestern Journal of Anthropology 11:345–354.

Niyekawa-Howard, Agnes M.
  1968   A psycholinguistic study of the Whorfian hypothesis based on the Japanese passive. Paper presented at the Thirteenth Annual National Conference on Linguistics, New York.

O'Barr, William M.
  1981   The language of the law. *In* Language in the USA. Charles A. Ferguson and Shirley Brice Heath, eds. Pp. 386–406. Cambridge, UK: Cambridge University Press.

O'Barr, William M., and John M. Conley
  1996   When a juror watches a lawyer. *In* Talking about people: readings in contemporary cultural anthropology. 2nd ed. William A. Haviland and Robert J. Gordon, eds. Pp. 42–45. Mountain View, CA: Mayfield Publishing Company.

Ochs, Elinor, and Bambi B. Schieffelin
  1982   Language acquisition and socialization: three developmental stories and their implications. Working Papers in Sociolinguistics, no. 105. Austin, TX: Southwest Educational Development Laboratory.

Ọlajubu, Oludare
1978   Yoruba verbal artists and their work. Journal of American Folklore
          91:675–690.
Parker, Frank
1986   Linguistics for non-linguists. Boston: Little, Brown.
Peñalosa, Fernando
1981   Introduction to the sociology of language. Rowley, MA: Newbury
          House.
Philips, Susan U.
1980   Sex differences and language. In Annual Review of Anthropology, vol. 9.
          Bernard J. Siegel and others, eds. Pp. 523–544. Palo Alto, CA: Annual Re-
          views.
Philips, Susan U., Susan Steele, and Christine Tanz, eds.
1987   Language, gender, and sex in comparative perspective. Studies in the
          Social and Cultural Foundations of Language, no. 4. Cambridge: Cam-
          bridge University Press.
Philipsen, Gerry, and Donal Carbaugh
1986   A bibliography of fieldwork in the ethnography of communication. Lan-
          guage in Society 15:387–397.
Pike, Kenneth L.
1954   Language in relation to a unified theory of the structure of human be-
          havior. Glendale, CA: Summer Institute of Linguistics.
1967   Language in relation to a unified theory of the structure of human be-
          havior. 2nd rev. ed. The Hague: Mouton.
Pike, Kenneth L., and Eunice Victoria Pike
1947   Immediate constituents of Mazateco syllables. International Journal of
          American Linguistics 13:78–91.
Pinker, Steven
1992   Review of Derek Bickerton: Language and species. Language 68:375–382.
Pi-Sunyer, Oriol, and Zdenek Salzmann
1978   Humanity and culture: an introduction to anthropology. Boston:
          Houghton Mifflin.
Plato
1961   The collected dialogues of Plato including the letters. Edith Hamilton
          and Huntington Cairns, eds. Princeton, NJ: Princeton University Press.
Postal, Paul M.
1969   Mohawk vowel doubling. International Journal of American Linguistics
          35:291–298.
Powell, John Wesley
1883   Second annual report of the Bureau of Ethnology to the Secretary of the
          Smithsonian Institution, 1880–81. Washington: Government Printing
          Office.
Premack, Ann James, and David Premack
1972   Teaching language to an ape. Scientific American 227:4:92–99 (October).
President's Commission on Foreign Language and International Studies
1979   Strength through wisdom: a critique of U.S. capability. Washington: U.S.
          Department of Health, Education, and Welfare/Office of Education.

Pride, J. B., and Janet Holmes, eds.
1972   Sociolinguistics: selected readings. New York: Penguin Books.
Propp, Vladimir
1958   Morphology of the folktale. Laurence Scott, trans. Indiana University Research Center in Anthropology, Folklore, and Linguistics Publications, no. 10. Bloomington. [The original was published in 1928.]
Roitblat, Herbert L., Louis M. Herman, and Paul E. Nachtigall, eds.
1992   Language and communication: comparative perspectives. Hillsdale, NJ: Erlbaum.
Romaine, Suzanne
1988   Pidgin and creole languages. New York: Longman.
Romney, A. Kimball, and Roy Goodwin D'Andrade, eds.
1964   Transcultural studies in cognition. American Anthropologist 66:3(part 2) (special publication).
Rosaldo, Michelle
1973   I have nothing to hide: the language of Ilongot oratory. Language in Society 2:193–223.
Roth, Walter E.
1897   Ethnological studies among the north-west-central Queensland aborigines. Brisbane: Edmund Gregory.
Salus, Peter H., ed.
1969   On language: Plato to von Humboldt. New York: Holt, Rinehart and Winston.
Salzmann, Zdenek
1950   An Arapaho version of the Star Husband tale. Hoosier Folklore 9:50–58.
1956a   Arapaho II: texts. International Journal of American Linguistics 22:151–158.
1956b   Arapaho III: additional texts. International Journal of American Linguistics 22:266–272.
1959   Arapaho kinship terms and two related ethnolinguistic observations. Anthropological Linguistics 1:9:6–10.
1983   Dictionary of contemporary Arapaho usage. Arapaho Language and Culture Instructional Materials Series, no. 4. Wind River Reservation, WY: Arapaho Language and Culture Commission.
Salzmann, Zdenek, and Joy Salzmann
1952   Arapaho tales II. Midwest Folklore 2:21–42.
Samarin, William J.
1967   Field linguistics: a guide to linguistic field work. New York: Holt, Rinehart and Winston.
Samovar, Larry A., and Richard E. Porter, eds.
1991   Intercultural communication: a reader. 6th ed. Belmont, CA: Wadsworth.
Sapir, Edward
1916   Time perspective in aboriginal American culture: a study in method. Canada, Department of Mines, Geological Survey, memoir 90; Anthropological Series, no. 13. Ottawa: Government Printing Bureau.
1921   Language: an introduction to the study of speech. New York: Harcourt, Brace.

1922   The Takelma language of southwestern Oregon. *In* Handbook of American Indian languages, part 1. Franz Boas, ed. Pp. 1–296. Washington: Government Printing Office.

1929   The status of linguistics as a science. Language 5:207–214.

1949   Selected writings of Edward Sapir in language, culture, and personality. David G. Mandelbaum, ed. Berkeley: University of California Press.

Savage-Rumbaugh, E. Sue

1984   Pan paniscus and Pan troglodytes: contrasts in preverbal communicative competence. *In* The pygmy chimpanzee: evolutionary biology and behavior. Randall L. Susman, ed. Pp. 395–413. New York: Plenum Press.

1986   Ape language: from conditioned response to symbol. New York: Columbia University Press.

Saville-Troike, Muriel

1982   The ethnography of communication: an introduction. Baltimore: University Park Press.

1989   The ethnography of communication: an introduction. 2nd ed. Oxford: Blackwell.

Schieffelin, Bambi B.

1990   The give and take of everyday life: language socialization of Kaluli children. New York: Cambridge University Press.

Schieffelin, Bambi B., and Elinor Ochs

1986   Language socialization. *In* Annual Review of Anthropology, vol. 15. Bernard J. Siegel and others, eds. Pp. 163–191. Palo Alto, CA: Annual Reviews.

Schoolcraft, Henry R.

1851   Historical and statistical information respecting the history, condition and prospects of the Indian tribes of the United States, part 1. Philadelphia: Lippincott, Grambo.

Schrier, Allan M., and Fred Stollnitz, eds.

1971   Behavior of nonhuman primates: modern research trends, vol. 4. New York: Academic Press.

Sebeok, Thomas A., ed.

1974   Current trends in linguistics, vol. 12: Linguistics and adjacent arts and sciences. The Hague: Mouton.

1977   How animals communicate. Bloomington: Indiana University Press.

Sherzer, Joel

1976   Play languages: implications for (socio) linguistics. *In* Speech play: research and resources for studying linguistic creativity. Barbara Kirshenblatt-Gimblett, ed. Pp. 19–36. Philadelphia: University of Pennsylvania Press.

1977   The ethnography of speaking: a critical appraisal. *In* Georgetown University Round Table on Languages and Linguistics 1977. Pp. 43–57. Washington: Georgetown University Press.

1986   The report of a Kuna curing specialist: the poetics and rhetoric of an oral performance. *In* Native South American discourse. Joel Sherzer and Greg Urban, eds. Pp. 169–212. Berlin: Mouton de Gruyter.

1987   A discourse-centered approach to language and culture. American Anthropologist 89:295–309.

1990   Verbal art in San Blas: Kuna culture through its discourse. Cambridge, UK: Cambridge University Press.

Sherzer, Joel, and Regna Darnell
1972   Outline guide for the ethnographic study of speech use. *In* Directions in sociolinguistics: the ethnography of communication. John J. Gumperz and Dell Hymes, eds. Pp. 548–554. New York: Holt, Rinehart and Winston.

Sherzer, Joel, and Greg Urban, eds.
1986   Native South American discourse. Berlin: Mouton de Gruyter.

Sherzer, Joel, and Anthony C. Woodbury, eds.
1987   Native American discourse: poetics and rhetoric. Cambridge, UK: Cambridge University Press.

Shuy, Roger W.
1984   Linguistics in other professions. *In* Annual Review of Anthropology, vol. 13. Bernard J. Siegel and others, eds. Pp. 419–445. Palo Alto, CA: Annual Reviews.

Siebert, Frank T., Jr.
1967   The original home of the Proto-Algonquian people. National Museum of Canada, bulletin 214; Anthropological Series, no. 78: Contributions to Anthropology: Linguistics I (Algonquian). Pp. 13–47. Ottawa.

Silverstein, Michael
1985   Language and the culture of gender: at the intersection of structure, usage, and ideology. *In* Semiotic mediation: sociocultural and psychological perspectives. Elizabeth Mertz and Richard J. Parmentier, eds. Pp. 219–259. Orlando: Academic Press.

Smith, William
1744   A new voyage to Guinea. . . . London: John Nourse.

Sorensen, Arthur P., Jr.
1967   Multilingualism in the northwest Amazon. American Anthropologist 69:670–684.

Stokoe, William C., Jr.
1960   Sign language structure: an outline of the visual communication systems of the American deaf. Studies in Linguistics, Occasional Papers, no. 8. Buffalo, NY: University of Buffalo, Department of Anthropology and Linguistics.

Stross, Brian
1974   Speaking of speaking: Tenejapa Tzeltal metalinguistics. *In* Explorations in the ethnography of speaking. Richard Bauman and Joel Sherzer, eds. Pp. 213–239. London: Cambridge University Press.
1976   The origin and evolution of language. Dubuque, IA: Wm. C. Brown.

Sturtevant, Edgar H.
1947   An introduction to linguistic science. New Haven, CT: Yale University Press.

Sturtevant, William C.
1964   Studies in ethnoscience. American Anthropologist 63:3(part 2):99–131.

Susman, Randall L., ed.
1984   The pygmy chimpanzee: evolutionary biology and behavior. New York: Plenum Press.

Swadesh, Morris
  1950   Salish internal relationships. International Journal of American Linguis-
              tics 16:157–167.
  1955   Towards greater accuracy in lexicostatistic dating. International Journal
              of American Linguistics 21:121–137.
  1971   The origin and diversification of language. Joel Sherzer, ed. Chicago:
              Aldine/Atherton.
Tannen, Deborah
  1986   That's not what I meant! How conversational style makes or breaks rela-
              tions with others. New York: Morrow.
  1990   You just don't understand: women and men in conversation. New York:
              Morrow.
Taylor, Douglas
  1951   Sex gender in Central American Carib. International Journal of Ameri-
              can Linguistics 17:102–104.
Tedlock, Dennis
  1972   (trans.) Finding the center: narrative poetry of the Zuni Indians. New
              York: Dial Press.
  1983   The spoken word and the work of interpretation. Philadelphia: Univer-
              sity of Pennsylvania Press.
  1985   (trans. and commentator) Popol vuh: the Mayan book of the dawn of
              life. New York: Simon and Schuster.
  1987   Hearing a voice in an ancient text: Quiché Maya poetics in performance.
              In Native American discourse: poetics and rhetoric. Joel Sherzer and An-
              thony C. Woodbury, eds. Pp. 140–175. Cambridge: Cambridge Univer-
              sity Press.
Teeter, Karl V.
  1964   "Anthropological linguistics" and linguistic anthropology. American
              Anthropologist 66:878–879.
Terrace, Herbert S.
  1979   Nim. New York: Knopf.
Thompson, Stith
  1928   The types of the folk-tale: a classification and bibliography. FF Communi-
              cations, no. 74. Helsinki. [Translation and expansion of Aarne 1910.]
  1932–1936   Motif-index of folk-literature: a classification of narrative elements in
              folk-tales, ballads, myths, fables, mediaeval romances, exempla, fabli-
              aux, jest-books, and local legends. 6 vols. FF Communications, nos.
              106–109, 116, and 117. Helsinki.
  1953   The Star Husband tale. Studia Septentrionalia 4:93–163.
  1955   Motif-index of folk-literature: a classification of narrative elements in
              folktales, ballads, myths, fables, mediaeval romances, exempla, fabliaux,
              jest-books, and local legends. 6 vols. Rev. and enl. ed. Bloomington: In-
              diana University Press.
  1961   The types of the folktale: a classification and bibliography. 2nd rev. ed.
              FF Communications, no. 184. Helsinki.
Thorne, Alan G., and Milford H. Wolpoff
  1992   The multiregional evolution of humans. Scientific American 266:
              4:76–79, 82–83 (April).

Thorne, Barrie, Cheris Kramarae, and Nancy Henley, eds.
1983 Language, gender and society. Rowley, MA: Newbury House.
Time-Life Books
1973 The first men. *Series* The emergence of man. New York: Time-Life Books.
Ting-Toomey, Stella
1986 Conflict communication styles in black and white subjective cultures. *In* Interethnic communication: current research, vol. 10. Young Yun Kim, ed. Pp. 75–88. Newbury Park, CA: Sage.
Todd, Loreto
1984 Modern Englishes: pidgins and creoles. Oxford: Blackwell.
Tomkins, William
1969 Indian sign language. New York: Dover. (Originally published by the author in 1926 under the title Universal [American] Indian sign language [of the Plains Indians of North America. . . .].)
Trager, George L.
1958 Paralanguage: a first approximation. Studies in Linguistics 13:1–12.
1972 Language and languages. San Francisco: Chandler.
Trudgill, Peter
1983 Sociolinguistics: an introduction to language and society. Rev. ed. New York: Penguin Books.
1984 (ed.) Applied sociolinguistics. Orlando: Academic Press.
Tyler, Stephen A., ed.
1969 Cognitive anthropology. New York: Holt, Rinehart and Winston.
Van Zandt, Howard F.
1970 How to negotiate in Japan. Harvard Business Review 48:6:45–56 (November-December).
Voegelin, Charles F., and Z. S. Harris
1952 Training in anthropological linguistics. American Anthropologist 54:322–327.
Voegelin, Charles F., and Florence M. Voegelin
1954 Obtaining a linguistic sample. International Journal of American Linguistics 20:89–100.
1957 Hopi domains: a lexical approach to the problem of selection. Indiana University Publications in Anthropology and Linguistics, memoir 14 of the International Journal of American Linguistics. Baltimore: Waverly Press.
1959 Guide for transcribing unwritten languages in field work. Anthropological Linguistics 1:6:1–28.
1966 (comps.) Map of North American Indian languages. American Ethnological Society.
Voegelin, Charles F., Florence M. Voegelin, and LaVerne Masayesva Jeanne
1979 Hopi semantics. *In* Handbook of North American Indians, vol. 9: Southwest, pp. 581–586. Washington: Smithsonian Institution.
Walter, Henriette
1988 Le français dans tous les sens. Paris: R. Laffont.
Wardhaugh, Ronald
1986 An introduction to sociolinguistics. New York: Blackwell.
Wardhaugh, Ronald, and H. Douglas Brown, eds.
1976 A survey of applied linguistics. Ann Arbor: University of Michigan Press.

Waterhouse, Viola
1962   The grammatical structure of Oaxaca Chontal. Indiana University Research Center in Anthropology, Folklore, and Linguistics Publications, no. 19. Bloomington.

Watkins, Calvert
1992   Indo-European and the Indo-Europeans. *In* The American Heritage Dictionary of the English Language. Pp. 1496–1550. New York and Boston: American Heritage and Houghton Mifflin.

Watson, O. Michael, and Theodore D. Graves
1966   Quantitative research in proxemic behavior. American Anthropologist 68:971–985.

Weitz, Shirley, ed.
1974   Nonverbal communication: readings with commentary. New York: Oxford University Press.

Wescott, Roger W.
1974   The origin of speech. *In* Language origins. Roger W. Wescott, ed. Pp. 103–123. Silver Spring, MD: Linstok Press.

Whorf, Benjamin Lee
1936   The punctual and segmental aspects of verbs in Hopi. Language 12:127–131.
1940a   Science and linguistics. Technology Review 42:229–231, 247–248 (April).
1940b   Linguistics as an exact science. Technology Review 43:61–63, 80–83 (December).
1941a   Languages and logic. Technology Review 43:250–252, 266, 268, 272 (April).
1941b   The relation of habitual thought and behavior to language. *In* Language, culture, and personality: essays in memory of Edward Sapir. Leslie Spier and others, eds. Pp. 75–93. Menasha, WI: Sapir Memorial Publication Fund.
1946   The Hopi language, Toreva dialect. *In* Linguistic structures of Native America. Cornelius Osgood, ed. Viking Fund Publications in Anthropology, no. 6, pp. 158–183. New York: Viking Fund.
1950   An American Indian model of the universe. International Journal of American Linguistics 16:67–72.
1956   Language, thought, and reality: selected writings of Benjamin Lee Whorf. John B. Carroll, ed. Cambridge and New York: Technology Press of MIT and John Wiley and Sons.

Wilson, Allan C., and Rebecca L. Cann
1992   The recent African genesis of humans. Scientific American 266:4:68–73 (April).

Witherspoon, Gary
1977   Language and art in the Navajo universe. Ann Arbor: University of Michigan Press.

Wolff, Hans
1952   Osage I: phonemes and historical phonology. International Journal of American Linguistics 18:63–68.
1967   Language, ethnic identity and social change in southern Nigeria. Anthropological Linguistics 9:1:18–25.

Wolfson, Nessa, and Joan Manes
  1979   Don't dear me. Working Papers in Sociolinguistics, no. 53. Austin, TX:
              Southwest Educational Development Laboratory.
Wonderly, William L.
  1951a   Zoque II: phonemes and morphophonemes. International Journal of
              American Linguistics 17:105–123.
  1951b   Zoque III: morphological classes, affix list, and verbs. International Jour-
              nal of American Linguistics 17:137–162.
Woolford, Ellen B.
  1979   Aspects of Tok Pisin grammar. Pacific Linguistics, Series B—Mono-
              graphs, no. 66. Canberra: Australian National University.
Yegerlehner, John
  1955   A note on eliciting techniques. International Journal of American Lin-
              guistics 21:286–288.
Zepeda, Ofelia
  1983   A Papago grammar. Tucson: University of Arizona Press.

Answers to Problems

Chapter 4

Problem 1. The sounds [c] and [ʒ] in Zoque are allophones of a phoneme because they are phonetically similar and in complementary distribution: The voiced alveolar affricate occurs after a nasal (as in 1, 2, 3, 7, 8, 9, 12), the voiceless alveolar affricate elsewhere (as in 3, 4, 5, 6, 10, 11). Rule: /c/→[+ voiced]/N____ (where N = any nasal).

Problem 2. All of the four Czech stops, [t, d, tʸ, dʸ], are separate phonemes, /t, d, tʸ, dʸ/, because they contrast, as is evident from the existence of minimal pairs in the sample (as in 1 and 3, 4 and 9, 11 and 13, 14 and 16).

Problem 3. The main stress in Araucanian is on the second vowel and hence is predictable by rule.

Problem 4. Phoneme /ð/ has two allophones: [d] occurring before [a] and [ð] elsewhere. Rule: /ð/→[d]/____a.

Problem 5. Vowel length in Mohawk is predictable: All vowels are short except those that are stressed and followed by a single consonant. Vowel length is therefore not distinctive.

Chapter 5

Problem 1.

Luiseño Morpheme	English Gloss
nóo	I
póy	him
čáami	us
q	PRESENT
n	FUTURE
ni	make
viču	want
wukála	walk
páaʔi	drink
temét	sun

Problem 2. The verb forms are pluralized by a prefix to the singular form; the shape of the prefix is the initial consonant and the following vowel of the singular form.

Problem 3. Allomorphs of the past tense morpheme: /-əd/ if the base ends in /t,d/; /-t/ if it ends in /p,k,č,f,θ,s,š/; and /-d/ if it ends in any other sound. Allomorphs of the third-person singular morpheme: /-əz/ if the base ends in

/s,z,š,ž,č,ǰ/; /-z/ if it ends in any voiced sound except /z,ž,ǰ/; and /-s/ if it ends in any voiceless sound except /s,š,č/.

Problem 4. The stems or roots are listed under 1–20. The first-person singular possessive is the prefix *an-*. The morphophonemics of this prefix may be stated as follows:

n→m/_____m, p (that is, *n* becomes *m* before *m* or *p* [bilabials])

n→ñ/_____y, č, š, tʸ (palato-alveolars)

n→ŋ/_____k, w

n→n/_____t, c, s, n, h (-elsewhere)

Problem 5. There are many possible solutions to this problem. Tree diagram (A) would be satisfied, for example, by the sentence "The dog in the house barks"; tree diagram (B) by "Father and the neighbor will camp in the woods"; and tree diagram (C) by "Mother's sister's husband says that turtles swim in the ocean."

322

Languages mentioned in the text

Europe

1	Albanian	11	Lapp
2	Czech	12	Magyar (Hungarian)
3	Dutch	13	Polish
4	Estonian	14	Portuguese
5	Finnish	15	Romanian
6	French	16	Romansh
7	German	17	Russian
8	Greek	18	Schwyzertütsch
9	Icelandic	19	Slovak
10	Italian (and Latin)	20	Spanish

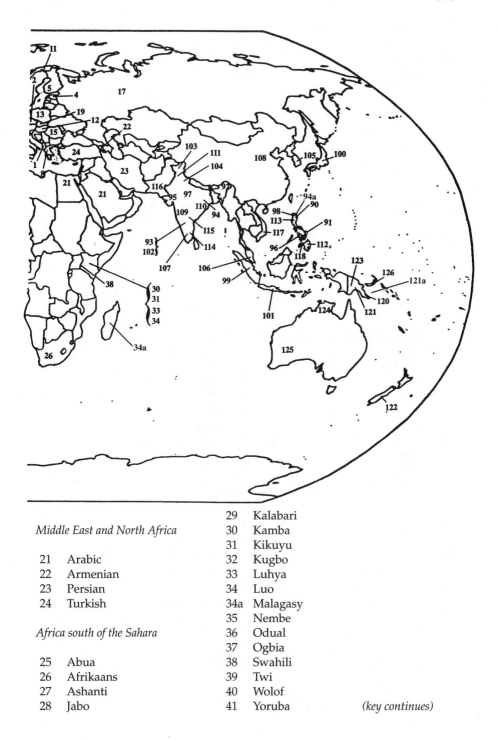

(key continues)

Latin America and the Caribbean

42 Aguaruna
43 Araucanian
44 Chontal
45 Guarani
46 Island Carib
47 Isthmus Nahuat
48 Jamaican Creole
49 Kuna
50 Mazateco
51 Otomi
52 Quiche
53 Sierra Popoluca
54 (Tenejapa) Tzeltal
55 West Indian Creole
55a Yucatec
56 Zoque

North America

57 Apache (and Western Apache)
58 Arapaho
58a Bella Bella
59 Blackfoot
59a Carrier
60 Cherokee
61 Cheyenne
62 Cree-Montagnais
63 Crow
64 Dakota
65 Eskimo
66 Fox
67 Gullah
68 Hopi
69 Hupa
70 Kiowa
71 Kiowa Apache
72 Koasati
73 Kwakiutl
74 Luiseño
74a Maidu
75 Menomini
75a Mescalero Apache
75b Mohawk
76 Navajo

77 Nootka
77a Northern Paiute
78 Ojibwa
78a Osage
79 Pawnee-Arikara
80 Penobscot-Abnaki
81 Sarcee
82 Shawnee
83 Shoshone-Comanche
84 Takelma
84a Tohono O'odham (Papago)
85 Tunica
86 Upper Chinook (and Wishram)
86a Walapai
86b Washo
87 Wichita
88 Yana
89 Zuñi

East and South Asia

90 Agta
91 Aklanon
92 Assamese
93 Badaga
94 Bengali
94a Bontok
95 Gujarati
96 Hanunóo
97 Hindi
98 Ilongot
99 Indonesian
100 Japanese
101 Javanese
102 Kannada
103 Kashmiri
104 Khalapur
105 Korean
106 Malay
107 Malayalam
108 Mandarin (Chinese)
109 Marathi
110 Oriya
111 Panjabi
112 Subanun
113 Tagalog   *(key continues)*

114　Tamil
115　Telugu
116　Urdu
117　Vietnamese
118　Yakan

Australia and Oceania

119　Hawaiian Creole English
120　Hiri Motu
121　Kaluli
121a　Kiriwinian
122　Maori
123　Neo-Melanesian (Tok Pisin)
124　Ngandi
125　Pintupi
126　Tolai (Kuanua)

Index